BIRKET FOSTER

Birket Foster 'stands as one of England's most popular landscape draughtsmen and as a painter in water-colour of great distinction'. This tribute came from the Dalziel brothers, whose fine engravings of the drawings of Birket Foster are represented in this comprehensive study of the artist's life and work.

Jan Reynolds has researched the subject in great depth and brings forward much original material, including extracts from over 80 unpublished letters, and information and photographs from family sources. There are detailed descriptions and illustrations of the artist's home (now demolished), extensively decorated by the firm of William Morris.

As well as a detailed account of the artist's career, there is a study of the books illustrated by him (over 100), with an annotated list of immense value to the collector. The question of faked work is examined in a sensible manner. Works by Birket Foster in public collections are listed, as well as exhibits with the Society of Painters in Water-colours and the Royal Academy, and the complete catalogue of the Christie's sale of the artist's work after his death in 1899 is included.

This is the first full study for many years of an artist whose work is now increasingly being sought by collectors, and whose water-colours in particular are frequently reproduced today.

Jan Reynolds is the author of *William Callow*, also published by Batsford, and of *The Williams Family of Painters*. She is the great grand-daughter of Sidney R. Percy, the Victorian landscape painter, and has distant family connections with Birket Foster himself. Coming from one of the oldest Quaker families in the country, she writes of the Quaker background of the artist with particular insight and knowledge.

BIRKET FOSTER

Jan Reynolds

B.T. Batsford Ltd, London

Copyright © Jan Reynolds 1984

First published 1984

ISBN 0 7134 3754 5

Made and printed in Great Britain by Butler & Tanner Ltd,
Frome and London for the publishers, B.T. Batsford Ltd,
4 Fitzhardinge Street, London, W1H 0AH

By the same author:
The Williams Family of Painters
William Callow

Frontispiece:
'Building the Hay Rick', from
Birket Foster's Pictures of
English Landscape

Contents

Acknowledgments

A very special dedication is due to Miss Sarah G.A. Glasson, grand-daughter of Birket Foster, who has made an invaluable contribution in allowing me to publish biographical details and family photographs of exceptional interest. One of the rewards of writing this book has been that it has brought me the friendship of Sarah Glasson, to whom I acknowledge my affectionate gratitude.

I would also like to express my deep appreciation for most important help received from William Glasson, great-grandson of Birket Foster, who has provided many family references of essential interest, including biographical notes, newspaper cuttings and photographs. My thanks are also extended to his mother, Mrs L.M. Glasson, for her kindness in making such material available and for permission to illustrate two portraits in her possession.

John F. Foster, great-grandson of Birket Foster, has also supplied family material and I am most grateful for his assistance. I would like to acknowledge information received from several other descendants and connections of the Foster family, namely: Charles Spence, Sarah Batchelor, N.M. Perry-Gore, Dorothy Mason, Sir Basil Nield, Simon Finch and Ann Finch.

A special acknowledgment is due to Brian and Rachel Moss, of Moss Galleries, London, who have greatly assisted me by making so freely available their private collection of books illustrated by Birket Foster, as well as original water-colours and other related references. Their help and encouragement has been so much appreciated.

The Central Library, Sheffield, has been unfailingly helpful, and a very warm acknowledgment is owing to the Librarian and staff of the County Library, Bakewell, for the friendly and efficient manner in which they have dealt with my numerous requests. I am particularly grateful to John Kirby, Library of Fine Art and Design, Sheffield City Polytechnic, for his always interested answers to my queries and for allowing me every facility in using the resources of this library. Recognition is also extended to: The Central Library, Newcastle upon Tyne, for permission to publish extracts from a valuable collection of Birket Foster correspondence; Eric Hollerton, Local Studies Centre, North Shields, also acknowledging information from Birket Foster of North Shields; R.A. Bowden of the Marylebone Library; Edward Milligan, Librarian, Friends House, London; The National Library of Scotland, Edinburgh, for permission to publish letters, acknowledging the individual help of Elspeth Yeo; and Brooke Whiting, Curator of Rare Books and Manuscripts, for permission to publish extracts from letters in the collection of the University of California. Andrew Ashton of the Bury Museum has allowed me to publish a Birket Foster example from his private collection of artists' letters; Alan Fleck of the Hitchin Museum has enabled me to add detail to the early background of Birket Foster, including in this respect the names of Pat Gadd and V.F. Davis.

Shirley Corke of the Muniment Room, Guildford has been most helpful with local references; I also extend thanks to P.M.J. Brewer of the County Library, Guildford and Avril Lansdell of the Weybridge Museum. Peter Davis of the Hancock Museum, Newcastle upon Tyne has drawn my attention to Foster family references. Thanks are also due to the Central Library, Richmond; Divisional Reference Library, Slough; and the Royal Library, Windsor Castle. I would like to thank Norah Gillow of the William Morris Gallery, Walthamstow, for her knowledgable interest; and acknowledgment is also due to Linda Parry of the Victoria and Albert Museum, and to Joyce Whalley and Lionel Lambourne.

My thanks are extended to over one hundred museums and art galleries for replying to my requests for information and in particular those named in Appendix 7.

The following individuals, whose help has been much appreciated are listed alphabetically: Professor G.N. Brown of the Betley Court Gallery, for permission to publish biographical material from his collection; Pauline Flick for the generous sharing of her own interest in Birket Foster and the loan of illustrated material; Robin Griffith-Jones of Christies; Ronald Huby for the loan of a first edition; Ray Layton of Tynemouth for the provision of local references; Ruari McLean for his kindness and assistance with introductions; A.G. Nevill of Frost and Reed for particular help with photographs; Paul Rich for research in the British Museum; R.A. Yardley and Edward Yardley for enthusiastic interest and the loan of books illustrated by Birket Foster. I would also like to thank the following for some part in supplying information or assistance (listed alphabetically): K. Barratt; C.K. Brown; John Christian; Stanley and Alethea Dawson; D.A. Down; Jenny Edwards; Robert and Elizabeth Gray; F.W. Greenacre; Gill Hedley; P.J. Jackson; S. Loveridge; R. and M. Maggs; B. Milton; W.C. Palmer; D. Phillips; N. Potter; Tom Rowney; Gill Schurer; Eric Stanford; Brian Stewart; Sheila Talbot; Julian Treuherz; J.A. Tyrell; C.W. Warwick; J. Watson; Selby Whittingham.

A special word of gratitude to my Mother for her loving

pride in my work and for so cheerfully managing not to take a toss on floors frequently made hazardous with a clutter of books, papers and folders.

I would like to dedicate this book to the memory of my much loved father, Kenneth Richard Reynolds. He was the grandson of Richard Reynolds, Quaker scientist, and of Sidney R. Percy, the landscape painter, and has thus passed to me an inheritance which is somewhat unusual

for the combination of Quakerism and professional art. It has given me a close sense of affinity with my subject to know that similar elements were essentially part of the life of Birket Foster.

Jan Reynolds
Baslow 1984

Incidental illustrations in this book are from the following sources:

page   6 *The Illustrated London Almanack*
        8 *Evangeline*
     18 *Beauties of English Landscape*
     86 *L'Allegro and Il Penseroso*
   174 *Evangeline*

page 186 *The Illustrated London News*
     216 *L'Allegro and Il Penseroso*
     217 *Evangeline*

The decorative motif on cover and spine is designed from an original Birket Foster book plate (by permission of William Glasson).

1
Family background and schooldays

'Myles Birket Foster, born 1825, on the fourth day of the second month, at the abode of his father, Myles Birket Foster, merchant, of Rosella Place, Tynemouth, Northumberland.'

These entries are recorded in a transcript copy of the Register of Births and Burials, with reference to the Newcastle Monthly Meeting of the Society of Friends. A connection of North Country families, including the Fosters, had for many generations been staunch adherents of this dissenting religious sect, whose members were more commonly known as Quakers.

The following short account of the antecedents of Birket Foster will provide a key to subsequent biographical references and is of importance to a full understanding of the life and work of this artist. Briefly:

Sir John Forster, Knight, son of Sir Thomas Forster, Knight, Marshall of Berwick on Tweed, was Lord of Bamborough Castle, by grant of the Crown, also Deputy-Warden of the Middle and Eastern Marches and Sheriff of Northumberland (died 1602). Robert Forster, brother of Sir Thomas, was given by his father property and lands in Cold Hesledon, County Durham and it was his direct descendant (also named Robert Forster) who was one of the early followers of George Fox, the founder of the Society of Friends. Foster was gradually adopted as the spelling of the family name from about 1730 and Birket Foster was descended from one of the first lines to use this version. Thus: Myles Birket of Birket Houses, a small estate in Westmorland, had a great-grandson who was also named Myles Birket and who was the owner of Hebblethwaite Hall near Sedbergh, Yorkshire and also of Sarthwaite, a property in the County of Lancaster. His daughter, Elizabeth, married Dodson Foster, who was the great-grandson of the Quaker, Robert Forster of Cold Hesledon.[1]

It was Robert Foster (1754-1827), their only surviving son, who was to become the grandfather of Birket Foster. In all but one aspect, the life of Robert Foster encapsulates much of the social environment of prosperous but pious Quakerism in which the Foster and Birket families had lived for many generations. After a good education, Robert Foster made several voyages on behalf of his grandfather and uncle, Myles and James Birket, who were merchants for the West Indies. At the age of 18, he was sent at very short notice to superintend their interests in Antigua, one of the Leeward Islands, but (just before the American War of Independence) he very unexpectedly closed the Birket stores and enlisted in the navy. This was a serious lapse from Quaker grace.

On 9 March 1776, James Birket of Lancaster wrote in his diary:

'There is an account in the town from the West Indies that Robert Foster, my nephew, has entered on board a Man of War's tender, called "The Endeavour", as mate and midshipman, to cruise against the American privateers, to the inexpressible grief, sorrow and anxiety of Father, Grandfather, relations and friends here. O! Foolish boy!'[2]

The extreme reaction of his uncle to this event serves to point up the attitudes held by the Society of Friends. In 1661 George Fox had been associated with a pamphlet in which it was stated: 'We utterly deny all outward wars and strife and fightings with outward weapons, for any end or under any pretence whatsoever.'

In 1779 James Birket wrote: 'Robert Foster came home on 1st Day (as we were going to Meeting) to see his father; he looks very thin, notwithstanding his fierce cockade and uniform. . . .' Robert Spence, R.E. was to produce over a century later a fine etching of this incident, entitled 'How Robert Foster, member of the Society of Friends, attended Brig Flatts Meeting, while serving as Lieutenant on [sic] the *Pelican*'; this shows the local Quakers in various states of astonishment and disapproval at the entry of Robert Foster into the Meeting House. Eventually the pleadings of his family and his own change of heart caused him to apply to the Board of Admiralty in London for his discharge and while waiting for this, Robert Foster stayed with relations in Wandsworth and had his Quaker clothes sent to him. All arrived, except the hat. His son, in an unpublished memoir, was later to relate that his father 'went to meeting with the family dressed as a Friend, but in his naval hat!' The Society of Friends had received Robert Foster back into the fold.

Soon after his return home, his grandfather made him tenant of the Hebblethwaite Hall estate. He was given the livestock and was also allowed to have the farm and 330 acres of land free of rent. Robert Foster then rather symbolically had his naval cutlass converted into a large domestic carving knife and set about life in the manner of his ancestors, wearing the plain grey Puritan-style garb of a Quaker, spun and woven from the fleece of his own sheep. In 1783, James Birket died and left him the Wood estate on Cartmel Fell, which had been in the family since 1679. In 1784, Robert Foster married Mary Burton, who had been his housekeeper and was the daughter of James and Mary Burton of The Hill, Sedbergh where he had lodged while he was still at school. Myles Birket Foster, son of Robert and Mary Foster (and later father of the artist) was born on 4 January 1785. He was named after his grandfather, who died shortly afterwards and left the Hebblethwaite and Sarthwaite estates to Robert Foster.

This industrious, scholarly, North Country Quaker was a man of many parts. He was able to dispense medicines and settle legal disputes and at the request of William Wilberforce gave evidence on the slave trade in the West Indies before a select committee of the House of Commons. He enjoyed spending his evenings studying Latin and Greek and could correspond in the former language, to which he was to add a good working knowledge of Dutch and German. Robert Foster also had an enthusiasm for botany and was a friend of the engraver and naturalist, Thomas Bewick. William Wordsworth stayed at Hebblethwaite Hall about 1805 and gave Robert Foster an introduction to Robert Southey, who was Poet Laureate from 1814-43. He wrote:

'O, Wordsworth sent me a man the other day who was worth seeing; he looked like a first assassin in Macbeth as to his costume - but he was a rare man. Had been a lieutenant in the Navy; was scholar enough to quote Virgil aptly; had turned Quaker or semi-Quaker [sic] and was now a dealer in wool about twenty miles off. He had seen much and thought much; his head was well stored and his heart was in the right place . . .'

- from a letter to the author, Richard Duppa, dated 23 February 1806.

Robert Foster had first established a small spinning mill to give employment to the local poor, but this business was later expanded to include several larger mills. His eldest son was to recall him as 'a sort of father, physician, lawyer and judge among his dependents and country neighbours'. He recorded that during a tour with his father in 1809, one night was spent at the home of Joseph Gurney, who was a relation of the celebrated prison reformer, Elizabeth Fry (née Gurney). Robert Foster is known to have been well acquainted with Bartlett Gurney, a member of the same Norfolk branch of Quakers. It may be of interest to note at this point that many of the Gurneys were what were known as Gay Quakers, who wore fashionable clothes and engaged in music and dancing. Elizabeth Gurney had turned Plain Quaker, reverting to traditional dress and attempting to adhere strictly to the original precepts of the movement. At the time of the birth of Birket Foster his family would definitely be in the category of Plain Quakers[3].

Robert Foster, in his very plain Quaker clothes, was rather pointedly ignored by a crowd of Gay Quakers in cocked hats, as he waited in the lobby of the House of Commons to give evidence before the Wilberforce commission. But, after a while, he was greeted with the utmost cordiality by a naval captain, with whom he had served and who was overheard to tell Foster that he would have been an Admiral if he had stayed in the navy.

'When they had parted, the Friends flocked around my Father and he had so many invitations to dine, that he need not have gone without a dinner for a week. But, he said "I'll dine with none of you, you have passed me several times and saw me, but you never spoke to me, or took any notice of me, what is it that has made you so kind all at once? I want none of your dinners."'

- from the unpublished memoirs of the father of Birket

Foster, who must often have heard this story repeated, with the splendid North Country crunch of the last line.

On 11 April 1811, Myles Birket Foster, son of Robert Foster, married Ann King, the daughter of Joseph King, a Quaker from Newcastle upon Tyne. It was their fifth son, also named Myles Birket Foster, who was to become Birket Foster, the artist. The fact that there were to be five generations in the Foster family with the same names makes for obvious difficulties of identity, but in this book care has been taken to refer to the father of the artist by all three names. As we have seen, the Newcastle Register records Tynemouth as the birthplace of Birket Foster but the exact location of 2 Rosella Place was in North Shields, an area with a separate identity, although an integral part of Tynemouth. 2 Rosella Place is still standing and forms part of a short terrace of Georgian houses, which cannot have changed much since the days of Birket Foster's childhood. These houses are about a quarter of a mile from the river and in 1825 would have been on the edge of the town.

In 1810, Mary Foster, daughter of Robert Foster, had married Robert Spence, who had been born at Whaitemill House, Darley, Yorkshire, but who was to become known in North Shields as one of the most respected public figures of his adopted town. His main occupation was that of banker, in partnership as Proctor and Spence, but he also traded as a wool and linen draper and had other business interests. Myles Birket Foster had commenced his career in the counting house of Proctor and Spence, but at the time of the birth of Birket Foster, he was a partner in the firm of Spence and Foster, timber merchants, Collingwood Street, North Shields.

Robert Foster had two surviving sons and three daughters and held that it would not be right for any of them to have a larger share in his property by reason of inheriting Hebblethwaite Hall. In 1812, as he approached the age of 60, it was decided to sell this property and the four other estates that he had by now acquired or inherited. He then retired to Northumberland Street, Newcastle upon Tyne, where he occupied himself as an active and reforming director of the Newcastle Savings Bank and continued as a devoted member of the Society of Friends, including attendances at their Yearly Meeting in London.

The earliest recorded drawing by Birket Foster is of an omnibus, which is said to have been done when he was four years old in 1829. This was the year in which such vehicles first appeared on the streets of London and it was also the year when Myles Birket Foster, sen., moved there with his wife and children, i.e. Robert - born 1812; Joseph - born 1813; Dodshon - born 1816; John Harrison - born 1818; Mary - born 1821; and Myles Birket - 1825. The address of the family was given as Maida Hill, London, at the time of the birth in 1830 of James Foster (who died in infancy). Myles Birket Foster was now establishing the firm which was to become known as M.B. Foster and Sons - the largest bottling concern in the country. Most Quaker families were essentially involved in commerce, owing to the fact that the Test Acts and the Corporation Act (1661) had prevented Nonconformists from holding public office or entering Oxford or Cambridge Universities. The education and intelligence which Quakers brought to trade, combined with their insistence on fixed prices and frugality of personal living, soon had the effect of building up small family businesses into large concerns, e.g. Cadbury, Fry, etc. The Quaker reputation for integrity also led neighbours to entrust money to them for safe keeping and it was this practice that resulted in the formation of many banks. The firm with which the Spence family was connected was eventually to be sold to Lloyds, which was also originally a Quaker concern.[4] The occupation of Myles Birket Foster, sen., can appear somewhat unexpected in view of the constrictions placed on Quakers with regard to the pleasures of the world, but the taking of alcohol was not forbidden. The circumstances of the founding of the firm came about by accident and the story reads as if it were apocryphal, but appears to be genuine. Just before Robert Foster left very suddenly for the West Indies, he was helping in the hayfields and had placed a bottle of home-brewed beer in a stream to keep cool. In the event, he did not retrieve it until about four years later.

> 'The cork was swollen by the water and seemed very tight, but at last he got it out and to his astonishment the beer came out bright and sparkling as he had never seen beer before and he knew that he had stumbled on a process of very great importance.'[5]

It was this process that his son, Myles Birket Foster, developed commercially and first established in premises at 87 Wimpole Street, London. In 1832, the business was moved to Queen's Bazaar, Oxford Street (now Woolworth's store, 150–54 Oxford Street). Beer had been placed in flasks and jars for centuries, but the bottling of beer was an entirely different undertaking and one in which the essential quality of the liquor depended as much on the skill of the bottler as on that of the brewer. The highly successful experimental bottling of a sample of Bass's India Pale Ale assured the fortunes of the firm of M.B. Foster and Sons. A pedantically humorous cleric (appropriately living in Burton upon Trent) is recorded as perpetuating the comment: 'He fosters Bass who fosters Foster's best. Long life may both in perfect friendship pass. Bass fostering Foster, Foster fostering Bass.'[6] Bottles not only bore the Bass label, but also the famous 'Bugle Brand' label, which was to become a household name. This trade mark of M.B. Foster and Sons was directly derived from a device which had formed part of the original Foster (or Forster) coat of arms on which there was a bugle horn suspended from a treble loop motive. The firm also had a vital association with Guinness and all their famous 'Harp' labels bore the name of M.B. Foster and Sons, as the bottlers.

At the age of about seven, Birket Foster was sent to a Quaker boarding school in Tottenham, at that time a satellite village of London, with a strong community of members of the Society of Friends. This preparatory school for small boys had been established by Deborah Forster and was considered the best, if not the only school of its kind near London. The numbers were limited to 20 boarders, who moved on at about the age of ten. It is obvious that this was a very happy establishment, with a homely atmosphere and ideas in advance of the period. By the time that Birket Foster arrived at the school it was being run by two Quaker sisters, Frances Sophia and Priscilla Coar, who were related to Deborah Forster. They were daughters of Thomas Coar, a schoolmaster and convinced Friend, who was the author of *A Grammar of the English Tongue* (1796) and was also clever with pen drawings. Frances and Priscilla Coar were intelligent and sympathetic teachers, who not only gave the children in their care a detailed knowledge of the Scriptures (required by Friends as a kind of spiritual insurance against the evils of the world) but also provided a general education within an interesting and unrepressive environment, with a

marked emphasis on art and craft work. No more ideal school could have been found for the young Birket Foster and there can be no doubt that it was important in encouraging his natural talent. Priscilla Coar, in particular, was very skilled in drawing and water-colour painting and it is recorded that a former pupil of the school, an East India merchant and something of a collector, would lend beautiful books of birds, flowers, shipping, etc. for the Coars to copy. Priscilla had a talent for pen-and-ink copies of wood engravings and these included frequent use of Thomas Bewick's famous *History of British Birds* – published in two volumes in 1797 and 1804.

A pervading influence from Thomas Bewick (1753–1828) occurs all through the childhood and early days of Birket Foster. No doubt he would tell the Coars that his father and grandfather had known Bewick and had often heard him relate some of the rather droll little incidents that were the subjects of many of the quaint little tailpieces in the illustrations of this celebrated Newcastle engraver, who was described by C.R. Leslie in his *Handbook for Young Painters* as 'a truly original genius, who, though not a painter, was an artist of the highest order in his way. ... The student of landscape can never consult the works of Bewick without improvement.' Adam Sedgwick, the noted geologist, was at school with Robert Foster and in later life described being taken to see Bewick by Foster, who remarked: 'We will now rest ourselves in the study of one of my friends. You will like to know him for he is a man of genius and a great humorist.'

Bewick's leafy vignettes of country scenes were to have an obvious influence on the early work of Birket Foster and he is reputed to have made a clever copy of one of these at the age of seven. The Coar sisters also distributed their own water-colour and pencil copies of birds and animals as 'Prize Pictures' at the end of each term. The illustrations in Bewick's *History of British Birds* were probably indirectly related to a letter Birket Foster was to write many years later to Theodore Compton:

> 'Perhaps you do not know that my first real desire to draw well was from seeing a picture of yours of a woodpecker, when I was at Miss Coar's school.'[7]

A few boys from outside the membership of the Society of Friends were admitted to the school, but the majority were Quakers, including two of the sons of William Foster Reynolds, Charles and Morris, first cousins of Richard Freshfield Reynolds, great-great-grandfather of the present writer. Birket Foster was just ten years old and soon to be leaving the care of Frances and Priscilla Coar, when he wrote this letter to Myles Birket Foster:

> '3rd. mo. 20th 1835
>
> My dear Father,
>   I hope that thou and Brothers are quite well. When thou writes to Mother give my very dear love to her, and when thou writes to Sister Mary give my love to her also. I shall be very glad to hear from you. I should be very much obliged to thee not to forget to send me my Skipping Rope and my knife. Cousin Elizabeth Foster came to see me, and brought me a bag of Oranges which were very nice indeed. I should be very much obliged to thee to send me a little writing paper. I have began [sic] to draw the Geometrical figures in a book. I have finished Reductions and am in Bills of Parcels. I have finished the Map of South America which I think looks very nice. If thou should go to Stannall [?] wilt

1 One of the earliest authenticated water-colours, inscribed on reverse: 'Birket Foster - Drawn when he was *eleven* years old. Given me by D. Foster, Esq. W.S.' - William Smith Bequest. Size: $7\frac{1}{2} \times 11\frac{1}{8}''$ - 19 × 28.2 cms.
Courtesy of the National Gallery of Ireland, Dublin, Eire.

thou give my love to Robert. I received the bride cake yesterday and I am very much obliged to Mother for sending it for me. Give my love to brothers, and Betsy, and accept it thyself from affectionate son,

Myles Birket Foster

F S, and P Coar desire their remembrance.'

It is interesting to note that Birket Foster does not write the *Misses* Coar, but in Quaker fashion leaves out what their movement considered to be 'vain titles of the world'. It will also be noted that he uses the Quaker form of date on this letter, i.e. '3rd. mo.' - meaning third month or March. Members of the Society of Friends also used these terms for naming days of the week, e.g. fourth day, instead of Wednesday (derived from the god Woden and therefore considered idolatrous). The original advice of 1697 had been strongly reaffirmed at the Yearly Meeting held in London in 1802. Quakers were advised: 'That all friends keep to the simplicity of truth, and our ancient testimony, in calling the months and days by scripture names and not by heathen.' Birket Foster also uses the biblical form of pronoun, as was the custom in the Society of Friends (both in speech and writing) although in this letter there is one lapse from this usage. A combination of the Quaker form and the ordinary pronoun was to appear in the personal correspondence of Birket for at least the next 30 years.[8]

The 'bride cake' that Birket Foster refers to would be from the celebrations of the double wedding of two of his cousins, daughters of Robert and Mary Spence of North Shields i.e. on 12 March 1835, Mary Spence married James Watson and Sarah Spence married Joseph Watson.

In later years, several of the children of these marriages were to have special links with the life of Birket Foster.

The first water-colour illustration in this book is part of the William Smith Bequest to the National Gallery of Ireland (Ill. I). It is inscribed on the reverse: 'Birket Foster - Drawn when he was *eleven* years old. Given me by D. Foster, Esq., W.S.' This inscription firmly authenticates the drawing, which was undoubtedly given to William Smith by Dodshon Foster, elder brother of Birket. It is a most charming and revealing piece of early work. Birket Foster, at the age of 11, had received some basic instruction in painting and drawing from the Coars, who were enlightened for their day, but it has to be remembered that the general Quaker environment was one in which the strict attitude was not only to frown upon the theatre, but also the visual arts and music. The thinking was that unless a great deal of time was spent on the arts the results were bound to be mediocre, if not worthless, and that both practice and discussion of the worthless was a waste of time. If good results were obtained then these must have been at the expense of energy which should have been spent on religious exercise. Some Quakers would not even have their portraits painted. Myles Birket Foster was a man of more relaxed views, but it is still doubtful if young Birket had been exposed to the type of pictures that could be expected to be found in the home of non-Quakers of his class. This drawing has obviously not been copied, but is a genuine observation of a landscape which strongly suggests that it was painted in Northumberland. The finely stippled technique of the adult Birket Foster is often directly attributed to his work for the engravers, but here in the light green of the foreground, touched with brown, are minute strokes of the brush, which prove that the stippling method was basically an expression of his own natural style. The colouring shows the left figure in red and blue and the taller figure on the right in blue. The trees in the middle distance are heavily painted in dark green with a little brown, and the buildings, tinted pale brown, are lightly delineated in ink. The trees on the right are yellowish brown and the mountains in the distance are blue, tinted with green. It will be noticed that there is a faint arc in the left background, which would appear to have been intended for a rainbow, but has been washed out. Birket Foster probably realised that the atmospheric delicacy of this was beyond his capabilities and showed a nice judgement in removing it. Most children would have carefully introduced all seven colours in stiff sequence and with bridge-like effect. This artless picture with its wood-toy farm animals provides a delightful glimpse of the unformed style of Birket Foster, in which we can see an inherent sense of composition and hints of his adult manner, with a marked ability to communicate his own pleasure in the scene.

About 1835, Birket Foster was sent to boarding school in Hitchin, a town with strong Quaker connections. There he attended Isaac Brown's Academy, a school for the children of members of the Society of Friends. This was a small and rather original establishment, which was run by a schoolmaster of many parts, with a particular interest in botany. Field studies were included in the curriculum and these rambles in the Hertfordshire countryside may

well have had a formative influence on the subsequent love of Birket Foster for wild flowers and the hedgerows. A fellow pupil with Birket Foster was Joseph Lister, son of a Quaker family, who was later to become Lord Lister, celebrated for his discovery of the value of antiseptics. This places Birket Foster in the context of the social times in which he was brought up: e.g. in 1837, Queen Victoria had just ascended the throne and the Penny Post was not yet instituted, the discovery of electric self-induction had taken place only three years previously, and it was to be another decade before James Simpson gave a demonstration of the first surgical operation to be performed under chloroform in Britain.

An entry in the diary of William Lucas, a prominent local Quaker, records: 'Had the whole of Isaac Brown's school to tea – with a young assistant – 31.'[9] William Lucas was the brother of Samuel Lucas (1805–70), the landscape painter, whom Birket Foster probably first met in his school-days, as the two men certainly knew one another in later life. It seems likely that the assistant mentioned may have been Charles Parry, who is known to have given Birket Foster his first academic instruction in drawing and painting. Parry later exhibited a 'View of St Albans Abbey' at Suffolk Street (from an address in St Albans, Hertfordshire).

Notes: Chapter One

1 Information from the Register of Births and Burials supplied by K. Barratt, Librarian of the Meeting, Friends House, Newcastle upon Tyne. Information also from *A Pedigree of the Forsters and Fosters*, first edition (1862) compiled at the age of 18 by Joseph Foster, nephew of Birket Foster. He was to become a well-known antiquary and genealogist and was awarded an Hon. M.A. Oxon. in 1892.

2 From a memoir of the Foster and Birket families by Myles Birket Foster sen. - as copied by his grand-daughter, Alice M. Foster, from the original ms. A version of this story also appears in *The Society of Friends in Scorn called Quakers*, J.W. Steel, 1899. Further quotation from James Birket from material supplied by Charles Spence, great-great-grandson of Robert Spence.

3 The interrelationship of members of the Society of Friends was such that there was nearly always some kind of link between those of the same name and frequently between families. Details recorded on the Reynolds pedigree in possession of Jan Reynolds show that in 1734, Thomas Reynolds of Southwark married a Mary Foster, daughter of William Foster. After this, the use of Foster as a first name became traditional on that line of descent. Their son, Foster Reynolds, named his son William Foster and he subsequently called his son Foster. In 1825, Rachel Reynolds, a cousin of Foster Reynolds, married John Gurney Fry, who was a son of Elizabeth Fry. Three years later, Richenda, one of her daughters, married Foster Reynolds. The latter was cousin to Richard Freshfield Reynolds, great-great-grandfather of Jan Reynolds. Research points strongly to a positive link between the

above Mary Foster and the Birket Foster family, with an undoubted connection in the fact that eventually Charles Reynolds, her great-great-grandson, was to marry a great-niece of Birket Foster.

4 The *Encyclopaedia Britannica* has an article on the Society of Friends by Edward H. Milligan, including reference to Quakers and the professions.

5 From *The History of M.B. Foster and Sons Ltd: The Greatest Bottlers of Bass and Guinness in the World*, issued by the firm in 1929 to celebrate 'Bottling Beers for a Hundred Years'. Copy in the Marylebone Library, London NW1.

6 See article in *Commerce*, 10 June 1896, p. 34, copy in Local History Room, Marylebone Library, London NW1.

7 Information with reference to Frances and Priscilla Coar from *Recollections of Tottenham Friends and the Forster family* by Theodore Compton, 1893. Supplied by Edward H. Milligan, Friends House, Euston Road, London NW1 2BJ. Birket Foster wrote the letter to Compton, referring to the woodpecker drawing, on 18 August 1865. Frances Coar, by then an old lady, returned this drawing to Compton, once its significance to the now famous Birket Foster had been realised.

8 Letter reproduced in facsimile in *Birket Foster* by H.M. Cundall, A. and C. Black, 1906. Information from the Minutes and Advices of the London Yearly Meeting (1802) supplied by E.H. Milligan, Friends House, London.

9 Quotation from the diary of William Lucas, Hutchinson, 1933. Information from Hitchin Museum, Hertfordshire.

2

Life in the studio of Ebenezer Landells: friendship with Edmund Evans

Birket Foster was to record that he had a holiday in Scotland with his father in 1841, which probably would be just after he left Isaac Brown's Academy. Now that he was 16 his education was considered complete and Birket Foster joined his brother Dodshon in the family firm, although with little inclination for this occupation. After only a short while, he gashed his thigh in an accident with a bottle and it was then decided that he should be allowed to pursue a career which had some connection with art. It is interesting to contrast the attitudes of Myles Birket Foster, the bottler, with that of William Lucas, sen., of Hitchin, the brewer and maltster. Both men were Quakers and both had sons with a strong wish to draw and paint, but the painting life of Samuel Lucas was made exceedingly difficult and his talent certainly much restrained by the sober rules of the Society of Friends. It has to be remembered that it was not until 1925 that the Quakers recognized the place of the decorative arts as a 'service of social and spiritual value'. In the period of the early life of Birket Foster it was their custom to frown upon the use of colour and decoration not only in their dress, but also in the furnishing of their homes. William Lucas only became reconciled to his son's being engaged in any form of painting and drawing when it was quite certain that he would follow him into the family business. Samuel Lucas achieved some success, as an amateur, but was always frustrated by the demands of the brewing trade. Myles Birket Foster displayed a very much more tolerant attitude, but the Quaker tradition of plain occupation probably influenced his decision to apprentice his son to an engraver, rather than have him trained as a painter. Myles Birket Foster first arranged to place Birket with a Mr Stone, a die-engraver, i.e. engraving the reverse impression for striking coins, medals, seals, etc. But, before these articles of apprenticeship could be signed the unfortunate Stone committed suicide and Myles Birket Foster then approached Ebenezer Landells, a fellow Northumbrian, who had been for a short time a pupil of Thomas Bewick. A lot is often made of the association of Landells with Bewick, but he did not stay long with this engraver, as his father could not agree terms, but served most of his apprenticeship under Isaac Nicholson, who was a *pupil* of Bewick[1].

Ebenezer Landell's first step in the instruction of Birket Foster as a wood engraver was to tell him to invent or copy some designs onto spare wood blocks, in order to practise on these. The quality of talent that Birket Foster displayed in making these drawings was so outstanding that Landells at once saw that Foster could have a very promising future as a draughtsman and it was this arrangement for his training that was made with his father. Birket Foster was never apprenticed as a wood engraver as such.

Many years later, in compiling a *curriculum vitae* for the Royal Berlin Academy, Birket Foster was to write:

'At the age of sixteen I was placed as a pupil with Landells the wood engraver, who was himself the pupil of Bewick of Newcastle the great reviver of the art. My master discovered that I had a faculty for drawing and advised me to abandon engraving and draw on wood for the engravers instead. Landells gave me every facility for studying nature in the fields around London and also for drawing from the Antique at the Government School of Art then held at Somerset House.'[2]

Jacob Bell, a prominent member of the Society of Friends and founder of the Pharmaceutical Society, was a friend of both the Foster and Reynolds families. (Note: Richard Reynolds, FIC great-grandfather of Jan Reynolds, was a past President of the Pharmaceutical Society and principal founder of the Yorkshire College of Science, now Leeds University.) Jacob Bell was also a friend of Edwin Landseer, RA, whose animal and sporting pictures were such favourites of Queen Victoria. Landells had recommended that Birket Foster should copy engravings as a means of learning to understand the methods by which colour is represented by line and tone. Jacob Bell discerned the potential talent in Birket Foster and arranged for him to borrow some of the proofs of engravings of work by Landseer. Bell was particularly pleased with a pen-and-ink drawing that Foster did after one of these proofs, and wanted Landseer to see it. He told Birket Foster that the painter was at that moment dining at an hotel in Oxford Street and urged him to take the drawing round at once to show to Landseer, but Birket Foster was too shy to go. Who knows how the course of his career might have been altered if he had met Landseer at this point? Birket Foster later sold the drawing for 20 guineas, which was a considerable sum for a Landseer copy by a totally unknown youth.

Birket Foster, a lad of only sixteen, was considered competent enough to re-draw and improve some amateur sketches by Samuel Carter Hall. This rather pompous man, who was reputed to have been the original of Dickens' Mr Pecksniff and was later to found *The Art Journal*, would most certainly have disapproved if the work had not been of a very good standard. These drawings were en-

14

graved by Landells, as part of the illustrations in *Ireland: Its Scenery and Character* - a book compiled by Hall and his wife, published by How and Parsons in 1841.

Another book which included engravings by Landells after the work of Birket Foster was *Richmond and Other Poems* by Charles Ellis published by Madden and Malcolm in 1845. There are two copies of this book in the Richmond Central Library and also a note supplied by the art historian H.M. Cundall (who lived locally for many years) in which he has recorded that the two illustrations entitled 'Richmond Park - Harrington's Retreat' and 'Richmond Park - view over Kingston' were wood engravings by Landells after the work of Birket Foster. There is no mention of the name of Birket Foster on the title page, in the preface, or attached to any of the drawings, but as Cundall was a friend of Sir J. Whittaker Ellis, brother of the author of *Richmond and Other Poems*, the information that this work contains probably the very earliest of original Birket Foster book illustrations is likely to be correct. 'Richmond Park - Harrington's Retreat' has the name of Landells in the bottom right corner (rather faint) but 'Richmond Park - view over Kingston' displays no trace of any signature of either artist or engraver. 'Ham House' is very clearly signed by Landells at the bottom of the print.[3]

Birket Foster was not only encouraged by Landells to get out into the country for the purposes of specific illustrations, but also as a general exercise in obtaining proficiency as a draughtsman. Landells instructed:

'Now that work is slack in these summer months spend them in the fields; take your colours and copy every detail of the scene as carefully as possible, especially trees and forground plants, and come up to me once a month and show me what you have done.'

It was while with Landells that Birket Foster first met Edmund Evans (1826-1905) whose later career as an engraver and colour printer was to be so closely associated with his own. Edmund Evans recalled:

'It was not very long after I was apprenticed that B.

Foster came into our circle. I well remember he would not tell us what the "B" stood for; we of course thought it was Benjamin or Bertram: if he had known how well "Birket" would stand afterwards in relation to book illustration and art generally, he might not have been so shy in telling us.'[4]

Edmund Evans was a quiet, delicate youth, with a slight impediment in his speech, who had first been employed in Samuel Bentley's printing office, but had been apprenticed to Landells in 1840. Evans continues:

'Birket Foster's coming to Landells was a great boon to me - we had evidently many tastes in common. He was one year older than myself. Landells soon found that drawing was his forte; in fact he engraved very little: he often made drawings on wood for me to practise before I could engrave parts of the block to be used. He copied parts of Scott's Bible illustrations after W. Harvey's drawing and a few birds from Bewick's "British Birds".'

Evans probably registered the birds, because these were the subjects on which he worked, but Birket Foster undoubtedly continued to absorb mannerisms from the more scenic aspects of the Bewick volumes, as he had done in his school-days, with special influence from the delicate use of leaf and branch to form a vignette (a term used to describe a portrait or landscape without any definite edge). Vignettes tend to be most associated with small illustrations, particularly end pieces, in which the outer lines of the picture form a rounded and framing effect. Bewick was inclined to moralize, particularly against cruelty to animals, which had the effect of introducing some unpleasant scenes into his work. The early farmyard illustrations and wooded vignettes of Birket Foster certainly reflect those of Bewick, but without that element of the coarser side of country life.

2 Edmund Evans, drawn by Birket Foster during the early years of their time with the engraver, Ebenezer Landells (about 1842). *By permission of the Library of the University of California, Los Angeles, USA.*

Portrait of Edmund Evans drawn by Birket Foster

Apprentices in the Landells studio would work at benches on which they steadied the engraving blocks on small bags of sand. A magnifying lens was often held to one eye by screwing up the face, and a cloth was sometimes used to cover the mouth in order that the damp of the engraver's breath should not smear the drawing on which he was working. It may be helpful at this point to distinguish between a wood-cut and a wood-engraving, as the two are not one and the same, although both are relief prints. Wood-cutting was the ancient method and in use until about 1800, when wood-engraving was developed and largely superseded it; the former term is often used where the latter is more strictly correct. Wood-cuts were made on soft wood, cut plankwise and using a knife that was pulled or drawn towards the engraver. Portions of the drawing on wood were cut away so as to leave the lines of the artist in relief and it was these that printed. It was Thomas Bewick who perfected the much more subtle method of wood-engraving, or white-line engraving as it was sometimes known, thus: the surface employed was almost always the end grain of boxwood and the tool employed was a graver or burin. The surface can be regarded as a black background on which the design was made in the form of white lines, i.e. a wood engraving is like drawing on a blackboard with white chalk, as compared to drawing with pen on paper. The implement was pushed away from the engraver and the precision of this, instead of the use of a knife (combined with the hardness of the boxwood), provided opportunity for great delicacy of line. Boxwood has such strength and durability that Bewick calculated that one of his blocks had printed 900,000 impressions and was still sound. The technique of wood-engraving, as developed by Bewick, had many subtleties of method, such as the lowering of parts of the block in order to obtain a lesser degree of printing, e.g. fading the edges of a vignette by lowering the block with a flat chisel, but full details of these methods are not the concern of this book. The above explanation is intended only to give an outline of the process with which Birket Foster was to be for so long associated. It is not possible to appreciate fully his illustrated work unless one has some idea of the methods employed in reproducing it.

In 1841, Ebenezer Landells conceived the notion that the English might appreciate a humorous magazine on the lines of the French publication *Charivari*. After a great deal of complication this project was put in hand, with Henry Mayhew, Mark Lemon and Stirling Coyne as joint editors; Joseph Last, printer; Ebenezer Landells, engraver and W. Bryant, publisher. It was first proposed that the title of this magazine (price threepence) should be *The Funny Dog - with Comic Tales*. There are many versions of how the title eventually came about, but, years later, M.H. Spielmann was to record that Birket Foster had told him: 'I remember Landells coming into the workshop and saying "Well, boys, the title for the new work is to be 'Punch'". When he had gone we said it was a very stupid one, little thinking what a great thing it was to become.'[5] The most frequent explanation of the title is that it was a pun on the name of Mark Lemon, the first editor of *Punch*. Someone had suggested that the magazine would be like a good punch with so much lemon - or words to that effect!

The first issue appeared on 17 July 1841 with a flourish of publicity, but with only indifferent financial results. Birket Foster, as one of the apprentices of Landells, was involved in drawing and engraving some work for the early

volumes. Most of this was in the form of decorated initial letters that had previously been intended for *Cosmorama*, a projected magazine that Landells had abandoned in favour of *Punch*. Work by Birket Foster was first included in *Punch* on 5 September 1841. For some time all the initials were his work or that of H.G. Hine (later to be Vice President of the Institute of Painters in Watercolours). These initials consist of such devices as the letter 'O' shown in the shape of a laurel wreath with a Lifeguardsman charging through it or as a circle of flowers, surrounding a hay cart and sunset. Birket Foster executed 13 initials in 1841, 11 in the following year and two appeared in 1843. The letter 'G' and a few other designs were drawn and cut by Birket Foster, after the work of the French caricaturist Gavarni (the pseudonym for Hippolyte G.S. Chevalier, one of the leading contributors to *Charivari*). The name of Birket Foster is recorded with those of A.S. Henning, John Leech, etc. as a cartoonist for *Punch* in 1841. In fact, Birket Foster executed only one such example, Punch's Pencillings no. 22 - an adaptation of Cruikshank's 'Jack Sheppard Cutting his Name on the Beam'. This represented Lord John Russell and was a parody on an illustration that had recently appeared in a novel by Harrison Ainsworth. Spielmann notes that Henning later touched up Birket Foster's work, but, even so, it was remarkable that any cartoon had been entrusted to a youth of not quite seventeen.

In addition to the Gavarni copies, Birket Foster also did other small engravings that were reproduced in silhouette (known in the printing trade as 'blackies'). For these Birket Foster was paid 18 pence each. Edmund Evans also did some 'blackies' for *Punch* and his name appears as the engraver for one of the designs of 'Phiz' (Hablot K. Browne), an early contributor and the celebrated illustrator of novels by Charles Dickens. Drawings by Phiz for *The Old Curiosity Shop* were being engraved in the Landells studio in the early days of Birket Foster's time there and it was one of his errands to take proofs to the home of Charles Dickens for the author to see.

Mark Lemon was a dedicated editor of *Punch* and Birket Foster recalled for Spielmann frequent visits to his lodgings, on some errand for Landells. Here Lemon and Mayhew would sit in a dusty, untidy room, shirt sleeves rolled up and scissors in hand, working desperately hard on a 'make-up' of the weekly edition. Landells was equally enthusiastic, but had rather an excitable temperament and became involved in squabbles and difficulties over financing the paper. Consequently, in December 1842, he severed his connection with *Punch* and also lost all the engraving work. This had the effect of terminating any further contributions from Foster, but Ebenezer Landells was soon to be associated with another new and important publishing venture.

In the early 1840s, Herbert Ingram, a printer, stationer and speculator, moved to London from Nottingham and established himself in Fleet Street with his partner Nathaniel Cooke. It was here that he conceived an idea for a new weekly newspaper, which was commercially inspired by the large number of copies of *The Weekly Chronicle* which he had been able to sell in Nottingham, during a period when that newspaper was relating (and illustrating with crude wood-cuts) the grisly details of a particularly horrendous murder. Ingram was greatly enthusiastic about illustrating not only murder, but every kind of crime, with a special predeliction for factory riots, rickburning, counterfeiting, horse-stealing and sacrilege. *The*

Weekly Chronicle had foundered, but a former owner of this newspaper brought Ingram and his scheme to the notice of Henry Vizetelly, the engraver, printer and publisher, a man of taste and discernment. Vizetelly was later to relate:

'The suggestion of a newspaper with every number of it more or less filled with engravings came as a sort of revelation to me, and I at once realised the vast field it opened up. I strongly combatted the notion of giving a general criminal tone to the illustrations, but although Ingram wavered a little I at first failed to bring him to my way of thinking ...'

Ingram pointed out that it was not engravings of the Houses of Parliament or the Queen taking an airing that had increased the circulation of *The Weekly Chronicle*, but it was eventually agreed that Vizetelly should produce a prospectus on his own lines. He envisaged illustrations that would include royal ceremonial, crowd scenes at great events, coverage of foreign wars and politics and also portraits (utilising the recent development of the daguerreotype). Ingram finally accepted this format and chose the title *The Illustrated London News* in view of the fact that the customers in his Nottingham shop had been indifferent to which paper they bought, specifying only that they wanted the one that contained the London news. It was certainly due to the intervention and wise counsel of Henry Vizetelly that *The Illustrated London News* was to be launched on course to become the respected journal that still exists to this day.

The Illustrated London News was first issued on 14 May 1842. Edmund Evans was later to write:

'I well remember Birket Foster buying the first number of the latter as we walked home through Red Lion Street, for Landells had moved from Thornhill Road to Bidborough Street, New Road, St. Pancras.'

The illustrations were all engraved by Vizetelly or his brother, from the drawings of John Gilbert (later Sir John Gilbert RA, President of the Water-colour Society and a close associate of Birket Foster), but after only a few months, a considerable amount of the engraving work for *The Illustrated London News* was given to Ebenezer Landells. The overtime worked by Evans, in order to have blocks ready for *The Illustrated London News* (often delivering these to Landells at four or five in the morning) would be considered gross exploitation by the standards of today, but Landells was a good master. He was a tall, handsome, kindly man and popular with his apprentices, who referred to him affectionately as 'The Skipper' or 'Old Tooch-it-oop' (on account of his strong Northumbrian accent), but to his friends he was generally known as 'Daddy Long Legs' or 'Daddy Landells'. A nineteenth-century engraver who allowed an apprentice to recover in the open air for a day or two after an overtime session must have been unusual in his consideration. Edmund Evans wrote:

'Landells was very good in letting me go out with Birket Foster on his journeys near and round London – for I was often knocked up and unfit for engraving after the drives to get work for *The Illustrated London News* and

Punch done to time, and the air revived me. Foster did an immense amount of sketching from nature this way.'

Evans chronicles many of these expeditions. There were railway journeys out to Croydon, walking then to Wadden water-mill or on to Beddington or Sanderstead. The pair often went to Rochester and once travelled by open third-class carriages on a day trip to Dover. When Landells' studio was in Bride's Court, Fleet Street, the two youths would go down to the riverside and watch the barges with their burnt-sienna coloured sails and wander about looking for picturesque subjects to sketch.

Edmund Evans related:

'There is one little incident I must tell – Foster and I went to Blackwall when the railway there was without locomotives! The carriages were drawn over the rails by ropes passed over grooved wheels by stationary engines, the carriages gripped the rope when it began to move. This railway made a terrible noise, a rumbling that could be heard for a great distance. On this occasion we went to Blackwall for the sake of the picturesque "bits" for sketching to be found there. I know we spent a considerable time in the "Isle of Dogs" close to Blackwall; it was then a pleasant meadow with dykes and trenches to allow the Thames to flow through it and supply the cattle and sheep with water; a large number grazed there. Anyhow, we wasted the day in looking for "bits" to sketch instead of doing some of the many objects, picturesque enough for anything, that were to be found there in those days, so Foster had no sketches to show Landells next morning. However, when he got home, he copied in a sketch-like way little scraps from *Etchings of Shipping and Craft* by E.W. Cooke. When Landells saw them, he said: "Capital, Foster, there is nothing like going to nature direct". This was the only incident of the kind, for Foster was a most conscientious worker; he loved the work too much to scamp or shirk it. I well remember an idle fellow-apprentice watching Foster at work in a room he had to himself – through the keyhole – and wondering how he could possibly work so hard without the eye of the master on him!'

The engraver, John Greenaway, was also a fellow apprentice with Edmund Evans. A pencil drawing by Birket Foster of John Greenaway, magnifying lens to his eye and block in hand can be seen facing page 40 in *Kate Greenaway* – a biography of this famous daughter of John Greenaway by M.H. Spielmann and G.S. Layard, published by Adam and Charles Black in 1905. The pencil sketch of Edmund Evans (Ill. 2) is a companion piece and was included with 20 loose items in an envelope, inserted into a notebook of drawings by Edmund Evans (some of which were executed when he was only fifteen years old). The inscription by Evans on this affectionately-observed portrait fully authenticates it as the work of Birket Foster and it was certainly drawn during the time that the two friends were with Landells. The gentle expression on the face of Edmund Evans and the sense of quiet concentration as he works with an engraving tool is beautifully suggested. This is how it was for Birket Foster in the studio of Ebenezer Landells and by looking at the simple lines of this drawing we are able to experience an intimate glimpse of the atmosphere of those days.

Notes: Chapter Two

1 See *The Brothers Dalziel*, B.T. Batsford reprint, 1978.
2 Printed minutes of the Committee of Management of the Government School of Design for December 1836–October 1847 are preserved in the Library of the Ministry of Education at Elizabeth House, York Rd, London SE1. A printed report of the proceedings of the School of Design from 1837 to 1840 survives amongst the Treasury Board papers (Ref. T1/4332 – paper number 9783). (Information from the Public Record Office, Kew, Richmond, Surrey.)

3 Information from the Central Library, Richmond, Surrey.
4 Quotation from *The Reminiscences of Edmund Evans: Wood Engraver and Colour Printer*, introduction by Ruari McLean, Oxford University Press, 1967. All quotations by Evans in this chapter are from this source.
5 From *The History of Punch* by M.H. Spielmann, 1895.

3
Early career as an illustrator

The family of Myles Birket Foster maintained a close involvement with their connections in the Newcastle area. Birket Foster's aunt, Mary Spence, bore children over a period of 21 years and this resulted in no less than 18 Spence cousins for the Fosters. One has to admire the hopeful optimism in naming twin daughters, Margaret and Anne, after the death at birth of another pair of twins of this same name in the previous year! By 1844, the surviving family of Robert and Mary Spence consisted of four sons and nine daughters.

The most usual form of transport between the Newcastle area and London during that period was by sea. Birket Foster was now 19 and after a visit to these relations in North Shields we have a charming glimpse of his return journey in a letter to Robert Spence. This is written from the new address of Myles Birket Foster at 4 Stranraer Place, Maida Hill, and is dated 14th 7th month 1844.

'My very dear Uncle,

I thought I should just like to send thee a note myself telling thee of my safe arrival at our new abode. We had a beautiful passage the sea was remarkably smooth a nice wind from the land carried us along famously. As Tynemouth lessened I really felt very dull I seemed leaving so many kind friends I might not see again for a long time. The beautiful light at Flamboro was lit as we passed it. I went to bed about 11 o'clock and slept without waking till 9 in the morning. When I got up I found that we had just come through Yarmouth Rd. We passed Gravesend about 6 in the evening and got to London about 9. There was nobody to meet me. They did not expect me till much later, so I took a cab and went straight home to Stranraer Place. I was much pleased with the house. We were extremely sorry to hear of dear Rachel's illness, but were glad to hear a better account in a letter from Polly and also such a good one of thyself. We were all delighted to see thy handwriting – perhaps either Meggy or Anne would just write us a line to say how dear R. is. We should be much obliged as we are very anxious to hear.

With my dear love in which all here unite to you all and believe me to remain thy truly attached nephew.'[1]

Birket Foster's cousin, Rachel, had married Henry Shewell Corder in 1842. '... dear Rachel's illness' was the tragic result of giving birth to a second son who lived only three months. She died five days after this letter was written.

Birket Foster writes in a neat flowing script, which has

not yet formed into the adult hand. The signature is interesting. This differs from the copper-plate style of the letter and suggests that the young Birket Foster had been consciously experimenting and aiming for a signature that would add a handsome flourish to his work. What must surely have been an unconscious influence is the fact that the capital lettering and general appearance has a definite hint of the facsimile signature of M.B. Foster on the label of 'Bugle Brand' beer! The eventual signature adopted by Birket Foster is similar in basic formation to the early version.

Birket Foster notes in an outline of his tours that he sketched in Scotland and the Shetland Isles in 1845. Edmund Evans must have been with him on this trip, as he writes: 'I forget how we left Edinburgh, but we stayed on our way home at North Shields, at the Bank House, with Mr Spence – Birket Foster's uncle. The memory of this friend [of the Society of Friends] with all his kindness remains fresh in me after so long an interval.' What has not quite been retained by Evans was the *year* in which he stayed with the Spences. He placed this as 1846, but the fact that the estimable Robert Spence died on 17 August 1845 proves that Evans must have made a visit there prior to this event. However, there is no doubt that Evans was also with Birket Foster on a further trip to Scotland. Evans recalled:

'... In early June 1846 I had a most delightful holiday with Birket Foster and his brother Dodshon [incorrectly spelt Dodgson by Evans]. We started from about the Tower on the Thames, by steamboat to Berwick-on-Tweed. The sea was absolutely calm all the way. Foster worked hard at sketching, his brother collected seabird's eggs. We had a boat to the Farne Islands ... we saw over the Longstone Lighthouse ... it is a wild desolate spot, the sea coming up to the base of the lighthouse at high tide, leaving an immense surface of weed-covered rocks when the tide is out. We went up the river Coquet to the hermitage there; the remains of the old Warkworth Castle are charmingly situated above the bank of the river, most picturesque.'[2]

'Coquet Island' in the Laing Gallery appears to be almost certainly dated about this period and there also exists a rather unusual informal study inscribed 'Quarry – 12th/6 '46/Warkworth' which shows the industrial workings of this scene, with pulleys and trolleys on rails, an interesting glimpse of Birket Foster sketching the pattern of these lines as they took his eye. The party continued their tour with a visit to Bamborough Castle and went by sailing boat to see Lindisfarne Abbey on Holy Island. They took a steamboat to Leith and then made a base in Edinburgh. Their explorations were to include a visit to Stirling, a sight of Loch Katrine and the Trossachs and an ascent of Ben Lomond.

Most of the standard works make mention of the serious accident that Birket Foster had during a visit to Scotland, but evidence as to exactly when this was is conflicting. He was thrown from a chaise and broke his right arm in two places and also received a severe spinal injury which resulted in a lumbar abscess. On his return home, Aston Key, an eminent London surgeon, advised resetting the limb, but Birket Foster (probably very wisely) refused and the arm eventually healed very well, but the back injury necessitated him being in bed for six months and it appears that his life was actually in danger at one point. However, Birket Foster was always one to take a philosophical view and regarded this enforced rest as positively beneficial to his career, enabling him to ponder constructively on his future. Some references say that he got up from his bed on his *nineteenth* birthday, i.e. 4 February 1844, which would have meant that he had the accident in the summer of 1843, but all other evidence points to a later date as we are told that the event was shortly before he was due to finish his time with Landells. This would mean that the accident happened during the 1845 tour or perhaps on a second visit in that year. It seems likely that Birket Foster would go to North Shields for the funeral of Robert Spence in August 1845 and if this was followed by a short trip to Scotland, it would fit in exactly with the six months he was in bed, but it would be his twenty-first birthday on which he got up, i.e. 4 February 1846. This theory appears to be the one that is the least contradictory. If so, we can discount any work purporting to be by Birket Foster between August 1845 and February 1846, although he is said to have attempted to use his left hand.

George and Edward Dalziel were two of the many engravers of this period who emanated from Northumberland and their records corroborate these dates. They had known Birket Foster since he was 'a little boy with a round jacket and a turn-down collar'. Writing of his early days, they recalled:

'It was during his illness that the period of his indentures expired, but, as soon as he was well enough to resume work he insisted on returning to his duties that he might make up the time that had been lost; and this he did without any request on Landells' part. On his return we well remember seeing him at work in a little top room in Birch [Bride?] Court, E.C. He was making small drawings of pots and pans, teapots, gridirons, and other such articles for an ironmonger's catalogue, and said in the most cheerful manner: "It is right that I should return here and do this work; it is good practice, and will enable me to draw all these sorts of things with some practical knowledge." '[3]

In 1845, Birket Foster had worked up drawings for *The Illustrated London News* from sketches sent to England by Landells, who was covering a visit by Queen Victoria to Germany. Other unsigned work had been used, but the first contribution on which his name appeared was a small insert illustration of 'The Ruins of Tynemouth Priory, near Newcastle', published on 18 July 1846. This was not signed conventionally, but the name Foster is introduced across an old gravestone, an integral part of the design.

Edmund Evans notes that Birket Foster left Landells in 1846, at which time he himself had another 15 months to serve. Birket Foster now set about obtaining work on his own account. He made several original drawings on wood and started to hawk these round the offices of various publishers and printers. He approached *Sharpe's Magazine* but was told rather crisply that they did not require any of his work. Robert Branston, who had a large engraving and printing establishment, congratulated Birket Foster on his drawings and offered to bear him in mind, but it was not until he contacted Henry Vizetelly that his success was assured. The publishing firm of Chapman and Hall had commenced a series, entitled 'The Boys' Own Library' and proposed a *Boys' Country Year Book* for which Thomas Miller, Lincolnshire basket-maker, poet and writer (and later failed bookseller and publisher) was engaged to write the text. Henry Vizetelly relates:

'. . . it was decided to make an important feature of its many illustrations. Edward Duncan, the water-colour artist, had already made a few rather uninteresting drawings for the work, when one day a young fellow called upon me with a large round of box-wood, which he had covered with cleverly pencilled sketches of rural subjects, as a specimen of his abilities. I saw at a glance that he was the very individual we were in want of, and after purchasing his specimen drawings there and then, promised him immediate and constant employment. The young fellow I speak of was Birket Foster, whose charming and truthful pictures of English rural scenes have long since been universally admired.'[4]

This would seem to be a suitable point at which to outline the method employed by Birket Foster in producing a drawing for the engraver, as follows: a wash of Chinese white was laid down on the wood block and then the clouds and distances were shown in graduations of Indian Ink. The other details were marked in with strokes of a very hard pencil and further applications of Indian ink from a fine pen. Illustration 15 shows a most attractive example of an uncut drawing by Birket Foster, in which one can see the natural marking of the wood underneath the basic wash of paint. It is interesting to note that illustration ideas worked out by Birket Foster in preliminary water-colour sketches on paper often have the characteristic addition of minute details, very firmly impressed in hard pencil strokes. These preliminary sketches can make very charming little pieces and are much sought after on the market.

The Country Year Book was published by Chapman and Hall in 1847 and was first issued in four parts: Summer, Autumn, Winter and Spring. Each part had a frontispiece and title printed in about four colours from wood blocks, with black and the addition of some gold. Some of the compositions have a strong influence from Thomas Bewick and the figures are inclined to a certain lumpiness of line and form which was very soon to be replaced by the more characteristic style of Birket Foster. This is already very apparent in the general effect of these attractive illustrations, which are among the earliest independent signed work by this artist. Ruari McLean has named *The Country Year Book* as a charming example of the best ordinary commercial production of the period and four black-and-white vignettes and the colour plates for 'Winter' are reproduced in his *Victorian Book Design and Colour Printing*. The frontispiece for 'Summer' is shown in colour in *English Children's Books* by Percy Muir.[5] These colour plates were probably the first in which Henry Vizetelly reproduced the effect of painting by the superimposition of translucent colours. *The Country Year Book* was later published in one volume under the imprint of Henry Bohn.

In May 1847, Edmund Evans kept a few diary entries in a little notebook of a visit that he made to the Lakes in the company of Birket Foster, who was with his brother John, and someone whom we must presume was their sister, Mary. The diary jottings of this shy young man provide a charming glimpse of these young Victorians on holiday. One is slightly surprised that Mary Foster did not have a female companion, but this is probably an example of our present-day lack of understanding of the amount of freedom that was actually allowed to women of the period, who were certainly most energetic tourists and equal to any mountain walk in spite of the unsuitability of their costume. In recording the places that the party visited, Edmund Evans has given a very useful record of subjects likely to have been sketched by Birket Foster at this date, including The Hill at Sedbergh. This farmhouse had been the parental home of Mary Foster (née Burton), wife of Robert Foster and grandmother of Birket Foster. The second wife of Robert Foster was Margaret Burton, widow of the brother of his first wife. His stepdaughter, Mary Burton, married Joseph Morton and it was she who was living at The Hill, Sedbergh in 1847. The reference in the diary to 'Mary's Aunt Morton' is slightly confusing. It seems in this case that Evans may not have been referring to the Mary in their party, although it would be very likely that Birket Foster and his brothers and sister did indeed refer to Mary Morton as 'Aunt' (see diary entry – 4 June). This tour was very much a pilgrimage to the area essentially connected with the roots of the Foster family. Robert Foster had inherited the Wood estate, near Windermere, from his uncle, James Birket, and later bought the Dovecote Gill estate, which was rather celebrated for its caves (see diary – 3 June). Hebblethwaite Hall is still standing, but the mill and many of the surrounding buildings have disappeared.

Extract from diary of Edmund Evans:[6]

'*May 31 1847*. Left the Euston Square Station at ½ past 8 am for Birmingham, whence we proceeded to Manchester, arriving at 5 pm Went to Mr. King's Moss Bank and remained all night.
[Note: Mr King would be related to Birket Foster's mother, née King.]
June 1. Went with John and Birket over their cousins Cotton Mill – was much interested in it – returned to dinner at Mr King's and left Manchester at 4 o'clock – A fine old Cathedral Church at Manchester – Over the altar hangs a piece of tapestry much faded – the carving beautiful – Went on by rail to Lancaster – took tea – visited the castle – now a prison – an old church stood picturesquely on the brow of the Hill. Came back into the Lady's Walk, along the winding river overhung on the side by a rich plantation. Mounted an aqueduct over the river – were serenaded by a party under the bridge – listened some time – crossed the river by the aqueduct & came back by the road. It was nearly dark when we reached the Inn.
Left Lancaster about 10 – June 2nd. Proceeded to Kirkby Lonsdale – took luncheon and sketched the bridge – left about 4 for Sedbergh. Walked in the churchyard till dark. Saw the tree where George Fox preached.
June 3rd. Visited Dove Cote Gill – whence we all crawled

like worms – the opening at the upper end was so extremely narrow. Went on to Hebblethwaite Hall where M.B. Foster and brother was born – a lovely spot – the beck was beautiful – I tried to sketch it. Next to Cantley Spout – the first fall I ever saw – took a slight sketch of it. Took tea with Thomas Hanley, wife and son – returned to Sedbergh, where we passed the night.
June 4. Visited The Hill belonging to Mary's Aunt Morton – drove to Dent Dale – visited the clergyman Professor Sedgewick's brother. Left Sedbergh for Kendal. Called at Parkside on the family of the Bensons: proceeded to Brownes – on the banks of Windermere.
June 5. After breakfast went on the Lake. Visited several of the islands on which we found the lily of the valley growing in wild luxuriance. Went up the Lake as far as Low-wood. Lunched and returned.
June 6th. Spent the Sunday at Brownes – attended morning and evening services.
June 7th. Breakfasted at 7. Crossed the Ferry and walked to Hawkshead and drove round Coniston – passing the lake – dined at a farm house on the mountains – passed Blea Tarn, Elterwater, Dungeon Gill, etc. Arrived at Low-wood for coffee.
June 8th. Visited Ambleside – Mounted to see Stock Gill Force (*sic*) – from there to Skelwith & Colwith – saw Lough Rigg Tarn – dined at Low-wood – went for a row from 9 till 10.
June 9th. Left Low-wood and enjoyed a delightful drive passed Rydal and Grasmere Lakes & round the foot of Helvellyn. Visited Rydal Mount where Wordsworth lives – also the falls – took sketches of both – passed Thirlmere. Came to Keswick in sight of Skiddaw and Saddleback – found a piano in our sitting-room. Saw Crosthwaite Museum and lead pencil manufactory.
June 10th. Left Keswick for Scale Force, a magnificent fall, passing on our way Honister Crag – visited Barrow and Lodore. We crossed Crummock Water to see the fall & had a rough passage – reached the Inn soon after nine.
June 11th. Took a car to within 6 miles of Wastwater. Went round by Styehead Pass on ponies – rowed the length of this beautiful lake & returned just in time to clear the pass by daylight. Kept our ponies till we were tired & then leaving them with the Guide, remounted the car and arrived at Keswick by ½ past 10 –
12th. A dull morning – so we did not set off till near the middle of the day for Skiddaw. We were 2 hours and ½ ascending and 2 hours in returning. Dined at the Inn & remained in the rest of the day which was rainy.
13. Sunday. Rainy. Went to the old Church in the morning. It has lately been renovated and beautified. Southey is buried in the Churchyard and a splendid monument is erected to him in the church. Birket sketched it before we left Keswick, as well as his house which was close to the town.'

At this point, Edmund Evans includes 18 lines of verse that had been written by Wordsworth for inscription on the tomb of Robert Southey. Obviously, Birket Foster must have been aware that both Robert Southey and Wordsworth had known his grandfather, Robert Foster, which would give him a special interest in these memorials, but it is to be noted that the party did not appear to make any approach to Wordsworth at the time when they visited Rydal Mount on 9 June. The diary of Edmund Evans continues:

3 'Rush for the Daily Newspapers' – from *The Illustrated London News*, 4 March 1848. Drawing by Birket Foster: engraved by Edmund Evans. Size: 9 × 5½″ – 22.8 × 14 cms. *By permission of Sheffield City Libraries.*

'The church has a good organ & the windows are very beautiful - the Vicar whose name was Lynn, was 75 years of age - he preached on the one thing needful - the desirableness of religion being the chief pursuit of life. I was much interested in the services. We had a wet walk back to the Inn. Remained in till the evening when we again went to service at the New Church - a pretty neat building.'

At this period the area round Keswick was a stronghold of Quakerism. Birket Foster seems to have made a preferred choice of attending the services of the established church, but it has to be noted that in 1839 two of his brothers, Dodshon and John (who was on this holiday) had resigned from the Society of Friends and been received into the Church of England. No doubt this had influenced Birket to consider his own feelings as a dissenter and the resignation of Myles Birket Foster was to be accepted by the Westminster Monthly Meeting on 15 March 1849. This must refer to Birket, as the likelihood of it having been his father is remote. But, resignation or not, Birket Foster came from generations of Quakers, whose religion had patterned the whole of their domestic and business life, so that anyone born into such a family was part of a veritable separate breed, with attitudes and customs that must always be an essential fact of this inheritance.

Edmund Evans later developed a deeply religious outlook and one wonders if this could have first been engendered in the church at Keswick. On the next day he noted:

'*June 14th*. A wet morning - wrote a letter. Packed up my things while Mary was gone with Birket to sketch. Walked out and did some shopping - went on the Lake - left Birket on an island to sketch the view of the distant hills while we visited Barrow and Lodore Falls. Returned to the Inn - dined - and left Keswick for Patterdale.

June 15th. A wet morning so were prevented attempting Helvellyn's height - but after an early luncheon left for Penrith, where we stayed a couple of hours before proceeding to Carlisle, where we slept.

16th. Visited the Cathedral & remains of the ancient castle. Left for Gilsland where we found the family of the Gilpins, & were joined in the evening by Robert F. and his cousins A. and M. Spence.'[5]

Here the diary ends. Robert Foster, eldest brother of Birket Foster was now aged 35 (and appears to have lived at one time in Kendal). Edmund Evans refers to Anne and Margaret Spence as cousins of Robert Foster, but ignores the fact that they were also cousins of Birket Foster, i.e. the twin daughters of Robert Spence of North Shields, who had married Mary Foster of Hebblethwaite Hall. It will later be seen that this meeting with his cousins was of special significance in the life of Birket Foster.

The seven-year apprenticeship of Edmund Evans with Landells had been completed in May 1847 and he was now determined to start up on his own, although he had been offered a permanent position with Landells. He obtained some engraving work for *The Illustrated London News*, including 'Rush for the Daily Newspapers', published 4 March 1848 (Ill. 3). The offices of the *London Telegraph* were then two doors from St Dunstan's Church on the north side of Fleet Street and this engraving now provides an interesting piece of social history. Edmund Evans was later to describe it as 'a picturesque wood-cut. I saw it exhibited in a frame in the King's Library a few years ago with Birket Foster's name attached to it.' Evans has a rather quaint style of writing, but this last comment points towards a practice that was to be very widespread, i.e. the wholesale removal of engravings from the pages of nineteenth-century periodicals. These were then handsomely mounted and framed to include the name of the original artist. The results were decorative, but often wrongly purported to be limited 'pulls' or of greater importance than was merited by what was basically a magazine cutting. But, although we may deplore the original practice (and particularly if this involved the removal of plates from books) time has had the effect of giving an acceptability to engravings detached from their first context. Many Birket Foster illustrations would have perished but for having been removed from tattered volumes, and can still be found loose in boxes of old prints. Such engravings can have real potential as charming framed pictures and examples of the craft and design of the period.

Notes: Chapter Three
1 Letter from Birket Foster in the collection of Newcastle upon Tyne City Libraries.
2 From *The Reminiscences of Edmund Evans: Wood Engraver and Colour Printer*, introduction by Ruari McLean, Oxford University Press.
3 *The Brothers Dalziel: A Record of Work* - 1890. Reprinted with foreword by Graham Reynolds, B. T. Batsford, 1978.

4 *Glances Back through Seventy Years* by Henry Vizetelly, Paul, Trench, Trübner and Co., 1893.
5 *English Children's Books* by Percy Muir, B. T. Batsford, 1954.
6 Diary entries by Edmund Evans are published from the original by permission of John F. Foster, great-grandson of Birket Foster.

4

The Illustrated London News and the success of *Evangeline*

By 1848, the name of Birket Foster was becoming known. He continued to keep up his links with the Quaker community in Hitchin and on 12 April 1848 an entry in the diary of William Lucas records: 'In the evening Birket Foster, a young artist, much engaged by the Illustrated News, etc. and his sister with H. Brown and the Pollards drank tea with us.'[1]

Joseph Pollard was from a Quaker family and had been at school with Birket Foster at Isaac Brown's Academy. He lived with his widowed mother and William Brown, his uncle, at High Down, Pirton, near Hitchin and it seems very likely that Birket Foster and his sister, Mary,[2] were staying there at the time of this visit to the home of William Lucas. In later years, Lady Nicoll, daughter of Joseph Pollard, was to write in *Bells of Memory* (a privately published autobiography) that Birket Foster was a lifelong friend of her father. Lady Nicoll commented on Birket Foster:

'... he literally drew with his brush, very dry and light. Many studies of trees he made from the dining room window at High Down, as he chatted to my father. There is a beautiful elm which I often think I recognise in his exquisite, caressing little pictures.'[3]

The elm tree was established from the very earliest days of the illustrated work of Birket Foster as a particularly characteristic feature. In later years, he was to live in a house surrounded by quantities of fir trees and was asked why he so seldom introduced this species into his pictures. Birket Foster replied: 'A fir always reminds me of a Noah's Ark tree, a stem in the middle, a pyramidical mass of foliage above with absolutely no variety. Now my favourite, "the hedgerow elm" as Milton calls it, has a magnificent bole, redolent of strength, and a superstructure which constantly varies, and it is as picturesque when shorn of leaves as when covered with them' (*The Art Journal*, 1890).

It is one of the special pleasures of the work of Birket Foster that his constant introduction of elms has preserved the beauty of a tree that is now sadly fast disappearing from the sight of our generation.

William Lucas in referring to the 'Illustrated News, etc.' almost certainly included *The Illustrated London Almanack*. The whole tone of this publication had been greatly improved in 1848 by the appearance of a series of 'Country Scenes' by Birket Foster, engraved by Henry Vizetelly. These beautifully detailed and atmospheric illustrations are of far too high a quality for the type of publication and the cheap pulp paper on which it was printed. Inking and indentation on the reverse of the page can be discerned through all the illustrations and this slightly spoils the general effect of what must be some of the most attractive collaborations between Birket Foster and Henry Vizetelly. 'February' and 'August' (Ills. 4, 5) are illustrated here to show the subtle craftsmanship that has produced two directly opposite effects of weather and season in compositions of very similar basic design. It is entirely by delicate manipulation of line that we can almost hear the boisterous spring-heralding wind blowing through the February trees and in the other illustration feel so well the mood of late summer and all the brooding stillness of a hot August afternoon.

The Illustrated London Almanack had first been produced in 1845, as an additional publication from the offices of *The Illustrated London News*. This included some very indifferent headpieces for each of the 12 months of the year, after vaguely zodiacal designs by Kenny Meadows, engraved by W.J. Linton, with other illustrations by John Gilbert, W. Harvey, etc. The format proved very popular, with nature notes, sporting features, domestic hints, scales of charges, time-tables and charts, and was imitated in 1846 by *The Pictorial Almanack and Year Book*.

In 1849, Birket Foster contributed another series of country pieces to *The Illustrated London Almanack* (Ills. 6, 7, 8). As before these were in the form of 12 large vignettes with 12 smaller ones on the facing page, and in this sequence the subjects were appropriate to the traditional activities of each month, with a detailed text by Thomas Miller. His first description for January rather tellingly states:

'Many of the old games and masques and mummings, which were in accordance with the simple habits of our forefathers, have long since passed away. A few only remain, out of those which it was their delight and amusement to witness; and even those are shorn of their ancient splendour; for though still picturesque, they have a faded look, and seem no more in keeping with the manners and customs of the present day, than murrey-coloured coats and slashed doublets would be ...'

But, Birket Foster's illustrations of Maypole Dancing, Whitsuntide Processions and Sheep Shearing Feasts, etc. are full of keen observation and some have almost a feel of Hogarth in lighter mood (Ills. 5, 6, 7, 8). The 24 large drawings and 24 vignettes in these two series form the best of the contributions of Birket Foster to *The Illustrated*

4 '**Country Scenes – February**' – from *The Illustrated London Almanack*, 1848. Drawing by Birket Foster: engraved by Henry Vizetelly. Size: 6½ × 7″ – 16.5 × 17.8 cms.
Collection: Brian and Rachel Moss.

London Almanack, but he also drew the cover illustrations for the 1853 edition, which is shown on page XI of *The Reminiscences of Edmund Evans* who was the engraver and also in that year for a series of drawings by Birket Foster of popular recreations, e.g. 'Skating on the ice in the Park', 'A Visit to the Zoological Gardens', etc. Copies of these supplements (sometimes to be found in bound volumes) provide a interesting aspect of the early work of Birket Foster, but the very nature of *The Illustrated London Almanack* made it particularly expendable and has induced rarity by comparison with work in *The Illustrated London News*.

In the summer of 1848, Birket Foster was sent to Portsmouth by the latter to cover the visit of Queen Victoria to open the new Steam Basin for shipping. This kind of illustrated reporting of topical events was very much in the spirit of the aims of the original Henry Vizetelly pros-

pectus, but was not very suitable to the style of Birket Foster, although the subsequent engravings by Edmund Evans show a faithful reproduction of events, as sketched at the scene. Queen Victoria came by sea from Osborne to perform the ceremony and entered the Basin in *The Fairy*. This scene and 'The Mayor of Portsmouth presenting the address to the Queen' appeared in *The Illustrated London News* on 3 June 1848. Ten years later, Birket Foster was still undertaking such assignments (see water-colour study for the 'Arrival of Queen Victoria at Birmingham Town Hall on 15 June 1858: Appendix 7 p. 207). Reproduced in *The Illustrated London News* 26 June 1858. But, such work

25

was not typical of the general style of Birket Foster for this periodical. Nathaniel Cooke told Edmund Evans that he was willing to give him engraving work for *The Illustrated London News*, but only if he could adapt his technique to a bolder method, more suitable to newspaper printing. Evans demonstrated his adaptability by engraving a drawing by Birket Foster that was particularly successful and reproduced well (Ill. 9). Evans recalled: '... the inscription they printed under it was "The Holly Cart" drawn by Foster. This was a joke against B.F. for some time!'[4] The engraving depicts the actual scene outside the home of Birket Foster at 4 Stranraer Place, Maida Hill, from the

5 'Country Scenes - August' - from *The Illustrated London Almanack*, 1848. Drawing by Birket Foster: engraved by Henry Vizetelly. Size: 6½ × 7″ - 16.5 × 17.8 cms.
Collection: Brian and Rachel Moss.

little room that was set apart for his studio. Stranraer Place (now the section of Sutherland Avenue between Maida Vale and Randolph Road) appears to have had the even numbers on the south side of the road and the odd numbers on the north side. If this is so, then 4 Stranraer Place has been demolished and the entire block is now taken up by St Joseph's Catholic Primary School, Sutherland Avenue. The houses opposite are numbered 190-200, Sutherland Avenue and would appear to be the original ones as seen in the 'Christmas Holly Cart' illustration.[5]

Birket Foster's sister, Mary (later Mrs William Atchison) added details about this engraving, which were included in the 1906 biography:

'Looking out of the window one winter's morning his attention was attracted by their servant purchasing some

holly from a cart drawn by a donkey. The subject pleased him and he made a hasty sketch, which he afterwards drew on a wood-block. His sister, admiring the rough sketch, Birket Foster worked upon it with water-colours and presented it to her at Christmas.'[6]

Edmund Evans had a flair for thinking up commercially successful ideas and it was his suggestion that *The Illustrated London News* should run a series on the 'Watering Places of England'. He and Birket Foster enjoyed travelling about the country in search of suitable subjects, although they were not paid any expenses by *The Illustrated London News*. They started to work on this project in May 1849 and the first of the series to appear was a view of 'Worthing, from the beach' (published 25 August 1849). This charming series was to run for several years and the happy collaboration between Birket Foster and Edmund

Evans is reflected in the quality of these beautifully composed scenes. 'Hastings' (8 September 1849) showed a downland view with the sea in the distance and was followed in October by 'Bridlington Quay'. This breezy scene is here Ill. 10. In 1850, they went to Folkestone (engraving published 13 July); Dover (engraving published 17 August) and Budleigh Salterton (engraving published 24 August). Birket Foster and Edmund Evans also visited North Shields in this year and a view of Tynemouth Harbour from the Priory appeared in *The Illustrated London News* on 24 August 1850. On their way back, they stayed in Scarborough and while there visited Doncaster,

6 'January – Plough Monday' – from *The Illustrated London Almanack*, 1849. Drawing by Birket Foster: engraved by Henry Vizetelly. Size: 6 × 7" – 15.2 × 17.8 cms.
Collection: Brian and Rachel Moss.

which resulted in two illustrations entitled 'Doncaster Races – the road to the course' and 'Doncaster Race-Course' (published 21 September 1850). These scenes contain the usual crowds and some sprightly horses, whose gait is obviously influenced by sporting prints, but the interest of Birket Foster appears to have been much more with the magnificent trees on the race course.

In 1851, six illustrations in the 'Watering Place' series appeared, i.e. Sidmouth, Star Cross, Margate, Broadstairs, Sandgate and another view of Tynemouth. In 1852, the view of Eastbourne (Ill. 11) was published. These trips to seaside resorts must certainly have provided Birket Foster

7 'May Day Games' – from *The Illustrated London Almanack*, 1849. Drawing by Birket Foster: engraved by Henry Vizetelly. Size: 6 × 7″ – 15.2 × 17.8 cms.
Collection: Brian and Rachel Moss.

with a very pleasurable way of gathering material and also included Blackpool, Lytham and Southport. In 1852, a view of Matlock Bath, Derbyshire, appeared in a series entitled 'Spas of England' but this was followed only by Buxton in 1854 and Harrogate in 1856.

Some of the most characteristic work by Birket Foster for *The Illustrated London News* was in the musical supplements and Christmas numbers. His first illustration for a musical supplement appeared on 10 June 1848. This was in the form of a three-part decorative heading for a ballad by Edward J. Loder, entitled 'Peace at Home'. The illustrations are appropriate, but otherwise not outstanding, showing a central harvesting scene (within a roundel) and a fireside scene and a busy quay on either side. Very much more distinguished were four major illustrations that followed in the supplements of 1849. The first of these was published on 14 April and depicted 'Spring – the country'.

This wayside scene (engraved by Edmund Evans) shows children gathering primroses and points forward to many similar subjects in water-colour that were to follow in the later period of the work of Birket Foster. 'Summer' was published on 4 August 1849 and there is an atmospheric somnolence about this river landscape with cattle under heavily foliaged trees. This was also engraved by Edmund Evans, as were all four in this series, which continued on 29 September with 'Autumn', an attractive harvesting piece, with the loaded hay cart that was to appear so frequently in the country scenes of Birket Foster. The Christmas supplement produced 'Winter' on 22 December 1849. This is shown here (Ill. 12) as a contrast to the more summery themes and for the fact that the figure of the horse has been obviously influenced by the last wood engraving on which Thomas Bewick was working at the time of his death. Birket Foster has plumped up his horse

as suitable to the illustration of 'sleepy Dobbin hangs his head/Or winks and dozes in his shed', but there can be no doubt that the pose is directly taken from Bewick's 'Waiting for Death' – published posthumously in 1832.

On 5 May 1849, *The Illustrated London News* published a double spread of illustrated poems by Charles Mackay, entitled 'May Lyrics'. Birket Foster provided nine illustrations for this presentation, which was engraved by Henry Vizetelly. The central theme on the first page is one of Birket Foster's idyllic cottage door pieces, enclosed in a roundel of flowers and leaves. Other subjects include ivy

8 'September – A Country Fair' – from *The Illustrated London Almanack*, 1849. Drawing by Birket Foster: engraved by Henry Vizetelly. Size: 6 × 7″ – 15.2 × 17.8 cms. Original sketch for this subject is now in the Victoria and Albert Museum. *Collection: Brian and Rachel Moss.*

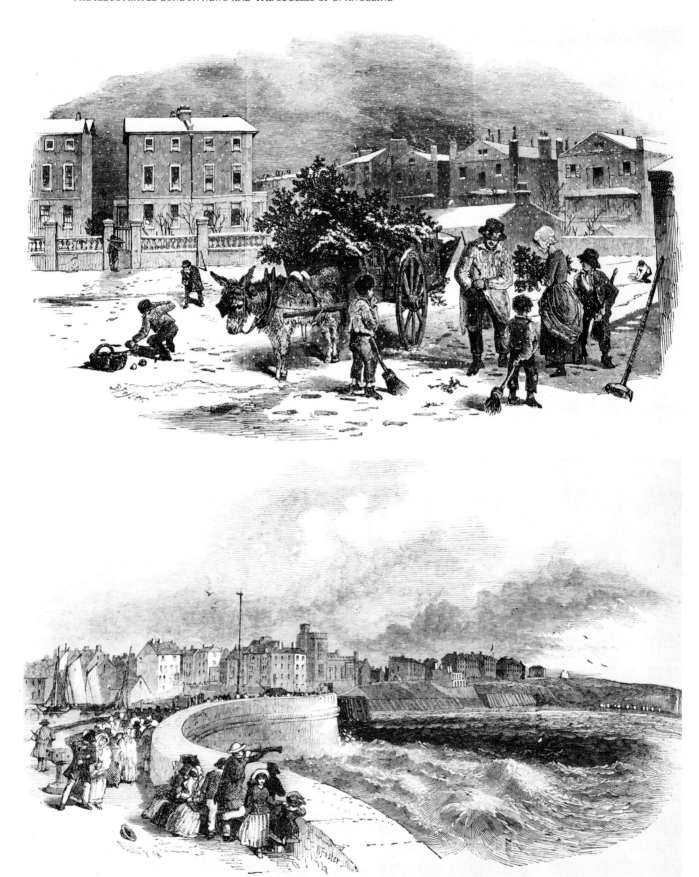

9 'The Christmas Holly Cart' - from *The Illustrated London News*, Christmas Supplement, 1848. Size: 5½ × 9″ - 14 × 22.8 cms. Drawing by Birket Foster: engraved by Edmund Evans. View from 4 Stranraer Place, Maida Hill, London, home of Birket Foster at this date.
By permission of Sheffield City Libraries.

10 'Watering Places of England - Bridlington Quay' - from *The Illustrated London News*, 20 October 1849. Drawing by Birket Foster: engraved by Edmund Evans. Size: 6 × 9¼″ - 15.2 × 23.5 cms.
By permission of Sheffield City Libraries.

11 **'Watering Places of England - Eastbourne'** - from *The Illustrated London News*, 1852. Drawing by Birket Foster: engraved by Edmund Evans. Size: 8½ × 6½" - 21.6 × 16.5 cms. *Collection: The Towner Art Gallery, Eastbourne, Sussex.*

twining up a crumbling wall, a mountain stream and an illustration of the poem 'My Garden Gate' which strongly suggests that it was probably based on a sketch from the window of his London home. As in the previous illustrations for the Seasons series, there is a touch of Bewickian influence in the smaller vignettes.

On 4 May 1850, Birket Foster illustrated another of the songs of Edward J. Loder, with the title 'A Song of Spring'. The work was engraved by Edmund Evans and these drawings were in the form of an attractive head- and tail-piece for the musical score: milkmaids and a ploughman with his team are in a background which suggests that it was influenced by the visit to Hastings in the previous year, as does the tail-piece of a pair of lovers wandering in a moonlit landscape.

The Illustrated London News, Christmas Supplement, published 21 December 1850, showed a Dickensian view of the season, with illustrations by Birket Foster of snow sweepers and unemployed gardeners and a particularly large engraving (10¾ × 8½") of a coach and horses racing a distant train, which now gives such an impression of the most hackneyed of traditional Christmas cards as to appear rather unoriginal; but one has to realise that some of these illustrations by Birket Foster were indeed the originals that played such a vital part in building up the Dickensian tradition of Christmas in the imagination of the general public.

In December 1851, the Birket Foster illustrations included a very charming vignetted piece entitled 'The Cuckoo' and an over-elaborate representation of 'The Christmas Hearth' in an octagonal holly wreathed frame, surmounted by a roundel and angels and with a square moonlit coaching scene below. 'Gathering Mistletoe' (Ill. 13) has far more of original observation.

The illustrations to a doleful ballad entitled 'The Mother's Lament' (*The Illustrated London News* - Musical

Supplement, 24 January 1852) are of particular interest as these are directly related to the uncut block illustrated in this book (Ill. 15). The size of the oval framing as marked on the block is identical to that of the published headpiece to this ballad and the features of the illustration are very similar indeed, but it will be noted that the seated figures of a mother and child have been replaced by a single figure of a woman in mourning, standing to the left, accompanied by a sympathetic dog (Ill. 14). The endpiece to the published ballad again shows many similarities with the uncut block. However, the drawing not used in *The Illustrated London News* is certainly the better design. Why was it not published? One can only put forward a theory that perhaps it was considered that the inclusion of the child might be too affecting for young sensibilities, as these musical supplements were very much intended for family use. It is interesting to speculate how it was that this block remained uncut and not utilized for some later purpose. It must have been retained by Birket Foster, as there is no way in which this could have come from the archives of *The Illustrated London News*, as their original blocks were kept until the Second World War, during which these and most other records were blitzed. It is fortunate indeed that this beautiful drawing should have been preserved in the pre-engraved state, as it was one of the less happy aspects of the work of an illustrator that he should see his original drawing destroyed for ever, once the block was cut.

Illustrations to a further musical supplement in May 1852 were in lighter vein and showed a flowery headpiece with children in the woods, as an illustration to 'Wild Flowers' - the endpiece in this case is not the work of

12 'Winter' – from *The Illustrated London News*, Christmas Supplement, 1849. Drawing by Birket Foster: engraved by Edmund Evans. The composition of this subject is influenced by Bewick's 'Waiting for Death'. Size: 6 × 9″ – 15.2 × 22.8 cms. *By permission of Sheffield City Libraries.*

Birket Foster, but is signed 'MW'. A ballad entitled 'The Dreams of Youth' (June 1852) shows a closely engraved moonlight headpiece, in which a pair of lovers look out across an estuary. The subject has a definite suggestion of having been based on the area near Tynemouth, with an endpiece that is very much a repetition of this theme. In all cases, these illustrations were engraved by Edmund Evans.

By 1853, it is obvious that Birket Foster is tiring of the work for *The Illustrated London News*, but he continued to be a traditional part of the Christmas Supplements until 1859, including a coloured plate in 1855, with the title 'Winter' and a large double-page colour illustration in 1857 in the series 'The Happy Homes of England', after which his contributions gradually ceased.

In 1850 Henry Vizetelly engraved and printed *The Illustrated Book of Songs for Children* (published Wm. S. Orr and Co., Amen Corner, Paternoster Row, London). This attractive book was reviewed in *The Art Journal* in 1851 as follows:

'The greater part of these songs are translations from the German – but nursery songs have the same set of ideas and feelings in all lands and these present no new features beyond a quiet yet graceful simplicity.'

Victorian taste was not offended by verses such as 'The Toyman comes from Germany/His shop contains rich stores/Both dwarfs and giants there you see/And Turks and Jews and Moors' although it was always the pictures that were the essential *raison d'être* for this type of book. *The Art Journal* continued:

'The illustrations by Birket Foster render the book an ornament to the drawing room table. They are both in style and execution amongst the most exquisite things produced in this country.'

It was only four years since Birket Foster had left Landells. This review serves to point up the exceptional progress that his career had made in so short a time and which was leading to his becoming one of the most popular and prolific illustrators of his day.

Henry Vizetelly noted in *Glances Back through Seventy Years*:

'Birket Foster, after completing the illustrations to Miller's *Boys' Country Year Book*, had made many miscellaneous drawings for me, exhibiting so much freshness, truth, variety and grace that it was obvious the clever young artist, whom I had so fortunately met with, was capable of something far beyond the shepherds and milk-maids, the reapers and threshers, and the haymaking and harvest-home scenes which so picturesquely illustrated Miller's descriptions of rural life, and I suggested him making some designs for an illustrated edition of Longfellow's *Evangeline* – a poem then scarcely known in this country – which I contemplated producing. I showed Foster's preliminary sketches to Bogue the publisher who readily embarked upon the enterprise.'

13 'Gathering Mistletoe' – from *The Illustrated London News*, 20 December 1851. Drawing by Birket Foster: engraved by Edmund Evans. Size: 6¾ × 9½″ – 17.2 × 24.1 cms. *By permission of Sheffield City Libraries.*

14 'The Mother's Lament' – from *The Illustrated London News*, 24 January 1852 (musical supplement). See link with Ill. 15. Drawing by Birket Foster: engraved by Edmund Evans. Size: 9½ × 7″ – 24.1 × 17.8 cms. *By permission of Sheffield City Libraries.*

Greenwich Fair   Birket Foster

15 Drawing by Birket Foster in pencil and Chinese white on a boxwood engraving block. The subject was obviously designed for use in illustration of 'The Mother's Lament', *The Illustrated London News*, 1852, but for some reason remained uncut. Size: 7½ × 9½″ - 19 × 24.2 cms.
Collection: City of Bristol Museum and Art Gallery.

16 'Greenwich Fair'. Pen and wash study for a book illustration (probably about 1848–50). This item was included in an album of sketches and drawings which Birket Foster later compiled for Polly Brown.
Collection: Manchester City Art Gallery.

17 'Under the sycamore tree were hives overhung by a pent house ...' - from *Evangeline: A Tale of Acadie* by Henry W. Longfellow, published by David Bogue, 1850. Drawing by Birket Foster; engraved by Henry Vizetelly. Size: 3½ × 3½″ - 8.9 × 8.9 cms.
From the collection of a provincial University.

18 'In that delightful land which is washed by the Delaware's waters...' from *Evangeline* by H. W. Longfellow, 1850. Drawing by Birket Foster: engraved by Henry Vizetelly. Size: 3 × 3″ – 7.6 × 7.6 cms.
From the collection of a provincial University.

Vizetelly is known to have recommended Birket Foster most enthusiastically to publishers, but there is a slightly different version of how he obtained this commission. David Bogue is said to have first given the work to certain unspecified Pre-Raphaelite artists, but was horrified by their unconventional style and wiped the drawing from the blocks, even though he had already paid for the work.

Thirty-one illustrations by Birket Foster were included in *Evangeline: A Tale of Acadie* (published in 1850). This lengthy narrative poem by H.W. Longfellow refers to the expulsion in 1755 of French settlers from the province of Acadie (or Newfoundland) by British forces for refusing to help them in operations against the Indians. 'This is the forest primeval . . .' – the opening lines are flanked by tall pine trees delicately traced in the Birket Foster manner, but these could just as well have been in Northumberland, as could any of the scenes of farming and countryside that are the main subjects illustrated by Birket Foster in Part I of *Evangeline*.

There is a story that Birket Foster was very anxious to know how the critics would receive this book and was slightly disconcerted, on arriving one day at Vizetelly's, to have a copy of *The Athenaeum* waved at him, with the somewhat ambiguous greeting: 'By Jove! They've given it to you!' In fact, *The Athenaeum* commented:

'A more lovely book than this has rarely been given to the public. Mr. Foster's designs in particular have a picturesque grace and elegance, which recall the pleasure we experienced on our first examination of Mr Roger's *Italy* when it came before us illustrated by persons of no less refinement and invention than Stothard and Turner. Anyone disposed to carp at our praise as overstrained is invited to consider the Boat on the Mississippi which to our thinking is a jewel of the first water.'

The illustration could be one of several in Part 2, which is set in America, but is most likely to be a group of figures in a boat, with a vignetted composition, enclosed by twining vegetation (see vignette, p. 174). A more definite sense of place had been created by Birket Foster in this section with characteristics of architecture, trees and costume which are recognisably American, although his source of information must have been derivative (Ill. 18). The remaining 14 illustrations in *Evangeline* are from the designs of Jane E. Benham and John Gilbert. These are exclusively figure studies and appear weak, uninteresting and lacking in depth by contrast with the intricate detail and harmonious balance of the Birket Foster compositions. *The Art Journal* commented:

'. . . the illustrations which ornament this new edition of the poem consist of between forty or fifty exquisite little engravings on wood . . . there are among these subjects many of very superior quality and all are engraved in first rate style; they look more like delicate etchings than wood cuts. The whole work is beautifully got up in illustration, type and printing.'

The sales for *Evangeline* were enormous and firmly established the individual style of Birket Foster as an illustrator.

Notes: Chapter Four

1 Entry from the diary of William Lucas, Hutchinson, 1933. (Information from the Hitchin Museum, Hertfordshire.)

2 Mary Foster, sister of Birket, was to marry William Atchison in London in 1852. Her third son, Thomas Percy Atchison, married Mary Reynolds, daughter of Charles Reynolds, on 1 June 1882. The latter was a direct descendant of Foster Reynolds, who was cousin to Richard Freshfield Reynolds, great-great-grandfather of Jan Reynolds.

3 In *Bells of Memory* it is stated by Lady Nicoll: '... my father was at school at Mr Abbott's, Hitchin ... school-fellows were Lord Lister and Birket Foster ...' This must be some kind of error, in view of the fact that R. Hine's *Hitchin Worthies* notes that William Ransom (1826-1914) was at Isaac Brown's Academy with Birket Foster, Joseph Lister and Joseph Pollard. The connection is further confirmed in an obituary for William Ransom which stated: 'Mr Ransom often referred to his school days and cherished memories of his contemporaries there, amongst whom was the late Birket Foster, artist ...' (Information from Hitchin Museum.)

4 From *The Reminiscences of Edmund Evans: Wood Engraver and Colour Printer*, introduction by Ruari McLean, Oxford University Press, 1967.

5 Information from the Marylebone Library, London NW1.

6 This charming early water-colour ($5 \times 6\frac{1}{2}''$) was reproduced in colour in the Cundall biography, as plate 15. Mrs Atchison (then in her eighties) had taken an interest in the preparation of the book, but did not live to see its publication. Production costs at the start of this century allowed a publisher to include many more colour plates than is now commercially possible and these form an attractive feature of the Cundall book. The large de-luxe limited edition (500) is today priced at about £100, but a descendant of Birket Foster has stated that the Foster family never much cared for this biography. The text is kindly in tone and provides a basic outline of the life and work of Birket Foster, but is lacking in depth and is in a form of presentation that is often confusing. Only in the case of a few quotations has Cundall been used as direct source material for this present book, which is otherwise entirely the result of recent research.

5
Marriage: established artist and family man

It was not customary for members of the Society of Friends to 'marry out of meeting' – i.e. to a non-Quaker. Intermarriage between those in some degree of relationship was therefore very commonplace, but the discipline of the movement advised strongly against the marriage of first cousins. There were to be many different affirmations on this somewhat vexed subject, varying from strong advice to binding rule, although it has to be accepted that well-concerned Quakers could sometimes conveniently forget the rule when declarations of marriage were made. Birket Foster adhered to the tradition of marrying a Quaker, but his bride was also his first cousin and it must have been for this reason that the ceremony took place, not in a Meeting House, but according to the rites of the established church. Myles Birket Foster was married by licence in Earsdon Parish Church to Anne Spence, on her 25th birthday, 13 August 1850. Anne was the twin daughter and tenth child of Robert Spence of North Shields whose wife was Birket Foster's aunt, daughter of Robert Foster of Hebblethwaite Hall. Birket Foster had resigned from the Society of Friends in the previous year, but he had not at this time been baptized into the Church of England. Quakers do not practise this rite and it would appear that the incumbent at Earsdon (about three miles from North Shields) was not strict in the enforcement of church rules, but was prepared to marry two people from dissenting families without first requiring any declaration of baptism.

Both of Anne's parents were now dead, but had they been alive, as Quakers, they would have been required by the rules of the Society of Friends at least to go through the motions of turning their back on such a marriage, owing to the first cousinship of the couple (even if the ceremony had been allowed to take place in a Meeting House). In the event, the marriage was witnessed by John Foster Spence,[1] one of the four brothers of Anne and by Robert Foster, eldest brother of Birket, also by Clement Kell. John Foster Spence had been educated at the Friends' School, York and was born in the same year as Birket's brother, John, who was also educated at this school. The latter had become a member of the Church of England in 1839 and it is possible that John Spence had resigned from the movement by the time of the wedding, but Anne's other surviving brothers, Joseph and Robert, were definitely still members of the Society of Friends. (Note: the marriage certificate and some other references spell the name of Anne Foster without an 'e', but Birket Foster *always* used the version shown in this book, which also appeared on her death certificate.)

There may have been some initial or token disapproval of the match among strict Friends on both sides, but there is no evidence of any lasting animosity, as the Spences and the Fosters had become virtually one family and remained in happy relationship. Birket Foster had a delightful sense of humour and liked company, but was also rather a shy man and one who needed the security of his family about him. In his marriage he not only strengthened these ties, but also chose a partner whom he had known since childhood. One senses that Anne was to be a much cherished companion to Birket Foster, as well as wife and mother of his children.

Birket and Anne Foster made their home at Marsden Villa, 45 Clifton Road, St John's Wood. On 1 December 1850, Birket Foster wrote from this address:

'My dear brother,
I send you 2 autographs – one of Crowquills – a good one as it has many sketches in it – the other is a rising painter and a great exhibitor. Anne and I spent a very pleasant evening last 4th day at Leslies. He is such a nice pleasant man full of Constable – he has a vast number of his sketches and many paintings and water-colour drawings. I should have liked to have prigged one of the small sketches for thee with his funny remarks written on the back. I thought of an autograph for thee but dared not ask as he so venerates every scrap. We are going to have them to tea soon so I will see what I can do.'[2]

Birket Foster wrote this letter to his cousin, Robert Spence of 4 Rosella Place, North Shields, who was also now his brother-in-law. It is the first of a series of letters that have survived from a regular correspondence (over a period of 30 years) between these two cousins. Birket Foster often writes to Robert Spence as 'My dear brother', which was a close form of Quaker address, not necessarily used to a relation, although in this case he is also acknowledging the fact that his correspondent was a brother of his wife. Robert Spence was a banker and a man of considerable literary taste and culture, with a valuable collection of books and manuscripts, including the original of the journal of George Fox, founder of the Society of Friends. He had inherited this document through Foster (or Forster) descendants of Margaret Fell, who married George Fox in late widowhood. The correspondence between Birket Foster and Robert Spence shows that the latter was interested in collecting autographs and important memorabilia. It is not recorded whether Birket Foster

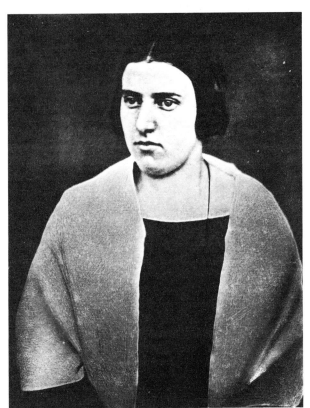

19 Birket Foster as a young man. Reproduced in *Robert and Mary Spence of North Shields* by Philip Spence, 1939. Printed from the negative of a photograph made by Philip Spence from the original daguerreotype and now published by permission of his son, Charles Spence, great-grandson of Robert Spence.

20 Anne Foster (née Spence), cousin and first wife of Birket Foster. Reproduced in *Robert and Mary Spence of North Shields*. Printed from the negative of a photograph of the original daguerreotype.
Collection: Charles Spence.

was able to obtain any item from the collection of Charles Robert Leslie, RA, the authority on Constable, who is mentioned above, but it is interesting to note that Foster was given an opportunity to examine Constable sketches at this stage in his career.

The letters to Robert Spence provide a unique glimpse of Birket Foster as husband, father, friend and artist. Some of the references strike a very poignant note. Anne and her twin sister, Margaret, known as Meggy, had not been separated when Anne married, because Meggy now lived with the Fosters. All the other Spence sisters were either married or dead and it is typical that Birket Foster should have agreed to this kindly shelter of Meggy, who was in an advanced state of tuberculosis. A further extract from the letter of 1 December presents a sad commentary on the lack of medical knowledge prevailing in 1850.

'The weather here is very bad just now damp cold and foggy. Anne is writing to John to propose a change for dear Meggy. She is very nicely and a friend of ours a medical man – very clever in consumptive cases – who has taken a great interest in *her* case and often comes to see her in a friendly way – says he thinks that it is of the utmost importance that she should get to the Isle of Wight. He says that instead of getting weaker as Dr Watson expected she would she is getting stronger and that she is at the turning point. If this be done at once he has great hopes of her recovery. He is a most kind man – a retired gentleman most desirous of benefitting any of his friends in that way afflicted so really we think it would be wrong not to give it the chance of doing her

good – he says it is a very peculiar case and change of air at this time is everything. Anne and I took a trip to Hyde Park the other day to see the Exhibition works. How fast they are getting on. We expect to see you all next Year. After seeing the Glass Palace we went to Kew Gardens to see the plants – the Victoria Regina Lily is in full flower and most beautiful. How are the autographs getting on? We are going to the Westalls in a day or two.

With dear love to Sarah and self in which Anne unites.

I remain thy affec. bro.
Birket Foster.'[3]

In spite of the hopeful diagnosis by the 'medical man' and the change of air, it was only three months later that Margaret Spence died, aged 25, on 8 March 1851.

The following letter to Robert Spence is undated, but must be after 25 December 1850 and later than 28 December of that year (or very early in 1851):

'Dear Robert,
Many thanks for thy letter. I shall be glad to help thee as far as I can – it is a very modest request this time. Men of my own cast and many that I am acquainted with. Dick Doyle I am pretty sure I can get thee. I know nothing of Gibson the sculptor or Egg. Thou asks Tennison's [*sic*] address. I do not know it But I should not wonder if have a good deal to do with him soon as Mr Moxon has been hinting at my illustrating his Poems – how it will terminate I know not.

39

21 Frontispiece and title page for *The Moorland Cottage*, 1850. Drawing by Birket Foster: engraved by Edmund Evans. Size: $2\frac{3}{4}$ × $4\frac{3}{4}$″ - 7 × 12.1 cms (each illustration).
From the collection of a provincial University.

The author of Mary Barton is a Mrs Gaskill [*sic*] I don't know her although she writes a deal about me to Chapman - indeed wanted me to entitle her new book. She first called it "Rosemary for Remembrance" but said it was only something for me to shoot at - we then had it called "A Fagot for Xmas" - however that did not do, so we called it *The Moorland Cottage* - it is a nice little tale.'[4]

Illustration 21 shows the frontispiece and decorated title page of the first edition published by Chapman and Hall, 1850. The book includes a further 18 illustrations in the form of decorated initials, head- and tail-pieces and illustrations set into the text. The headpiece for Chapter I occupies all but six lines of text and is a vertical composition of trees, overlooking a church in a valley. The book was printed by Bradbury and Evans (not to be confused with Edmund Evans). All the engravings were the work of the latter, but he cannot have seen proofs of the plain title page, on which it is stated: 'Illustrations by Birkett Foster'. The addition of an extra 't' to the first name of this artist was (and still is) a frequent mistake by individuals, but is not so often met with in books. The British Library does not hold a copy of *The Moorland Cottage*, but an illustrated novel would have a more expendable life than an elaborate

gift book and consequently this attractive little volume is now in the rare book category. The combination of a story by Mrs Elizabeth Gaskell and illustrations by Birket Foster (with additional interest in the fact that it was he who gave the work its title) has produced a most worthwhile item for collectors.

Birket Foster continues his letter:

'Met Wm. Howitt on Xmas Day as Anne and I were strolling over the fields near Hampstead so we had a long chat - he said Mrs Gaskill [*sic*] was going to tea at their house that night and that from her repeated visits to town from Manchester (where she lives) he thought something was brewing.'

William Howitt (1792-1879) was a writer on poetry, history and social subjects. He had been at school with Joseph Watson, who was married to Sarah (née Spence) sister-in-law of Birket Foster. His works included *The Rural Life of England* and illustrations by Birket Foster were an attractive feature of his *Year Book of the Country* which was published in late 1850. Charming vignettes (Ill. 22) form the headpiece for each month of the year and the text provides a very readable commentary on life in that period.

In the opinion of *The Standard* the illustrations were 'very beautiful' and the *Morning Advertiser* remarked that the 'exceedingly clever and pretty designs, by Mr Birket Foster, are quite worthy of the pages on which they appear'. But a more important book than this was illustrated by Birket Foster to appear in 1850. After the success of *Evangeline*, Henry Vizetelly had at once obtained for

THE YEAR-BOOK

OF

THE COUNTRY;

OR,

THE FIELD, THE FOREST, AND THE FIRESIDE.

BY

WILLIAM HOWITT,

AUTHOR OF

"THE BOOK OF THE SEASONS," "RURAL LIFE OF ENGLAND," &c.

WITH

ILLUSTRATIONS FROM DESIGNS BY BIRKET FOSTER.

LONDON:

HENRY COLBURN, PUBLISHER,

GREAT MARLBOROUGH-STREET.

1850.

22 Title page from *The Year Book of the Country* by William Howitt, 1850. Drawings engraved by Edmund Evans. Page size: $7\frac{1}{2} \times 4\frac{1}{2}''$ – 19 × 11.4 cms.
Collection: Derbyshire County Library.

23 'Anglo-Norman Carol' – from *Christmas with the Poets*,
published by David Bogue (1852 edition). Drawing by Birket
Foster: engraved by Henry Vizetelly. Page size: $7\frac{1}{2} \times 4\frac{1}{2}''$ – 19
× 11.5 cms.
Collection: Brian and Rachel Moss.

Birket Foster a commission to produce all the illustrations for a major anthology.

Christmas with the Poets, 'a Collection of Carols and Descriptive Verses, relating to the Festival of Christmas, from the Anglo-Norman period to the Present Time' was published by David Bogue in 1851, but was produced in time for the 1850 Christmas season. This was illustrated with 53 designs by Birket Foster and was engraved by Henry Vizetelly and according to him was selected by the Trustees of the British Museum for display in the Great Exhibition of 1851 as an example of contemporary book illustration and printing. It is certainly a most handsome volume in the tradition of the illustrated gift book. The title page is printed in two neutral colours and gold, with some bright colours touched in by hand. Each page of text is outlined in gold, with frequent additional decoration in the same medium. The illustrations are printed in black and neutral tints, i.e. very pale ochre or coffee beige shades. The text presents a decided emphasis on the Wassail Bowl and Boar's Head aspect of Christmas.

The Art Journal commented (in a review of the 1855 edition): 'This is, *par excellence*, THE book for Christmas' but went on to criticise (as did many other opinions) the inclusion of several other poems that were considered a mite too robust for family reading. Certainly Birket Foster is not always at his best in the illustration of such lines as 'A bone, God Wot! Sticks in my throat without I have a draught of cornie ale' – four men seated at a table in vaguely sixteenth-century dress, waving aloft drinking glasses of unlikely size in which the contents is set flat like jelly. Even so, the general portrayal of Christmas atmosphere is attractively done and was to break new ground. It has been suggested that *Christmas with the Poets* was a contributory factor in the popular revival of this conception of the event and the resulting fashion for Christmas cards. The illustration in this book (Ill. 23) gives some idea of the general style, but much of the rich effect is inevitably lost without full representation of the gold embellishment and the subtle quality of the neutral tones on cream-tinted paper cannot be adequately shown in black-and-white reproduction. The book has a red cloth cover, which is elaborately blocked in gold with a holly leaf design.

Birket Foster must be referring to *Christmas with the Poets* in the letter to Robert Spence, when he writes:

'I have got my large book out at last. It has been well reviewed by The Athenaeum, Examiner, Express, Morning Herald, Chronicle, Observer, Art Circular and the Lit. Gazette promise in next number an elaborate review. The Illustrated News also praised it. I hope that wealthy brother of mine'

– and here Birket Foster has inserted 'Robt' above, in order that the purport of his little joke should not be missed –

'will get a copy. I should like thee to see it – as specimen of printing it is very beautiful. As to the rest I cannot say as I am so sick and tired of the sight of it and really cannot judge, the papers say it is good so I suppose it is not bad....'[5]

As Birket Foster indicates, the book was certainly well reviewed in *The Athenaeum*:

'... The illustrations are of great elegance and variety and take us back to the periods which they severally illustrate. Admirably drawn and composed – they have been very successfully cut by Mr Vizetelly; and the printing by tinted blocks produces a very novel and satisfactory result...'

– p. 1383, 28 December 1850.

Two editions of *Christmas with the Poets* appeared in 1851 and another in 1852, followed by one in 1855 and an edition printed by Edmund Evans in 1862. In the edition of 1869 (printed by Vincent Brooks, Day and Son) the title page vignettes are still hand-coloured, but in the edition of 1872, also printed by Vincent Brooks, these are printed in colours.

In 1979, a copy of *Christmas with the Poets* (ed. 1855) appeared on the market with a piece of Windsor Castle writing paper inserted, signed 'Duchess of Teck' on the reverse side. This had the inscription: 'To my dear sister Augusta from her very affectionate sister Victoria.' Thus, the book would appear to have been a gift from the Duchess of Kent, mother of Queen Victoria, to her sister-in-law, the Duchess of Cambridge, whose daughter became the Duchess of Teck after her marriage. The work of Birket Foster was to be much admired by members of the royal family, as will be seen in later references. *Christmas with the Poets* is an essential item in any collection of books illustrated by Birket Foster. In 1979, the above edition was priced at £35, but had some loose pages. The binding of books of this period is one of the most frequent causes of their total loss and contributes greatly to the scarcity of copies available. *Christmas with the Poets* had a sewn binding which makes for a more secure page but many of the books illustrated by Birket Foster had what is known as a caoutchouc binding, i.e. instead of the pages being several sections of folded (then sewn) paper, all the sections were guillotined down the back and the edges gummed with an adhesive called caoutchouc or gutta-percha and made to adhere to the casing or cover of the book. Unfortunately gutta-percha had constituents which were not stable, but cracked under pressure and came apart in damp conditions. Also, because the pages of many illustrated books were like thin boards, it was inevitable that such a binding could not stand up to the stress and strain of time, but caused many Victorian books to disintegrate. Renovations are sometimes attempted by placing a piece of canvas down the opened spine of the book and sewing from the inside, but the stitching will always be obvious on examination and in a way that a true sewn binding never will be. It is important to check that any book that has been subject to renovation does in fact have all the original pages. But, those interested in the illustrated work of Birket Foster should not reject a book that is only an untidy bundle of loose pages, because this does not necessarily mean that any are missing and can be an opportunity to obtain a very satisfactory collection of engravings for a modest price. The actual pages often stand up to wear and tear better than the binding.

Birket Foster continues his letter to Robert Spence:

'I am rather more at my ease now than I have been and am going on steadily with the minor [?] poems of Longfellow – and after that I have another book proposed of a very splendid sort to be taken up as soon as that is done. I fear I shall have tired thee with my histories of myself. I will endeavour to procure as many of the autographs mentioned as I am able. We have pretty good accounts from Hastings. We hope sometimes to pop down and see them but I don't think it will be yet

24 Heidelberg – from *Hyperion* by H. W. Longfellow. Drawing by Birket Foster: engraved by Henry Vizetelly. Size: 2¼ × 2¾″ – 5.7 × 7 cms.
Collection: Brian and Rachel Moss.

a bit. How fast they are getting on with the Crystal Palace. I want to walk over there with Anne some day and see it. It will be one of the most marvellous things there I think. I called at the cellars the other day to see Dodshon – he is very fat and I think he has forgotten all about his autographs.

'We had a visit from Joseph Pollard a friend of ours and his sister is collecting autographs. I gave him a few for her but they are what thou has in abundance.

'Well I will end now wishing you a *very* happy new year and many of them. Believe me with love to you all.

Thy sincerely attached bro.

Birket Foster.'[6]

In 1851 M.B. Foster and Sons was to be extended to include 27 Brook Street, Grosvenor Square. This move would be about to take place at the time of the mention by Foster of visiting his brother Dodshon 'at the cellars'. Disraeli and Gladstone was both to patronize the firm in its new locality, for the purchase of the famous 'Bugle Brand' beers.

On 29 November 1851, Anne Foster gave birth to their first child, who was named Myles Birket Foster after his father and grandfather. The child was not baptized, an indication of the fact that Anne and Birket were still following the basic precepts of the Society of Friends, as is shown in the continued use by Birket Foster in his letters of the biblical pronoun. They did not now dress as Friends, but certainly followed some of the customs of their Quaker upbringing, although this should not be equated with solemnity. Birket Foster had a great sense of fun and with his kindly nature and unassuming ways was to be a very devoted and much loved parent. In the Victorian era, the children of Quakers were often brought up in a manner that was in advance of the period.

Sarah Glasson, a grand-daughter of Birket Foster, has allowed some fascinating and delightful glimpses of the family life of Birket Foster to be published in this book. Her mother, Ellen, was the youngest of the five children of Anne and Birket Foster and some of the stories that she was later to relate to her own children provide us with vivid pictures of the happy and tolerant atmosphere generated by the personality of her parents. These recollections have a touching reality and are often very amusing.

Ellen remembered the lively fun of the days when the family were living in St John's Wood. Birket Foster was a shy, undeclamatory man, but for many years he made an effort to continue the custom from his own childhood of assembling for family prayers every morning before breakfast. Sarah Glasson has told me that her mother always declared that what finally finished off family prayers was the almost inevitable appearance of the milkman, at the top of the basement steps, just below the dining-room window, rattling his cans and calling out 'Milko'. The daily speculation as to how far Birket Foster would get in his reading of prayers before being interrupted by this loud and inappropriate cry was too much for the solemnity of the children – and for his! Very sensibly, the custom was gently allowed to lapse, but we are left with a glimpse of just how happy and relaxed life in Victorian England could be for those in an intelligently progressive family.

Notes : Chapter Five

1 The three Spence brothers all became prominent in civic duty and philanthropic works and when Alderman John Foster Spence, JP, died, he was described as 'full of years and honours ... the best-known gentleman on Tyneside' - *Shields Daily News*, 22 July 1901.

2 Published by permission of Newcastle upon Tyne City Libraries. 'Alfred Crowquill' was the pseudonym of Alfred Henry Forrester (1804-72) who had been one of the original *Punch* cartoonists and illustrators. He is reputed to have advised the young Birket Foster that he should first make dots for the head and principal joints as an aid to figure drawing.

3 Quotation by permission of Newcastle upon Tyne City Libraries.

4 Quotation by permission of Newcastle upon Tyne City Libraries. In this letter Birket Foster is referring to Richard Doyle who was the designer of the best-known cover for *Punch*. In the next sentence the reference is to Augustus Egg, the historical painter. In the event the work of Birket Foster was not included in the famous *Illustrated Edition of Tennyson's Poems*, published by E. Moxon, 1857.

5 Quotation by permission of Newcastle upon Tyne City Libraries.

6 Quotation by permission of Newcastle upon Tyne City Libraries.

6
Tour with Henry Vizetelly for *Hyperion*

In 1851 Edmund Evans moved his engraving and printing office to 4 Racquet (or Raquet) Court, off Fleet Street. He was to be there for nearly 50 years and become recognised as the most successful engraver and printer from wood of his generation.

The first signed colour blocks from Edmund Evans are thought to be those for *A Visit to the Holy Land, Egypt and Italy* by Ida Pfeiffer, translated from the German and published by Ingram Cooke and Co. in 1852. The frontispiece states: 'Printed in tints by E. Evans'. The colours employed were brown, pale blue and pale yellow and the eight plates were after the drawings of Birket Foster. 'Mount Carmel' (a representation of the subject in which ships on a stretch of wind-ruffled water predominate) is shown on p. 23 of *The Reminiscences of Edmund Evans*. Birket Foster would appear to have worked up the illustrations from the original sketches of Ida Pfeiffer.

It was in the 1850s that innovations in book publishing created an entirely new reading public as advances in colour-printing techniques made it possible to print large quantities of cheap and attractive books. W.H. Smith's first railway book stall was established at Euston on 1 November 1848 and this was the forerunner of a vast new outlet for books sold in wrappers or paper boards. Edmund Evans was soon involved in the printing of colourfully pictorial book covers to catch the eye of the general public. *The Log of the Water Lily* was designed by Birket Foster (original sketch now in the Manchester City Art Gallery) and printed by Evans in a dark blue-grey and strong warm tints on a thick white paper. The firm of George Routledge was in the forefront of the new trend and produced a 'Railway Library' of such books. It was their request for a tinted paper that did not soil easily that led Edmund Evans to print on a yellow enamelled paper with outstanding success for such covers, which quickly became known as 'Yellow-backs'. Also in an album of sketches by Birket Foster (Manchester City Art Gallery) are several other book cover designs, including *Wild Sports in the Far West* and *North Pole* which were not exactly in his line and *A Quiet Street* and *Books for the Country* which were more so. Birket Foster made these book cover designs as part of his association with Edmund Evans, but this work was never of any significance. It was the establishment of their mutual strength as book illustrator and printer/engraver that was of particular importance at this time. *Fern Leaves from Fanny's Portfolio*, published in 1853 by Nathaniel Cooke, Milford House, London, was illustrated with seven semi-coloured plates by Birket Foster, engraved and printed by Edmund Evans. This was an English edition of a collection of short stories and articles by the American writer, Miss G.P. Willis.

Most of the pieces in *Fern Leaves from Fanny's Portfolio* had previously appeared in such periodicals as the *Boston True Flag* and the *New York Musical World and Times*, but, in spite of the flowery title and an inevitable preponderance of motherless children and brave widows, one is struck by the readability of the text. The pious tone and gently improving message is put over with a naturalness of style and genuine observation that makes for an interesting view of life in America at this period. The first edition proved immensely popular, and only two weeks after publication 30,000 copies had been sold and continued to sell at the rate of 1,000 a day. Nathaniel Cooke had a flair for knowing what the public wanted and his English edition also proved very successful and had the added attraction of illustrations by Birket Foster. These were printed as separate plates on a better quality paper than used for the text and were produced in dark sepia brown and pale ochre as follows:

1 'The Nightwatch' – church seen across a stile with trees in the foreground
2 'The Stray Lamb' – destitute immigrant child being befriended by lady benefactor
3 'Night' – rather murky and Dickensian moonlight scene showing a man with a lamp in the foreground
4 'Lilies of the Valley' – mother and child in a woodland glade
5 'Fern Glen' – old man with a bald head and fringe of long white hair, surrounded by a group of children in a summer house
6 'Sweet Briar Farm' – scene inside a stable, showing a man and woman with a farmyard beyond
7 'Little May' – pert child in a large hat standing under a tree and holding a basket.

The impression is that Birket Foster himself was probably not too interested in the subject matter, but the general effect of the half tone is attractive and some of these illustrations have subsequently become detached from the book and been sold as framed prints. *Fern Leaves from Fanny's Portfolio* was brought out as part of Nathaniel Cooke's National Illustrated Library, which appeared in monthly volumes usually priced at 2/6d (or with gilt edges 3/6d and 7/6d in morocco). This book went into another English edition in 1854 and in this year *Fern Leaves from Fanny's Portfolio – Second Series* also appeared, but this was *not* illustrated by Birket Foster, but by George Thomas. The two books are uniform in green cloth covers, blocked in gold and blind, and provide the collector with an item that has something of the charm and spirit of the world of Louisa M. Alcott. *Little Ferns for Fanny's Little Friends* also followed in 1854 and was described as 'The Juvenile Book of the Season', it was again illustrated by Birket Foster, with eight plates in dark brown and ochre, printed by Edmund Evans. It is more difficult to obtain this volume than the two earlier books that were meant for reading by older girls and adults.

The success of any engraving by Edmund Evans after the work of Birket Foster was almost a certainty, but Evans made a telling point in his reminiscences:

'I engraved a considerable number of drawings by various artists who had not made their name and they got me to engrave their drawings and were very disappointed, and even disgusted, because their drawings when engraved did not come up equal to those drawn by Birket Foster, and they evidently thought I, as the engraver, was alone to blame! I could not help thinking, "You cannot make a silk purse out of a sow's ear." '[1]

The other engravers of special significance in the career of Birket Foster were George and Edward Dalziel. In *Victorian Illustrated Books* (B.T. Batsford, 1971) Percy Muir notes in his comments on what he terms the Dalziel era: '... the scale and comprehensive nature of their activities make them exemplars of the movement. They were artists, engravers, printers and publishers. They discovered young artists to work in the medium, and by the excellence of their results they attracted artists already famous in other spheres to join them.'

The Dalziel brothers state that their first business connection with Birket Foster was in 1851.

'We commissioned him to make a set of 8 illustrations to *Kirke White's Poetical Works* for Messrs George Routledge and Co. After this he illustrated several small books in a similar manner for us, as well as becoming a constant and very liberal contributor to many of the "Fine Art Books" we produced'.

The Poetical Works and Remains of Henry Kirke White included a life of this Nottinghamshire poet by Robert Southey and was illustrated with eight black-and-white engravings after the drawings of Birket Foster. This is a small, thick book ($6\frac{1}{2} \times 4''$) of a rather uninteresting design, with a cloth cover, mostly blocked blind, but with a little gold decoration and gold page edges. The illustrations are printed as separate plates on better quality paper than the closely printed text, but the effect is generally cramped. A better feeling was obtained when some of the illustrations were later reprinted in *Beauties of English Landscape* (1874).

In *Glances Back through Seventy Years* by Henry Vizetelly there is a long account of a tour abroad with Birket Foster in 1852. Vizetelly has a somewhat original way of constructing some of his sentences, but he comes over as an amusing man and one can see that he and Birket Foster were congenial companions. He wrote:

'When Mr Bogue had issued all of Longfellow's poetical works, then published in an illustrated form, I suggested producing an edition of *Hyperion* with engravings of the different scenes in which the hero of the romance figures, from sketches to be taken by Mr Birket Foster on the spot.'

Hyperion was to be an important book in the career of Birket Foster as an illustrator and the initial journey to obtain material was the longest he ever undertook for the purpose of a single publication. Vizetelly and Birket Foster set off for the Rhine in the summer of 1852, accompanied by a man named Fry (probably from the Quaker family) who was supposed to act as their interpreter, but who proved more of a hindrance than a help owing to his somewhat eccentric personality.

Longfellow's *Hyperion* was described as a romance, but in fact it was a fictionalized account of one of his own tours, with pauses for the recital of local legends, etc., and the addition of a very slight love interest between the hero, Paul Flemming, and Mary Ashburton. Henry Vizetelly recorded:

'When traversing the Odenwald we entered the woodland dell, which Longfellow lauds as the "enchanted valley of Birkenau" [Ill. 25] and were perplexed, I remember, in our search for the mill referred to by the poet, owing to there being three mills in the valley, and all within the space of a mile. We discovered, however, that only one served the double purpose of a mill and an inn, and as it was evidently here that the poet had stayed, we visited it with the intention of passing the night there.'

Henry Vizetelly and Birket Foster went to considerable trouble to identify the exact location of the scenes, buildings, etc. as described in the book, and at Interlaken had a long search for the apartment in a convent where Longfellow had stayed. They questioned an old crone in charge of part of the building and an old soldier who had a room there and obviously greatly appreciated the quite useless attempts to help by a gentleman and his two 'pretty, fair-haired, limpid-eyed daughters'. Next day, they were still determinedly tackling the problem and enlisted the aid of the police who had an office in part of the old convent buildings, only to discover that the interior of the room they were looking for had been so much altered as to make it totally different from the description in *Hyperion*. One cannot help wondering if it was more the journalistic instinct of Vizetelly that took authenticity to such lengths, rather than enthusiasm on the part of Birket Foster. The prettiest illustration of Interlaken is one of an avenue of walnut trees – an obvious subject to take the eye of Birket Foster, but not specially connected with the text of the book.

Henry Vizetelly continues:

'I remember that during our sojourn at Interlaken, we made the ascent of one of the lesser mountains of the Bernese Oberland - the Wengern Alp, I think it was - and that while resting at a chalet near the summit we had a splendid view of an avalanche careering down into the valley with a roar of thunder. After Mr Foster had made all the sketches he required in the valley of Lauterbrunnen, and other places around Interlaken, we took the steamer along the Lake of Brienz and landed near the famous Geissbach cascade.'

The route followed by Birket Foster and his companions to Innsbruck was one not much used by tourists. The three men sometimes rode on horseback or trudged on foot beside a single pack animal, often ending the day at inns where there was little food but rye bread and the beds were infested by bugs. Vizetelly wrote:

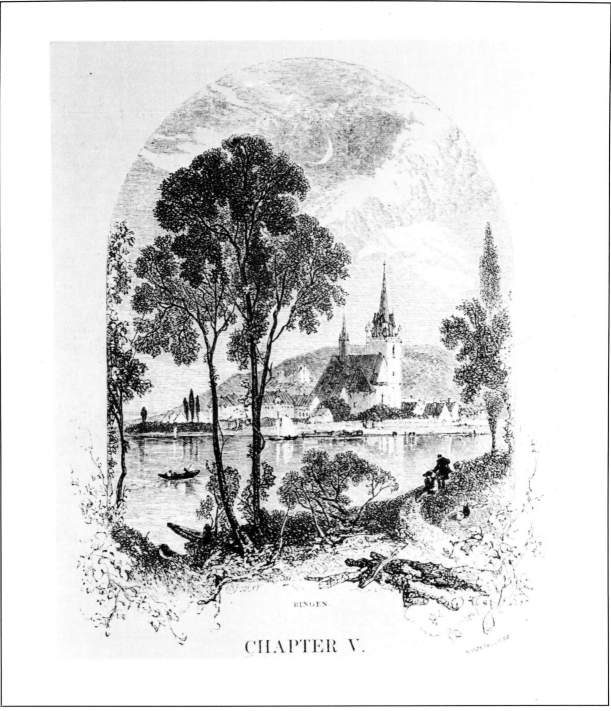

BINGEN.

CHAPTER V.

'At Ilanz the villagers all came to their doors to catch sight of the new and to them strange looking arrivals, for we wore neither tourist's suits nor wide-awakes, but the same top hats and black frock coats in which we were accustomed to perambulate the streets of London.'

The image of Birket Foster dressed thus for riding over mountains is somewhat unexpected, as one is inclined to picture him already in the wide-awake hat and more casual garb of an artist, as a direct transition from the Quaker costume of his youth.

Birket Foster and party were obviously the subject of much curiosity and on the following day the entire village turned out to see their departure for Reichenau, including the priest, the schoolmaster and the mayoral equivalent, who made a formal speech.

'We found ourselves spinning along, over green turf

strewn thickly with huge boulders and unpleasantly near the edge of the precipitous rocks forming the gorge of the Rhine. Our driver went merrily on, leaving his horses to thread their way as best they could among the masses of rock. This they did apparently to their own satisfaction, but not entirely to ours, for one of the wheels of the vehicle came in violent contact with a boulder which shattered it, overturned the waggon, completely wrecking it and sending one of our travelling bags flying over the brink of the precipice into the Rhine, which was rushing along, several hundred feet below. Fortunately, we saw the impending collision and jumped off before it occurred, otherwise we should most likely have accompanied the lost travelling bag in its gymnastical descent . . .'

After this mishap, Birket Foster and party were forced

48

VALLEY OF BIRKENAU.

CHAPTER VII.

25 From *Hyperion* by H. W. Longfellow, published by David Bogue, 1853. Drawings by Birket Foster: engraved by Henry Vizetelly. Size: 4 × 3″ - 10.2 × 7.6 cms and 5 × 3½″ - 12.7 × 8.9 cms.
Collection: Brian and Rachel Moss.

to walk, struggling with their baggage until they reached Reichenau. After a night there they continued to Coire, which was comparatively civilised, but it was in a village just beyond that the incompetent interpretation of Fry caused the inhabitants to get it into their heads that Birket Foster and his party intended some insult (or worse!) to the local womenfolk and knives were drawn with obvious menace.

> '... the driver whipped up his horses and the band gave us chase, flourishing their knives and gesticulating

frantically. One of the fleetest of them caught us up, but we kept them at bay with our alpen-stocks, while the driver lashed his horse into a gallop, and Fry, who was in a mortal funk, and perspiring nervously, prodded the animals with the sharp spike, which while we were on our Alpine journey he had fixed into an ordinary walking stick. In spite of our perilous position, Foster and I could not resist shouting with laughter at the energy Fry was displaying, and at the anxious way in which he every now and then glanced round to see whether our irate pursuers were gaining on us. After an uncommonly exciting quarter of an hour, the speed of our horses told, the angry villagers treated us to a volley of oaths and a parting flourish of their lethal weapons, and gave up the chase, leaving us to congratulate ourselves on having escaped a serious danger.'

As well as being chased by peasants with knives, the party had now survived raging torrents, bugs and bad food, a carriage crash and the loss of luggage over a precipice, but the hazards of the journey were not over. An almost inevitable part of Victorian continental travel was an encounter with some kind of armed political ferment, if not outright warfare. After a few days in Innsbruck, they engaged a private carriage to take them on the three-day ride to Salzburg. Troops were massing on the Italian side of the Austrian frontier, which had to be crossed and re-crossed several times. Vizetelly describes constant personal and baggage searches, detention for questioning and the confiscation of their passports, but with a calm air of confidence that their English nationality conferred an absolute protection from harm, if not from the petty irritation of being suspected of conspiracy against the Austrian Government – although there was one rather tricky moment when the Italian derivation of Vizetelly's name made him very suspect indeed.

During all this time, Fry had been attempting to interpret and put over the reason for their journey. The true facts that they were following the steps of an American poet in order to make sketches did not impress their interrogators and it was all rather too much for the highly strung Fry. They stayed a night at the village of Waindring in the Tyrol and Vizetelly writes:

'... not only did he lie awake himself, but did his best to disturb the rest of us. In the dead stillness of the night fancying that he heard someone stealing softly into his room and calling to mind the many stories current of cut-throat inn-keepers in lonely places dispatching their guests, he jumped out of bed flung open the window and frantically shouted "Murder! Murder!" much to the perplexity of the slumbering inhabitants of the little Tyrolean village whom he roused with his terrified cries. Next morning the good-natured inn-keeper asked us if our friend was right in his upper storey, while as for Fry he simply chuckled over the whole affair as if it was an excellent joke.'

From Salzburg they went to St Gilgen, where Birket Foster made some sketches, including the rather Swiss-looking inn and a depressing chapel in a graveyard full of wooden crosses. From Gilgen they made an excursion to St Wolfgang and passed under the 'Mighty precipice of Falkenstein', which Foster also sketched and where they tried out the famous echo, as described in *Hyperion*. These places form some of the last illustrations in the book and the journey was completed via Munich and Stuttgart.

The first edition of *Hyperion* proved to be a handsome volume in maroon leather covers, with a gold-blocked design, gold-edged pages and a ribbon marker. The title page states that the work is illustrated with nearly 100 engravings on wood from the work of Birket Foster and the Preface adds:

'This, the first illustrated Edition of Longfellow's famous Romance comes before the public with some claim to its attention. Independently of the beauty of

the Illustrations, it furnishes the first example of a lengthened journey being expressly undertaken to depict from nature all the varied scenes amid which a writer of fiction has laid the incidents of his story. And when it is considered that between two and three thousand miles – out and home – had to be performed for this purpose, and that every local illustration contained in the volume was sketched on the spot, and is a perfectly faithful representation of the place described or mentioned, the book cannot fail to be regarded with some additional interest, if not higher feelings of satisfaction. – London 1853.'

Hyperion retailed at 25/- in morocco and 15/- in cloth and was to be several times reprinted. Birket Foster was pleased with the reviews of the book and retained many of the original pencil drawings for the rest of his life. (See Appendix 6, p. 201, 'Views of the Rhine'.) *The Art Journal* (1857, p. 374) in a review of an edition published in that year commented:

'... Hyperion, illustrated with nearly 100 engravings on wood, by H. Vizetelly from drawings by Birket Foster, whose aid has become almost a necessity in every work claiming a pretention to be ranked among the best class of illustrated literature ... the volume is produced with taste and elegance and if it pleases us less than those already noticed it is only because even Mr Foster's pencil cannot give to such materials as Germany has supplied him with, the beauty and richness which his own fancy forms out of the characteristic features of English landscape.'[2]

Birket Foster has been criticised for the repetitive style of his illustrations, but if he attempted to travel (literally) over new ground there would always be critics and public hankering after the English vignettes that had first made his name. Forrest Reid in *Illustrators of the Sixties* (1928) said, rather unfairly:

'They are often charming in Foster's somewhat finikin way, but they are so little experimental as to suggest that the artist, having once invented a formula was ever after too timid to depart from it. In any true sense of the word, he was not an illustrator at all. He had no imagination and apparently took little account of the imaginations of others ...'

In defence of Birket Foster one has to point out that illustration is an art form most usually executed to the commission of a publisher. David Bogue or George Routledge were not looking for innovation or subjective commentary, but only for the popular manner of Birket Foster that had earned him the admiring recognition of the public. He was not being commissioned to produce experiments, even if it had been in his nature to do so. But Birket Foster was most conscientious in aiming to show the correct topographical detail if this was required, and this is again proved in the series of illustrations which he undertook for Adam and Charles Black of Edinburgh.

Notes: Chapter Six
1 *The Reminiscences of Edmund Evans: Wood Engraver and Colour Printer*, introduction by Ruari McLean, Oxford University Press, 1967.
2 This issue of *The Art Journal* had also been reviewing a reprint of Milton's *L'Allegro and Il Penseroso*.

7
England's most popular illustrator of poetry

On 20 December 1852, Birket Foster wrote to Adam Black:

'... I have to thank you for copies of The Lady of the Lake for Mr Gilbert, Messrs Evans and Whymper and myself. I like the volume very much. Some of Mr Whymper's landscapes are not so well engraved – owing to the time being short but altogether it is very satisfactory.'[1]

The Lady of the Lake was published in 1853 with 34 illustrations from the work of Birket Foster. The book included two frontispiece illustrations, engraved by W. Miller, after the work of J.M.W. Turner, with John Gilbert as the other illustrator for the text. Most of his drawings were engraved by J.W. Whymper, whom Birket Foster seems to be singling out for a little gentle criticism, although one cannot quite see why, as his own work appears to be just as competently engraved by Whymper as by Evans. 'The Combat', for example, is one of the most attractive pieces in the book.

Birket Foster continues in his letter of 20 December to Adam Black:

'... I shall be glad to undertake the views. I am sorry that I have not got sketches of very many of the places, but such as I have I shall be glad to get engraved for you in 2 months – if you could procure sketches for the remainder I think I could do them all in that time – I enclose a list of subjects marked on map, with X marked to show those I have sketches for. I have also got a good sketch of Dunbarton Castle, but that you do not mark so I suppose it does not come into the district you describe. If I had had the slightest idea that the work was contemplated I would have got sketches for the whole when I was in Scotland for The Lady of the Lake, but as time was no object then, I only did such views as were necessary for the Lake.'

The purport of the above is that A. and C. Black had asked Birket Foster to do the drawings for *A Picturesque Guide to the Trossachs*. Edmund Evans went to Scotland with Foster on some of his sketching trips, in connection with the Black publications and described these journeys with Foster as 'the greatest treat of my life'. Birket Foster wrote to Adam Black on 28 February 1853: 'Have you any subjects to send me for the Guide Books? I have done all that I had sketches for and they are very nearly finished engraving. In about a week you shall have them all.' On

28 April 1853 Birket Foster submitted an elegantly scribed account to Messrs Black for:

'Drawing and engraving on wood
   27 Illustrations for A Guide to the Trossachs at £5. 0. 0.
               £135. 0. 0.'

Birket Foster acknowledged receipt of this money on 8 May 1853. Part of the payment would be due to Edmund Evans for the engraving work. The sum of £135 represents the equivalent of many times that amount in present day values.

In an undated letter Birket Foster says:

'I have to thank you for a copy of the Trossachs Guide which I think very nice. It would have been improved with a little more margin and some of the eng. (*sic*) are I think a little too heavily printed but on the whole it is a pretty little book. Mr Evans tells me he has received one or two commissions from publishers from their approval of the cuts in this volume.'

Birket Foster was right in his opinion that some of the engravings for the Trossachs Guide were rather over-inked, but these illustrations were popular and some were later used in *Memento of the Trossachs: Loch Katrine, Loch Lomond and the neighbouring scenery* which was published by A. and C. Black in 1854, as the sort of small gift book that might appeal to the tourist.

Birket Foster was also working on illustrations for *The Lay of the Last Minstrel*, a poem in six cantos by Sir Walter Scott. In his letter of 28 February 1853 he asks of Adam Black:

'Can you tell me whether there is any old view of Branksome Tower to be procured or seen? – as I understand it is now a modern residence. I am very unfit for the scenes in the Lay of the Last Minstrel – I should prefer a correct view of the old castle to making an imaginary place of it. I understand that there is one tower remaining but that all the rest is like a modern villa – which would not do at all. The scenery of course is the same – so if I could procure a view of the old building I would have all I want. I should be greatly obliged if you could give me any information.'

Birket Foster seems to be suggesting in this letter that he would imagine the contours of the landscape if he had the outlines of Branksome Tower in correct period, but the

Canto First.

I.

THE feast was over in Branksome tower,[1]
And the Ladye had gone to her secret bower;
Her bower that was guarded by word and
by spell,
Deadly to hear, and deadly to tell—
Jesu Maria, shield us well!
No living wight, save the Ladye alone,
Had dared to cross the threshold stone.

headpiece for the first canto has rather the appearance of a compromise (Ill. 26). Another illustration of this subject (p. 116 – first edition) shows a charming little vignette in which only the tower is visible against a wooded background at daybreak (Ill. 27). In a further letter on 4 April 1853, Birket Foster tells Adam Black: '... I have not received the parcel yet but no doubt the sketches etc. will be sufficient. If all be well I hope to leave on Thursday morning for Melrose.'

Prints of the ruins of Melrose Abbey must have been available at that time, but Birket Foster conscientiously set off to see for himself. 'If thou would'st see fair Melrose aright/Go visit it by pale moonlight.' The headpiece for these opening lines of the second canto shows a careful representation of Melrose Abbey which is painstakingly correct in architectural detail and rather stiff in effect. The other illustrations of this subject are full of authentic details, but it seems that it is only when he is once again in a more open landscape that Birket Foster ceases to hold his breath in concentration and reverts to his usual relaxed manner, although a definite impression comes across that

26 From *The Lay of the Last Minstrel* by Sir Walter Scott, published by Adam and Charles Black, 1854. Drawing by Birket Foster: engraved by Edmund Evans.
Collection: Aberdeen Central Library.

27 '**Branksome Tower**' vignette from *The Lay of the Last Minstrel*. Drawing by Birket Foster: engraved by Edmund Evans. *Collection: Aberdeen Central Library.*

Birket Foster was always slightly fussed about the illustrations for this book. In an undated letter to Adam Black (almost certainly August 1853) he writes:

'Have you seen the cuts for the Lay of the Last Minstrel? How do you think it will look? I am very anxious to see a sheet. I hope sometime before the leaves are off the trees to get the sketches for Marmion – so as to have plenty of time for it. I have been sadly pinched for the Lay.'

The Lay of the Last Minstrel was published in 1854. The first edition had strong gold-blocked covers in green, with a sewn binding, which has made for a sturdy volume. Thirty-one of the illustrations are after drawings by Birket Foster and 51 from those of John Gilbert. The frontispiece and illustrated title page are after the work of J.M.W. Turner. J.W. Whymper engraved illustrations by John Gilbert and Edmund Evans those of Birket Foster. Appendix 1, p. 191, gives further details of other subjects illustrated by Birket Foster from the works of Sir Walter Scott, e.g. *Marmion* (published 1855). Every one of these volumes provides illustrations of quality, and indeed Birket Foster himself stated that the drawings he made for Adam and Charles Black in illustration of Scott's poems and for the various Picturesque Guides were some of his best work and the best engraved. Advertising matter at the back of one of the Guides quotes from a publication called *Atlas* which had commented that the *Picturesque Guide to the English Lakes* was 'Charmingly written, its intelligence is ample and minute and its illustrations are admirable specimens of art'. In view of the personal opinions of Birket Foster the claim does not seem as biased as might have been supposed. All these books went into countless editions. A 28th edition of *Black's Picturesque Guide to Scotland* appeared in 1889 and a 26th of *Black's Guide to the Trossachs* in 1903, by which time the picturesque description had been dropped, together with all but nine of the original Birket Foster illustrations.

Illustration no. 38 is from *Black's Picturesque Guide through North and South Wales*, tenth edition, published in 1860. This contains 44 very charming and accurately observed drawings by Birket Foster, engraved by Edmund Evans, as were the main illustrations for these Guides, with the exception of some frontispieces and insertion plates, e.g. the above guide shows two engravings by W. Miller after the work of Montague Stanley, which are printed on better quality paper than the main text. In a book of over 400 pages, plus folded maps, but still compact and light enough for the pocket, it was inevitable that the paper should be flimsy and this has been to the detriment of some of the illustrations which are indented with letterpress on the reverse side, but the two views illustrated here are from pages printed on a single side only. The average price of these informative little volumes was 5/-. It might be thought that the large number of editions (during a period of well over half a century) would provide an item readily available for the collector, but this is not so, as such guides were very expendable. The basic history and topography of an area may not be subject to change, but the information on trains, hotels, roads, etc. would quickly date and these books must often have perished in many a Victorian spring-cleaning before they had time to acquire any kind of rarity value. Those that survived would be even more obsolete with the coming of motoring and an obvious choice for re-pulping during the Second World War. Consequently, in the light of present day appreciation of the work of Birket Foster, *Black's Picturesque Guides for Tourists* (if illustrated by this artist) can be expected to fetch a price far above the level of the very mundane commercial purpose of the original.

In 1854, Birket and Anne Foster travelled for six or seven weeks through Belgium, Germany and Switzerland, during which tour Birket Foster gathered much of the material for *The Rhine and its Picturesque Scenery* (published by David Bogue in 1856). They were accompanied by Anne's nephew, Robert Spence Watson, who was then 17 years old and acted as interpreter. It was from the wedding breakfast of his parents that Birket Foster had received the 'bride cake' in 1835; that is, he was the eldest son of Joseph Watson a solicitor, of Gateshead, who had married Sarah Spence, a sister of Anne. Joseph Watson had a rather unexpected claim to literary fame in that as well as anti-slavery treatises, etc. it was he who wrote 'The Ballad of the Lambton Worme' - a piece that with its well-known tune has become inalienably associated with the Newcastle area. His son, Dr Robert Spence Watson, LL D, DCL, solicitor and philanthropist, was to achieve

high academic and political esteem.[2] As a young man, while studying in London, he was a frequent visitor to the home of the Birket Fosters and it was there that he recalled meeting Frederick Walker and Charles Keene, whose names are so closely associated with the life of Birket Foster.

Frederick Walker (1840-75) has been described as a nervous, timid, sensitive man, frail of body and excitable in temperament. He was born in Marylebone, the son of a moderately successful jeweller and at the time of his introduction to Birket Foster was enrolled at the Royal Academy Schools, but was also studying drawing on wood with J.W. Whymper. This talkative, engaging little man, who was well below average height, was recalled by Robert Spence Watson as 'always playing tricks and always so charming that you could not be vexed with him'. The shy, mercurial personality of Fred Walker endeared him to Birket Foster, who was to act as something of a guide and mentor to this talented artist. The fact that R.S. Watson remembers seeing him at the home of Birket Foster during his student days shows that the two had met earlier than is often stated.

Charles Samuel Keene (1832-91) was the son of a solicitor, but after making unsuccessful attempts at the law and architecture, he was apprenticed to the Whympers for five years. Keene has been described as very nearly the greatest English black-and-white artist since Hogarth. He had an absolute devotion to the art of drawing and practised constantly, often carrying a bottle of ink attached to his coat for instant use. His was rather an original personality and he was regarded as slightly eccentric, although examples of this are only mildly unusual, e.g. he did not like shaking hands, but did like to live in a clutter and was so fond of animals and birds that he regularly fed the rats in his studio and once kept a pet carrion crow. This musical, kindly, humorous, but sometimes taciturn man was to become a close friend of Birket Foster. R.S. Watson first met Keene at the time when he was just approaching his most famous period as an illustrator for *Punch*, but he thought him 'grave and solemn, his pockets filled with curious little old pipes which only held about three draws'. Charles Keene was such a constant smoker of small clay pipes that this habit was an essential part of his personality and led to his sometimes being referred to as 'Old Dottles' - after the plugs of wickedly strong tobacco that he kept in an old sardine box.

The Sunday-evening gatherings at the home of Birket Foster were always a very happy memory for Robert Spence Watson, who also recalled meeting there Thomas Miller, who had compiled the text for *The Boy's Country Book*, etc. and Albert Smith, a rather colourful character, whose *Story of Mont Blanc* had been illustrated by Birket Foster for David Bogue in 1852, as also *A Month in Constantinople* by the same author.

In 1855, Milton's *L'Allegro and Il Penseroso* was published by W. Kent and Co. (formerly David Bogue). Forrest Reid continues his criticism of Foster: 'Whatever poet he may be illustrating - whether it be Edgar Allan Poe, Wordsworth, Milton or the amazingly geographical James Montgomery - he gives precisely the same delicate little Birket Foster idyll.' Certainly this volume of Milton

28 From Milton's *L'Allegro and Il Penseroso*, published by W. Kent and Co, 1855. Etchings on steel by Birket Foster (illustrated from the 1860 edition). Engraved area: 6¾ × 4¼" - 17.1 × 10.8 cms.
Collection: Jan Reynolds.

While the ploughman, near at hand,
Whistles o'er the furrow'd land,
And the milkmaid singeth blithe,
And the mower whets his scythe,
And every shepherd tells his tale,
Under the hawthorn in the dale.

And, missing thee, I walk unseen
On the dry smooth-shaven green,
To behold the wandering moon,
Riding near her highest noon,
Like one that had been led astray
Through the heaven's wide pathless way ;
And oft, as if her head she bow'd,
Stooping through a fleecy cloud.

presents the usual vignetted style, with wooded landscapes and glimpses of country pursuits, but the 29 illustrations are of particular interest for the fact that these were etched on steel by Birket Foster himself, showing his work without the intervention of the engraver (Ills. 28, 29). The illustrations were first printed onto the pages from the steel plates and the text was then over-printed in red, with Caslon type face. The name of the printer is not recorded, but it is the opinion of Ruari McLean that this was probably Richard Clay, who was to print Goldsmith's *The*

29 From Milton's *L'Allegro and Il Penseroso*. Etching on steel by Birket Foster. Engraved area: 5 × 4¼″ – 12.7 × 10.8 cms. *Collection: Jan Reynolds.*

30 From *The Poetical Works of George Herbert*, published by James Nisbet and Co., 1856. Drawing by Birket Foster: engraved by Edmund Evans. Reproduced from *The Reminiscences of Edmund Evans*, 1964, by permission of the Oxford University Press. *Collection: Derbyshire County Library.*

Traveller for Routledge in 1868, with etchings on steel by Birket Foster.

The work of an indifferent artist can be enhanced by a clever engraver. These etchings prove that the many drawings made by Birket Foster were indeed reproduced (notably by Edmund Evans) very much in the spirit of his original conception. He may have been trying to prove such a point in undertaking the engraving of this book, although the critics considered the steel engravings were an improvement.

'... as examples of Mr Foster's art, they possess an advantage over wood-cuts, however well executed, for his free and delicate touches could never be so produced by the most skilful wood engraver ... Often as these poems have been the themes of our artists, they appear inexhaustible, and Mr Foster's fertile imagination and ready pencil have extracted new sweets from the flowers of poesy that everywhere abound; whether the subjects be figures only, or landscapes only, or a combination of the two, he is alike happy in each and all ...' (*The Art*

31 From *Sabbath Bells Chimed by the Poets*, an anthology published by Bell and Daldy, 1856. Drawing by Birket Foster: engraved by Edmund Evans and printed by him in black and four colours (illustration from the first edition). Size: 8¼ × 6″ – 21 × 15.2 cms.
Collection: Ronald Huby.

Journal, part of a long review of a reprinted edition, 1857.)

Birket Foster works his way steadily through the text of the Milton poems, illustrating each page with a suitable subject, but his sense of humour has allowed him to enliven a jousting scene by emblazoning 'B. Foster' across the shield of a knight who is kneeling to receive an accolade. Faces in the work of Birket Foster can be weak in modelling, with a characteristic that suggests features painted onto a hazel-nut, endearingly recognisable, but rather repetitive in effect. An interesting point emerges from a

study of the sixth plate (Ill. 28). It will be noted that the figure of the milkmaid is the obvious basis for the now famous water-colour of 1860 (Victoria and Albert Museum, Ill. 40). The preliminary sketch for the latter was posed by Mary (known as 'Polly') Brown, who was the daughter of Anne Foster's sister, Elizabeth, who had married Henry Brown in 1837. Thus, Polly Brown was a niece of his wife and first cousin to his children. Polly Brown (whose father died when she was six) was to become a permanent member of the Foster household from about 1855 and later recalled posing for the milkmaid sketch in the fields near Hampstead. Comparison of detail shows that Birket Foster had drawn the Milton illustration from this location, but must have later returned, with Polly Brown, in order to re-sketch the scene and make a detailed observation of the figure, in which the stance has been slightly altered. An inspiration from work commissioned as illustrations in the 1850s was often to be a source of later water-colours.

'L'Allegro and Il Penseroso' proved popular and was much reprinted. *The Art Journal* concluded: '... We have no space to enlarge, though we could readily find something to say by way of commendation on each plate; and can only regret that we cannot introduce a specimen of these charming engravings, as they are on metal ...' This substantial volume and earlier editions have an ochre-coloured cloth cover, with a handsome decorative title blocked in gold and additional decorations in blind. Unhappily, the book had a gutta-percha binding and this has proved inadequate to hold the stiff card-type pages and many copies have collapsed as a result, although the number of reprints has made it still one of the more obtainable of collectors' items. In 1979, a first edition, with Birket Foster's own book plate inserted, was on the market for £35.

It was almost entirely in collaboration with Birket Foster that Edmund Evans worked on the books that were to establish his reputation as the foremost engraver and printer of high quality illustrations in colour. *Sabbath Bells Chimed by the Poets* was the first book engraved and printed by Evans in full colour. The text of this anthology was designed and printed by Charles Whittingham at the Chiswick Press and 16 illustrations after the drawings of Birket Foster were engraved and over-printed by Evans on the cream-toned Chiswick Press sheets, employing colours of dark brown, pale yellow, blue-grey and reddish brown. The initial letters were hand-coloured – a tedious occupation that was often done by young children for very poor rates of pay. *Sabbath Bells Chimed by the Poets* (published by Bell and Daldy in 1856) is not only a delightfully pretty book, but also has a pious theme – a sure recipe for success with the Victorian public, although *The Art Journal* chose to carp at the very ingredient that gives this attractive volume its essential interest and quality (Ill. 31):

'A book that requires not the help of the reviewer to lift it into notice if once seen. It was a happy thought to bring together what a multitude of poets have sung in harmony with the sound of the "church-going" bells, so as to make, as it were, a chorus of sweet and solemn music, floating across streamlet and valley, from "distant towers and antique spires" presented by the pencil of so charming a sketcher of rural scenery as Mr Foster ... we have, however, one fault to find with the artistic portion of this otherwise elegantly "got up" volume; it is a great pity the illustrations are coloured; the beauty of Mr Foster's designs are by no means increased by the tintings, while the delicacy of the engraving by Mr Evans is altogether lost; they would have been far more acceptable left plain. It was quite a "mistake" to send them forth in their present garb.' (*The Art Journal*, 1856, p. 31.)

It was perhaps legitimate to use the term 'tintings', but this criticism of the use of colour showed a lack of appreciation of the trend of the day. The book was a success and later editions (published by Ward Lock) were to be re-set and printed entirely by Edmund Evans (from 1861 onwards, but not often dated). The cover of the first edition in red or blue morocco has 'Sabbath Bells' blocked in gold, but in the Evans editions the full title appears, although within a design that does not have the subtle quality of the original Chiswick Press decoration, i.e. Charles Whittingham used bell-like flowers as part of his motif but later editions show actual bells of very undistinguishable design. There is a marked difference between the first edition of this book and the re-set work by Edmund Evans, including a variation in the former text and the colouring of the illustrations. It must be a matter of personal opinion as to which is the more attractive. The original printing shows more differentiation of colour, but subsequent editions under the entire direction of Evans had a more integrated effect and less of the appearance of 'tinting' complained of by *The Art Journal*, although with a result that tends towards an overall impression of ochre. Evans also introduced a new plate as a frontispiece with the title 'Sunday Morning' from a drawing that does not appear in the first edition. The initial letters are more ornamental in treatment, but are not coloured either by hand or otherwise.

At the time of the publication of *Sabbath Bells Chimed by the Poets* the market was exactly right for the appearance of high-quality mass reproduction methods in the field of book illustration. Edmund Evans was not only a skilled craftsman, but was a man of taste and creative ideas, who was able to recognise commercial potential and originality in the work of individual artists and could initiate projects to suit their particular style. That his collaborations with Birket Foster were so successful could be expected as part of their personal friendship, but many other artists were to owe an inestimable debt to Edmund Evans. He virtually discovered Walter Crane and printed all the famous Toy Books that followed and which were to have such a radical effect on the design and style of Victorian coloured books for children. Randolph Caldecott owed much of his success to the promotional ideas and colour printing of Edmund Evans, but his most famous protégé must always be Kate Greenaway, the immortal illustrator of books for children. A later reference will show that her work was also indirectly linked with the life of Birket Foster (see p. 146).

It was early in 1857 that Birket and Anne Foster moved from Marsden Villa to another address in St John's Wood, at 12 Carlton Hill East. This road ran between Abbey Road and Loudoun Road and was a continuation of Carlton Hill, which ran between Maida Vale and Abbey Road. Birket Foster's parents were by this time living at 12 Carlton Hill, i.e. at the opposite side of what is now the same road, as Carlton Hill East became part of Carlton Hill in 1867, when the house where Birket Foster had lived was no. 30.

Birket Foster wrote to Robert Spence from 12 Carlton Hill East on 24 May 1857.

'My dear Brother,
    Some time ago, you proposed spending a few days with us in Yorkshire. As the time is getting near for our trip, I thought I would just write a line to say how very glad we shall be to have your company for as long a time as you can spare. We quite hope to leave here on the 1st of June – go to Manchester to see the pictures which we hope to accomplish in 2 days or 3 at the most as I am very desirous to get into the country to sketch – we propose going from there to Bolton Bridge when our stay is uncertain from then – we think of going to Barnard Castle – Rokeby &c and then perhaps to Shields visiting Middlesboro on the way. Now at any or all of these we shall be most glad to have you with us. There is some small uncertainty as to the day of our leaving as I have a great deal to do before I can leave but we look to the first of June. Perhaps you will write us a line to say what you propose doing. We are having most delightful weather ...'[3]

32 Left: From *Birds, Bees and Blossoms* by Thomas Miller, published by Routledge and Co., 1858. Size: 5¼ × 3½″ – 13.3 × 8.9 cms.
Right: From *The Seasons* by James Thomson, published by Nisbet and Co., 1859. Size: 4½ × 3½″ – 11.5 × 8.9 cms.
Drawings by Birket Foster: engraved by 1 – Edmund Evans, 2 – W. Palmer.
Collection: Brian and Rachel Moss.

Birket Foster was well justified in saying that he had a great deal to do. He was now so popular as an illustrator of books of poetry that the publishers were continually searching about for the work of any poet, even if only vaguely suitable, in order to publish this (often in reprint) with the sole object of using the text as a vehicle for Birket Foster illustrations. Anthologies abounded. 1857 was to see the publication of 12 books of poetry that were either wholly or in part illustrated by Birket Foster and these were followed by at least 16 such volumes in 1858. Birket Foster tackled this stream of commissions with steady Quaker industry, although one is a little surprised at the nature of some of the work that he was still prepared to accept at this stage of his fame as an illustrator. For instance, in 1857 George Routledge published *Aldershot and All About It with Gossip, Literary, Military and Pictorial* by Mrs Young with illustrations from original sketches by the author.[4] These were engraved by Edmund Evans, but it was not until the second edition in 1858 that the cover actually states 'With illustrations by Birket Foster'. *Aldershot and All About It* cost only two shillings and was probably produced as a guide to the district for officers and wives who were stationed at this recently opened army base. One cannot help thinking that George Routledge and Co. were fortunate indeed to obtain the services of Birket Foster to work up amateur sketches for this type of

publication, but his association with the firm in the illustration of books of high quality may have made Foster consider that it was hardly worth complaining if asked to undertake a certain amount of hack work, particularly if this was engraved by Edmund Evans. The views in *Aldershot and All About It* were at least in keeping with his general flair for landscape, but Birket Foster admitted that some of the subjects that he was asked to illustrate were not at all his style and was recorded as saying that the Fallen Angels in 'The Unfathomable Lake' from Pollok's *Course of Time* (1857) reminded him of eels being thrown out of a bag! It is typical of Birket Foster that he could see with an objective and amused eye what must surely be the most unsuccessful drawing ever credited to his name. It is the last plate in the book and these creatures slithering over a cliff into an unlikely hell are completely out of keeping with the Birket Foster style – and he knew it. (See also list of illustrated books, p. 192.)

Birket Foster usually achieved a happy result in illustrating the work of Thomas Miller. *Birds, Bees and Blossoms: Original Poems for Children* was published in 1858 by J. and C. Brown, London and engraved and printed by Edmund Evans. This slim volume (5 × 7½″) had a sewn binding with a blue cloth cover, blocked in gold and blind. There are three separate colour plates on good quality paper, printed in black, blue and ochre, and these represent the three sections of the book, e.g. frontispiece – showing five children bird's-nesting in a wood. The top corners of a square composition are rounded and coloured in with ochre, with a surrounding border in ochre, which is also used for the title 'Birds' under the picture. All three colour plates are to this design and have a very pleasing harmony of tone, but perhaps the most attractive is 'Bees' (Ill. 32). The text is printed on rather thin paper and this is heavily indented, thus spoiling the effect of the delicate little black and white vignettes which appear on each page. *Birds, Bees and Blossoms* was the type of book that might have been given as an inexpensive birthday present for a young girl, but will now be found in the range £10-£15, owing to the quality of the colour plates, which are likely to have survived in better condition than the rest of the book and sometimes appear as very charming framed prints. The book was reprinted, including an edition in 1861 which gives the name of the printer as W. Clowes and Sons, Stamford Street, although the illustrations are from the original blocks by Edmund Evans.

In the following letter to Robert Spence, Birket Foster mentions James Watson, who was to be closely associated with the Dalziels in their engravings for *The Lays of the Holy Land from Ancient and Modern Poets* (1858) which included 15 illustrations by Birket Foster considered by the Dalziels to be 'Exquisite examples' of his work.

> '12 Carlton Hill East
> 23rd. Sept. 1857
>
> My dear brother,
>
> I found this note in my pocket and as the writer of it is the author of the Memorials of Capt. Hedley Vickers fancy it may be acceptable to thee. If it is not just put it in the fire. Anne is still up and pretty nicely. She sends her love and many thanks for thy note ... James Watson is here from Paris. I had a delightful trip into the Lake District and Wales - and have bagged no end of sketches.
>
> How is Robert after his descent into the cellar?
>
> With very dear love in which Anne and Polly Brown unite.
>
> I remain your affec. bro
>
> Birket Foster.'

He explains in a postscript that James Watson is 'not our brother, but of the firm of James Nisbet and Co.' By the term 'brother' he means fellow Quaker. Birket Foster then

33 Birket Foster (probably aged about thirty).
Photograph by permission of the Glasson family.

follows with another postscript in a very excited scrawl:

> 'I just open this to say that Anne and daughter *Ellen* are doing very well indeed - the baby was born at 10 minutes past 12 - 2 hours after James Watson left.'[5]

The birth of Ellen on 24 September 1857 meant that Birket and Anne Foster now had a family of five children. Ellen had three brothers and a sister: Myles Birket, born 29 November 1851; William - 6 June 1853; Henry - 6 November 1854 and Margaret Ann - 27 January 1856.

Notes: Chapter Seven

1 Quotations in this chapter from correspondence between Adam Black and Birket Foster are reproduced by permission of the Department of Manuscripts, National Library of Scotland, Edinburgh.

2 This distinguished nephew of Anne Foster was a most prominent and influential Liberal. He several times refused offers of a title, as Quakers do not accept such honours, but in 1907 did agree to take a Privy Councillorship with one proviso. As a member of the Society of Friends and President of the Peace Society he felt it against his principles to wear the ceremonial sword that went with the official uniform of a Privy Councillor. King Edward VII was consulted and issued a very kindly worded dispensation to this immensely respected old Quaker. For further information see *The Life of Robert Spence Watson* by his nephew

Percy Corder (published by Headley Brothers, Bishopsgate, London, 1914). Percy Corder (1863-1927) was the son of Anne's niece, Lucy, who had married Alexander Corder in 1859. Thus Percy Corder was second cousin to the grandchildren of Birket Foster.

3 Letter published by permission of Newcastle upon Tyne City Libraries.

4 Information with reference to *Aldershot and All About It* from Divisional Library Headquarters, Farnborough.

5 Published by permission of Newcastle upon Tyne City Libraries. The author of *The Memorials of Captain Hedley Vickers*, published in 1856, was Catherine M. Marsh, a writer of no particular fame.

8
A change of direction: The Society of Painters in Water-colours

Birket Foster was so popular as an illustrator that he could well have continued in that role to the end of his career, but for the quality of his talent that made inevitable the need to progress in the direction of a more individual and creative expression. The Dalziel brothers record:

'Birket Foster was a constant visitor to our office in High Street, Camden Town, generally bringing a parcel of drawings with him. On one of these occasions the conversation turned upon water colour painting and the great demand there was for that class of art, when, having seen some of his slight sketches in colour, we expressed a little surprise that he did not go in for it. He replied that his wife had suggested the same thing, but – and he shrugged his broad shoulders saying, "Um – I don't know – but we shall see – we shall see." He did see and all the art world knows with what result.'

In 1858, Birket Foster was still working on commitments in hand, but had virtually ceased to accept any further illustrative commissions and was making deliberate moves towards becoming an exhibiting water-colourist. He spent a lot of time that summer in the Dorking area, where he worked in solitary concentration on the problems of mastering technique. The use of colour as the finished form of presentation (rather than as a sketch medium) proved to be a liberating, but somewhat heady experience. The Surrey countryside was always to be a source of spiritual uplift and a constant joy to the eye of Birket Foster, but he could not convey this by means of conventional water-colour washes, with the result that his early works were almost certain of opposition from exponents of the established style.

Birket Foster chose three drawings from the Dorking summer and submitted these to the Society of Painters in Water-colours with an application to become an Associate member. His anxiety about the outcome is brought vividly to life in the following letter to Polly Brown, which is such a charming mingle of Birket Foster the family man and artist. It is dated 5 February 1859 and was written while Polly was on a visit to her mother in North Shields:

'My dear Polly,
    I have undertaken to write you a note this week as your Aunt Anne is quite laid on the shelf with a bad arm. It is a gathering under the arm and till it has come to a head will make her feel weakly and poorly. She gets about however & reads a good deal but being her right arm she cannot do anything else. I quite hope that in a

few days she will be quite well again. She wishes me to thank you for your letter and the Crochet and to beg that you will write her a good long one this week as letters are very acceptable now. Mary Ann is really going, but we have heard of another housemaid – one that Mary Atchison has had for a short time. The children are all quite well again and very good. There was great excitement yesterday amongst them owing to its being my birthday. They presented me with an ivory penholder which was a tremendous event. My pictures are now finished and ready to send. They have to go on Monday for the artists to see for a week and on the following Monday the election takes place which of course will be a time of much interest to us. We have such lots of people to see them, crowds of people! I shall be quite glad that they will be gone on Monday. I fear I shan't get in as there are 22 candidates – and I want two-thirds of the votes. But we can't help hoping.
    What a gay life you seem to be leading at Shields. Yesterday we had Thos. Miller the poet and his daughter and had a very amusing visit from him. He was well acquainted with Campbell, Tom Moore, Sydney Smith, etc. and he told us many amusing stories about them. We are having delightful weather. The Queen is in town and we look very nice just now. . . . How does the music get on? I expect when you return we shall be astounded. . . . We expect Willie Watson to walk in any-time – we have had a letter from him and he may turn up anytime' [i.e. William Joshua Watson, son of Anne's sister Sarah and brother of Robert Spence Watson.] 'Grandmamma has just come in and sends her very dear love to you all and now dear Polly I must end as the paper is done. With dear love to you all, believe me, your very affec. uncle,

Birket Foster.'[1]

This letter shows how keenly Birket Foster hoped that he would be accepted by the Water-colour Society, but on 15 February 1859 he wrote to Robert Spence:

'My dear brother,
    No go! No election took place – or rather no candidate was elected not even Leitch! It has produced a tremendous sensation. It is a conspiracy as they have invited Leitch to send drawings for the last 6 years.
    Anne is much better
    In haste with dear love
        Your affec. bro.
        Birket Foster.'[2]

The selection committee is purported to have rejected the candidature of Birket Foster with the comment: 'We have had quite enough of these wood engravers ...' That may have been the opinion of the 'Old' Water-colour Society stalwarts, but others were more perceptive and the art world was about to enter on a long period in which neither the dealers nor the public could have enough of the water-colours of Birket Foster. In that year, some of the water-colour drawings made in 1854 for *The Rhine and its Picturesque Scenery* were sent for sale by auction. Birket Foster had been more or less a novice in the medium at the time of the execution of these illustrations, but the attractive quality of the work drew considerable interest and the items realised 12 guineas each. (Birket Foster had originally been paid £5 each. Later in the century, the same items were to reach up to 150 guineas apiece.) Henry Wallis of the French Gallery, one of the most enterprising of the London art dealers, immediately recognised in these drawings the potential of Birket Foster, the water-colourist. Apparently, Wallis called on Birket Foster just after he had received the disappointing news of his rejection by the Water-colour Society and promptly suggested that Foster should set to work at once on a large water-colour drawing for him, with a view to completing this in time for submission to the Royal Academy. The plan was very successful and Birket Foster had the satisfaction of seeing 'A Farm - Arundel Park in the distance' accepted and hung in the 1859 Royal Academy exhibition.

But, the year which brought his first establishment as a water-colourist was to be a tragic one for Birket Foster. The letter that he had written to Polly Brown in February is made all the more poignant by the knowledge that Anne Foster was soon to be become very ill with tuberculosis – the disease from which her twin sister had died eight years before.

Polly Brown nursed her aunt most devotedly, but a Change of Air was prescribed, although this was to prove anything but remedial. Anne Foster had been married for just under nine years when she died, aged 33, at Little-hampton on 3 July 1859. The cause of death was not certified as tuberculosis, but as 'Gastric Fever' - a some-what vague term often used by local doctors to conceal the fact that the horrific state of the drains and general lack of sanitation in the area was the frequent cause of death from typhoid, cholera and similar diseases.[3]

The death of his wife was a cruel blow for Birket Foster. There can be no doubt that this had been a most happy marriage and the loss of Anne was to leave a quiet sorrow in Birket Foster for the rest of his life. But he was not a naturally depressive man and he took great comfort from his family. Polly Brown, who was then 19, agreed to stay to manage the household and continue to care for the five children. His eldest son, Myles, was not quite eight years old and his youngest child, Ellen, was just under two. Polly Brown was a lively, intelligent and happy personality and the Foster children already looked upon her as a mother figure.

It was some time in the immediate years after the death of Anne, while his children were still small, that Birket Foster used to amuse them with a game that they called the Scrap Book. They played this every evening when they came down to be with their father. In turn, one child each day was allowed to choose a subject, which could be anything - an omnibus, a person, an animal - the versatile pencil of Birket Foster was equal to all requests. The fascinated children would then watch the subject taking

34 Anne Foster, with their elder daughter, Margaret, and second son, William (who wears skirts as was the custom for boys, until they were 'breeched' at the age of about five). From an album in possession of the Glasson family.

shape and the result was a scrap book composed of some 40 or more very attractive drawings of great spontaneity. Many years later (in 1924) the Scrap Book was to come onto the market, as part of the estate of William Foster, second son of Birket Foster. A member of the family spoke to the dealer who had bought the item and he confirmed that this was to be split up and the drawings mounted and framed as individual pictures. Any collector is fortunate who has one of these original drawings in his possession.

In October 1859, Birket Foster took Polly Brown on a tour through Belgium to the Rhine and back by way of Paris, accompanied by Joseph Cundall and his wife.[4] Cundall had first met Birket Foster at some time during the apprenticeship of the latter and the two became close friends. The Cundalls now lived almost opposite Birket Foster in St John's Wood. The name of Joseph Cundall, who had been trained as a printer, was of some significance in the field of Victorian illustrated books. He was a man of enterprising ideas, which he carried out in the publication of many books of excellent design and original conception. In 1851, in partnership as Cundall and Addey, his firm had exhibited examples of books and colour printing at the Great Exhibition and had been awarded a medal. In that year, their publications included *The Poetical Works of Oliver Goldsmith* with 30 illustrations by John Absolon, Birket Foster, James Godwin and Harrison Weir. These were black and white engravings in which the subjects illustrated by Birket Foster were the 'cooling brook, the grassy vested green ... tangling walks and ruined grounds ...' and similar themes that were suited to his delicate leafy style. Five further books of work by Oliver Gold-smith were to be illustrated by Birket Foster for various publishers.

In 1856-7, Edmund Evans had commenced a long

35 From *The Hamlet* by Thomas Warton, published by Sampson Low, 1859. Etching on copper by Birket Foster. Size: $3\frac{1}{4} \times 2\frac{3}{4}''$ – 8.2 × 7 cms.
Collection: Pauline Flick.

association with the firm of George Routledge. 1859 saw the publication by Routledge of *The Poems of Oliver Goldsmith*, with illustrations by Birket Foster and decorative designs by H. Noel Humphreys. The book ($6\frac{1}{2} \times 9''$) had a sewn binding and the first edition was produced in a dark blue cloth cover, attractively tooled and blocked in gold, with gold-edged pages. The back cover has a certain curiosity value in that it is blocked in gold, as follows: 'With illustrations by Birket Foster in colors (*sic*) Edited by R. A. Willmott'. We are inclined to think of this spelling of 'colour' as a modern Americanisation, but in fact it was a valid form at the period, although not met with very frequently. It is certainly not a misprint. The title page also reads: 'Printed in colors (*sic*) from wood blocks'. This was decorated in black and two shades of grey with a gold border and was the work of Noel Humphreys, as were all the designs for headings, etc. The pages throughout are surrounded with two lines in gold and the general effect of the book is very handsome, although many would consider that *Christmas with the Poets* is more aesthetically pleasing.

The 40 illustrations to the text are from the drawings of Birket Foster and were printed in about eight colours by Edmund Evans. Martin Hardie in *English Coloured Books* (1906) quotes a letter written to him by Edmund Evans describing the methods employed:

'Birket Foster made his first drawings on wood. After I engraved each, I sent him a pull on drawing paper, which he coloured as he wished it to appear. I followed this as faithfully as I could, buying the dry colours from the artists' colourmen and grinding them by hand.'

Some nine or ten printings were used and the resulting strength and variety of tone represents a milestone in Victorian mass-produced colour printing, although certain of the illustrations give an appearance that could have been achieved by the application of slightly crude tints by hand. It is the blue tones that Edmund Evans has managed with the most subtlety and many of the skies are full of delicate and attractive effects, but there is a harshness about some of the colouring of dresses and flesh tints and a very unvaried green that tends to obscure the essential delicacy of the Birket Foster line. One of the prettiest of the illustrations with a very harmonious use of colour shows a stag and some deer under trees, in a half moon-shaped presentation. This is a variation of the last illustration in *The Lady of the Lake*, but is minus the mountains in the

36 From *The Hamlet* by Thomas Warton. Etching on copper by Birket Foster. Size: 3¼ × 2¾″ – 8.2 × 7 cms. *Collection: Pauline Flick.*

distance which have been replaced by more gentle slopes. The title page for the poem 'The Deserted Village' was obviously a favourite of Birket Foster's as he was later to repeat a similar version of this in his *Pictures of English Landscape*, but Edmund Evans adds, in reference to *The Poems of Oliver Goldsmith*: 'Birket Foster never liked this book, though it sold very well indeed' (Ill. 37). Another edition with 12 extra colour illustrations was issued in 1860 and further editions were to follow in later years.

Common Wayside Flowers (George Routledge and Son) was published in 1860, with a prose text by Thomas Miller and water-colour paintings by Birket Foster, which were reproduced by Edmund Evans in six or seven colour printings. The format was an unusual one in the illustrative work of Birket Foster, but the fluent treatment of violets, wood anemones, cowslips, buttercups and daisies, convolvulus and campion, etc. has produced a refreshingly uncontrived effect. There is no hint of the stylised botanical print about these pretty illustrations, but all the affectionate observation of an artist, who genuinely loved and cherished the simple flowers of the wayside – an enthusiasm inherited from his father and grandfather and nurtured by his old schoolmaster, Isaac Brown. The typography of the book is plain and unfussy, although the cloth binding of the first edition, signed by Albert Warren, is one of the richest of the period. An overall design in

gold contains four pasted-down sections of colour printing on paper (of flower designs not in the book) and this is repeated on the back. The book proved popular and was several times reprinted, but later editions do not have the elaborate binding but a dark blue cover with *Common Wayside Flowers* and *Illustrated by Birket Foster* blocked in blind and decorated with a design of wild flowers and other embellishments in gold, with gold-edged pages. It should be noted that in the 1880 edition the colour printing of the illustrations is inclined to be very slightly out of register, so that there is a repeated shadow of outline, e.g. on the wild hyacinth and wood anemone.

1860 also saw the publication of *A Book of Favourite Modern Ballads – Illustrated by Modern English Artists* which was another fine example of the work of Edmund Evans and the 50 engravings included 11 illustrations after drawings by Birket Foster. The first edition is thought to have been the one printed by W. Kent and Co (formerly David Bogue). The presentation of this book shows an influence from the Bogue house style and *Christmas with the Poets*. Line borders and ornamental designs in gilt (by Albert Warren) surround each page and Edmund Evans

EMOTE, unfriended, melancholy, slow—
Or by the lazy Scheldt, or wandering Po,
Or onward where the rude Carinthian boor
Against the houseless stranger shuts the door,

37 Illustration for 'The Traveller' in *The Poems of Oliver Goldsmith*, published by George Routledge, 1859. Drawing by Birket Foster: engraved and printed in colours by Edmund Evans. Size: 6½ × 4″ – 16.5 × 10.2 cms.
Collection: Brian and Rachel Moss.

makes an integrated effect of the engravings in spite of dealing with the styles of many varying artists. Another edition of *Favourite Modern Ballads* was published by Ward, Lock and Tyler in 1865 and is identical except that the illustrations were all printed in six or eight colours and the decorations and type in a neutral tone.[5] The colour-printed version was also issued in two halves, with the titles *Choice Pictures and Choice Poems* and *The Illustrated Poetical Gift Book* (both undated).

'Mr Foster ... especially seems to have reached a point beyond which it would be impossible to go ....' This statement in a review of *The Seasons* by James Thomson, published 1859 (Ill. 32) had a particular significance to the work of Birket Foster which was now approaching a time of vital change. For an artist of his undoubted talent and integrity it had to come.

'Carlton Hill East
19th Feb. 1860

My dear brother,

I thought you would like to hear of my success. The gallery at Pall Mall East is the best place to have Water Colour drawings exhibited and it has been a great desire of mine to get into the Society that I might be enabled to send pictures there. I am only an Associate at present which entitles me to send 8 pictures to the Exhibition

– more than I shall ever do. The members of course fill up their number from the Associates according to their merits that sometime I hope that I shall take the higher step – and that at present is as far as a Water Colour painter can go. Keep Duncan's card if you like. You would see the mention of my election in the Athenaeum. I expect when the Exhibition opens I shall come in for a torrent of abuse in the papers as my drawings are very peculiar – but I must take my chance as I believe it is the right road – at least for me. There is no distinguishing mark attaching to the name of members of the Society. I cannot tell thee how I have longed for dear Anne – it makes me think of poor Constable who was made ARA just after his wife died – he said "it has been delayed until I am solitary and cannot impart it" speaking of the pleasure it gave him.

Dear little Myles is quite nicely again and all the rest are well.

I have my pictures to paint for the exhibition – the 3 candidate drawings I had to borrow for the occasion – one belonging to Mr John Morley – another to Mr Coleridge of Eton – and the other just finished for Mr Vokins, but sold so I can't have them for the gallery. This of course makes me very busy as I have only till the 17th of April to finish them. I have entirely given up the old work. I have given notice to all my friends that I have given up all drawing on wood. It is a bold step but commissions for pictures pour in – and it is far more delightful working in colour. We look forward with great pleasure to visiting the North in the summer.

I must end this now as I have some other notes to write.

With my dear love to all in which Polly unites.
I am thy affec. bro
Birket Foster.'[6]

We can feel for Birket Foster in his state of mingled sadness and pleasure. He was right to be quietly proud of his achievement, but his election had not much pleased J.D. Harding, who was then one of the elders of the Society. In later years, it amused Birket Foster to relate that the formal congratulations of Harding had been delivered in a most patronising manner with a definite implication that he considered Birket Foster was very fortunate to have been elected.

James Duffield Harding (1798–1863), who was the author of many instruction books (and whose style is reflected in that of William Callow), probably felt his authority was being threatened by the innovative methods of Birket Foster, as these were so far removed from the mainstream of pure water-colour technique. Harding is reported to have said to Birket Foster, after much pontification about the need to study from nature: 'If you will do as I suggest, I have no doubt you will one day take a good place amongst the best of us.'[7].

In fact, the water-colours of Birket Foster were to be an instant and phenomenal success and achieved a popularity and acclaim far beyond anything accorded to the more conventional style of J.D. Harding, in spite of the latter being very well known through his lithography. A review of 'The Royal Academy and other Exhibitions' in *Black-*

38 From *Black's Picturesque Guide through North and South Wales* (tenth edition, 1860). Drawings by Birket Foster: engraved by Edmund Evans. Size: 4½ × 3½″ – 11.4 × 8.9 cms.
Collection: Brian and Rachel Moss.

CARNARVON CASTLE.

CADER IDRIS

39 'Tynemouth'. Water-colour, signed B. Foster and dated 1855. Size: 5¼ × 12″ – 13.3 × 30.5 cms.
Collection: Laing Art Gallery, Newcastle upon Tyne.

40 'The Milkmaid'. Water-colour, signed and dated 1860.
Size: 11¾ × 17½″ – 29.9 × 44.4 cms.
Collection: Victoria and Albert Museum, Crown Copyright.

wood's Magazine for July 1860 notes the sunburnt flints and chopped-up chaotic foregrounds of P.J. Naftel, which 'give the sense of earthquake uneasiness and volcanic uproar, so fearing a fever or a sunstroke we gladly quit the neighbourhood altogether and join company with Mr Birket Foster or Mr Harding in the quiet retreats of home-loving England. Mr Harding has been long known by his capital handbooks on landscape drawing, and for power and dexterity of hand he is not surpassed. Mr Birket Foster, the graceful illustrator of popular poets, is in execution equally dextrous and in study has the advantage of greater detail...' One cannot help wondering what Mr Harding thought about this review in the light of his remarks to Birket Foster!

On 27 April 1860, Queen Victoria wrote in her journal:

'After breakfast we went to the Old Water Colour Exhibition with the four eldest children, etc. Some very fine landscapes by Branwhite, Newton, Fripp, B. Foster and Callow, four very fine ones by Carl Haag.'[8]

Queen Victoria expressed a wish to purchase one of the Birket Foster exhibits, but this was already sold. Representations were made to the new owner, but he was not prepared to part with his picture, even to please the Queen!

The reviewer in *Blackwood's Magazine* returned to the subject of Birket Foster in a later passage:

'... the exquisite little drawings of Mr Birket Foster, so remarkable for their finished detail. All the beauties which our readers may have doted over in the wood cuts of this most successful of book illustrators, are recognised with fresh delight in these wonderful studies. The execution is, in fact, almost the work of the graver; the usual sweep of the full and flowing water-colour brush is here exchanged for the lines and dots of the pointed pencil. Yet the result is in nowise Pre-Raphaelite. The detail is well kept together, the taste is most refined; only we would desire in the colour greater fervour. The general tone is indeed almost as passionless as the simple light and shade of the wood-engraving itself.'

The Art Journal commented:

'The rejected candidates of last year, Birket Foster and Frederick Smallfield, do ample honour to their election.... No. 30 "Feeding the Ducks". We have observed that if drawing upon wood leads to any power in painting at all, that power is generally characterized by originality. This drawing is very beautiful in its minute manipulation; every leaf of the willows is given, every blade of grass at the brink of the pool has its place and asserts its individuality, but effect is forgotten; when the drawing is removed from immediately before the eye we feel it wants force.'

It will be noticed that at this time the critics were still seeing the work of Birket Foster very much in terms of the illustrations that they knew so well. This was only to be expected and perfectly fair. The traditional use of wash methods would not come naturally to an artist who had been constantly employed in producing minutely detailed drawings for the engraver.

The personal collection of Birket Foster testifies to his admiration for the work of William Henry Hunt (1790-

41 'Young Gleaners Resting'. Water-colour, signed with monogram (left). Size: 11⅞ × 17⅝" – 30.2 × 44.8 cms.
Collection: Victoria and Albert Museum, Crown Copyright.

1864). His later technique of painting on a ground of Chinese white is reflected in the methods of Birket Foster, although the latter had already received an influence in this direction from his work for the engravers. Unfinished work by Birket Foster shows that he first made a detailed pencil drawing and followed this by covering some parts of the paper with pure colour wash and some with solid patches of Chinese white, over which he worked with stipple and hatched strokes of pure colour. This method of working over Chinese white with very light brush strokes did not disturb the ground pigment, but induced into the result a brilliance and crisp finish to the work, not to be confused with the admixture of body colour to water-colour, although Birket Foster also employed this method. His early skies were so thickly worked with body colour that the effect is almost as of impasto, showing the raised lines of the brush strokes. Some water-colours by Birket Foster have become damaged, not by fading or foxing, but owing to the pigment literally flaking off the surface of the paper. He worked with an exceptionally fine brush and is reputed to have used less water than any artist before. The exact delicacy of point to the brush was a constant requirement and he would pass this between his lips as he worked – a habit that led to the saying that the paint came out of Birket Foster's head!

Some biographical notes in possession of the Glasson family include the following:

'B.F. was an extraordinarily rapid sketcher and a friend who constantly went out with him used to complain that while he was deciding what to pencil in, B.F. had not only settled to his subject and drawn it in, but had half finished the colouring. He was also when sketching insensible to cold or heat, so wrapped up was he in his drawing, although others who were with him were nearly frozen or baked. He was never in the habit of carrying the mass of paraphernalia that most artists and especially amateurs set out with. People often said, We see you going out, we suppose, sketching but we never see you carrying anything. Oh, B.F. would say, I've got it all concealed about my person and often this was quite true. A water-colour folding palette ready charged with all the needful colours, a brush or two and a sketch book as large as his coat pocket or possibly a piece of Chalon board in brown paper was all he took on many occasions. He borrowed chairs at the cottages he loved to draw. He occasionally carried a sketching bag and camp stool, but never an umbrella. He used to chaff his friend the late J.H. Robinson (examiner of private bills in the House of Commons 6 months of the year and amongst other things a very enthusiastic amateur artist the other 6 months) about the amount of tackle he went out with. He said, You look as if you were going to discover the North West Passage with all those harpoons and things.'

It is very fortunate that we have an exact description of Birket Foster's palette from this same family source, as follows:

Scarlet vermilion	Permanent yellow	Green oxide of
Rose madder	Aureolin	chromium
Rubens madder	Cadmium orange	Cyanine blue
Purple madder	Yellow ochre	Cobalt blue
	Golden ochre	Cobalt green
	Red sienna	Ultramarine
	Burnt sienna	Terra verte
		Vandyke brown
		Sepia

42 'The Hill, Sedbergh'. Water-colour with monogram and inscription (left). This was the parental home of Birket Foster's grandmother, the former Mary Burton, who married Robert Foster. Size: $8\frac{1}{4} \times 12\frac{1}{2}''$ - 21 × 31.7 cms.
Photograph: Abbey Antiques and Arts, Hemel Hempstead.

43 'The Sheep Fold'. Water-colour, signed with monogram (left). Size: $13\frac{7}{8} \times 27\frac{1}{2}''$ - 35.3 × 70 cms.
Photograph: Christie's.

44 'Near Streatley on Thames'. Water-colour, signed with monogram (left). Note the similarity in compositional elements and atmosphere to 'The Sheep Fold'. Size: $10\frac{1}{8} \times 20\frac{1}{4}''$ - 25.7 × 51.4 cms.
Collection: St Helen's Museum and Art Gallery.

One has to add to the above notes the Chinese white that Birket Foster so obviously used, but which is not mentioned in this list, as it may not have been considered as a colour. At the time of compiling this book, Birket Foster's palette is on loan to the British Council from the Royal Society of Painters in Water-colours and in China as an exhibit in 'British Water-colours and Drawings 1750-1980 – China Exhibition'.

'His paint box was only a small one – $7\frac{1}{2}'' \times 4''$ – and his palette would have astonished most people as it did the late E. W. Cooke, RA who called in the absence of Birket Foster one day and was shown the studio by his son. Catching sight of the palette, Cooke exclaimed: "You don't mean to tell me that your father gets the lovely pure colours he does off a palette as dirty as that!" He could hardly be persuaded that it was just as Birket Foster had used it the day before. It certainly did look dirty, but B.F. knew his way about it and probably no palette ever provided such pure bits of colour.'[9]

Birket Foster could manipulate an acceptable drawing from the most unlikely materials. He once went out to make a water-colour drawing of a particular location, but discovered that he had left his water bottle behind and none was to be had. However, he had a small flask of sherry in his luncheon box and promptly decided to use this as an improvised medium. He thought it extremely nasty to work with, but the result was a drawing with an interesting mellow tone. On another occasion, a friend sent him for a joke a penny box of children's 'safe' paints, which contained about eight cakes of exceptionally poor quality colours. Using only these, Birket Foster still managed to produce a beautifully delicate and attractive little drawing. It was said that he could work with almost anything.

The Dalziels add to the many anecdotes about Birket Foster and his work:

'It was Foster's invariable custom to make small water-colour sketches for his more important black and white work; sometimes they were partly pencil, or pen and ink tinted. Some little time before he seriously took to water-colour painting a West End publisher frequently asked him for some of these sketches, so he gave his friend a "bundle" of original drawings, for which the publisher thanked him, saying that one day, when he could afford to do so, he would have them bound in a nice book. It was after Foster won distinction as a painter that he said to us "Those drawings would now represent a money value of some hundreds of pounds." His mother, a dear old Quaker lady who was present, said: "Thee mustn't mind that, Birket, Thee gave him the drawings and they are his now, not matter what the value of them may be now".'

The use of 'Thee' in the nominative, instead of 'Thou' varies in Quaker custom and the version given by the Dalziels was probably the one more frequently met with in North Country speech. The Dalziel brothers also related:

'Birket Foster naturally spent much of his time in the country, often locating himself at farm houses, and being of a genial nature always became friendly with the people. On one occasion an old farmer took the greatest interest in the work as it went on, in fact to the extent that the old boy seemed to feel that he had a sort of partnership in the production of the picture. Some time after this a friend of Foster's, who stayed at the same farm, found the old man most anxious to know all about Foster, but particularly as to how much money he had got for the picture, "that we done down here". The friend said, "A hundred pounds at least". The old man was incredulous, in fact he would *not* believe it. When assured that such an amount was small for a picture by so clever and popular a man, he seemed unable to grasp it, saying "Why, it would be like pickin' up sovereigns as if they were turnips or eggs; and if it were so, all I can say is, he must ha' sold it to a friend."'

It is perhaps not surprising that this old country yokel was unaware of the importance of Birket Foster, as the

45 '**Cottage at Hambledon**'. Water-colour, signed with mono-gram (right). Size: 16¾ × 25″ - 42.5 × 63.5 cms. *Collection: The Tate Gallery.*

46 '**At Bonchurch, Isle of Wight**'. Water-colour, signed with monogram (right). Size: 9¼ × 14″ - 23.4 × 35.5 cms. *Collection: Warrington Borough Council, Museum and Art Gallery, Warrington.*

artist himself did little to promote his name, but retained a charming lack of pretension and a modest amusement in the knowledge of his fame as an artist. He used to tell a story of an encounter with a fellow passenger on a voyage up the west coast of Scotland, during which they got into interesting conversation. At the end of the day, his companion said: 'May I ask with whom I have had the pleasure of travelling?' On being told, he remarked, with a twinkle: 'Ah, a very well known name, but not as well known as mine.' Birket Foster then asked who he was and got the reply, 'I am Cadbury of the Cocoa!'

Another story that Birket Foster used to relate was of setting out to do a water-colour drawing of a cottage in a field near Betws-y-Coed and finding a sketcher already at work nearby. He strolled up to Birket Foster and told him that it was no good starting on his subject in the prevailing light and proceeded to give him detailed instruction in the art of water-colour painting. Many artists would have been very huffed and instantly explained who they were, but one has to remember that Birket Foster was basically a shy man, so he merely said that he proposed to settle down and work in his own way. Some time later, when his fellow sketcher caught sight of his drawing, he exclaimed: 'Hello, your work reminds me of that man who exhibits in London, but I can't think of his name.' B.F. quietly suggested 'Birket Foster?' and was told, 'Yes, that's the man!' The artist then revealed his identity to this unfortunate amateur, who replied with astonishment and a good grace: 'By Jove! And to think that I have been trying to teach you how to paint in water-colour!'[9]

Birket Foster is known to have photographed landscape subjects, like so many artists of the period, but this would appear to have been more of an experiment and confined to his earlier years. There is a story in the Birket Foster family that one day he had a large camera rigged up outside a picturesque cottage when a woman came out and asked; ''Ow many tunes does it play?' thinking that it was a barrel organ. Or this is what the story relates, although one cannot help wondering if the tale gathered in the telling by Birket Foster, who had a definite sense of humour.

In later years, Birket Foster was often asked to give lessons in water-colour painting, but always replied that he had never had any and could not instruct anyone else. As it was, his method of feeling his way into the use of water-colour from the engraving block evolved into a style of genuine originality. The public was instantly captivated by the beautiful intricacy of detail in his work and it was this, allied to a natural sense of colour harmony, that laid the foundations of the career of Birket Foster as one of the most popular water-colourists of the Victorian era.

Notes: Chapter Eight
1 Letter to Polly Brown published by permission of the Library of the University of California, Los Angeles, USA.
2 Letter published by permission of Newcastle upon Tyne City Libraries.
3 Local information from Stanley Jepson, Superintendent Registrar, Worthing District. See also *Glimpses of Old Worthing* by Edwin Snewin and Henfrey Smail (1945).
4 Places visited on this tour included Ostend, Bruges, Ghent, Antwerp, Brussels, Cologne, Rolandseck, Andernach, Coblenz, St Goar, Mainz, Saarbruck, Metz, and back by Boulogne to Folkestone. The weather was not suitable for much outdoor sketching and few subsequent works are related to this trip.

5 A colour illustration of the title page and frontispiece of *Favourite Modern Ballads* (1865) is reproduced in *Victorian Book Design* by Ruari McLean, published by Faber and Faber, 1963.
6 Letter reproduced by permission of the Newcastle upon Tyne City Libraries.
7 *The Brothers Dalziel*, B. T. Batsford reprint, 1978.
8 Extract from the journal of Queen Victoria reproduced by Gracious Permission of Her Majesty the Queen.
9 Information from the Glasson family.

9

Birket Foster's Pictures of English Landscape

In the autumn of 1860 Birket Foster went again over much of the same ground as he had travelled in 1859. This time he was accompanied by Polly Brown and her aunt, Sarah, with her husband, Joseph and their son Robert Spence Watson, who had been with Birket and Anne Foster on the tour of 1854.

Robert S. Watson contributed 15 articles to the *New-castle Daily Journal* based on this trip, with the title 'A Three Weeks' Ramble in the Autumn of 1860 – the diary of travels in the Rhineland, Switzerland and France with Birket Foster'. H.M. Cundall includes some details of the itinerary:

'The party left Newcastle by steamboat and crossed the North Sea to Rotterdam; thence went by rail to Dentz, and from Cologne to Coblenz, where they took the steamer up the Rhine to Castel. After visiting Frankfurt and Heidelberg, they proceeded to Switzerland, stopping at Basle and Lucerne. From the latter place they ascended the Righi; and afterwards crossed the Grimsel to Interlaken. All the party were on horseback with the exception of Dr Watson, who was a good pedestrian and preferred to trust himself to his own legs. In his narrative in dealing with the mode of progression, he lets a little side-light into Birket Foster's equestrian powers as he says "the only drawback to the perfect happiness of the party were the horses. They were certainly quiet animals, but I have always observed that, however excellent in this respect, they can tell immediately whether he who straddles them is used to his position. If he is not, they at once conceive a cool contempt for him, and evince it by looking round in a sneering manner, standing still to eat grass by the way-side; nay, Mr F's brute even went so far as to commence to lie down, and but for the timely assistance of one of the men engaged to look after them, would doubtless have accomplished its intention". They continued their journey to Geneva by way of Berne, Freiburg and Vevey, and afterwards returned home through Macon and Paris. This being a pleasure trip to see as much as possible in three weeks, Birket Foster had little or no time to make many drawings, but his spare moments were always engaged in making pencil notes in one of his sketch books without which he never travelled.'

(For some details of sketch books, see Christie's sale, 26-7 June 1899 – Appendix 6.)

On 2 February 1861, the following rather surprising announcement appeared in *The Athenaeum*: 'Mr Birket Foster, an artist whose delicate pencil has been the delight of Christmas homes for many years, died at his house in St John's Wood last week.'

In fact, it was Myles Birket Foster, father of the artist, whose death at 12 Carlton Hill on 21 January had been announced in *The Times*. Owing to their names being identical and their addresses almost so, there was a great deal of unfortunate confusion. Two elderly ladies are said to have been much disconcerted to have the door opened to them by Birket Foster, on calling at 12 Carlton Hill East to condole with his supposedly orphaned children. Birket Foster was both amused and embarrassed by the error, which was repeated elsewhere. On 17 February he wrote to Robert Spence, who had obviously seen one of these notices:

'... I was much entertained with the scrap from the catalogue. What an awkward mistake it was. I had a great many letters of one sort or another – one from the Editor of the London Review to the family wishing for particulars of my life, etc., but the thing is all set straight now in a very clumsy paragraph in The Athenaeum.'[1]

The breezy correction that appeared under 'Our Weekly Gossip' in *The Athenaeum* on 9 February 1861 might have been more tactfully worded.

'We are pleased to hear that the Mr Birket Foster, who died in St John's Wood last week, was not the artist, but his father. The identity of name and place of residence doubtless led to the confusion between father and son.'

Birket Foster continues his letter to Robert Spence:

'... I am keeping the house today to try and get rid of a bad cold that has been hanging about me for some time. We have very nice weather just now.

My mother seems very nicely. I call to see her whenever I have an opportunity. I think she is feeling (in its full force) her stripped condition – but at the same time is so calm & even cheerful – that it is quite a pleasure to see her. I should be very glad to hear from thee now and then – though I am such a bad correspondent – I am *very fond of getting letters*.'

The character of Birket Foster's mother (1790-1884) always comes over as serene and strong and must have contributed much by inheritance and example to the same qualities in her son.

The 1861 exhibition of the Society of Painters in

Water-colours contained an example of work based on Birket Foster's early background - a subject to which he was frequently to return, both in person and in paint.

'Birket Foster's "Wark's Burn, Northumberland" (no 7) is pleasantly mellow in colour; he may be congratulated on the breadth he gets into his work when it is remembered that the entire surface of his paper is worked over in stipple, though it is not so apparent in this drawing as in some others. The practice of stippling out every item of a landscape composition places the painter under a dead weight that is for ever bearing him downwards; for instance, in "Gleaners" (192) whatever weakness may be found in this drawing is the result of stipple. It appears only in close examination, but the effect of it is seen as far as the drawing is visible. "Down Hill" (212) is another drawing by Mr Foster; and all these works have peculiar beauties, but their good qualities could be produced by a more generous execution, whence must follow greater effect.' (*The Art Journal*, 1861, p. 174.)

Birket Foster was by this time earning a considerable amount of money and his work had brought him into a prosperous position. On 5 February 1862 - perhaps mindful of the lingering cold he had the previous year - he writes that he has decided to take his family for a long winter holiday. 'We go to-morrow to Bonchurch Isle of Wight - bag and baggage. I have taken your friend Bicknell's house (Winterbourne). It is a most delightful place looking right on to the sea. I expect we shall stay three months there' (letter to Robert Spence). Ill. 46 may be linked with his visit, although it was a place to which Birket Foster frequently returned. However, some illness to one of the children or whatever must have delayed their departure, because on 13 February Birket Foster is still in London for the receipt of important news.

> '12 Carlton Hill East
> St John's Wood
> 13th Feb. 1862
>
> My dear brother,
> I was this day elected by the Water Colour Society. I enclose Duncan's card as it may interest you. Mr Smallfield and I were the successful candidates.
> With dear love to you all
> I am your affec. bro.
> Birket Foster
> Will write again soon.'

Birket Foster's establishment as a full member of the Society of Painters in Water-colours meant even more commissions, but he did complete some illustration work after his announcement that he would not undertake any further drawings for engraving. In 1858, he had written to the Dalziel brothers:

> 'Dear Sirs,
> I shall be most glad to do the 50 drawings for £300, and the vignettes at your own price. I will do them for £50 if nothing is said about it. You must give me this week, as I have a good deal to get done, but next week you shall have some "Minstrels".'[2]

The Dalziels had asked Birket Foster to make a series of larger pictures, which were to be the best and most perfect work he could do, and they were, as far as possible, to be thoroughly representative subjects of rustic English scenery. He commenced the work, but soon fell behind with the project. He was now totally captivated with the excitement of using colour and the translation of his skills into a new medium. The popularity of his water-colours surprised and delighted him, both for the recognition of his 'very peculiar' style and for the potentially lucrative rewards. Birket Foster was a conscientious man. He could have completed 50 hurried drawings for the Dalziels and 50 vignettes, but instead he worked to the standard required, but reduced the illustrations to 30 and omitted the vignettes.

Percy Muir in *Victorian Illustrated Books* (B.T. Batsford, 1971) gives a helpful description of the techniques involved in the reproduction of an illustration from an original drawing. This explains how the artist was involved in the various stages and had the opportunity to comment, as will be shown in the case of Birket Foster and *Pictures of English Landscape*. Muir notes:

> 'The woodblock was given a thin coat of Chinese white on which the artist would work with pencil, pen or brush. The engraver then cut away the drawing with a graving-tool that was pushed, the direct opposite of the knife technique, and proofs were then pulled. The proofing was a special job. The block was inked with a special ink and this was applied, not with a roller, but with a dabber similar to those used by the early letter press printers. By a mixture of dabbing and wiping the proofer achieved the depth of inking required. Proofing was then completed, using a special paper with a slightly glossy surface called in France papier de chine and here India paper, probably to indicate its relationship to the fine papers used in the Orient.
>
> Impressions were taken, not in a press, but by laying the paper down on the inked block and rubbing the back of it with a burnisher. Proofs were sent to the artist, who frequently retouched them or wrote instructions in the margins for recutting. When the cutting was completed a proof was sent to the printer to show him how the finished result should appear.'

The Print Room of the British Museum holds a complete set of annotated proofs for *Pictures of English Landscape* on which it is interesting to note the pencilled comments and instructions of Birket Foster. These could sometimes be quite sharply critical of the engraving, e.g. of 'The Ferry Boat' - referring to the centre left, the sky just above the trees, he wrote: 'The cross hatching in the sky is not right and to my thinking quite out of place . . .' and he adds that the delicate sky above the distance is 'just like a nutmeg grater', but having made his points, the kindly Birket Foster frequently then adds such notes as: 'It will be very nice with the touching'. A full descriptive list of each plate in *Pictures of English Landscape* is shown on pp. 193–4.

In view of the reduction of the number of plates it was decided that the pictures should be augmented with some kind of text. The Dalziels recalled:

> 'When our work was drawing to completion, we submitted some of the proofs to Sir [*sic* - not knighted until 1885] John Millais and it is, perhaps, hardly necessary to say that he was charmed with the pictures, and warmly entered into the idea of having poetic descriptions to them. When asked his opinion whether he thought Lord, then Mr, Tennyson would be likely to co-operate with us, he immediately, in the most gracious manner, offered to write to him on the subject, saying:

47 '**Donkeys on the Heath**' - from *Birket Foster's Pictures of English Landscape* published in 1862 by George Routledge and Sons. This illustration and the following five are photographed from the 1881 edition. All engravings by the Dalziel brothers. Size: $7 \times 5\frac{3}{8}''$ - 17.8×13.6 cms.
Collection: Sheffield City Polytechnic Library.

48 **'The Farmyard'** – from *Birket Foster's Pictures of English Landscape.*
Collection: *Sheffield City Polytechnic Library.*

49 '**The Country Inn**' – from *Birket's Foster's Pictures of English Landscape.*
Collection: Sheffield City Polytechnic Library.

50 '**The Market Cart**' – from *Birket Foster's Pictures of English
Landscape*.
Collection: Sheffield City Polytechnic Library.

51 'At the Cottage Door' – from *Birket Foster's Pictures of English Landscape.*
Collection: Sheffield City Polytechnic Library.

52 **'The Cottage on the Beach'** – from *Birket Foster's Pictures
of English Landscape.*
Collection: Sheffield City Polytechnic Library.

"I wish I could give sufficient time to the subject, for to tell the truth there's nothing I should enjoy more than to do the verses myself. But, of course, my pictures place that idea entirely out of the question. But, I'll tell you what I'll do" he continued, "I'll write to Tennyson and ask him to take the matter up – he's rather particular, you know, and perhaps he might the more readily consent to do it for me, than if you wrote to him".'

The following letter from Lady (*sic* – not until 1883) Tennyson to Millais will show how the proposition was received:

'Dear Mr Millais,

Alfred was in the New Forest when your kind letter came, or it would have been answered yesterday, although I am sorry to have to answer the thing is impossible. Poems do not come to him so, and if they did not *come*, you are, I flatter myself, too much his friend to wish to find them there or anywhere.

May I ask you to do him the favour to decline the offer as you will best know how to do with all courtesy....'

This letter was accompanied by the following note from Millais:

'My dear Dalziel,

I enclose Mrs Tennyson's answer to my note. I said not to bother him if he couldn't say "yes" to write himself. It is just what I expected; however, we have lost nothing by the attempt. I should have thought it easy enough to write a few lines to each, as I should find it easy enough to illustrate anything. I am sorry to have kept you so long for the two fellows seated on the gate. Cut it with all your might.[3]

Yours sincerely,
J.E. Millais.'

Tom Taylor was then approached. He was at that period art critic of *The Times* and a frequent contributor to *Punch*, of which he was subsequently to become editor. While at Cambridge he had been one of the Tennyson set, had won a Trinity Fellowship, was called to the Bar and was for two years Professor of English Language and Literature at London University. Tom Taylor was a gruffly kind, able and energetic man, always ready for a new challenge. He wrote to the Dalziels and agreed to undertake the text for Birket Foster's drawings, at a price of £100 for 30 poems. ('This is putting the work at *Once a Week* terms and is the lowest price at which I could write and do justice to both you and myself..... P.S. I send you two samples of the kind of illustration I should supply to the drawings....')

Tom Taylor obviously had an inflated idea of the importance of the verses, with which he proposed to 'illustrate' the drawings of Birket Foster, but terms were agreed and he wrote to the Dalziels: 'I accept this with great pleasure, for independent of the beauty of the work, Foster and I are both "Tyne-siders" and that will give an additional pleasure to me'.

Birket Foster's Pictures of English Landscape, engraved by the Brothers Dalziel, with Pictures in Words by Tom Taylor' was published by George Routledge and Sons in 1862. This is one of the best and most highly regarded of all the books illustrated by Birket Foster and essential to any collector of this aspect of his work. Forrest Reid states

that copies of the book dated 1863 are the earliest, although the book was issued for the 1862 Christmas season. The binding was the work of Owen Jones, the Welsh architect and designer, who was responsible for many important covers of the period.[4] *Pictures of English Landscape* was handsomely blocked in gold on blue cloth, but it is unfortunate that the pages are held by the insecure method of caoutchouc binding. This has led to the total disintegration of many copies of this book which might otherwise have been preserved, if the stiff card pages had been first stuck to strips of linen and then sewn. Framed prints often originate from this volume, with later hand-colouring sometimes added. The plate number immediately under such examples may be masked with a close-up mount. Tom Taylor's preface to *Birket Foster's Pictures of English Landscape* reads:

'It is fair that the public should be informed of the relation of the designer and the writer who have contributed to this volume.

Birket Foster's drawings were made quite independently of the verses I have attempted to set to them. I am, therefore, the more free to express, in the first place, my admiration of the singular grace, fertility and facility of invention, felicitous arrangement of line, and harmonious distribution of light and shadow which distinguish the compositions of this charming artist.

The verses which I have associated with his designs are meant to harmonise with and illustrate without pretending to describe, the inventions·of the painter. In this free way, I believe pen and pencil will be found to work best together. The painter, as a rule, succeeds as ill in painting after the writer's descriptions, as the writer who tries to produce a picture in words after the painter. But picture may be set to poem, or poem to picture, as music is set to words, with an effect that enhances the enjoyment of both one and the other. I have attempted such a setting of poems to Mr Foster's pictures – with what success the public must determine.

The poems of "The Smithy" and "At the Brookside" are my wife's, with whom I am anxious to be connected in the first serious original poems to which I have attached my name.

It may be worth mentioning – I do not know if Mr Foster is aware of the circumstance – that he and I are, if not precisely fellow-townsmen, near neighbours in our birthplaces. We must have been familiar in our earliest years with the same nature on the sea coast of Durham and Northumberland. But, as he has not, in this series of designs, laid his early impressions under contribution – except perhaps in two designs, "The Mill" and "The Farm Yard" – so I have drawn upon my later experiences of the south of England for my illustrations. Still I believe we are the better fitted for such an association as the present by having played among the same fields and deans, and breathed the same keen air of the Northern Sea. I believe I can trace in much of Mr Foster's work the influence of his Northern nature, though his singular amenity and gracefulness of design, both in landscape and figures, may seem, at first sight to savour little of the rude North. He has, indeed, both in his drawings and in his designs for the wood engraver, carried suavity and grace to the very highest point to which they can be carried without falling into effeminacy, as he has pushed delicacy of execution to a pitch beyond which it seems impossible to go without pettiness and loss of unity. It is one of the mysteries of Mr Foster's art how he manages to conciliate such finish with such breadth of effect.

In this series of designs Mr Foster has been, I think, exceptionally fortunate in his engravers. The Brothers Dalziel have devoted to the reproduction of his drawings an amount of labour very seldom bestowed on woodblocks, with an aim at combined freedom and force of effect which gives their work much of the character and charm of etching.

It is still a moot point among the best critics of the art how far wood engraving can profitably be carried; – whether it can attempt, with success, such freedom and subtlety of workmanship as are employed, for example on the skies throughout the series, or should restrict itself to simpler effects, and a broader and plainer manner of execution. Whichever opinion may be the sounder one, those who claim for wood engraving the widest variety of means and the greater power of attainment, have never, I think, been supported by such strong evidence in their favour as this series supplies.

The designs should have the more interest for the public as they are the last works for wood engraving likely to be produced by the artist.

Tom Taylor
Lavender Sweep, Wandsworth, July 1862.'

The rather ingenuous tone of these comments is continued in the verses, which have been called 'embarrassingly homely' and generally not of a fitting standard for the illustrations, but such opinion is essentially subjective. Would these quiet scenes of farm and countryside have been suitable for 'illustration' by better poetry? It is possible to find a simple charm in the verses of Tom Taylor, if one takes this text as a gentle background commentary, in which the thought is in tune with the actual subject matter of the pictures, e.g. 'Donkeys on the Heath' –

'Wandering thralls of wandering master
Hobbled, harness-galled and rough
Round the gnarled thorn we pasture
Picking scanty fare and tough. –
What to us are wind and weather
Who ask no man's pains or pity?
Better toil through gorse and heather
Than through shrill and stifling city. –
Better wood-smoke sharp and fragrant
Than the alley's odours foul
Better serve a merry vagrant
Than bear coster's stripe and scowl. –
Like our gypsy lords, disdaining
City comfort city care
Leave us, rough but uncomplaining
To our scanty moorland fare.'

The Dalziels sent a pre-publication set of the engravings to John Ruskin, who replied:

'Geneva August 12 '62
Gentlemen, – I am much obliged by your having sent me those beautiful proofs. They are superb specimens of the kind of Landscape which you have rendered deservedly popular, and very charming in every respect. I wish, however, you would devote some of your wonderful powers of execution to engraving Landscape which should be better than "charming", and which would educate the public taste as well as meet it. These pieces, however, are peculiarly good of their class – rich,

gracefully composed, exquisite book illustrations, and very precious as examples of wood illustration.
Believe me, sincerely yours,
John Ruskin.'

The first notice to appear in *The Art Journal* (December 1862) was rather inappropriately placed under 'Minor Topics of the Month', but the tone of the mention was very much in a major key:

'*Birket Foster's Pictures of English Landscape* is the title of an exquisitely beautiful volume just published by Messrs Routledge, Warne and Co. As we expect to be in a position next month to include some of the engravings into our journal, we shall at present merely announce its appearance, with the remark that Mr Foster and the engravers and printers, Messrs Dalziel Brothers, seem to have outdone all their previous efforts in the production of this book – the last we regret to hear from the pencil of Mr Foster . . .'

The book was received with universal acclaim. The painter, Frederick Leighton, in acknowledging the receipt of a complimentary copy of the book, wrote to George Dalziel:

'Dear Sir,
When your messenger came yesterday I was unable to write and thank you and your brother, as I do now, for the very handsome present you have made me, of the extent of which I own I had not the slightest notion when I accepted it with such alacrity the other day. I have looked through the volume with great interest, and am much struck with the great talent displayed in very many of the designs – some, I think, quite excellent – and with the great spirit and brilliancy of your rendering of them.
Once more with best thanks,
Yours ever faithfully,
Fred. Leighton.'

The Dalziels quote from reviews:

'When our book appeared the Press was unanimous in its praise. *The Times* said: "It would be difficult to do justice to these delineations of rural life and scenery without seeming to fall into extravagant praise". . . *The Sunday Review* spoke of the "subtile feeling for rustic character and his sympathy for the poor, his curious love for unsophisticated company in sequestered places". . . .'

Birket Foster's Pictures of English Landscape not only entrances the eye with beauty of line, but also provides a reference to the many water-colours that were based on subjects in the book and also indicates some of the previously engraved illustrations from which certain of the pictures were derived, e.g. the title page for 'The Deserted Village' in *The Poems of Oliver Goldsmith* is shown with very little alteration as 'The Mill' in *Pictures of English Landscape* and the stooping figure with the jug from 'The Hamlet' (Ill. 36) was again featured in a similar composition entitled 'The Dipping Place'. This last illustration was also made into a water-colour, as was 'The Ferry' – here shown in very close version (Ill. 95). See also 'The Village Churchyard'. The colour illustration of 'The Old Chair Mender' is one of a series of very fine water-colours of this subject, which were directly related to the engraved illustration. *Pictures of English Landscape* was to be republished as a De Luxe edition (limited to 1,000 copies) in July 1881. The illustrations were then printed on heavy quality India paper, with a slightly tinted surround and deckle-edged pages (11 × 15½"). The result was very handsome indeed and it is this edition that has been used for the illustration of the engravings shown in this book, as follows: 'Donkeys on the Heath' – 'The Farm Yard' – 'Building the Hay Rick' – 'The Country Inn' – 'The Market Cart' – 'At the Cottage Door' – 'The Cottage on the Beach' (Ills. 47–52 and frontispiece). Birket Foster commented:

'The Hill Witley
Surrey
31 Augt. 1881

My dear Dalziel,

Accept my best thanks for the three copies of the 'English Landscapes'. It is really a splendid volume, admirably printed, and the get-up is altogether charming.

I sincerely hope it may prove a success.
With kind regards,
Believe me,
Very sincerely yours,
Birket Foster.'

Notes: Chapter Nine

1 All extracts in this chapter from letter's to Robert Spence are published by permission of Newcastle upon Tyne City Libraries.
2 Birket Foster is here referring to his illustrations for *The Minstrel* by James Beattie, engraved by the Dalziels and published by George Routledge in 1858.

3 This refers to a drawing for *The Cornhill Magazine*.
4 Design for the cover of *Pictures of English Landscape* is illustrated in *Victorian Book Design and Colour Printing* by Ruari McLean, Faber and Faber, 1963.

10

The Hill, Witley, Surrey: the building and interior

A criticism levelled at Birket Foster was that the children in his water-colours did not look like true rustics, but were too graceful of limb and pretty of face. For Birket Foster this was something more than a slur on his artistic integrity, but struck a deeper chord. As a Quaker he had been taught one of their most essential beliefs which was founded on the need to see 'the true Light, which lighteth every man that cometh into the world'. His upbringing was totally opposed in thought to the eighteenth-century tradition that regarded the poor as oafs and sluts and unworthy subjects for the artist. Birket Foster was aware that squalor and poverty had distorted the faces and bodies of many of the city poor, but the children that walked in the Surrey lanes did not work in factories or live in crowded back streets. The faces of the children playing on a cottage step could be just as happy and lively as those of his own children, although it must be accepted that the figures in many pictures were worked up from sketches of his own family. Certainly Birket Foster was electing to see the more pleasant and picturesque side of life, but it was a perfectly valid aspect. It could be argued that his Quaker upbringing might have led him to use his art in a reforming role, in order to reveal the Dickensian horrors of the town, but his charmingly pretty subjects were not without an element of thoughtful purpose. Birket Foster was a genuine conservationist and before his time in many of his views. He realised that much of the natural beauty and pattern of the English countryside was under threat in an era of unprecedented industrial growth.

'He was almost the first to see beauty in the wayside cottage, with its tiled roof ridged with moss and houseleek, its timbered sides half hidden in vines, its apple trees pushing their blossoms almost in at leaden lattices; the first to put on paper the hedgerows decked out with honeysuckles and wild rose, and the woods gay with hyacinth and primroses.' (M. Huish, *The Art Journal* – Christmas Supplement 1890.)

But the Victorians greatly admired clever artifice and ornamented their homes with wax flowers under glass domes and automaton birds in gilt cages – why, then, did they also so much admire the buttercup fields of Birket Foster?

His grandson, Lancelot Glasson,[1] the painter, wrote:

'... at a rather earlier period, the painting of the poor and their surroundings had been considered unworthy as a subject for the artist. Reynolds had made a slighting reference to Hogarth for this very reason. But the attitude to the peasant had undergone a change. The public were ready to see beauty in the humble cottage and in those who lived in it, and, as usual, it only required the necessary genius for everyone to recognise the thoughts as his own. In this case, it was Birket Foster, and the public recognised in his drawings something which they themselves had already half felt. Not that his popularity and success merely rested on his choice of subject. Many artists, contemporary and later, dealt with the same subject, for the most part weakly and ineffectively. But he had an outlook which was sincere in its appreciation, sincere in its technique, original and truly poetic in its feelings. On this rests his popularity.'[2]

It was also the strength of the trend towards upheaval and change that had the effect of drawing attention to the reverse mood of rustic tranquillity in the pictures of Birket Foster. Tom Taylor's 'Illustration' to 'The Country Inn' in *Pictures of English Landscape* includes the following lines:

'The time has been, e'er railways began
When the Red Lion swung from a stout oak tree
That whereso highway or byway ran
Such hostelries greeted the wayfaring man ...
But now we are ruled by the iron ways
Where no Red Lion swings from its old oak tree
At the Station Hotel the traveller stays ...' etc.

A rather unfairly rumpty-tumpty example of the style of Tom Taylor, but the incongruity of the sudden introduction of Station Hotels provides a jolt of social comment. Already Birket Foster was depicting scenes that were fast disappearing and it was the rapid advance of the railways in the previous two decades that had caused more radical alteration to the countryside than ever known before. Birket Foster did not entirely ignore contemporary life, e.g. in his London scenes and townpieces or in the band-stand bustle of a seaside resort, but one of the salient features of his most popular work was the fact that it gave no hint of the changes caused by the insidious spread of industry and housing that was rapidly coalescing into towns all along the routes of the railways. A new type of art patron had emerged from the wealthy manufacturing classes, who owed much of their prosperity to this social upheaval and industrial invention. No doubt they still preferred to think that life in the countryside was a rural idyll, an unchanging scene, even if their own mill chimneys

53 Tigbourne Cottage, Witley, Surrey, of which Birket Foster held the tenancy from 1860 to 1876 (sub-letting to Charles Keene from 1865).

Above: behind fence – 'Old Wilson' and his wife, Birket Foster with Polly Brown, who has Ellen and Meggie clutching at her skirts and Henry standing nearby with Ann Dennyer (probably the children's nurse) slightly to side.

Below: Mrs Wood, Myles, Ann Dennyer, Birket Foster with Polly Brown (shown here as Mary, which was her real name), also William (holding cat) and Henry (at the window). From an album in possession of the Glasson family.

A
'THE HARROW' (13¾ x 33¾″ – 35 x 85.8cms)
Water-colour. Signed with monogram (left) c. 1860-65.
Collection: City of Bristol Museum and Art Gallery.

B
'ROTTINGDEAN, NEAR BRIGHTON' (13½ x 28¼″ – 34.3 x 71.7 cms)
Water-colour, signed with monogram (left) Inscribed 1865.
Collection: Metropolitan Borough of Bury, Bury Museum and Art Gallery.

C

'A PEEP AT THE HOUNDS: HERE THEY COME!' ($8\frac{7}{8}$ x $13\frac{7}{8}$" — 22.5 x 35.2 cms)

Water-colour, signed with monogram (left) c. 1875.

Photograph: Christie's.

D

'THE STEPPING STONES' ($11\frac{1}{4}$ x $15\frac{1}{2}$" – 28.6 x 39.4 cms)

Water-colour, signed with monogram (left) c. 1880.

Photograph: Frost and Reed, Ltd.

E
'THE OLD CHAIR MENDER'
Print by The Cavendish Collection Limited from the original water-colour in
possession of Borough of Hyndburn, Haworth Art Gallery, Accrington.

and the ugly houses of their workers were fast destroying the reality.

The wooded lanes and tangled hedgerows of Surrey provided a landscape that was exactly suited to the style of Birket Foster. He was particularly attracted to the village of Witley, near Godalming, where his friend the painter, James Clarke Hook RA was already living. In 1860, Birket Foster decided to rent Tigbourne Cottage, which was situated by the corner of the road leading to Hambledon at the foot of Wormley Hill. Trees straight from a Birket Foster illustration surrounded this ivy-clad house, with its wooden latticed porch and quiet lawns. (Ill. 53)

On 17 February 1860, Birket Foster wrote to Robert Spence:

'Our cottage will soon be ready for us. Polly and I were down on Wednesday and Thursday. We have J.C. Hook RA for a neighbour and in a little while we shall have Henry Cole, who was the great name of the 1851 Exhibition. He sometimes goes by the name of "Felix Summerley". Saml. Redgrave brother to the RA is close to us so that we are in an artistic atmosphere.'[3]

Tigbourne Cottage was to be used as a summer residence, but Birket Foster had soon acquired a large and beautiful site on which to build a more permanent home. He discovered three acres of building land for sale while out for a ramble with Sir John Gilbert and J.W. Whymper, but subsequently persuaded the owner to sell a much more extensive area and this finally produced a total estate of about twenty acres. Part of this he then sold to Edmund Evans and the two old friends made plans to erect adjacent houses. A stone marker peg inscribed with the initials 'B.F.' still stands on the old boundary between the two properties. M. Huish was later to describe the site:

'A constant and rapid climb brings the visitor ultimately to a terrace, on one side of which stands the house, and on the other is unfolded a marvellous panorama. Over a rolling champaign, almost hidden by woods, is seen to the right Hindhead, the highest point in the prospect, its barren summit standing out a deep violet against the sunset sky. Somewhat to the left, but apparently not much lower, comes the spur which terminates in Blackdown, the topmost houses of Haslemere peeping over its crest, and on its flank the Poet Laureate's house, and Lythe Hill, where so many of Sir F. Leighton's best works are stored. Beyond the Weald – here called of Surrey, but for the most part in Sussex - can be discovered the spire of Petworth, recalling memories of Turner; and far off on the horizon the heights above Goodwood, and the range of the South Downs, broken midway by Arundel, and away to the east by Shoreham Gap. That most assertive of South-Down beacons, Chanctonbury Ring, is of course visible.' (*The Art Journal*, 1890.)

The architects of the house were officially W. Tasker and the painter W.P. Burton, but in fact Birket Foster was wholly responsible for planning much of the essential design. The house was named The Hill and some opinion has linked this with The Hill, Sedbergh, the home of Birket Foster's grandmother (the former Mary Burton), but it seems more likely that it was merely considered a suitable name for a house on an elevated site.

George Eliot described this part of Surrey as '... a land of pine woods and copses, village greens and heather-covered hills, with the most delicious old red or grey brick

54 The five children of Birket Foster. Left to right: Margaret, Henry, Myles, Ellen and William, photographed at Tigbourne Cottage about 1862. Note the similarity of their dress to that of many of the children in the early water-colours of Birket Foster. From an album in possession of the Glasson family.

timbered cottages nestling among creeping roses'. Birket Foster was environmentally sensitive and had no wish to place an inappropriate building in the Surrey landscape. The tall brick chimneys and half-timbered style of The Hill was very much in keeping with the basic design of the cottages that so frequently appeared in his drawings. Birket Foster deliberately attempted to soften any jarring effect of newness by using old weather-worn cottage tiles on the roof and incorporated other such materials in the general structure. An architect's report in 1971 (in connection with the historic buildings of Surrey) described The Hill, Witley, as having been 'an essay in Victorian Tudorism, red brick and decorative timber framing'. The builders of The Hill were Holland and Hannen of London (and Warne and Son for later additions). The house which Edmund Evans built on the adjoining site was named Leybourne and was similar in style to The Hill, but on a smaller scale.

The design of the interior of The Hill might appear rather unexpected. The firm of Morris, Marshall, Faulkner and Co., Fine Art workmen in Painting, Carving and Metals, was established in 1861. William Morris (1834-96), painter, craftsman and idealist, had made the first commercial step in a movement that was to have a revolutionary effect on Western art and the interior decoration of the home. The Hill must have been one of the earliest houses in England to be extensively decorated with this unique blend of myth and modernity. It is interesting to speculate as to what it was that attracted Birket Foster to such an 'avant garde' style, which was still the subject of criticism and ridicule. He was an unassuming person and not fashionable in the manner of the wealthy manufacturers now building opulent new mansions all over the countryside, but it may well be that we should look to his Quaker background for an explanation of his taste. The homes of members of the Society of Friends were essentially plain and functional and some Quaker houses were even entirely devoid of pictures. Furniture was of good quality, but unostentatious, as were the walls and draperies. It was an event to be remarked upon in the family when Robert Foster allowed carpeting of a parlour in

55 Polly Brown in the drawing room of The Hill, Witley, Surrey, home of Birket Foster from 1863 to 1893. The water-colour over the mantelpiece is a version of 'The Hhareem' by J. F. Lewis and some of the pictures on the wall behind Polly are by J. M. W. Turner. Note the monograms on the grate and the date '1863' – the year in which The Hill was completed. From an album in possession of the Glasson family.

Hebblethwaite Hall to accord with what his frequent non-Quaker visitors were accustomed to. There was an element of the principles of William Morris in this dislike of the non-functional and in the reverence for craftsmanship. William Morris drew his inspiration from the Middle Ages and the notion that this represented a time when the craftsman was contented because he was able to see a project through from first to last, rather in the manner of Robert Foster who wore the wool from his own sheep. Medievalism was essentially reflected in the designs of Edward Burne-Jones, who with Philip Webb, Ford Madox Brown, P.P. Marshall, Charles Faulkner and Arthur Hughes was very closely associated with the firm of William Morris and Co. In Birket Foster we have a man whose upbringing had been in a home environment that was different from the contemporary Victorian style, and

in his career we find an artist whose favourite illustrative work had been for the poems of Sir Walter Scott, with their tales of legend and knightly deeds. Against this background, his enthusiastic reception of the decorative ideas of William Morris comes across as very genuine, as opposed to the response of those who wished only to be daringly new in adopting the wallpapers, tapestries and stained glass panels that were so entirely different from the current mode of Victorian decoration.

Birket Foster probably first met William Morris through his acquaintance with the painter, Dante Gabriel Rossetti. Morris went down to Witley in the early months of the building of The Hill and drew up a most ambitious scheme for the interior decoration of the house. Some of it did not get beyond this stage, but the imprint of the ideas of William Morris was to be one of the most characteristic features of The Hill.

The effect of the numerous stained glass windows must have been both dramatic and beautiful. A representation of the jewel-glowing colours can be found in *The Stained Glass of William Morris and His Circle* by A.C. Sewter (Yale University Press, 1974) in which one of the major pieces from The Hill is illustrated in colour. This was known as 'King René's Honeymoon' and consisted of four

56 The Hill: the library (facing the terrace). The stained glass panels depict 'King René's Honeymoon' and were executed by Morris, Marshall, Faulkner and Co. Now in the collection of the Victoria and Albert Museum. Below: enlarged detail showing 'Painting' (from the design of Burne-Jones) and 'Architecture' (Ford Madox Brown). From an album of photographs by William Foster in possession of Sarah G. A. Glasson.

panels which formed the upper part of the library windows facing the terrace (Ills. 56, 57). The designs were originally executed as paintings for the decoration of a cabinet made to his own specifications for the architect, John P. Seddon. This was shown by Morris, Marshall, Faulkner and Co. at the International Exhibition, South Kensington in 1862 and is now in the Victoria and Albert Museum (Ref. W 10 - 1927), as are the four panels from The Hill (C. 516-519 - 1953). It was apparently at the suggestion of Ford Madox

Brown that the subjects were treated as a series of imaginary incidents from the honeymoon of King René of Anjou, whom Walter Scott had popularised in *Anne of Geierstein*. The panels represented: 'Painting' (Burne-Jones), 'Architecture' (Ford Madox Brown), 'Music' (Dante Gabriel Rossetti) and 'Sculpture' (Burne-Jones). The colours show the decorative border with a soft yellow effect and the main background of the subjects in deep blue glass, which is repeated in the blue of the dress of the female

57 The Hill: part of the large studio. Below: the library – third and fourth stained glass panels of 'King René's Honeymoon' in which these subjects are 'Music' (Rossetti) and and 'Sculpture' (Burne-Jones). From an album of photographs by William Foster in possession of Sarah G. A. Glasson.

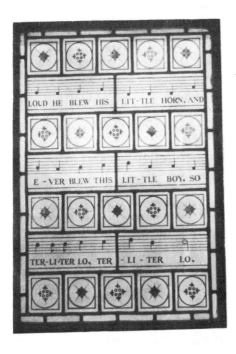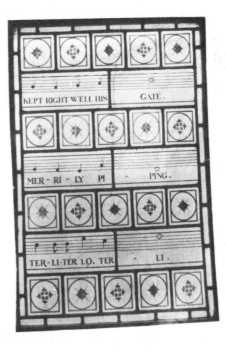

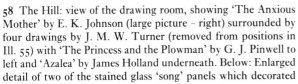

58 The Hill: view of the drawing room, showing 'The Anxious Mother' by E. K. Johnson (large picture – right) surrounded by four drawings by J. M. W. Turner (removed from positions in Ill. 55) with 'The Princess and the Plowman' by G. J. Pinwell to left and 'Azalea' by James Holland underneath. Below: Enlarged detail of two of the stained glass 'song' panels which decorated the upper half of one of the drawing room windows. These are now in possession of Sarah Batchelor, great-granddaughter of Birket Foster. From an album of photographs by William Foster in possession of Sarah G. A. Glasson, granddaughter of Birket Foster.

figure in 'Music'. Gold, green and red predominate in the clear unshaded colouring of these splendid pieces of stained glass. It should be noted that the horizontal line that appears across the panels in the illustrations shown here is not part of the leading, but the saddle-bar, i.e. an iron rod inserted into the stone-work on either side of a window, on the inside, to which the lead joints or edges of a glass panel are attached by copper wires for purposes of support. William Foster could not avoid photographing this, but in the illustrations in *The Stained Glass of William Morris and His Circle* the photographs are of the glass after removal from The Hill and in consequence without the saddle-bar.

It has to be remembered that themes for stained glass, tiles, etc. were often used more than once by Morris, Marshall, Faulkner and Co. and that virtual duplicates were produced in some cases. Designs by Burne-Jones have presented problems in identifying exactly how many of these were eventually used and for what locations. Deliberately grumpy, half-joking comments were a feature of the account books of Burne-Jones, in which he recorded in 1866: 'to touching up some Good Women and I would rather have been boiled ten times over – £1-1'. This entry must refer to versions that were executed after the original commission for Birket Foster. Chaucer's 'Dream of Good Women' was depicted in seven stained glass windows which were incorporated in the original building of The Hill as the centre lights of one of the main bedroom windows. A complete set of cartoons for these windows is in the Birmingham City Art Gallery (517–523 '04). The original stained glass was photographed in detail by William Foster, but has now been dispersed and partially lost. A duplicate of 'Chaucer Asleep' and also the panels entitled 'Amor and Alcestis' and 'Cleopatra and Dido' (dated 1864) are in the Victoria and Albert Museum.

The Chaucerian theme was also featured at The Hill in a set of five roundels showing Chaucer, Griselda, Dorigen, Constance and Creseide, with the names in decorative scrolls, each roundel on a diamond patterned background. The female heads were executed by Morris, Marshall, Faulkner and Co., from designs by Burne-Jones. (Original cartoons in the Birmingham City Art Gallery.) A duplicate set of these roundels, but without the head of Chaucer is to be found in the staircase window of Oakwood Hall, Bingley, Yorkshire. These pieces are dated 1865, slightly later than those commissioned for The Hill, which were sited in the entrance hall windows.

The stained glass panels, also in the form of roundels, as seen in Ill. 59 were situated in a window on a staircase landing (looking towards the porch). These Chorus Angelorum subjects (all in white and pale gold, against green backgrounds) were repeated in windows installed in St Edmund Hall Chapel, Oxford in 1865 – designed by Burne-Jones and executed by Morris, Marshall, Faulkner and Co.

A.C. Sewter also illustrates four stained glass panels of 'The Seasons' (designed by Burne-Jones) and now in the Birmingham City Art Gallery. A similar, but not duplicate set was sited in one of the staircase windows at The Hill. Each panel shows a woman in flowing robes, standing by a tree appropriate to the season. The panel 'Autumn' can be glimpsed in Ill. 61. The full set from The Hill is now in America in possession of Sarah Batchelor, a great-granddaughter of Birket Foster, who also owns the madrigal panels (Ill. 58). These designs for the drawing-room windows added a most original touch which has nothing

59 The Hill: (1) upper landing, with enlarged detail showing Chorus Angelorum windows designed by Burne-Jones.
(2) A landing and William Foster's bedroom. From an album of photographs in possession of Sarah G. A. Glasson.

to do with William Morris. The upper part of the windows consisted of panels of glass on which were placed the words and music of various madrigals and songs that were often sung by the Foster family. This charming idea was entirely the original suggestion of Charles Keene and followed on from his notion that the words of these songs should be painted on large boards for communal singing. He was a close friend of John Clayton, who was prominent in reviving the art of glass painting, and it was the firm of Clayton and Bell that carried out the work, which included 'Would gentle evergreen to form a shade' and the roundelay illustrated here, which had been discovered by Charles Keene in the British Museum. Detailed photographs of these windows show that the musical bars were marked as part of the formation of individual panes and each line of music alternated with a decorative pattern of simple roundels within squares.

'A Jol-ly Shep-herd up- / on a Hill as he sate, so / loud he blew his lit-tle horn and, / kept right well his gate./

This line (in capital lettering throughout) ran across four windows as shown by the division marks, and the ditty continued:

'Ear-ly in a morn-ing / late in an even-ing and / e-ver blew this lit-tle boy, so / mer-ri-ly pi-ping /
'Ter-li-ter-lo, ter-li-ter lo / ter-li-ter lo, ter-li / ter-li-ter lo, ter-li-ter lo / ter-li-ter lo, ter-li.'

One has a vivid picture of Birket Foster and his family and friends collapsing into breathless laughter after singing this window, with its hilariously folksy final line, but music was also appreciated on a deeper level and the grand piano was no mere ornament but an instrument frequently played with real talent.

60 The Hill: bedroom. The eight panels over the mantelshelf were painted by H. Stacy Marks, RA. The wallpaper appears to be of a later date than the original decoration. From an album of photographs by William Foster in possession of Sarah G. A. Glasson.

Tiled fireplaces were a feature of The Hill. The account books of Burne-Jones have an entry for 26 July 1863, as follows: 'Set of subjects for tiles – Beauty and the Beast' and below 'ditto – two extra – £2'. Ill. 62 shows a detail from this set of six tiles that were used to decorate an overmantel for a bedroom fireplace (now in the William Morris Gallery, Walthamstow (ref. C. 75)). Each scene from the story occupies two tiles in a surround of blue and white tiles, which are painted with the 'Swan' pattern, designed by Philip Webb (the architect, who was one of the original members of the Morris 'firm'). Below the scenes runs a scroll inscribed: 'How a Prince, who by enchantment was under the form of a Beast became a man again by the love of a certain Maiden'. The example illustrated in this book is of the final episode: 'Beauty kissing the Beast who reveals himself as a Prince'. Enamel colours were used to decorate these earthenware blank tiles and each scene is signed with the initials of Lucy Faulkner in the right hand corner. Lucy was a sister of Charles Faulkner and helped with the work of the firm in the early years, especially painting tiles and other ceramics, as well as doing some embroidery work with her sister, Kate, who later designed wallpapers for William Morris.[4] A number of the more finished drawings for 'Beauty and the Beast' are in the Victoria and Albert Museum and some preliminary drawings in pencil are in the Tate Gallery. The fireplace overmantel and surrounds as shown in Ill. 61 were also designed by Burne-Jones and painted in this case by Kate Faulkner. The lettering that runs across the main panel reads: 'This is the Story of the Maid with the Shoe of Glass and how she became Queen that was before called Cinder Wench'.

In March 1865 a further account book entry by Burne-Jones notes: '2 designs Birket Foster charged vide 1864'. Turning back to that date the entries read: 'to 10 designs of Sleeping Beauty at the mean and unremunerative price of 30/- each – £15. To 7 windows of Good Women at ditto ditto price of £3 each – £21'. These tetchy remarks are not an indication of parsimony by Birket Foster, but were all part of Burne-Jones playing out a comic role, in which he complained of poor payment and pretended stinginess by Morris. The Sleeping Beauty designs were executed in the form of tile panels set above the fireplace in bedroom number four. These are now in the Victoria and Albert Museum (ref. circ. 520 – 1953).

It is perhaps significant that it was Birket Foster who went in February 1864 to the home of Burne-Jones to give him the news of his election as an Associate member of the Society of Painters in Water-colours. It had been a controversial decision and many members and also the public continued to be much affronted by the paintings of Burne-Jones, but Birket Foster championed him, in spite of the ridicule of the critics. For instance, *The Art Journal* wrote of 'The Merciful Knight' shown in the 1864 exhibition:

61 The Hill:
(1) Bedroom known as the nursery.
(2) Landing with glimpse of the third stained glass panel in the series 'The Seasons' – designed by Burne-Jones for Morris, Marshall, Faulkner and Co.
(3) Bedroom fireplace decorated with painted tiles, designed by Burne-Jones on the Cinderella theme. The legend (behind porcelain vases) reads: 'This is the Story of the Maid with the Shoe of Glass and how she became Queen that was before called Cinderwench'. From an album of photographs by William Foster in possession of Sarah G. A. Glasson.

ofa whtain maiden

'... The painter has actually ventured to represent Christ, or rather the wooden effigy of Christ on a carved crucifix, in the act of bowing down from the cross to embrace the good knight, who far from being comforted seems to shake in his clattering armour...'

And of the 'Annunciation' (commissioned by the always tolerant brothers Dalziel) the reviewer comments, with acid wit:

'... here is a bedstead set above a garden at which the Virgin kneels in her nightdress; the angel Gabriel in his flight appears to have been caught in an apple tree; however he manages just to look in at a kind of trap door opening, to tell his errand ...'

What then was it that attracted Birket Foster to these paintings? Was it perhaps that we are inclined to admire skills that we do not ourselves possess? Symbolism, allegory and drama were not in the range of his own art, but perhaps some aesthetic deprivation in his early background may have given him a longing for colourful treatment of romantic themes and a fascination with the very strangeness of any kind of decorative presentation of religion. Quaker tradition objected to anything that excited rather than calmed the senses.

Burne-Jones thought poorly of most contemporary engraved illustrations which he described as '... scribbly work ... Nearly all book illustration is full of it ... stupid senseless rot that takes an artist half a minute to sketch and an engraver half a week to engrave ...'; he continues: '... of course people will generally prefer Birket Foster illustrations to anything else. They have all the sole qualities that are cared for – delicacy, smoothness, or rather woolliness and prettiness ...' (as quoted in *Burne-Jones* by M. Harrison and W. Waters, 1973).

62 The Hill: detail from tile panel decoration for a bedroom fireplace. From 'The Story of Beauty and the Beast' designed by Burne-Jones and painted by Lucy Faulkner for Morris, Marshall, Faulkner and Co.
Collection: William Morris Gallery, Walthamstow, London.

Burne-Jones may not have admired the illustrations of Birket Foster but he obviously respected him sufficiently to be gratified when Birket Foster commissioned him in 1865 to paint the legend of 'St George and the Dragon'. The wife of Burne-Jones later commented in her *Memorials* (1909): 'It was not the first time that Edward's pictures had been wanted by brother artists and that they cared to possess them gave him purest pleasure.' It was decided that Burne-Jones should paint seven canvases depicting 'St George and the Dragon' to be inset in a continuous band of decoration round three walls of the dining room at The Hill (Ill. 63). The subject was based on some stained glass that Rossetti had designed for Morris on the same theme and the work was executed in oils, a medium which Burne-Jones had only recently taken up.[6]

In this version of the St George and the Dragon story, a crowd of citizens petition the King of Egypt to find some means of ridding them of the scourge of the Dragon and they show him the blood-stained clothes of girls already devoured by the beast. A soothsayer divines that the Dragon can somehow be permanently propitiated by the offering of a deliberate sacrifice from amongst the circle of the Princess and her maidens and with inevitable drama it is the Princess who draws from a crimson bag the fateful lot inscribed 'Moritura'. Princess Sabra is then led away by a guard from her life in a flowery garden, with her maidens following behind with lighted tapers and mournful attitudes. She is abandoned in a clearing in the forest, chained to a still living tree and waits, drooping, innocence personified, for mutilation and death (Ill. 64). Meanwhile

the good citizens have approached St George and he arrives to the rescue in the proverbial nick of time. The sixth panel depicts a rather unpleasant Slaying of the Dragon, which appears as a slightly unfortunate, lizard-like creature, a very small dragon, having a massive sword thrust between its gaping jaws and through its throat by the gallant St George. Princess Sabra clasps her hands together in admiration of this deed and the series ends with scenes of rejoicing and a happy-ever-after ending.[7]

The strong colours of these panels in oils reflected the drama of the subject, an illustration of Good and Evil, with a definite element of sensuality, even if the artist may not have been fully aware of the underlying implications. The young captive Princess in threat of violation by a beast was transformed by Burne-Jones into a kind of purified symbolism and considered by Birket Foster as quite suitable adornment for his dining room, although the Slaying of the Dragon must have been enough to put the more sensitive guests off their soup!

Burne-Jones completed the first three panels and these were installed at The Hill by the end of 1865, but in August 1866 Burne-Jones was still making preliminary tree studies for the backgrounds which he sketched while on holiday in Lymington. The commission was very much behind and in consequence the last four panels were worked with the aid of his studio assistant, Charles Fairfax Murray, who joined Burne-Jones in November 1866 and enabled the series to be completed. The last panel 'The Return' (City Art Gallery, Bristol) is acknowledged as almost entirely the work of Fairfax Murray. All seven panels have now been dispersed, but Ill. 64 shows number five – 'The Princess Tied to the Tree'. This is monogrammed 'E.B.J. 1866'. Burne-Jones did some re-painting of the panel when it was later removed from The Hill and in the centre of the stretcher is a hand-written note: 'If this picture ever needs to be re-varnished it must be with *pure mastic varnish only*. Edward Burne-Jones, 1895'. The panel was bequeathed to the Newark Museum, New Jersey, USA in 1944 by Louis Bamberger, who bought the painting from Lord Leverhulme. 'The King's Daughter' (the second panel) is in the Louvre Museum, Paris and 'St George Kills the Dragon' which can be glimpsed in the illustration of the dining room (Ill. 63) is in the Art Gallery of New South Wales, Sydney, Australia, after having been in the collection of Sir Ernest Moon from 1902 – donated to the gallery by his son in 1950, in memory of his mother who was born in Australia. The painting is now magnificently framed and takes on an individual importance that it could never have had in the original position at The Hill. The whereabouts are not at present known of 'A Petition to the King' and 'The Princess Drawing the Lot', but 'The Princess Sabra led to the Dragon' re-appeared recently at Christie's, New York in a sale of '19th Century European Paintings' (Lot 288, 27 October 1982), obtaining a record £58,479. (For further references to the 'St George and the Dragon' panels, see the letter from Birket Foster

64 'The Princess Tied to the Tree' – oil on canvas (42 × 36½" – 106.7 × 92.7 cms). Inscribed: E. B.-J. 1866. Fifth in a series of seven panels illustrating the legend of St George and the Dragon which were painted by Edward Burne-Jones for The Hill.
Collection: The Newark Museum, Newark, New Jersey, USA.

to Edmund Evans (p. 176) and also Appendix 8.)

'Celebrities at Home – No. DXXVII – Mr Birket Foster at The Hill, Witley' (an article from an un-named source, which has been pasted into an album of cuttings) gives a general description of the drawing-room and adds life to our picture of the house. The article must refer to a period after 1880.

'On the solid oaken door encrusted with iron-work ornamentation, being opened, you pass into the carpeted hall, panelled, like the whole interior of the house, with dark wood, efficiently relieved here by the blue and white china arranged on shelves. After traversing a long corridor, hung with an indigo-coloured dada curtain, above which, on a flowered wallpaper are suspended etchings after Mason's "Harvest Moon", Walker's Marlow and a couple of Gainsborough landscapes, you reach the drawing room. While awaiting your host, you cannot fail to be charmed by the comfort and elegance of this room. It is lighted by two grand oriel windows, looking south and west, the deep embrasures being furnished with cushions of a russet-tinted velvet, the prevailing material and colour of the upholstery of this and of the other sitting-rooms throughout the house. The ceiling is of panelled oak, as is also the wainscotting, which is surmounted by a plain gold paper with a light frieze, on which arbutus flowers and berries are figured. On these walls, admirably adapted to show off paintings, there are eight water-colour landscapes by Turner arranged round 'The Anxious Mother', a drawing by E.K. Johnson; some inimitable studies of still life by W. Hunt; 'The Hhareem' by Lewis; some figure sketches by Millais; two groups of flowers by Holland; and several examples of John Linnell, Fred. Walker and Samuel Palmer.'

63 The Hill: the dining room. Picture to left of mantelpiece depicts 'St George Kills the Dragon' – one of a series of seven oil panels painted by Edward Burne-Jones and set round the dining room walls. 'The Princess Tied to the Tree' can be seen to the far left (as enlarged illustration). 'St George Kills the Dragon' is now in the Art Gallery of New South Wales, Sydney, Australia. From an album of photographs by William Foster in possession of Sarah G. A. Glasson.

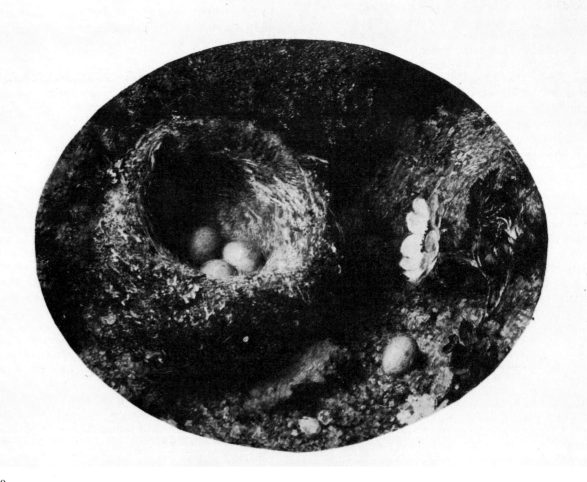

The Hill certainly contained an interesting collection of pictures by artists other than Birket Foster (see list on pp. 213–15). Birket Foster was particularly fond of the work of William ('Birdsnest') Hunt, and a typical example of his style is shown in the enlarged detail of a picture entitled 'Chaffinch's Nest and Wild Rose' which can be discerned on the wall behind the grand piano in Ill. 65. In 1860, Birket Foster commissioned William Hunt to paint three water-colour drawings, which were mounted in one frame, thus: 'May Blossom and Eggs'; 'Primroses and Egg'; 'Wild Roses and Egg'. Other examples included 'Black Grapes, Peaches and Strawberries' and 'Greengages and Orleans Plums' which displayed the soft bloom which Hunt painted onto fruit with such realism. Birket Foster owned ten examples by this artist. He possessed two Venetian pieces by Fred. Walker and two scenes in Venice by James Holland, also one by George Cattermole, which can be noted above 'Chaffinch's Nest'. 'The Princess and the Ploughman' by G. J. Pinwell was also in his collection. The work of this artist was thought by Kate Greenaway and others to have owed much to the influence of Birket Foster, as did that of Fred. Walker, whose 'Chaplain's Daughter' is shown in Ill. 75. One of the most beautiful examples by Walker in the collection of Birket Foster was the study of Ellen Foster, as a young child (Ill. 74). 'A Pastoral Scene' – dated 1853 – and 'The Barley Harvest' – dated 1863 – by John Linnell, sen., were specially commissioned by Birket Foster from this artist, who with William Hunt had been a pupil of John Varley.

Birket Foster also owned a Turkish interior by John Frederick Lewis, entitled 'The Mendicant' and a version of 'The Hhareem', one of the most famous of all the works from Lewis. This caused a sensation when exhibited with the 'Old' Water-colour Society in 1850 and was pronounced by *The Art Journal* to be '... the most extraordinary production ever executed in water-colour ... the work is unique in the history of water-colour art ...' The amazing quality of the finely stippled technique (using body colour throughout), would probably appeal to Birket Foster, although the subject does not quite fit in with his usual taste. 'The Hhareem' as owned by Birket Foster was exhibited in the Arts Council Exhibition of 'Great Victorian Pictures', 1978 and illustrated in the catalogue. The subject shows a Turkish pasha, surrounded by voluptuous women, all of whom are staring with much interest towards some point almost out of the picture. The work is in the Victoria and Albert Museum and at one time some opinion favoured the theory that this was the original water-colour that had been cut down to please a stiff Victorian, who did not consider it suitable that the pasha and his women were in fact inspecting a prospective addition to the hareem who was being smilingly unveiled by a jolly negro eunuch. This full version was illustrated in *The Souvenir* of the Franco-British Exhibition in 1908 and the work is documented as that exhibited in 1850 and can be traced to 1909, but the present whereabouts are unknown. In the water-colour from the provenance of Birket Foster, the woman and the eunuch and some of the upper half of the composition have all been excluded so

that the pasha and his ladies appear to be riveted by a piece of drapery to the extreme right of the picture. This bears direct similarity to that of the excluded woman, but there are enough minute differences between this water-colour and the work illustrated in 1908 to confirm that the one owned by Birket Foster may either have been a commissioned version of the respectable half of the original picture or (as seems more likely) a version that was subsequently cut down.[8] The picture in possession of Birket Foster appeared in a loan exhibition at the Royal Academy in 1891, when it was rather coyly described as 'Interior of a room in which a pasha is seated on a divan, surrounded by his family – a slave stands behind'.

The photograph of Polly in the drawing room (Ill. 55) shows 'The Hhareem' over the mantelpiece, with a charming arrangement of little curtains for protection of the water-colour against strong light. This illustration also includes 'Tinted paper drawings by J. M. W. Turner' which are positioned on the wall above her head. A later hanging of the drawings described them as being on a background of roughened gold, as in 'Celebrities at Home' and in the positions shown in Ill. 58. Birket Foster himself always considered that the Turners were the jewels of his collection. Marcus Huish (at one time Managing Director of the Fine Art Society) wrote of a visit to The Hill in 1890:

'... Not only in duty bound, but with a sense of delight, we at once make our way across the room to worship at the shrine of the great master of water-colour art and revel over a group of Turners, for the most part of the grey paper kind, which form a wonderful bouquet of colour, as full and rich as the day in which the artist stayed his hand upon them. The names of the Rhine, Switzerland and the Moselle and Sidon will convey to those who are familiar with Turner's work an idea of the pleasurable anticipations which the thought of a prospective quiet study of these induces.' (*The Art Journal*, 1890.)

The reverential enthusiasm of Marcus Huish is in sharp contrast to that of a decidedly nouveau riche couple from Manchester. The amusing story of their calling at The Hill has passed into Foster family legend. The husband asked patronisingly, 'Foster, who built your cottage?' and he and his wife then proceeded to adopt a very nose-in-air attitude to everything that they were shown, including a magnificent view across the Weald of Surrey. Birket Foster no doubt accepted all this with his gentle, good humour, but it was when the wife was looking at his treasured Turners that the situation finally collapsed, as, turning to her husband, she remarked: 'S-, you must get me some of these for my scrapbook ...'

The airy and subtle atmosphere of Birket Foster's Turners does not come out well in black and white photographs taken over a hundred years ago, but one example in particular with the sun swirling in misty clouds gives a hint of the colour that would have so much appeal for the discerning eye of Birket Foster. Certainly it seems that it was this factor in particular that so much attracted him to the work of Turner. Unlike the water-colourist William Callow, who was also a great admirer of Turner, his influence is not obviously felt in the work of Birket Foster, although 'Return of the Lifeboat with St Michael's Mount in the distance' (Ill. 80) is an example of the freedom of line and wash that can be found in some of his more unfinished works. This would not be considered a typical

65 The Hill: the drawing room. Pictures to right (above piano) are 'Venice' by George Cattermole and 'Chaffinch's Nest and Wild Rose' by William Henry Hunt, which is shown in the enlarged detail. From an album of photographs by William Foster in possession of Sarah G. A. Glasson.

example of the style of Birket Foster, although it is in a manner more frequently used than is often realised and one which may perhaps owe an unconscious debt to Turner. There is a passing reference comparing of these two artists in *The Private Papers of Henry Ryecroft* by George Gissing:

'If any man whom I knew to be a man of brains confessed to me that he preferred Birket Foster [to Turner] I should smile . . . but I should understand.'

This was said à propos of Turner's genius not being 'truly English' and those who look for an evocation of subject that is the quintessence of Englishness have a genuine right to prefer Birket Foster and to be understood.

Two entries from accounts kept by Philip Webb for William Morris and Co. read:

'1 January 1866: Cabinet for B. Foster's
pictures   £2.0.0.
8 February 1867: Design for B. Foster's
bookcase   £1.0.0.'

Birket Foster was a keen bibliophile and the library at The Hill contained many rare books, including a special case of first folios and quartos of Shakespeare, Caxton and works by the early printers.

A statement of an account with a London book dealer shows that Birket Foster spent £595/10/- on bibliographical items from this one firm during the comparatively short period between January 1865 and March 1866. It is a pointer to the financial success of his work that he was able to lay out nearly £600 in this manner, so soon after building The Hill. Details from this account may be of interest to present day antiquarian book collectors:

'Caxton's *Myrrour of the World*', dated 1491, bound in red morocco, imperfect, but very rare - £52.10/-: *Shakespeare's Poems: First Collected edition* - dated 1640, portrait by Marshall inlaid - £31.10/-: Holinshed's *Chronicles of England, Scotland and Irelande* - 2 volumes, first edition folio, dated 1577, in red morocco - £31.10/-: four Shakespeare folios, dated 1623, 1632, 1664 and 1685 - £367.10/-: Shakespeare's *Midsummer Night's Dream* - large, extremely rare copy, dated 1600 - £63: Shakespeare's *King Lear*, good copy in green morocco, dated 1608 - £42 [this had been George Dalziel's copy]: *Memoirs of John Evelyn* - second edition (in two volumes) dated 1819 - £6.6/-: *Blades list of Works Printed by Caxton* - £1.4/-.'

All these items were later to be sold on 11 June 1894 by Sotheby, Wilkinson and Hodge as 'A Select Portion of the Choice Library of Birket Foster' (Lots 1–45). The prices then obtained were £77, £40, £25, £466, £122, £100, £19 in order as above (final item not in sale). A perusal of the Sotheby catalogue gives more detailed information on these works and also adds to our knowledge of other books in the collection of Birket Foster. One of the volumes he specially treasured was Milton's copy of *Lycophronis Alexandra* bound in the original calf and dated 1601. It is described in the catalogue as follows:

'John Milton's copy with his autograph and 1634 on fly-leaf and numerous marginal MS notes in the great Poet's handwriting. A most interesting volume, accompanied with a long MS note by Lord Charlemont, respecting the price Milton paid for it, etc. It was bought at Lord Charlemont's sale by the present owner,

for £60. Noticed by Mr S. Leigh Sotheby in his work on the autograph of Milton.'

It is pleasant to know that Birket Foster was able to possess this book, in view of the success of his illustrations to some of the poetry of Milton. The book reached £90 in the 1894 sale. Representative examples of other items from the library of Birket Foster (as listed in the sale catalogue) included the following: a total of 11 Shakespeares included a first edition of *The Merchant of Venice* dated 1600 - £146 (for which Birket Foster is recorded as having paid £52/10/- in 1868) and several books of poetry by Edmund Spenser including a first edition (1590) of *The Faerie Queen*, imperfect - £9/10/-; also a first edition of Izaak Walton's *The Compleat Angler*, 1653, a very rare copy - £150. The collection included *The Booke of Common Prayer and Administration of the Sacraments - the First Book of Edward VI*, dated 1549 - £30 and *The Collected Works of John Taylor, The Water Poet*, dated 1690 - £15. On a more contemporary level Birket Foster also owned a first edition of Ruskin's *Seven Lamps of Architecture*, with a selection of odd volumes and editions from *Modern Painters* and *The Stones of Venice*, all bound into one volume - £30, but no doubt one of his special favourites would be J.M.W. Turner's *Liber Studiorum*, which was described as follows:

'A complete set of seventy one plates, all in fine condition, with full margins. Many of the plates are in early states, some of them being Touched Proofs. Each plate separately mounted; in oblong folio volume, bound green morocco, dated 1812.' [A note adds that there is in the volume a duplicate impression of the plate "Interior of a Church" in a peculiar state, signed by the artist - £100.]

Birket Foster also possessed several other editions of Turner engravings including *Picturesque Scenes in Richmondshire* (32 large engravings, dated 1843) and 24 India proof engravings of illustrations to the *Poetical Works of Sir Walter Scott*, 1852, some of which had of course appeared in conjunction with Birket Foster's own illustrations.

One of the most unusual manuscript treasures in the library was a large parchment document, with seals attached, dated 10 February 1617, which was the form of conveyance of the entail created by Shakespeare's will, in respect of property left to his daughter, Susanna Hall. Receipts show that Birket Foster had paid £65 for this in 1865. The item is included in the details of a regular account which Birket Foster had with Frederick Startridge Ellis, a dealer in manuscripts and rare books, of 33 Covent Garden. William Morris had been introduced to this shop by Swinburne and first took Burne-Jones there in 1864. In all probability it was the latter who introduced Birket Foster to Ellis, who later became a publisher for Rossetti and at one time held the joint tenancy with Morris of Kelmscott House. The Library of the University of California holds a rather interesting letter which Birket Foster wrote to Frederick Ellis on 30 November 1868, as follows:

'My dear Sir,
    I will send you the cheque next week, as I am rather short just now - if it makes no difference to you I shall be quite as well pleased to pay the money as to make the drawing, as I am very much engaged at present.
    'I am yours very truly etc.'

It is obvious that Birket Foster had over-reached

66 Birket Foster on the terrace of The Hill, Witley, with Polly Brown. Photograph about 1863. From an album in possession of the Glasson family.

himself financially and that Ellis, who was a collector of paintings, had suggested that he would accept a water-colour from Foster in lieu of payment. This is the only time we have any indication of Birket Foster being in any kind of financial difficulty and this was almost certainly due to what he later calls 'so many pulls in the building way' – the large extension of The Hill. As might be expected, the library at The Hill contained all the books illustrated by Birket Foster and in addition there were albums of sketches by Fred. Walker, Charles Keene and Orchardson, as well as plenty of good novels and light reading. Birket Foster was a refreshingly genuine book collector.[9]

The armorial device of the Foster family, including that used by Robert Forster of Cold Hesledon, had the motto 'Persevere' and showed a lance with allied accoutrements, a greyhound, oak leaves and a shield emblazoned with three bugle horns. The latter were thought to represent the foresters' horn, from which the name Forster was a

derivation. In his *Pedigree*, Joseph Foster states that the first known ancestor of the family was one Gilbert de Buckton – also called Forrester, alias Forster, who was a landowner and chief forester to the Bishop of Durham in 1342. Birket Foster incorporated the main features of this coat of arms into personalised devices of his own design. One showed a large 'F' interlocked with a smaller 'B' and both entwined with a decorative version of the Foster crest, including the motto, but rather deliberately omitting the lance. Another made a main feature of one bugle draped with the motto and with the name 'Birket Foster' appearing below a monogram in which the initials are not interlocked. Birket Foster had these designs printed from wood-cuts on heavy India paper and used these as book plates. A simpler version of the monogram and crest was also incorporated into the structure of The Hill (Ill. 55).

Most of the photographs of The Hill shown here were taken about 1880, by which time it is reasonable to suppose that many of the original William Morris wallpapers had been covered with others of a later date. The Victorian equivalent of a fitted wash-hand basin can be seen in an unpublished photograph of the bedroom known as 'The Nursery'. This appears to be plumbed in and is backed by Dutch tiles, but the immediate surrounding wall space is decorated with a wallpaper that can clearly be identified as the design 'Pomegranate' by William Morris. The second wallpaper in this room has the appearance of being 'The Bower' (1877) by William Morris, but other patterns were probably by Lewis F. Day, who was a follower and fellow founder with Morris of the Arts and Crafts Exhibiting Society. The decorative frieze in the billiard room is not by Morris, but owes more to the influences felt by the Aesthetic designers than to the Arts and Crafts Movement.[10]

A very characteristic feature of the ornamentation of The Hill was the appearance of blue-and-white porcelain on every available shelf and mantel, nook and cranny and often at table in the form of serving bowls, plates, etc. The illustrations in this book give some impression of this porcelain and other ornamental ware, but more precise descriptions can be found in Christie's catalogue for 30 April 1894, when the major part was sold as 'A Valuable Collection of Old Nankin Porcelain, Gres de Flandres, Majolica and Enamels'. Birket Foster was started on an enthusiasm for blue-and-white porcelain (before this became fashionable) by Dante Gabriel Rossetti and the most valuable set of items in his collection had formerly been owned by Rossetti. This was described as: 'A Vase and Cover, and a Pair of Beakers, painted with Lange Lysen, vases of flowers, nine figures of deities in raised compartments - 18½ inches high' (Lot 69 in the 1894 sale – £294). The total figure obtained for the 117 lots was well over £1,000, with 71 being Old Nankin Porcelain, including two dinner services. Of the other types of ornamental ware, the central group of china figures, as shown in Ill. 67, is obviously 'A Derby-Chelsea group of a nymph holding a lyre, and two children standing by a column' (Lot 115) and on either side of this are two Staffordshire pieces, showing a woman with two children and a dog (Lot 109) and of Dr Syntax and the Highwayman (Lot 110). A

67 The Hill: the billiard room. The large blue and white porcelain vase on top shelf of overmantel was one of three originally in the collection of Dante Gabriel Rossetti. Below: Derby-Chelsea group, with Staffordshire jugs either side. All items later included in sale at Christie's, 30 April 1894. From an album of photographs by William Foster in possession of Sarah G. A. Glasson.

further 25 items of Oriental porcelain from The Hill were to be sold at Christie's on 1 December 1921.[11]

The decorative candle sconces that were fixed to many of the interior walls of The Hill remind us that oil lamps and candles would be the only means of lighting this large house. The candle sconces were obvious products of the firm of William Morris and Co. and were in the form of round or square brass plaques, embossed with knights and their ladies, flowers, vines and in one case a very elegant flamingo.

Extensions to The Hill were commenced in 1866, with the addition of more rooms under an extra gable and also a billiard room beyond. The latter was also used as an oil painting studio and later for amateur theatricals and to house a large eight-fold painted screen – one of the major works of Edward Burne-Jones. Birket Foster had first seen this screen in the home of Burne-Jones in 1864. The panels were some of the designs Burne-Jones had originally made for a window showing scenes from the life of St Frideswide for the Latin Chapel, Christ Church Cathedral, Oxford – 1859. The artist subsequently put more finish on certain of these oils and framed them into a screen. The general composition presents a very overcrowded and rather confusing effect, but the colour and treatment must have appealed to Birket Foster and he was later able to acquire the piece. A somewhat faded photograph of the screen taken at The Hill about 1882-6 (Ill. 68) gives the impression that by then it was regarded as a slightly cumbersome item and had been banished to the stage end of the large studio. An interesting light has been thrown on the subsequent history of this screen by the painter Walford Graham Robertson, ROI (1867-1948) in his autobiography *Time Was* (1931). Robertson went to live at Witley in 1888 and was obviously a very genial and amusing personality, as shown in his writing and in a photograph of him at The Hill, which appears in one of the Foster family albums. In his reminiscences of Burne-Jones (whom he

had known since childhood) Robertson states:

'His pictures always appealed to me strongly, but more especially his early work, so colourful, so steeped in romantic suggestion, and I had been lucky in securing most beautiful examples in the eight panels setting forth the Life of Saint Frideswide, painted very early in the artist's career as designs for a great window in Christ Church Chapel, Oxford. These lovely panels, perhaps the most spontaneous and fascinating of all his works and far finer than the window for which they were designed, were made into a screen by the artist and were for long in his own house in Kensington Square, until his friend Birket Foster, persuaded him to part with them and bore them off to The Hill, Witley, which already boasted stained glass by the same hand and a series of decorative paintings from the history of Saint George.

Birket Foster was then *the* water-colour painter of the day, and there are still traditions at Witley of heavily laden trains disgorging swarms of dealers at the station who would race each other up to The Hill and sit patiently on its doorsteps to waylay the popular artist and extract from him the promise of a "little gem". When in course of time I came to make my home at Witley I did not notice any racing dealers, but found the kindly Lord of The Hill still painting and tramping about the countryside which he so loved and fought hard to protect against the "improving" and destructive jerry-builder. Alas, what would he think of it now? The great Frideswide screen stood in a seldom-used studio, and I finally induced Birket Foster to pass it on to me; when I detached the panels, framing each one separately in a narrow band of black, under Burne-Jones's direction.

Then came a difficulty which nearly always occurs when an artist comes across his early work after losing

68 The Hill: two opposite ends of the billiard room/large studio. Fresco above fireplace depicts 'The Feast of the Peacock' by John Dawson Watson, RWS, brother-in-law of Birket Foster. Below: Unfinished fresco shows 'The Raising of the Maypole' by J. D. Watson. Also eight-panelled screen painted by Burne-Jones with scenes from the life of St Frideswide (now as separate paintings and in possession of Cheltenham Ladies' College). From an album of photographs by William Foster in possession of Sarah G. A. Glasson.

69 General view of The Hill, after extension in 1866. From an album in possession of the Glasson family.

sight of it for many years. He at once wished to restore and repaint.

Now this puts the owner of a picture in a most awkward position. It would seem ungracious, nay unfair, to deny the creator of a picture the right to work his will upon it, yet to deliver it into his hands is to court disaster.

If a picture actually wants retouching in order, for instance, to hide an accidental injury, the artist who produced it many years ago is the last man who should be allowed to touch it, because, quite erroneously, he imagines himself to be the man who painted it and therefore falls upon it without mercy or respect. No artist should ever be allowed to see a picture painted by himself more than twenty years ago . . . I fought for my panels. "There's hardly anything to be done" I pleaded. "Only those little joins to paint over. Let *me* do it. Let us get a man from Whiteley's to do it. Don't let us do it at all – but *please* don't do it yourself!"

Burne-Jones was kind, but quite firm. I was respectful (I hope) but quite firm too. I left town for a few days, and Burne-Jones raided the house in my absence, carrying off four panels. I, on my return, raided the Grange and got all the panels back again. Finally, under stress of other work, the painter forgot about the matter and six of the eight panels remain in their original condition.'[12]

The smaller studio (leading off the hallway) was the one in which Birket Foster usually worked. Here he was surrounded by portfolios of sketches and the accumulated references of many years (some of which were kept in a

huge brass-bound walnut box, known in the family as the Armada Chest)[13] but one of the most important references was outside the window. Just far enough away to avoid blocking the light was a high, grassy bank. This had been purposely allowed to grow into a tangled profusion of gorse, ferns, cow parsley, wild flowers and brambles. The gardeners were forbidden ever to touch this part of the grounds and many a charming dog rose in a Birket Foster picture must have bloomed on this delightful bank.

Quaker family tradition actively encouraged the cultivation of gardens and much otherwise thwarted creative talent was channelled into their design. Birket Foster had obviously inherited the enthusiasm of his father and grandfather; the illustrations in this book and descriptions by Freddy Walker give some idea of the extent and beauty of the garden and grounds at The Hill. Here Birket Foster built a lodge and at least three rosy-brick, diamond paned cottages for members of the outdoor staff and their families. Gardeners in billy cock hats tended the acres of flower beds and grassy lawns, which later included a tennis court, with a raised bank for spectators.

'Then, following winding paths down the hillside, studded with ornamental conifers of exceptional luxuriance, past borders of gay flowers, through a lane of filberts, along terraces of standard roses, you presently arrive at an old-English garden with a sundial in its midst; then entering the cool shade of woods, you may rest awhile by a pool, on the surface of which a mass of white water-lilies are in full bloom. Before returning to the house you must visit the grape and peach houses, and the abodes of tropical fern and orchid and pass through

106

a conservatory filled with rare plants. . . .' ('Celebrities at Home'.)

Photographs show hyacinth, tulips, daffodils and many other varieties of flowering plants massed in large containers, not only in the conservatory, but placed about the house in a manner much less formal than the stiff (often artificial) floral decorations of the period.

The landscape painter, Edwin Edwards (1823-1879), who was a friend of Charles Keene, wrote in his diary for 2 September 1865, as follows: 'CK about to undertake some "tempera" painting of a medieval subject for a summerhouse of Birket Foster's at Witley.'

This project does not appear to have been carried out, but H.S. Marks RA certainly painted for the loggia seven panels with gold backgrounds, representing Shakespeare's 'Seven Ages of Man'. After some years these were removed indoors for the sake of preservation and placed in a hallway. The panels were eventually sold to Sir Squire Bancroft, the actor and theatrical manager.

Notes: Chapter Ten

1 See pp. 107-8 for details of the life and career of Lancelot Myles Glasson (1894-1959).

2 Extract from *Birket Foster* by Lancelot Glasson, 'Old' Water-colour Society Club, Vol. XI, 1933.

3 Extract from letter published by permission of Newcastle upon Tyne City Libraries.

4 Information with reference to tiles from Norah Gillow, Curator, William Morris Gallery, Walthamstow, London.

5 Quoted in *Burne-Jones*, by M. Harrison and W. Waters, Barrie and Jenkins, 1973.

6 The St George and the Dragon series of stained glass designed by D.G. Rossetti and executed by Morris, Marshall, Faulkner and Co. is now in the Victoria and Albert Museum. Readers should be aware that titles given to the Burne-Jones panels may vary according to source.

7 An engraving of St George Kills the Dragon was published in *The Art Journal* (Christmas Supplement, 1890, p. 26). This engraving was also reproduced in *Country Life* on 4 December 1975, in an article entitled 'A Victorian Artistic Haven' by Pauline Flick, noting the position of Birket Foster in the centre of a colony of artists at Witley.

8 The source of some of the information with reference to 'The Hhareem' is from the catalogue notes by Rosemary Treble for the Arts Council Exhibition of Great Victorian Pictures (1978).

9 The final total obtained in the 1894 sale of books was £1,869. Further items from the collection of Birket Foster appeared at Sothebys on 27 May 1904 (lots 311-362) which consisted of a large proportion of bird books, collections of engravings by Turner, Etching Club folios, etc. Prices were very modest and the total received was only £112/12/-.

10 Information from the William Morris Gallery and Victoria and Albert Museum.

11 Information from catalogues, receipts, etc. in the collection of William Glasson.

12 In 1950, the St Frideswide panels were presented by the executors of W.G. Robertson to Cheltenham Ladies' College. These paintings are much valued by the College and in 1983-4 are scheduled to be removed from their present site in the Music Wing to a more prominent position in the Council Meeting Chamber.

13 This chest was said to have been taken by Captain Vansittart Earle from one of the ships of the Spanish Armada, in the engagement under Admiral Howard on 29 July 1588 (Lot 117 in the 1894 sale - £25/4/-).

11
'A painter in water-colour of great distinction'
(the Dalziel Brothers)

The photograph of Birket Foster and Polly Brown (Ill. 66) shows them on the terrace in the early days of life at The Hill. Birket Foster writes on 12 April 1863 to Polly, who was staying with the children at Brighton and gives an amusing difficulties of the hassles of hanging the annual exhibition of the Society of Painters in Water-colours:

'The first day's work over, thank goodness. I am nearly worn off my legs; however, I think we have got on tolerably well. I found my companions very agreeable and we have had great fun; we dined in the Haymarket together. This evening I have been to see Holland, who sent such a lovely drawing that I went up directly and bought it – one of the finest he has ever done. We invited the President to come and see where we have placed his drawing, for he cannot come without our permission. We have been most bothered with Carl Haag's drawing – a most uninteresting one, like London in a fog; the subject is the Ruins of Palmyra; it has taken us half a day to hang it. Hang it! We meet at breakfast tomorrow at eight for another hard day.'

The water-colour by James Holland which had so taken the eye of Birket Foster was mentioned in *The Art Journal* review of the exhibition as follows:

'Mr Holland with his rapturous love for colour, makes "The Rialto" (No. 84) span with its single arch of grey the emerald green of the canal beneath, set off by the caps of the Venetian boatmen.' [See also Appendix 8.]

Two days later, Birket Foster continued his letter:

'We have done hanging, and tomorrow we are going to put the finishing touches to it, and to hang a few others we have got as the gallery is not full. If I have not mentioned getting the letters, it has been from utter prostration after my work, – I have hardly known what I have been about.'[1]

Birket Foster scribbled off another note to Polly on 15 April 1863.

'Another day over very comfortably, but I find I shall not be able to come to Brighton till Saturday. We shan't be done till Friday night and we have to receive the members and hear what they have to say on Saturday morning, so that I shall try and get away by the 4 o'clock train on Saturday. I was delighted to get your letter and to hear you and the children are well and alright. *Take*

care of Dodshon. I shall have an amusing account to give you of our doings.
　　With dearest love to you and the chicks,
　　　I am your affec.
　　　　Birket Foster.'[2]

The public and the critics were enchanted with the pictures by Birket Foster as displayed in this exhibition of the Society of Painters in Water-colours and *The Art Journal* commented:

'Lane Scene, Hambledon' (no. 228) and 'Cottage at Chiddingfold' (no. 284) highly elaborated by Mr Foster, composed after the manner of Vignettes, are perfect in their kind. Each point in these compositions is thoughtfully studied and carefully balanced, even to the placing of a group of fowls feeding. Each light and every shadow falls precisely in its fitting position, and the strokes of the facile pencil, infinite in multitude, are playful as a wind-dancing leaf. Colour, however, is lacking.'

Birket Foster and his family were well settled at The Hill by the autumn of 1863. On 18 November of that year, he wrote to Robert Spence, with regard to some family portraits that the latter had allowed him to have. The letter continues:

'We are beginning to look very autumnal now & are busy planting trees again. I do hope next summer you will pay us a visit. I am sure thou would be pleased with the country and it would be a great delight to me to have you for a while.
　　With dear love to you all in which Polly joins
　　　I am thy affec. bro.
　　　　Birket Foster.'
I hope Sarah is better.
I have not forgotten 'Loch Leven' (i.e. a painting that he was doing for Spence).

Included in the collection of letters to Robert Spence is a cutting from an unidentified newspaper, dated 7 December 1863:

'Mr Birkett Forster (*sic*) who has given up working for the booksellers, having come into a handsome fortune by the death of his uncle (Mr Forster by the way is a North Shields man) has two charming coast scenes in the Winter Exhibition of Water-colours. "Marsden Rock" says the London Review "is one of the most beautiful renderings of cliff and rock we have ever seen". The critic speaks of "Dunstonboro" 'by Birkett Forster (*sic*) in the same flattering manner.'³

It is not within the brief of this book to ascertain as to whether Birket Foster was indeed left a fortune at this time by an unidentified uncle, but it seems likely that the report was somewhat exaggerated and we know that it was totally incorrect in giving this supposed inheritance as the reason for his ceasing work as an illustrator.

The critics were almost always kind to Birket Foster and watched with interest as his style evolved:

'Mr Birket Foster, if we mistake not, is striving to mass into unity the infinite dots of which his landscapes have been so dextrously composed. He, too, like others, may be in transition, for none are so perfect as not to strive after something as yet unaccomplished. However, to our liking 'Flying a Kite' (125) can scarcely be surpassed. The composition of the figures with the landscape is adroit; the story is pretty. The details are sufficient for their purpose and have, above all, been kept duly subordinate to the general effect.' (*The Art Journal* 1864, p. 170.)

The Art Union of London had been established in 1837. This was a society for the fostering of interest in the fine arts and encouraging British artists and the manufacturers of decorative ware. Members paid an annual fee of one guinea and for this their basic entitlement was to receive each year a large engraving and the right to participate in a 'draw' for pictures. Winners in this lottery could choose a painting to the value of their prize from one of the current exhibitions. The work of Birket Foster seldom appears in the list of these prizes because his pictures were frequently sold almost as soon as the doors of an exhibition were open. It is said that on one occasion there was the usual rush by dealers at a private view of the 'Old' Water-colour Society to select from the Birket Foster exhibits, but while they were making their choice, another dealer quietly went up to the Secretary's desk and purchased every one of the Birket Foster paintings on view.

The work of Birket Foster is linked with the Art Union by way of the prints or engravings that were presented to each member. In 1864, *The Art Journal* (p. 273) commented:

'... the chromolithographs of Mr B. Foster's "Wild Roses" and Mr Fripp's "Young England" are the best examples of printing in colours we have ever seen. Both prints have much softness – the result of the use in one case of twenty-five, and in the other twenty-six stones – that it is necessary to look into them very closely to determine that they are not drawings.'

The term chromolithography had been coined by G. Engelmann for the process of full-colour printing by lithography which had been patented by him in 1837, but which was now greatly improved. 'Gathering Wild Roses' was executed by M. and N. Hanhart of Charlotte Street and is indeed a fine example of chromolithography (Ill. 70.) Many otherwise good prints were spoilt by an over-emphasis on red in the skin tones, but in this example all the values are in balance and reproduce very faithfully the original colours as used by Birket Foster. The face of the elder girl is not a correct representation of the style of the artist, but the general effect of line and texture is very well

imitated. Collectors should be aware that a smaller version (8 × 10¾″) of this chromolithograph exists, which is *not* the one presented to Art Union members, but a very inferior example using at the most six colours and having a much weaker and less detailed effect. The latter is inscribed with the title and marked 'Printed in Germany'.

Chromolithographs of the work of Birket Foster were to become immensely popular and the verisimilitude of these prints was such that even the artist himself could mistake one for the original. Birket Foster related that he once saw a picture of his in a dealer's window and was rather surprised, as he thought the owner prized it too much to sell it. It was only on closer inspection that he realised it was a chromolithograph. In view of the many examples of work by Birket Foster which were reproduced by this method it may be helpful to give a brief description of the method employed to produce these colour prints.

The original drawing was traced and then transferred on to a lithographic stone by retracing over a piece of paper which had been primed with red chalk. The lithographer then drew upon the stone the basic outlines of the subject (and indications of shading) with greasy chalk or ink. Black-and-white prints were run off on to thin paper and these impressions were laid in a moist state onto the same number of lithographic stones as colours required. The artist used a separate stone to indicate each individual colour and the subsequent printing of these in sequence was a most skilful job. Exactly the right amount of ink had to be applied and the paper placed so as to achieve a perfect 'register', e.g. the colour of a red scarf must fit exactly into the space outlined for it without overlapping or leaving the undertone exposed. The 25 stones mentioned in the review of 'Wild Roses' refers to the fact that this print would have to be pulled through the press that number of times in order to print each colour from the appropriate stones. It is part of the quality of this chromolithograph that the colours are all in perfect register. The best contemporary account of chromolithography is to be found in *The Industrial Arts of the XIX Century* by M. Digby Wyatt (Day and Son, 1853).

George Rowney and Co. produced many of the best chromolithographs of work of Birket Foster (Ill. 71). *In Rustic England* (Hodder and Stoughton – 1906) is a useful source of reproductions of these prints, although it should be noted that the quality of the colours is not quite up to the standard of the originals. Rowney's catalogue for 1883 lists the following Birket Foster chromolithographs (or 'Fac-simile water-colour drawings') thus: 'Returning from Pasture – evening' – 'Making Hay while the sun shines' – 'Sunny Glade' – 'The Cottage Nurse' – 'The Boat Race' – 'Rustic Stile' (Ill. 71) – 'Summer Time' – 'Ride Home' – 'Bringing Home the Calf' – 'Cullercoats' – 'Pet of the Common' – 'Fisherman's Cottage' – 'A Surrey Lane' – 'On the Beach' – 'Blackberry Gatherers' – 'Birds' Nesting' – 'Gardener's Cottage' – 'Old Mill, Godalming'. All but five of these are illustrated in *Rustic England*, with the addition of 'A Peep at the Hounds'. The original water-colour (colour ill. C) was bought by Rowney at Christie's in 1888 and issued as a chromolithograph. The firm suffered much loss of archive material during the Second World War, but the above list gives a general idea of many of the most popular of the Birket Foster chromolithographs, as published by George Rowney and Co. These make admirable collectors' items, but have become relatively scarce.

70 'Gathering Wild Roses' – print after water-colour. Chromolithograph presented to members of the Art Union of London in 1864. Executed by M. and N. Hanhart of Charlotte Street, London. See p. 109. Size: 10½ × 14″ – 26.6 × 35.5 cms.
Collection: Pauline Flick.

71 'The Rustic Stile' – print after a water-colour. Chromolithograph executed by George Rowney and Co. Reproduced in *In Rustic England*.
Collection: Tom Rowney.

The wheel has now turned full circle in that modern reproductions of water-colours by Birket Foster have in recent years proved exceptionally popular subjects for greeting cards, etc. and have also been very successfully published in the form of separate prints for framing, just as in the lifetime of the artist.

Birket Foster was both a rapid and a constant worker, but he was soon to have difficulty in keeping up with the demand for his water-colours, in spite of raising his prices. He told the Dalziels: 'When I sit down in that chair after breakfast it means at least twenty guineas before I get up again'. The stories that W. Graham Robertson had heard about hordes of eager buyers continually appearing at The Hill in the earlier years at Witley were not exaggerated. Lancelot Glasson relates an amusing anecdote about the competition between dealers to obtain the work of Birket Foster:

'One story deals with a well known picture dealer of the time, Monsieur Gambart, who arrived at Waterloo en route for Witley. To his chagrin he saw on the platform his rival Mr Tooth also obviously bound on the same errand. Having taken certain precautions, he got into the same compartment as Mr Tooth and they travelled down to Witley together. Arriving at the station, Mr Tooth placed himself by the door, and springing out, ran down the platform to the solitary cab standing outside. M. Gambart followed with leisurely step, and approaching the cabby, just as Mr Tooth was climbing in, said – "My name is Gambart, I think you have had a wire from me from Waterloo engaging this cab? Yes? I thought so. Now my dear Mr Tooth, if you happen to be going to Mr Foster's I shall be most pleased to give you a lift, and after I have had a little talk with Mr Foster you can see him". Mr Gambart got the best drawings that day.'[4]

The Dalziels have a version of this incident, but their ending has it that Gambart bought every disposable drawing in the studio. In fact Gambart was on rather more friendly terms with Birket Foster than just those of dealer and artist, as he appears dressed in costume in a photograph taken on the terrace steps at The Hill, with Birket Foster, J.D. Watson and W.P. Burton. Obviously, he was on this occasion a guest at one of the large house parties during which Birket Foster and his guests would garb themselves in elaborate Tudor costumes. It is an unexpected view of Charles Keene to see him showing a shapely pair of legs in doublet and hose. It is possible that it may have been he who took the photograph shown here of one of these costume sessions (Ill. 73).

1864 was to be a year of great change in the life of Birket Foster. On 8 February he wrote to Robert Spence:

'My dear brother,
    As I know thou takes an interest in what befalls me I thought I would like just to send thee a line myself to tell thee of my prospects. I am engaged to be married to Fanny Watson a sister of J.D. Watson the illustrator of Bunyan's Pilgrims Progress and Robinson Crusoe, and whose name I daresay you know very well. You will have heard all about it but I thought I should like to write and tell you myself. After much serious consideration I believe it is a right thing and I am sure it will add to my happiness. I quite hope very shortly to come

north for a day or two so I shall hope to see you and then we can have a chat.
    With my dear love to you all,
        I am your affectionate brother,
            Birket Foster
I go up this morning to the Election of Associates. I expect the successful ones will be F. Walker and J.D. Watson. I believe they are safe and there are two more vacancies, but it is doubtful who will get them.'[5]

The future brother-in-law referred to in this letter was John Dawson Watson RWS (1832-92). He was a painter, water-colourist and illustrator, who had studied at the Manchester School of Design and at the RA Schools. J.D. Watson was one of a band of illustrators for the periodical Once a Week, but some of his best magazine illustrations are to be found in Good Words and London Society. When George Routledge asked the Dalziels to find an illustrator for Pilgrim's Progress, he stipulated that the drawings should be undertaken by 'a new man'. The Dalziels had been impressed with some drawings by J.D. Watson that they had engraved for Good Words and therefore commissioned him to do 100 illustrations for the new work. Pilgrim's Progress was published in 1861 and was followed by Robinson Crusoe in 1864. These illustrations brought the name of J.D. Watson to the notice of the public and Pilgrim's Progress proved to be one of the most successful of all the fine art books from the house of Routledge.[6]

It was not only Birket Foster who became engaged in 1864. Polly Brown, at the age of 24, was to marry Edmund Evans, who was 14 years older. One has to presume that there had been some attachment between them before the engagement of Birket Foster to Fanny Watson, but it does appear that one event must have precipitated the other. Birket Foster's grand-daughter remembers Polly Brown as a most attractive personality. She knew her only as an old lady, but also heard her mother's recollections of the woman who played such a vital part in that young life. Polly was lively and full of fun, kind and gentle with the Foster children, interested in everything around her, but also rather untidy and haphazard and none too capable in her management of the Foster household. Birket Foster had been very happy to have Polly to care for his children and relieve his loneliness with her cheerful ways, but he needed a competent mistress for The Hill, where he employed at least seven indoor servants, in addition to the outdoor staff, who lived in cottages on the estate. Frances Watson was in fact younger than Polly, having been born on 17 April 1841 (the year that Birket Foster had started at Landells). She was now only 23 and very pretty, but also a very capable woman, with a decided presence, who had been brought up in more socially sophisticated surroundings than the Plain Quaker background of Polly Brown. She was a sister of a friend with whom Birket Foster had much in common and seemed ideal for the role of hostess in the entertainment of an increasingly wide circle of friends who now frequently visited The Hill.

It was about this time that Birket Foster made a formal break with his Quaker background and became a member of the Church of England. He was the most unpompous of men and his children inherited his outlook on life. One of the many charming recollections of his daughter Ellen was that Birket Foster and his five children all trooped up to London for the day and combined their christenings with a visit to the dentist and the zoo!

'Augt. 1st 1864

My dear Robert,

I am writing you a line to say what very great pleasure it would give us if Sarah and you would come to Polly's wedding on the 23rd. We can house you nicely and it would be a very great delight to us all – and should so like you to see Witley and where I am settled. Do give it your serious consideration and come if it is in anyway possible. I enclose 2 cartes of Fanny – they are not very good but they are the best I can get. I am going to Sedbergh tomorrow with J.D. Watson to bring her back to London. Our place is suffering fearfully from the drought – the grass is entirely gone and many of the evergreens are withered.

With very dear love to you all,
I remain your affec. bro.
Birket Foster.'[7]

The second name of John Dawson Watson came from a branch of the family in Lancaster. John Dawson of Lancaster was a solicitor and Under Sheriff for the North Riding. He moved to Sedbergh in 1829 and his diary relates details of the families of Watson, Seed, Gray and Foster, all of whom were connected. In his memoirs, Myles Birket Foster, sen., noted that there were some 41 cousinships linking other families with his own. In view of the close associations of the Foster and Birket families with Lancaster and Sedbergh (and the confirmation in the diary of John Dawson) there can be no doubt that Birket Foster was in some manner related to his second wife, although in a much more distant sense than the full cousinship to his first wife, Anne Spence.

On 25 August 1864, John Dawson copied the following announcement into his diary:

'On the 25 inst. at St Mark's Church, Regent's Park, London, by the Rev Joseph Lupton, MA Fellow of St John's College, Cambridge.

Birket Foster, Esq., of The Hill, Witley, Surrey to Frances, third daughter of Dawson Watson, Esq., Solicitor of Sedbergh, Yorkshire.'[8]

Notes: Chapter Eleven
1 Reproduced in *Birket Foster* by H. M. Cundall – but incorrectly dated in that book.
2 Dodshon Foster must also have been in Brighton with Polly and the children, hence the joking reference to him. Reproduced by permission of University of California, Los Angeles (Dept. of Special Collections.)
3 Letter and newspaper cutting reproduced by permission of Newcastle upon Tyne City Libraries.
4 'Old' Water-colour Society Club, Vol. XI, 1933.
5 By permission of Newcastle upon Tyne City Libraries.
6 For further reference to J.D. Watson see the obituary in *The Graphic*, 8 January 1892, and *Historical Notes on Cullercoats, Whitley and Monkseaton* by W.W. Tomlinson, published by Walter Scott, London, 1893.
7 By permission of Newcastle upon Tyne City Libraries.
8 Entry from the diary of John Dawson published by permission of Sir Basil Nield, a great-nephew of Frances Foster.

12

Life at The Hill, Witley: Frederick Walker, Charles Keene and William Q. Orchardson

'The Hill Witley
29th Nov. 1864

My dear Robert

Will you kindly send me – by return of post – an impression of the seal you have with the Birket arms upon it. I have mislaid those you gave me. You will have your pictures shortly.

With love to you all
I am your affec. bro.
Birket Foster

You would hear David Roberts was dead.'[1]

From about 1860, the correspondence between Birket Foster and Robert Spence is increasingly concerned with an exchange of details in reference to the many painting commissions that Birket Foster executed for his cousin, but a letter on 16 September 1862 mentions another side of the collecting interests of Robert Spence. Birket Foster wrote:

'I am very much obliged for the trouble that you have taken to get me the Bewick. I have looked through it and it is in beautiful condition & it is beautifully bound. I enclose 7. 0. 0 but hope that if you have been at any other expense in the purchase you will let me know.'

Two previous letters suggest that Birket Foster was intending this book as a present for his friend James Hook, RA, but he adds: 'The copy is so nice that I am not at all sure that I shall let Hook have it.' An admiration for the work of Thomas Bewick continued to be a basic principle for Birket Foster and it was a manner from which he never tired, even while being able to appreciate more fashionable styles as they appeared on the art scene.

In October 1862, Birket Foster sent a receipt to Robert Spence for £31/10/- for a water-colour drawing of 'The Little Nurse' and followed this less than a fortnight later with another receipt for £63 for a water-colour drawing of 'Edinburgh Castle' and one of 'Tynemouth from the North Pier'.

'May 6th. 1864

My dear Robert,

I shall be very glad indeed to make the drawing you name. Will you send up the sketch or print and I will do my best with it. I should have answered thy note sooner but I have been moving from Brighton.

In great haste and with very dear love to you both
I am your affec. bro.
Birket Foster.'

'28th May 1864

My dear brother,

I should have answered thy note sooner but many things have come in the way. The Photographs will do very well I think – the one showing the foreground is too indistinct – however I will try and make it do. It appears to be taken from a considerable elevation, so that I shall not get the quay as a foreground, but I dont think that matters as it makes a very good picture. With the material at command I could perhaps be more *correct* if I took the view from the shore – like I have indicated on the other side. The Photograph of it is much more distinct and perhaps on second thoughts it would be better – the only thing is I couldnt show the house you occupied – but I fear the detail of them is so indistinct that I could not make anything of it. All the distant hills of course are quite easy to understand. I will send you an outline for correction very shortly.

With dear love to all,
I am your affec. bro.
Birket Foster.'

The sketch on the back of this letter shows a sweeping bay, with a small village nestling on the left shore, with mountains in the distance. Birket Foster has indicated the left foreground with the query: 'What should this be? It is quite black in the Photograph.'

Robert Spence has sent Birket Foster some photographs of an unnamed location which obviously had sentimental, but sad associations for the former. The photographs had been sent to Robert Spence by an acquaintance in a letter addressed from Rothesay and mentioning a bereavement. It seems that this must have been the death of Robert Spence's daughter, Rachel, aged 12, in August 1863. Even if the subject in hand cannot be identified, the response of Birket Foster provides a glimpse of his approach to the commission and his willingness to work from photographs in this entirely objective manner.

'We ought, perhaps, to have noticed Mr Birket Foster among the painters of the figure; but the fact is that an artist of this lively versatile mood is never out of place, put him anywhere or everywhere. "On the Beach at Hastings" (no. 12) he is on the verge of the sea, whereunto do congregate the fishermen and their families, grouped together with boats, nets and other seafaring properties. We have heard it objected that this and other

114

scenes are a little spotty. Mr Foster certainly sacrifices repose for the sake of vivacity and sparkle.' (*The Art Journal* p. 175, 1865.)

'The Donkey Ride' as exhibited with the Water-colour Society in 1864 was subsequently re-sold in 1865 for 300 gns. – an indicator of the swift commercial recognition of pictures in a new medium for this artist. Birket Foster was now well established as a water-colourist, with a position even more esteemed than that which he had held as an illustrator, although his methods still made the purists uneasy.

'Mr B. Foster contributes a pleasant picture "Winterbourne, Bonchurch" (321) – a garden where children feed peacocks; this is sounder in execution than is common with the painter, not mannered. "River Scene, Evening" (273) is one of those capital representations of river vistas with which Mr Foster sometimes indulges us; it is nearly free from chalkiness and finely coloured, very solid in the artist's way.' (*The Athenaeum*, 19 May 1866.)

The Art Journal did not agree with this opinion:

'What can have befallen Mr Birket Foster is beyond our power to conjecture. He is not at all himself this year. That "River Scene" might have been a "hayfield" so little surface or transparency is there in the water. In the dramatised sunset sky, there is a grand array of clouds; but surely atmosphere and light would more abound if opaque colour were not quite so obtrusive'

– and in the later part of the review the critic returns to his theme:

'By way of conclusion may we add a word on the present state of the art of water-colour painting, as displayed in the present exhibition. In the first place we are glad to observe a reaction from the immoderate use of opaque colour which some time since threatened to corrupt the purity of the practice of former years. There cannot be a doubt that Mr Birket Foster's drawings suffer in colour, quality and tone from the too liberal employment of body colours...'

The original rules of the Water-colour Society forbade all use of body colour (i.e. the admixture of white), but the dictum was now widely disregarded, although this continued to be a touchy point with critics. The idea still lingered that only the pure wash of classic tradition was considered fit for the highest esteem and that all else was adulteration or trickery. But, most of the public cared little for such academic quibbles and bought pictures for their pretty effects, with no interest in the technique by which they were achieved.

In September 1864, Robert Spence purchased for £60 another view of Edinburgh and also a piece entitled 'The Little Winter Grave'. On 7 May 1866, Birket Foster writes about a further commission:

'Vokins is just packing up the picture to send off today. I do hope you will like it though I am very nervous about it – if you don't send it back and I will try again.

With regard to the doctor. I had hoped to have seen him today, but I cannot manage it, but if I have time before I leave I will do it. A letter will reach me at Witley on Thursday morning – we sleep Thursday night at Carlton Hill at my mothers and leave for Dover on Friday evening. I know you will like to know something about the price. I fear I shall have to charge £200 – but this will include the two sketches.

Yours very affecly.
Birket Foster.'

The correspondence makes it clear that Birket Foster was at this time arranging to take out a life insurance policy and that Robert Spence was to handle the matter for him. Many of the subsequent letters are dated January or July and note 'I enclose my premium' – it is probably for this reason that some have been preserved that do not otherwise have much import, but nevertheless they contain many delightful glimpses of homely events in the life of Birket Foster. A reply to the above letter exists and is very surprisingly headed: 'Dear Birkett'. If such a close relation could misspell the name it makes more understandable this frequent mistake on the part of others. But, what is this letter doing in a batch of correspondence, otherwise all from Birket Foster *to* Robert Spence? The idea that it might be a copy kept by Spence has to be considered, but it provides a certain interest in showing us the other side of the correspondence and the totally Plain Quaker style of Robert Spence, who was to remain a convinced Friend all his life (1817–90):

'4, Rosella Place, North Shields
May 9th. 1866

Dear Birkett (*sic*)

I enclose a draft for £200 pounds in payment for the picture of Rothesay Bay and the two sketches. Thou dost not mention whether the two sketches are finished and sent also. If they are not will thou finish them on thy return – putting in different skies from the other pictures as I should wish them to vary from it in this respect. The picture has not yet reached me but I hope it will do in time for me to write to thee before thou goes away. Please send me a receipt for payment for the three drawings – I thought thou would be glad to have the matter settled before thou left home and if the sketches are not finished and sent already – a little work on thy return will complete them. I shall be glad to hear that this has reached thee safely – Thy letter dated the 7th. did not reach me until this morning & I thought it best to telegraph to thee at Witley as it was impossible for me to write thee there. I hope this settlement will be satisfactory to thee and I am sure that when I have seen my three pictures I shall have great reason to feel pleased with them.

Thine affectionately
R. Spence.'

On 11 May 1866, Birket Foster acknowledged the receipt of £200 for 'Rothesay Bay' and two sketches of the same made on the spot. In a letter written from Morley's Hotel, Charing Cross (in which this receipt was enclosed) he comments:

'I am glad the picture has arrived safely and you are pleased with it. I began to get rather anxious about it being so long on the road. I have only one unpleasant feeling in connection with it and that is that you have sent the money before the sketches are done. Of course, I will send them as soon as I get home – my reason for naming the amount was that *I myself* am always anxious to know what a thing is likely to cost me. The money arrived quite safely for which I am much obliged.

I had just time to run over to Dr Peacock – and he has put me through my paces – and I fancy he doesn't think badly of me so that perhaps you will kindly get the thing done for me. I cannot tell what the premium may be so that I don't know what to do unless you will kindly pay it for me and send me word to Heidelberg that I may remit. We shall be there till Monday morning and that is following the Wednesday you name.'

In a letter addressed from Brook Street, Bond Street, on 11 January 1867, Birket Foster encloses a cheque for £62/6/8d in half-yearly payment of his insurance premium and adds: 'I am delighted to hear such good accounts of Sarah. The two sketches are at the framers and will be sent off either tomorrow or Monday.'

Robert Spence bought two unnamed Birket Foster sketches in 1867 and offered his cousin another book by Thomas Bewick. A letter dated 29 January 1867 shows that construction work was still in progress at The Hill.

'I have been away in London for a few days or I should have answered sooner. I have so many pulls just now in the building way and having got all the Bewicks (though not first editions) I do not incline to purchase. Many thanks for the opportunity. I am very glad you are pleased with the sketches. Of course, they are left in a sketchy way, but I think on the whole they are the better for it.

I don't seem to remember about the Bamboro. drawing. I shall be very glad to do it however and I have a good sketch of it – I have no street view – that is an actual locality but I made a drawing of the subject for Barry Cornwall's Dramatic Scenes and if you have no objection to its being a fancy scene I shall be able to accomplish it very well.'

(Later that year Birket Foster forwarded a receipt to Robert Spence for the sum of one hundred and five pounds for three drawings in water-colour – of 'Loch Leven', 'Bamboro', and 'Durham' – 23 September 1867.)

'"The Old Breakwater" (no. 150) by Mr B. Foster although it shows no novelty in painting or peculiar brilliancy of atmospheric effect and is in the rather chalky manner of the artist, is, nevertheless, pleasant in its breadth of sunlight over the sea. The subject, an old groyne on a beach, with children at play. The bright opalescent tinting of the sky is noteworthy here.' (*The Athenaeum*, 11 May 1867.)

The first major exhibit by Birket Foster of a foreign subject appeared with the Society of Painters in Water-colours in this year, but an exposure to more dramatic scenery and different light had not produced any radical effect on his work.

'Mr Birket Foster continues to charm by the pretty play of his execution. His stippled skies have as many lines or threads as a piece of lace or a cambric handkerchief. He weaves his details even into water, so that a river or a lake becomes less of a fluid than a textile fabric. The neatness of his manipulation has been carried over a novel surface in his picture of "Bellagio" (86). The Italian Palazzi have been touched with a ready, dainty hand.' (*The Art Journal*, 1867, p. 147.)

'The Hill Witley Surrey
June 29th 1867
My dear Robt.
    I enclose a cheque for my premium. How you will

enjoy Wales if the weather is only what it is now, but it is terribly hot here.
    Fanny and I intend taking a ramble northward in about 6 or 7 weeks time after the boys return to school.
    We are very glad to have a nice account of Sarah.
        With love to you all from us all,
            I am your affec. bro.
            Birket Foster.'

Birket and Frances Foster had now been married for nearly three years. This letter suggests that Fanny was paying due attention to the needs of her step-children and that the marriage was working out in a pleasantly companionable way, but it would be some time during the summer of 1867 that W.Q. Orchardson was painting a portrait of Frances Foster.

William Quiller Orchardson (1832–1910) had been included in their party when Birket Foster visited Tynemouth in 1864. This talented Scottish painter of historical subjects and life *à la mode* had come to live in London about two years previously and was probably first introduced to Birket Foster by Charles Keene. Orchardson was a good looking, amusing and sociable man, who liked to hunt, fish, play cricket and tennis and was exceptionally skilled at billiards. He was a frequent house guest at The Hill and invariably spent Christmas there, but it was not only good talk and billiards that attracted Orchardson to Surrey, but a more subtle charm in the person of the young Mrs Birket Foster. Orchardson was still a bachelor and known for his attachments to pretty women, with whom he had a series of romantic flirtations, which produced a great deal of love poetry, but appear to have left him emotionally unscathed. A delicately conducted episode between William Orchardson and Frances Foster was at its height during the time when he was painting her portrait (Ill. 72). The expression on the face of Fanny has a revealing awareness and the portrait shows not only her emotions, but also those of the painter. The style of dress and simple colouring are essentially characteristic of the Orchardson manner, but the beautiful pose was not contrived by him, but was entirely natural to the sitter. The portrait was exhibited in 1868 at the Royal Academy in the year that William Q. Orchardson was elected an ARA. *The Art Journal* commented: '... we observe with pleasure that G.D. Leslie and William Q. Orchardson bring into the dry routine of portrait-painting a freedom and variety caught from fancy. Mrs Charles Dickens, jun., by the former and Mrs Birket Foster by the latter, are as novel in treatment as they are pleasing in effect.'

The picture was later set into a panel above the chimney piece in the library at The Hill. In spite of Fanny's little dalliance, Birket Foster and Orchardson remained friends, which must provide an insight into the relationship between Birket Foster and his second wife. She was only 10½ years older than his eldest child and one suspects an element of paternalism on his part. There is a letter in the Victoria and Albert Museum that Birket Foster wrote to J. Spielmann in 1897, with reference to pictures in the British International Exhibition. It contains only one line, thus: 'These drawings are lent by *Mrs Birket Foster*, not Mrs Frances Foster as I said'. Birket Foster in his Quaker way had obviously been seeing his wife as a person in her own right and the correction to the more formal version can only have been at the instigation of Fanny, who even sent a wreath to the funeral of her own brother-in-law as Mrs Birket Foster. One senses that this was a role that was

very important in her life, but how much was it detrimental to her relationship as Fanny, wife of Birket? In later years, photographs of Fanny show her with an expression which is not unhappy, but with a certain look that is not quite content, in spite of her beautiful clothes and the ideal surroundings of The Hill. The Foster family regarded the childless marriage as successful enough in its way, but Fanny was never to replace Anne in the affection of Birket Foster.

William Orchardson was eventually married in 1873 at the age of 40 to a girl of half his age. They were to be a most happy and devoted pair, but it was his bachelor habit of constantly visiting The Hill that led to one of their few quarrels. His young wife gave birth to their first child on Christmas Eve 1873. Later she was to recall: 'Do you remember? You had for years spent Christmas with the Birket Fosters at Witley; they asked you again although you were married and I was unable to go. You did go for a week some time after Christmas, which distressed me, as I was alone'.[2]

Frances Foster was a woman who understood the social niceties and could perfectly well have arranged not to ask Orchardson under the circumstances. The fact that the invitation was extended at all must point to her influence and personal inclination.

Frederick Walker was another friend of Birket Foster for whom The Hill was a very special place. After successfully illustrating for *Once a Week*, etc. he had been elected to the Water-colour Society in 1864, the year in which he received great praise for his exhibit of 'Spring'. This much-acclaimed work showed an influence from Birket Foster in a background which Walker himself described as 'primrosey' with the figure of a young girl as the main subject in a woodland scene. Fred. Walker was

72 Frances Foster (née Watson), second wife of Birket Foster. This portrait in oils by William Quiller Orchardson, RA, was inset above the library mantelshelf. Exhibited no. 223 'Mrs Birket Foster' at the Royal Academy in 1868. Photographed by William Foster. Original in possession of Mrs L.M. Glasson.

a painter of figures in landscape, rather than a landscape painter as such. 'Spring' was purchased by William Agnew, the much respected dealer and collector, whose patronage and friendship was always to be extended to this artist. Walker was made a full member of the Society in 1866. 'The Lost Path' – a classic Victorian narrative piece, depicting a young woman struggling through a blizzard with a baby in her arms – was his first exhibit at the Royal Academy in 1863 and is now a widely recognised example of his work in oils. But it was not until 'Bathers' was exhibited at the Academy in 1867 that Walker produced the oil painting that was later to be described as 'one of the finest and the best works that was ever lifted from an English painter's easel'. But, in spite of his success, the highly strung temperament of Frederick Walker was constantly causing him to be in a state of self-doubt and anxiety.

The Hill was a haven for Walker, who had made several previous visits when, on 17 February 1868, he wrote to his mother:

'I've just returned from a long drive, which we, B.F., Mrs F., and Miss Brown (F's niece) have had, to see Mr Hook, RA. *This is paradise*. If I had but some money! I am half mad with envy and other feelings. There is a beautiful little cottage within a stone's throw of the house Hook has left, with a studio and four or five bedrooms, which I would this day buy if I had money enough (it is £1,200). The situation is perfectly romantic – such a sweep of glorious country! Alas, I could sell *myself* to be doing what I might do here. The cottage has two acres of ground, with beautiful heather, etc. stretching down from it, and altogether I do not think you have any conception of the wondrous beauty of this place. As for the house Hook has left, it is simply splendid; but like the cottage – which he built as a kind of retreat – it is to be sold, not let. I shall stay here as long as I can, and work as much as I can. B. Foster says: "My dear boy, why don't you paint a picture and buy it?" – meaning the cottage. He is most kind and begs me to stay here and work. Gambart is coming to-morrow or Wednesday, and I think I have a subject already. I am very glad I came, and trust that, with Heaven's help, I may now have turned the corner. How you would revel in this place!'

During this visit, Frederick Walker thought that his mother and sister might have returned home from a stay in Brighton and went up to London to greet them. The following extract from a letter is dated 19 February 1868:

73 In the garden at The Hill: house party in Tudor costume (must be dated between 1864–6). From left to right: Elizabeth Brown; Alfred W. Cooper (whom Elizabeth married in 1870); Polly Evans (formerly Brown); Birket Foster; Frances Foster; Lindsay Watson (nephew of Anne Foster) and his wife Katharine; Mrs J. D. Watson and J. D. Watson (seated), brother-in-law of Birket Foster, with Edmund Evans, also seated. From an album in possession of the Glasson family.

'My dears, in case this finds you here to-morrow, know by it that I came up hoping to find you both here, and jolly; and lo, the place is desolate, as you will find it, I fear; but no matter, only a few minutes could I spend with you, in any case, for now it is 8, and the last train leaves Waterloo at 9, and the Foster's carriage has to then meet me at Godalming. However, I cannot help feeling sorry not to have met you once more in the old crib, but let this represent me. . . . This morning was too lovely at the Fosters'. I am doing my own wonderful bedroom window there, with the stained glass, and comfortable recess with cushioned seats – that Fan recollects no doubt – and a figure . . .'[3]

Walker is referring to a previous visit to The Hill, when his sister, Fanny, accompanied him. The picture was exhibited as 'The Bedroom Window' in the 1868 exhibition of the Society of Painters in Water-colours. Another water-colour by Walker which was based on a visit to The Hill was 'The Well-Sinkers' (also exhibited 1868). This shows a woman and a little girl peering into the dark hole of a newly constructed well, with labourers and wheelbarrows and other such navvying touches in evidence. The female figures are shown almost back view, but the woman has a definite look of Fanny Foster about the set of her head and her hairstyle. Marcus Huish recorded that she had told him that Walker kept her and one of the Foster girls out in the pouring rain for two hours while he sketched them in, but as both figures are in summer

74 Ellen Foster (1857-1946), younger daughter of Birket Foster (aged about 12). Water-colour painted at The Hill by Frederick Walker, ARA. Ellen was to marry Lancelot Thompson Glasson in 1886 and the portrait is now in possession of her son's widow, Mrs L. M. Glasson.

dresses this does sound like a mild exaggeration.

Fred Walker wrote another letter to his mother on 23 February:

'I suppose you have at last returned, and have found my letter and explanation.... No news; I am well and happy, and getting on well with my work. It will be finished next week, as early as possible, and another begun, so I can't say anything about coming home, but will come up to see your old faces and show you mine if you like – only say when, and I'll be with you.
[24 February] 'B. Foster wants me to finish the little subject of the workhouse children for him, and at some later time to do an important work for him, for he believes in your boy's work, and has much comforted me in the unconscious signs of respect he shows ... My room here is not the one I occupied before; it is the chief room for visitors, and from it I see the Brighton Downs, and the "Devil's Dyke", 30 miles off, so you know the kind of prospect there is above the beautiful fir trees that enclose the grounds. But I hope you will see it, for I do think you ought to fetch me home from so lovely a place. I have worked pretty hard today and successfully.... Birket Foster and I went for a beautiful walk yesterday morning, finishing up by visiting a little church. In the churchyard they laid poor Lindsay Watson, who first came with the news of my election to the Water-colour Society, and which I remembered as I stood there yesterday.'

Fred. Walker is referring to William Lindsay Watson, eldest son of Mary and James Watson (from whose wedding Birket Foster had received the 'bride cake' 32 years before). W.L. Watson (see Ill. 73) was a frequent visitor to The Hill, but had died in 1866, at the age of 30 while staying at Tigbourne Cottage, after having been married only three years, but leaving two infant daughters. Helen Lindsay Watson, the younger daughter, was to marry Percy Corder, author of *The Life of Robert Spence Watson*.

Walker's letter to his mother continues:

'26 February – I am glad, dear, that you are both pretty comfortable, both of you, and this weather will help Fan surely. Today here is a fine spring one, the downs in the far horizon tinted with gold by the setting sun at this moment. F. and one of the little girls are on the charming lawn playing at bowls and the birds are going like mad ...'

The chatty style of Fred. Walker frequently brings a glimpse of life at The Hill into vivid focus, as if we were watching the scene. On 29 February 1868, he wrote to his married sister, Mary (wife of J.G. Marks, his subsequent biographer):

'I have just received your nice long letter and the neckerchief, which I have put on and mean to wear this evening. This has been an awful day, rain and wind no end – very different from the lovely days ever since I have been here. We have just had dinner and coffee has been brought in; and though I mean to touch upon the water-colour (which is all but finished) I look upon the evening, and indeed all the evenings here, as leisure time, for I have worked very well since coming here, resisting many a temptation to take a jolly walk. I wish I could tell you how dainty the place is, from the delightful little drawing-room we're now in, with its walls covered with water-colours – little gems by old

Hunt, Millais, &c, &c. [see Ills. 58, 65] to the bedroom I occupy, and in which I paint, for the subject is the window, which is in a large recess, with stained glass and diamond shaped panes, and I am doing a woman brushing her hair. It is just the house you would revel in, my Poll. Part of the garden is a gentle slope, with its shrubs and bushes covering the beautiful lawn, on which the blackbirds promenade in the sun of a morning. There are two smaller flat lawns on which we play bowls or croquet; and above, and around down below, plantations of firs and pines, and so many evergreens that one forgets that this is the leafless season; and from my bedroom as I sit on the cushions in the recess, I can see across to the Brighton Downs, and "Devil's Dyke" 30 miles off. Foster is very jolly and kind, with a great sense of humour in a quiet sort of way. He makes me very comfortable and I know he likes my being here, and he admires my work very much; and by the way he asked me to finish the workhouse kids and your kid for him, so you will have me down upon you again. On Thursday evening, I went up to town, as I dare say you know, and took the Missis by surprise, and we had a little bit of dinner together – we three – and then I came back by the last train, the carriage waiting comfortably outside Godalming station for me, as the last train does not go on to Witley... I shall be sorry to leave this place. As you say, there are lots of new ideas and if I could, I'd stay here until the summer. Old Keene shares a cottage with another man named Bridger, close to this. He comes down now and then, and there is a dog at the cottage with a short tail that reminds one of old dottles himself ... Foster is glaring at my picture, which I brought into the room at dusk.'

In 1865, Charles Keene (or 'Old Dottles') had been persuaded by Birket Foster to become the sub-tenant of Tigbourne Cottage, in order that the Fosters would be sure of having a congenial neighbour. Keene had lodgings and a studio in London, but frequently went down to Tigbourne Cottage, where he continued his unconventional style by always sleeping in a hammock. He was to write to a friend:

'The stillness here after London is delicious. The only sound is the ring of the village blacksmith's hammer in the distance or the occasional cluck of a hen, and the wind roars through the trees at night which lulls me pleasantly to sleep.'

On 26 January 1865, he wrote to his friend, Alexander Macdonald:

'... This is a pleasant retreat to fly to for a day or two from the row and turmoil of London, and gives my friends too the opportunity of calling it my "country house" and the pleasure of making me wince by hinting at the wealth that enables me to afford such luxury!
It's a bosky-copsey country, very picturesque and English, with just a suggestion (compared to Scotland) of hills on the horizon (the Hog's Back) but from there being so many trees, when the glass does fall the rain comes down with a vengeance. Last night there was a furious gale, which kept everybody awake but me....
We've a small aristocracy of artists too down here – Birket Foster, Burton, Watson and Jones – and amongst our surroundings there's a good deal of fun to be picked up ... I heard of a Belle of the nearest town remarking of the curious manners and customs of these artists, that

she had actually seen them in Society in evening dress up to the waist, and a velveteen jacket and any-coloured necktie a-top!'[4]

Certainly the rather Bohemian figure of Charles Keene, with his saturnine good looks and wide-awake hat on curly black locks would have an interesting and artistic air. He had a strong objection to carrying any kind of luggage and would present himself as a guest at fashionable houses with only a rucksack slung over his shoulder. Birket Foster's daughter Ellen remembered him taking her on one side, with a twinkling and slightly conspiratorial smile and remarking: 'I say, Nellie, look, I've got three jackets on under my cape ... saves all that packing ...' – but, it also led to occasions when Charles Keene was known to appear wearing an evening jacket with entirely inappropriate trousers. From the early 1860s he would frequently tell friends that he was going 'to run down to Witley' and from that time he was increasingly in the company of Birket Foster. Keene was basically a shy man, but he had an original and amusing way of talking, so that his long recitals of funny incidents were to become legendary entertainment at The Hill. Birket Foster was one of the friends who was always on the lookout for suitable little anecdotes to tell Keene, as possible subjects for his inimitable drawings in *Punch*. One of the most famous of all the humorous drawings by Charles Keene for *Punch* (5 December 1868) was based on an incident that was witnessed by Sir John Gilbert and told to Birket Foster, who thought it might suit Keene and sent him the story: a Glaswegian was heard to say that he found London so

awfu' expensive that he had not been there more than a few hours when 'bang went *saxpence!*' The success of this joke was such that the punch line became an immediate catch phrase and Birket Foster himself was highly amused to hear a flashy young man on Brighton pier calmly informing a barmaid that he was the originator of the joke

75 The Hill: a corner of the drawing room photographed by William Foster about 1880. Below: enlarged detail showing water-colour by Frederick Walker, entitled 'The Chaplain's Daughter'. From an album in possession of Ellen's daughter, Sarah G. A. Glasson.

– and had the original drawing!

As we have seen, Charles Keene and Frederick Walker had been known to each other ever since the days of the Sunday evening gatherings at the Birket Foster home in London, where R.S. Watson remembered meeting these two artists. Both were men who were loyal in their friendships and this characteristic was also true of Birket Foster.

In another letter, written to an acquaintance during the 1868 visit, Walker gives a very vivid idea of just how welcoming The Hill was for guests:

'I am staying with Birket Foster ever since Sunday week, and I shall, I expect, remain a week longer, for I am at work, and am happier here than I have been for a long time ... This place is the most lovely and snug that I ever stayed at; all the horrors of winter, and all discomfort of every kind, seem done away with. I can see 30 miles from my bedroom window, across the most beautiful part of Surrey. The house (which B.F. built himself) is the most perfect; the eye is continually refreshed by good colour.'

On 5 March, Walker wrote the last of his letters to his mother, which relate to this particular visit:

'I shall in all probability be in town to-morrow evening, or Sunday morning, and spend Sunday with you, although I think I had best return here to finish up. Gambart came yesterday, and carried off the work I have done, and I only wished that the other had been ready and so did he ... Thank you, my dear, for the little wallflowers, it is as good as anything can be, and makes me feel that the same sun that gilds this place so wonderfully, does not forget to look upon the place you are in ...'

Freddy Walker left The Hill about a week later. In April, his study of 'The Well-Sinkers' attracted considerable attention at the annual exhibition of the Society of Painters in Water-colours and the work was much praised by that formidable and influential art critic, John Ruskin. *The Art Journal* noted:

'Birket Foster has of late been giving greater prominence to figures, as seen in two compositions, charming as ever, "The Convalescent" and "Snowdrops". The figures are placed in the midst of landscape and cottage-door surroundings with the knowledge, tact and taste for which the painter has been long proverbial. Perhaps for this happy combination "The Convalescent" is unsurpassed.' (For a later version see Ill. 90.)

This subject is one such as might have been conceived by Fred. Walker. It certainly appears that Birket Foster introduced more importance to the figures in his landscape during these years of close friendship with Walker, although his work never purported to be of such narrative emphasis. Birket Foster had a genuine admiration for the work of this artist, but it was the content and spirit of the paintings that attracted him, rather than the originality of technique. The piece which Walker had described in a letter to his sister as 'the workhouse kids and your kid' can be seen hanging in the sitting room of The Hill in Ill. 75. The work was entitled 'The Chaplain's Daughter' and the enlargement shows this water-colour in clearer detail. It will be noticed how effective is Walker's treatment of the group of workhouse children, who have about them a shy wonder and subtle thoughtfulness, as they stare at the figure (modelled by Walker's niece) of the prettily dressed girl, a child of their age and yet so totally of another world. The theme obviously appealed to Birket Foster and one has an insight into his personal attitudes that it should be so. The early teachings of the Society of Friends always remained with him and his kindly manner to all classes of people was certainly in the Quaker tradition of attempting to see 'the light of God which is in every man'. Walker had seen this in the workhouse children and so had Birket Foster.[5]

Notes: Chapter Twelve

1 All extracts in this chapter from letters to Robert Spence are reproduced by permission of Newcastle upon Tyne City Libraries as is the letter from Spence to Birket Foster.

2 From *The Life of Sir William Quiller Orchardson, R.A.* by Hilda Orchardson Gray, Hutchinson, 1930.

3 All appropriate extracts in this chapter from *The Life and Letters of Frederick Walker, A.R.A.* by J. G. Marks, Macmillan and Co., 1896.

4. From *The Life and Letters of Charles Samuel Keene* by George Somes Layard, Sampson Low and Co., 1892.

5 'The Chaplain's Daughter' was sold for £320/5/- in the sale of Birket Foster's pictures at Christie's on 28 April 1894.

13

First visit to Venice and Christmas festivities at The Hill

Frederick Walker and William Orchardson met at The Hill and the two men became friends – no doubt their mutual enthusiasm for angling would be a frequent topic of conversation. It was during the time that Walker was staying with Birket Foster in the spring of 1868 that Orchardson suggested that he should accompany them on a trip to Venice.[1] Walker went by sea for the outward journey and finally reached Venice on 18 May and booked in at the Grand Hotel de l'Europe, from where he wrote to his mother: '... I did think of going round to the hotel where the Fosters must be by this time, but the storm and my aching limbs forbid. This is a wonderful old place, but more of it in my next.'[2]

Birket and Fanny Foster set out on 11 May 1868, accompanied by W.Q. Orchardson and Birket's cousin, Mrs Elizabeth Foster Brown (who was the mother of Polly) with her youngest daughter, Elizabeth. Elizabeth Foster Brown gives a charming account of the early days of this tour in a letter which she wrote to Birket Foster's daughters, Margaret and Ellen, then aged twelve and ten.

'St. Remo – 19th May 1868
My dear Meggy and Ellen,
I think you will be surprised to hear we have not reached Venice yet, as Papa & Mr Orchardson wished to visit some places on the Mediterranean before going there, but we are now in Italy & expect to reach Venice in 3 or 4 days, We had a delightful voyage from Dover to Calais, even Mamma kept well & was able to enjoy walking upon the deck of the steam boat. We went from there to Paris & from Paris to Macon, where there are so many vineyards – then we came to Lyons where silk is made – and from there we had a very beautiful ride amongst olives & figs & vines. We got to Marseilles in time to see the place in the evening & then we had an open carriage & went round by the cliffs & saw such a lovely blue sea & very fine rocks. From Marseilles we came to Nice where we staid over Sunday. In the afternoon all the people promenaded in a square, while a band of music played delightfully. As we drove between Nice and Mentone we saw hedges of roses & geraniums & cactus & such wonderful trees, palms and figs, oranges, lemons, peppers & almonds – the lemon trees are quite as sweet as the oranges – and the air is full of scent – I wish you could have seen the funny dresses & hats the children wore. After we left Mentone we very soon entered Italy & our carriage was stopped for the baggage to be examined, but De Beer manages these things so

cleverly, they never unlocked our boxes; we came along by the sea all day, sometimes almost on the shore & then on high cliffs from which we saw snowy mountains. I think you would have been amused to have seen our party some in blue spectacles and Papa & Mr Orchardson with white veils on their hats & even I wear a hat, the sun is so very hot. Thursday – May 21st. Savona – We are now at a town which is on the Gulf of Genoa – it seems very musical – & the women are walking about in white veils which hang from their heads almost down to the ground. Tomorrow night we reach Genoa & then 2 days railway will bring us to Venice when Mamma hopes to write to you. We shall be very glad to hear you continue to get on well at school. Night before last we saw a great many fireflies – they flash about in a mysterious sort of way – & Papa saw a little girl in the street wearing one as a brooch. Now I must say no more but very dear love from Papa, Mamma Coz. Lizzy & myself. Believe me, Dear M & E your affec. Aunt,
Eliz. Foster Brown.'[3]

Via Genoa and Bologna, the party eventually reached Venice on 25 May. On the following day, Freddy Walker[3] wrote:

'The Fosters and Orchardson are here in this very hotel. Yesterday morning I was coming in to lunch and found the whole party on the steps. They had arrived on Sunday night without my knowing anything of it; the other hotel where they intended putting up was full ... The F's are very jolly and kind, and all's going on first rate...'

The letters of Freddy Walker often seem to reveal a kind of surprised gratitude at finding himself accepted into the Foster circle and there is a certain underlying anxiety, as if he were afraid of doing anything to jeopardise the relationship.

A diary kept by Elizabeth Foster Brown describes days spent in delighted sight-seeing, visits to churches and art galleries and a trip by steamer to Chioggia, about twenty miles away, but always it was the charm of the canals which held the most fascination. It is evident that Birket Foster, Orchardson and Walker were assiduous in attempting to make good use of their time in Venice in spite of the intense daytime heat.

'This morning Birket and Mr Orchardson went off in the gondola, which we have hired during our stay, in search of subjects to paint, whilst our courier took us

76 'A Venetian Gateway'. Water-colour, signed with mono-gram (left). Size: $11\frac{1}{4} \times 8\frac{3}{4}''$ – 28.5 × 22.2 cms.
Photograph: The Leger Galleries, London.

ladies into St Marks and to look at the shops. I am now writing this diary in the gondola which is fastened up to enable Birket to sketch ... Today we have been in the gondola to the Church of the Jesuits, an old disused place, but still splendid. Now and then we stopped, whilst Birket made some sketches, but he found it impossible to do much work, as the heat was so over-powering.'

Walker also writes '... I must tell you the heat is something tremendous, though I still go on with my work, and my picture is going on very well, I think – I haven't let the F's see it ... Well, I've disappeared without saying good-night to the F's, so must go down and do a little cool drink, and so to bed....'

'The Gondola' by Frederick Walker was very success-fully exhibited at the Old Water-colour Society Exhibition in 1869. An illustration of this subject is shown in *The Life and Letters of Frederick Walker*, but a variation of 'The Gondola' was also acquired by Birket Foster. This shows one of the Venetian palaces with W.Q. Orchardson framed

77 '**Burano**', Venice. Water-colour, signed with monogram.
Size: $11\frac{1}{4} \times 8\frac{1}{2}''$ – 28.6 × 21.6 cms.
Photograph: The Leger Galleries, London.

in a window (it is now in possession of Mrs L. M. Glasson); Birket Foster also owned a water-colour drawing by Walker of the Lido, which the latter particularly liked because he considered it 'so Thamesey' and the little streams between the mud 'so lizardy'.

The Foster party was intending to go on to Switzerland and the Alps. On 6 June, Walker wrote:

'I left Venice yesterday morning with the Fosters, and went with them to Verona. We got there about two and spent the afternoon quietly driving about the place ... I took leave of them finally at Bergamo, where they had to change carriages, for they are going to the Lakes, and cross the Alps at St Gothard, and finish up with the Rhine. They were all very sorry to lose me, I think, and I am sure I was to leave them, for they have been most jolly.'

In Verona, on 5 June, Mrs Elizabeth Brown continued her account of the journey:

'It seemed very odd once more to come to a region of cabs, omnibuses, and horses again, after not seeing any for so long ... We passed through Padua and Mantua ... this afternoon we had a drive round the town and saw some of the churches and an amphitheatre, which is considered more perfect than the Coliseum at Rome though not so large. This is the oldest-looking town we have visited, with narrow streets like all Italian towns.'

From Lecco the party sailed on Lake Como to Bellagio and continued from there to Lugano, although not without a hitch. The stamina displayed by the Victorian tourist has to be admired. Elizabeth Brown was then 53, but she hardly ever appears fatigued or discomforted with the travelling, except for a slight dismay when they found on arriving at Menaggio that all the available carriages were booked. Nothing daunted, Fanny Foster, who would be dressed in layers of hooped skirts, set off with Orchardson and young Elizabeth to walk *six* miles over a mountain road to reach the boat for Lugano! Mrs Brown and the burly Birket Foster hesitated and wondered what to do, but were much relieved to be offered a lift in the carriage of an acquaintance. Mrs Brown wrote:

'The road was so hilly that we did not overtake the walkers until they had gone nearly four miles; soon after we had passed them they fortunately met an empty carriage, so we all managed to catch the steamer to Lugano. During the passage another storm came on with torrents of rain, but it now looks like fine weather again. This is a lovely place and a delightful hotel.'

On 14 June, after reaching Lucerne:

'Here we are safely over the St Gothard after a most pleasant journey. The drive from Lugano to Bellinzona, where we slept the night, was very fine, with beautiful views of Lake Maggiore. We started the next morning at 8 a.m. and stopped to rest the horses at Faido, where there is a grand waterfall. We saw it to the best advantage owing to the recent snowfall on the mountains.

Yesterday we reached Airolo, which is about 4000 feet above the sea. The mountains covered with snow towering above the little village are very grand. This morning we left at 7 a.m. and commenced climbing St Gothard at once. We all walked for about two thirds of the way up. During the descent we left our carriage to

walk across Devil's bridge. It was magnificent indeed, the scenery all the way very grand.

We passed through Hospenthal, Armsteg and Altdorf. ... Here we took the steamboat to Lucerne, which we reached in about two hours, all very tired after twelve hours travelling through such exciting scenery. It is so nice to settle down for a quiet Sunday here in such delightful rooms in the most perfect of hotels.'

The trip continued by way of Zürich, Schaffhausen, and Heidelberg, after which there are no more diary entries, but the journey was concluded as the Foster's party went down the Rhine, stopping at Coblenz and Cologne and back to England, by way of Ghent.

On 10 December 1868, Freddy Walker wrote to his brother-in-law:

'I've had to send my flute up to town to be mended, one of the springs broken (servant of course) but, I shall have it to-morrow I expect. I am improving, I think, especially in tone; while here, I seldom practise anything but exercises. We are going to spend the Christmas at Birket Foster's, as perhaps you know. I am not quite certain about Mamma, though I want her to go very much; there'll be so much going on that she won't have time to be desponding. ...'

Christmas festivities at The Hill were on such an enthusiastic scale that one wonders if Mrs Walker was quite suited to this continuous round of celebration and entertainment. Charles Keene was to be one of the large house party and shortly before that Christmas he wrote to Birket Foster's eldest son who was just embarking on what was to be a very successful musical career.

'Dear Myles,
I send you a "screaming" melody that I have lately become acquainted with and am much taken with. It seems to me to be so quaint and characteristic with all its "tipsy jollity", the way in which the tune never swerves from a sort of timorous dependence on the key-note. I think it very funny. It is very peculiarly "Newcastle", so I want you to keep it to yourself till some evening when your father is quietly at work to play it on the piano and note the effect on him. I think it must strike his early recollections and please him. I hope to be down at Christmas.
Yours very sincerely,
Charles S. Keene.'[4]

It will be noticed that Keene refers to Birket Foster working in the drawing room. This was his habit, as he liked to be near his family and would often paint with a board on his knees, by artificial light, with all the talk and laughter of the company about him. The quality of the results he produced by such a method of working are a tribute to the confidence of his basic skill and touch.

Charles Keene duly joined the Christmas house party and later wrote from Tigbourne Cottage to Edwin Edwards on New Year's Day, 1869:

'... I hope you've had a jolly Christmas; and in saying this to you I mean, principally, fine weather for painting, My joviality has been of a more vulgar character, for instance, the pleasant sensation of not being very hard at work after several weeks of "fag", the being in the country, not seeing any newspapers and with no means of knowing what day of the week it is, and therewithal the regular festivities of the season carried on by my friends down here with an old fashioned vehemence that carries you away and fatigues you very effectively. I got down here on the Monday before Christmas Day, and kept quiet and did a little work, and on Christmas Eve the guests came in a body down by the afternoon train, and we all dined at The Hill at six o'clock in the big room.

The fiddle and 'arp came at the same time, and soon after dinner we set 'em to work, and danced until about three in the morning, including supper, which is sine qua non at The Hill whatever time you dine. I had heard from the Chaplain of the King Edward School that they were going to sing "noels" on Christmas morning. The schoolmaster had coached up a choir from among the boys, and I volunteered as a bass, so I was up again at 5.30, and we started at six to sing carols under our friends' windows. Such a sluggard as I may be allowed to boast of this feat. It was pitch dark, so we had to read our parts by the light of our lanterns, and it was very picturesque. The boys, wrapped up in their bed-blankets, were in high spirits, and, ye gods! how they did sing! I shan't forget the sound of those sturdy young trebles in the still morning in a hurry; it was splendid! Everybody was delighted. It was said we were heard a mile off. We had lots of music at The Hill – can't say much for the vocal, but we did our best. Little Walker with his flute, and Long Jones with his violin, and another friend of Foster's with his tenor – it was a perpetual "consort of viols". A general tuning was very effective, and then Cooper used to come out with

"apples, oranges, ginger-beer, bill of the play" – very excellent fooling; and so it went on, breakfast, lunch, dinner, dancing, supper, and then dancing again; a comic song between whiles, followed by a violin concerto. Cooper was very great. It was very funny, one day; when the three instrumentalists were talking serious shop, he took up the violin and played very slowly and laboriously and half out of tune about half a page of the Kreutzer Sonata. On Saturday, we all dressed up in costume, down to the children, and so to dinner and then dancing again; but now the fiddle and 'arp got the best of us; at twelve o'clock they looked at their watches, pleaded religious scruples and gave in! Then there was a comparative lull for a few days, broken only by the fitful scrapings of Jones and Walters in some remote apartment. We flared up again last night, and hailed the new year with the usual ceremonies, and today all the guests have departed and I've come back to my hermitage here. . .'[4]

The part of Fanny Foster has to be admired for the excellence of the domestic arrangements that must have been required in order to give such successful house parties. There is no doubt that Birket Foster genuinely enjoyed seeing all happy about him, but one cannot help wondering if he was not slightly over-compensating for his Plain Quaker background by hosting such very merry celebrations. On Christmas Day, 18 years ago, he had been content to stroll quietly with Anne on Hampstead Heath.

Notes: Chapter Thirteen

1 Birket and Fanny Foster had been to Switzerland in 1865 and in the following year they made a first attempt to see Venice. On that occasion they were accompanied by Polly Brown's sister, Elizabeth and Mr Bridger of Tigbourne Cottage, who acted as a secretary and courier. The journey commenced through Belgium by way of Ghent and Antwerp to Luxembourg, then to Trèves, where they spent three days. The tour continued by way of Coblenz, Mainz, Heidelberg, Strasbourg, and on through the Black Forest to Schaffhausen and Zürich, over the Splügen Pass to Bellagio and Como and then on to Milan. But the outbreak of the Austro-Italian War prevented any further travel and the plan to visit Venice had to be abandoned until 1868.

2 All appropriate letters in this chapter from *The Life and Letters of Frederick Walker, ARA*.

3 Letter from Elizabeth Foster Brown published by permission of Sarah G.A. Glasson, grand-daughter of Birket Foster. De Beer was the personal courier who was engaged to travel with the party. Diary entries from *Birket Foster*, H.M. Cundall, 1906.

4 From *The Life and Letters of Charles Samuel Keene* by George Somes Layard, Sampson Low, 1892.

14

Oil painting, amateur theatricals and tours in England and abroad

'The Hill Witley Surrey
Jan 27th 1869

Dear Robt.,
    I send a cheque for my premium.
        Hoping you are all well
            I am yr. Affec. bro.
                Birket Foster
Vicat Cole ARA!!! It isn't right. Peter Graham should
have had it.'[1]

The crisp asperity of this postscript is the nearest thing
to a sharp remark that one ever finds in the letters of Birket
Foster. Peter Graham was a Scottish painter of landscapes
and coastal scenes, who had leapt to fame with his first
exhibit at the Royal Academy in 1866. He was not elected
ARA until 1877 and RA until 1881.

It was about this time that Birket Foster himself took
up oil painting. Even the most venerable and respected of
water-colourists always had a sense of their works being
slightly over-shadowed by the often massive and highly
colourful paintings that were shown at the Royal Academy,
the Society of British Artists and other such exhibitions.
Birket Foster was no exception and in 1869 he exhibited
an oil painting of 'A Surrey Lane' at the Royal Academy
and was to follow this with exhibits until 1877, but the
medium was one in which he never felt properly at ease.
He recorded: 'From 1869 to 1877 I painted a few pictures
in oil which were exhibited at the Royal Academy but I
found I could not express myself as well in that medium
as I could in Water Colours, so I gave it up.' Birket Foster
also stated that 'The Mussel Gatherers, Isle of Wight' and
'The Pedlar' were two of his most important works in oils
(from information supplied to the Royal Berlin Academy[2]). 'The Girl with the Orange' (Ill. 78) is an attractive
example, although it is to be seen that this is very much a
translation of his water-colour style and that he has not
gained any originality of expression by using a different
medium.

Working in oils can have an effect on an artist's water-
colour painting but in the case of Birket Foster there was
little change. A tendency to produce bigger works and
bolder brushwork can result, but if Birket Foster exhibited
a larger-than-usual piece it was to be remarked upon. In
the 1869 exhibition of the Society of Painters in Water-

colours he showed 'The Meet', which measured $27\frac{3}{4} \times 59\frac{1}{2}''$. The Art Journal commented:

'The place of honour among landscapes has been as-
signed for size and possibly also for merit, to Mr Birket
Foster's highly elaborated picture "The Meet". Yet, we
may be excused for preferring the artist's smaller works.
This composition strikes us as scattered, it seems
chopped up into several distinct subjects, each certainly
charming in itself, yet taken together scarcely proving
satisfactory as a whole. But, of course, we need scarcely
add that this large effort in common with smaller works
shows exquisite manipulation and an absolute command
over detail.'

The Athenaeum of 8 May 1869 (p. 643) was less impressed:

'Mr B. Foster's "River Scene" (no. 291) is one of his
happier pictures – less spotty than has been frequent
with him – and, with a sky which, notwithstanding its
shallowness of effect, treatment and feeling, is pleasant
to look at. In all qualities it is superior to the larger
landscape, which is styled "The Meet" (no. 75) and
differs only in bigness from scores which the painter has
exhibited for many years.'

'The Meet' was illustrated in colour in the Cundall
biography and in monochrome in Lancelot Glasson's
article in the 'Old' Water-colour Society volume. This
horizontal composition showed a Surrey landscape in
autumn, with a group of colourful children on a raised
bank, who are looking down on the hunt as it passes
through the valley below. In spite of the opinion of the
critics, the water-colour appears admirably arranged to
show the subject in full panorama and one feels that Birket
Foster was justified in his use of a large paper and was in
no way doing this in an attempt to create a more important
impression. At this time, many of his fellow water-colourists were being positively induced to do just that by the
policy of the Water-colour Society which offered an annual
premium to several members if they would execute a larger
than usual work for exhibition. The results were often
mere enlargements, which lost both in detail and essential
atmosphere, but Birket Foster was never influenced into
this mistaken trend and much of the fascination and charm
of his handling of the medium was due to the fact that he
kept his dainty treatment on a scale that exactly suited his
particular style.

In May 1869, Birket Foster set off with his son, Myles
and his friend, Alfred Cooper, to visit Belgium, Holland

78 'The Girl with the Orange'. Oil on canvas, signed with
monogram. Size: $38\frac{3}{4} \times 59\frac{1}{4}''$ – 98.5 × 150.5 cms.
Collection: City of Bristol Museum and Art Gallery.

and the Rhine. He had been commissioned by E. Moxon and Co. to illustrate two volumes of poems by Thomas Hood and the journey commenced via Ostend, where Hood had lived for a number of years. This trip included visits to Bruges, Ghent and Antwerp, with excursions to The Hague, Amsterdam and other towns in Holland and afterwards up the Rhine to Coblenz. The first volume of *Poems of Thomas Hood* illustrated by Birket Foster was published in 1871. This and the companion volume (1872) are the only examples of any major book illustration by Foster, after his decision to give up drawing for the engravers (excepting *Pictures of English Landscape*). Both the Hood volumes were engraved by William Miller of Edinburgh, who was very nearly eighty when he undertook this last commission, which he called 'a work after my own heart'. Two of the blocks used in the illustration of these poems by Hood had originally been drawn by Birket Foster in the early 1850s as illustrations for Tennyson's 'Break, Break' and 'The Reapers'. Moxon had intended that Birket Foster should illustrate all the poems of Tennyson, but differences arose between Moxon and Tennyson over copyrights and this particular project was shelved. Each volume of the Hood poems is illustrated with 23 delicate little black-and-white vignettes, in which the fineness of line and minute cross-hatched strokes are a remarkable achievement on the part of Miller. The actual measurement of each drawing is an average of about $2\frac{1}{2} \times 3\frac{1}{2}''$, but each engraving is presented on the large page size of $8\frac{1}{2} \times 10\frac{3}{4}''$. The engravings have been printed onto very fine paper and laid down with exceptional skill, so as to be almost imperceptible from an embossing of the page. Each volume contains some attractive topographical subjects, full of careful observation of architecture and detail e.g. a quayside scene in Ghent (Vol. I) and some rather more homely studies of Margate and Hastings in Vol. 2. The latter subjects are obviously based on the sketches which Birket Foster did for the early 'Watering Places of England' series in *The Illustrated London News*. Hood's Poems make for a handsome pair of books, with cloth covers blocked in gold (1) and gold and some colour (2), designed by John Leighton.

It was during 1869 that Birket Foster became involved in a local dispute – one of the few times in which he entered into such matters. In 1869, it was proposed that St Mary's Parish Church, Chiddingfold (about two and a half miles from Witley) should be renovated. Plans for this restoration were drawn up by Henry Woodyer, an architect much admired for his buildings in the Modern Gothic style. Birket Foster was not a natural protester or a man with any wish to become involved in local public affairs, but the alteration to Chiddingfold Church was for him an emotive issue. The signature has become detached from a letter, dated 15 June 1869, addressed from 'Fernside', Witley (home of John Harrison Foster) to the Rev. L.M. Humbert, Vicar of Chiddingfold:

'My dear Sir,
    I have asked Mr Birket Foster's opinion of the intended alterations at Chiddingfold Church; he says "do not touch the tower, it will quite spoil it – there are so very few like it now left". The rumour that reached you respecting the matter was quite correct – *all* the artists in the neighbourhood are united in their protestations that its picturesque character will be gone if the tower be at all altered. I only wish you could have sooner been made acquainted with their opinion, for I know you

would not willingly rob this lovely district of one atom of its attractiveness. Some of the lookers-on are quite *unhappy* about it, but as it is a question of accommodation for the parishioners I fear you will not be able to give artistic reasons their full weight. Mr Foster told me to tell you that his name [J.H.F.] might be added to your list for £20 – perhaps Mr B.F. might be induced to give you something too, if you do not spoil the structure in his idea of it. Believe me, etc.'

Two days later, Birket Foster himself writes to the Rev. Humbert:

'On behalf of the artists I write to say that we do hope if it is possible that the tower of Chiddingfold Church may remain as it is. It is one of the most picturesque towers in the country (though not perhaps very old). It has been our admiration and pride for so long that the prospect of having it spoilt is a source of great distress to us. I am, Dear Sir, etc.'

It is interesting to note that the sensibilities of Birket Foster were offended on purely aesthetic grounds. His letter shows that he had no real knowledge of the history of the building, although his efforts to prevent alteration were very determined. On 7 July, he informed the Rev. Humbert that he had taken an eminent architect to see the church and now enclosed his opinions on the subject (as written in a letter to Birket Foster). The architect in question was John Stevenson, a founder member of the Society for the Protection of Ancient Buildings. His long exposition fully supported the view of Birket Foster and would be very much in accord with the standpoint of modern preservationists. One reference gives a telling idea of what Henry Woodyer thought of Birket Foster and his fellow artists. Stephenson writes to refute this: '... I think his argument that architects would not think of interfering with painters works – so they should not interfere with architects is not to the point ...'

The Rev. Humbert duly forwarded Stephenson's viewpoint to Woodyer, who was not impressed and came back sharply with a sanctimonious and somewhat tetchy reply, which included the comment: '... do not let us think of our Churches as if things of the past, but of the present for all of God's people to His Honour ... not moss grown models for painters to work into ideal landscapes ...'

The tower of Chiddingfold Church appears little changed from pre-1869. Receipts and expenditure for the restoration and enlargement of the building show that John Harrison Foster honoured his promised £20, but Birket Foster did *not* contribute. Detailed records of the specifications for the work are deposited among parish records in the Guildford Muniment Room, as are the above letters, with many others from Henry Woodyer.[3]

Birket Foster and his brother, J.H. Foster, were personal friends of Rev. John Chandler, Vicar of Witley, who had some part in the compilation of *Hymns Ancient and Modern*. Photographs of him and his family are included in those taken by Willie Foster, as well as groups of Bible Class lads in billycock hats and the 'Workus' men enjoying an outing on the Vicarage lawn. The grounds of The Hill were sometimes used for local fetes and other charity events and no doubt Fanny Foster would grace these with an elegant presence.[4]

John Harrison Foster (1818–1905) had built 'Fernside' in 1862. This large residence in a fine shelter of trees was near to 'The Heights', home of the novelist George Eliot.[5]

J.H. Foster had a more overt character than Birket Foster and took a very prominent part in local affairs. He and his brother Dodshon had resigned from the Society of Friends in 1839 and from that time John H. Foster had been a particularly devout and committed member of the Church of England. He was an outstanding benefactor in the Witley area and among his donations was £2,000 for the erection of a Village Institute in 1883 and the responsibility for the total cost of the complete restoration of Witley Parish Church in 1889, as well as additions and improvements before and after this date. After his death, it became known that he had been the anonymous donor of £6,000 for the installation of the organ in Peterborough Cathedral as well as many other acts of generosity. Birket Foster appears as a frequent, but rather more modest public subscriber, although one piece of local restoration in which he actively participated is somewhat unexpected. In 1870, Elizabeth Brown (sister of Polly) married Alfred W. Cooper, son of Alfred Cooper, RA. About 1875, Birket Foster and the former re-painted the inn sign of The White Hart, Witley. This oil painting on panel is now in the Victoria and Albert Museum, but a photograph of it was reproduced on p. 33 of *Inn-Signia* (Whitbread and Co. Ltd, produced by Adprint - 1948).

On 27 July 1869, shortly after the contretemps over Chiddingfold Church, Birket Foster wrote to his cousin:

'My dear Robert,
I enclose cheque for premium £56-11-9.
What weather! Our grass has departed altogether for the present.
I am just off for a few days sketching with Fanny and the boys. I had the pleasure of dining with the Lord Mayor the other day and meeting everybody.
Hoping you are all well
I am affectionately yours,
Birket Foster.'

It would appear that this sketching tour must have been one during which they visited on their way Ely, Grantham, Lincoln, York and Durham. They stayed for a few days in North Shields and then went on to Melrose, Abbotsford and Edinburgh. At Lanark, Birket Foster painted the Falls of Clyde and afterwards sketched Dunblane Cathedral. At Pitlochry, he converted a cottage into a temporary studio and while there made a large water-colour of the Falls of Tummel - a frequent subject. The return trip was made through the picturesque scenery of the Trossachs.

'The Hill, Witley
July 25th 1870
My dear Robt.,
I enclose a cheque for my premium. The heat is fearful. We are all off to the Thames at Eton. I have taken a small house that was formerly Sir Henry Wottons and where Iz. Walton used to stay. We take up our abode on Friday next.
With love to you all
I am your affec. bro.
Birket Foster.'

An engraving by J.H. Engleheart has been preserved in the Foster family, showing a pleasant house by the river, painted in 1841 by W. Smith, with the print being titled 'Black Potts - Sir Henry Wotton's in 1639, frequently visited by Izaac Walton'. H.M. Cundall states that Birket Foster stayed at 'Black Pots' (*sic*) as if it were a house and gives the location as almost on an island below Windsor

railway bridge. Black Potts applies to a point on the north bank of the Thames, about a quarter of a mile downstream from Eton College, where a small stream marks the boundary between Eton and Datchet. The island close to the bank is called Black Potts Ait or Eyot. Sir Henry Wotton did indeed build some kind of structure here for the benefit of his angling friends. This is variously described as a fish-lodge and a cottage (later occupied by Verrio, the ceiling painter). Another source attributes a second building (of the summer-house type) to Verrio. Both structures have now quite vanished.[6] A sketch by Fred. Walker captioned 'The Island of Black Pots' (*sic*) is reproduced in the Cundall biography and shows a jokey representation of the black-bearded Robinson Crusoe-like figure of Birket Foster sitting under an umbrella, sketching on the island where there is an undoubted house. Walker sent this sketch in a letter to Myles Birket Foster, in which he wrote: 'Your description of your own favoured isle is indeed refreshing, especially that referring to the number of crabs caught by certain members of your family ...'. In the foreground of the sketch are two young girls in dire boating straits, with their legs in the air, while further down stream a sandcastle flag flies over a toy Windsor Castle.

Birket Foster must certainly have been staying in the house depicted in the Engleheart engraving and is known to have returned to the Black Potts area several times and sketched on the Thames and in the surrounding countryside (Ill. 79).

'41 Marine Parade, Brighton
Winter Weather again. I am hard at work for the Exhibitions [26 January 1871].'

Comments in letters to Robert Spence show that Birket Foster was often in a state of anxiety about the sheer volume of work in hand. So much was commissioned or literally bought from the brush by dealers that Birket Foster sometimes found it difficult to reserve sufficient examples to have on public view. His membership of the Society of Painters in Water-colours obviously meant a great deal to Birket Foster and he gave thought and time to his annual exhibits, but he was not on the exhibiting circuit in the manner of many of his contemporaries. For instance, an unsold picture exhibited at the British Institution by a member of the Williams Family would often be forwarded to such displays as the Norfolk and Norwich Association for the Promotion of Fine Arts in order to see if it might find a provincial buyer. Birket Foster did not need the bother of exhibiting in the provinces. The Royal Liverpool Academy was a very popular exhibition to which many of the well-known names frequently contributed, but the catalogues record only four exhibits by Birket Foster: no. 110 - 'Sunrise' and no. 126 - 'Sunset' exhibited in 1864; and 'Highland Cottages' and 'Barbogle Castle' - nos 155-6 - exhibited in 1867 (both pictures were on loan from a private collection).

The Art Journal praised the works by Birket Foster in the 1870 exhibition of the Society of Painters in Water-colours: 'Mr Foster contributes sparkling gems, such as 'The Greta at Rokeby (48)' and 'Houses at Eton' (79). The execution is far too clean and neat for sketches outdoors; the presumption becomes strong that these are studio works.' And in an 1871 review: 'Mr Birket Foster's drawings are up to accustomed excellence; indeed in treatment of figures set in landscape or by cottage door, he has never

79 'Eton'. Water-colour, signed with monogram (right).
Photograph: Frost and Reed Ltd, London.

80 **'Return of the Lifeboat with St Michael's Mount in the distance'.** Water-colour and pencil, heightened with white, signed with monogram (right). Size: 8 × 11½" – 20.3 × 29.2 cms. *Collection: Bedfordshire Borough Council, The Cecil Higgins Art Gallery, Bedford.*

surpassed "Rabbits" (235) and "River Scene with Sheep" (243)'.

Robert Spence had obviously spoken for two water-colours entitled 'Newcastle from the Windmill Hill, Gateshead' and 'Newcastle and the Tyne from Crawhall's Ropery'. ('£35 each is what I should charge a dealer. I should like to have them for the Winter Exhibition if you have no objection' – 4 October 1871.) 'Your cheque for £70 has arrived safely. I am very much obliged for it. I am glad you have got the Newcastle drawings, for those who have seen them like them very much. I will be sure to attend to your instructions about the framing, &c.' – 6 October 1871.

His exhibits shown in the 1872 exhibition of the Water-colour Society included important works on the Newcastle theme, which must have been inspired by the commissions that he had executed for Robert Spence. *The Art Journal* commented:

> 'Those by Birket Foster are numerous, considering the labour bestowed upon them. The subjects vary from scenes of immense complication, as "Newcastle from Gateshead Fell", "Newcastle and the River Tyne" (192) and "The Falls of Tummel" (162) to the very modest rural sites, rendered attractive by the neatness of their dressing.'

It was in 1871 that the Christmas festivities at The Hill included the first of a long series of amateur theatricals. These were held in the billiard room (Ill. 68) where a good stage was constructed at one end.

On 5 December 1871, Frederick Walker wrote to A.S. Stevenson: '... the Fosters intend to have another jollification at Xmas, and, entre nous, something on a complete scale in the theatrical line is contemplated, into which your humble servant is drifting.' (*Life and Letters of Frederick Walker*.) The artist, Robert Dudley, was another close friend of Birket Foster and particularly associated with the organisation of these plays. Dudley, who lived in London, was a frequent Christmas guest at The Hill with his family (see Ill. 97). He was a painter and illustrator of only moderate ability, but one of his best achievements was *The Wedding at Windsor*, published by Day and Son, which celebrated the marriage of the Prince of Wales (1863) in a folio of very fine chromolithographs, which were all either from drawings by Dudley or those under his supervision, in illustration of a text by W.H. Russell, who was war correspondent of *The Times*. This was followed by another collaboration with Russell in producing *The Atlantic Telegraph* (1866) – also published by Day and Son. As well as illustrating this elaborate volume, Robert Dudley also designed the binding and others of this period. He appears as something of a jack-of-all-art-trades, who seems to have found yet another interest in the production of amateur theatricals. The first of the plays that he produced at The Hill was called 'Whitebait at Greenwich' and the characters were played by Robert Dudley and Myles Birket Foster (now 20 years old) with Fanny Foster and her brother, J.D. Watson. Birket Foster painted much of the scenery for these theatricals, but did not use the usual distemper type paint, as he felt that he did not understand the effects and so worked with his normal water-colours. An assistant at Newman's colour shop is said to have been utterly astonished on receiving an order from Birket Foster for a vast quantity of his usual medium, obviously wondering how an artist who produced such delicate little water-colour drawings could need so many tubes of colour.

In 1872, Birket Foster and Walker worked hard on the scenery for 'Fish out of Water' and 'The Birthplace of Podgers'. Freddy Walker took the part of Mr Erasmus Maresnest – a Literary Enthusiast, in the first play and appears to have been one of those people who can overcome their natural shyness when assuming another character. Not so Birket Foster. He liked to dress up in costume and delighted in all the excitement and fun of the preparations for these plays, but none but the cast lists show him as a performer. Freddy Walker threw himself into the spirit of these somewhat exhausting Christmasses at The Hill, but on 2 January 1873, he is obviously somewhat overdone by all the effort. '... I am feeling the result of last week a good deal today, slightly languid and low – shall be alright in a day or so, but wonder that I feel so well, considering how little rest I had – won't do it again in a hurry' (*Life and Letters of Frederick Walker*). He had painted a backcloth for the library scene in 'Fish out of Water' and had locked himself into the billiard room while doing it. He was there all day and refused all entreaties to rest or to allow anyone to come in and rehearse. Finally, just before dinner, the door was flung open and Fred. Walker emerged, a grimy, tired little figure, covered in distemper from head to foot. Behind him could be glimpsed a superb piece of scenery. This showed a magnificent fireplace, with a fine portrait of Charles II above it. Shelves appeared to be filled with books in rich bindings and over a doorway there was a bust of Minerva, realistically dusty in places, as if just missed by the housemaid's brush.

But, on 4 January, Frederick Walker (with very good reason) wrote to a friend: 'I have just returned in a perfectly *battered* condition, from a terrible bout of private theatricals and scene painting ...'.

One of the most successful of the backcloths produced by Birket Foster was a Venetian scene, which was afterwards damaged while being rolled up, but was later stretched into a frame, re-touched and sold to Vokins, the dealer, from whom it was purchased by a nobleman who hung it on his staircase. The Foster family particularly remembered the scenery for 'A Chimney Corner' which Birket Foster painted and which was described thus:

> 'It was a scene in which a small grocer's shop is seen through the parlour door and was a marvellous piece of painting done on stretched brown paper with water-colour. The shop contained a medley of candles, pickles, cheese, herrings, tea, coffee, treacle, sweets, etc. broadly treated and very effective; a piece of work that he really enjoyed. Of this same sort of work may be mentioned a small panorama painted for his children of views picked here and there – many of them moonlights lighted from the back and one ship on fire (lighted in the same way) that was extraordinarily effective. The whole was mounted on a small stage and accompanied by appropriate music and an amusing account of the views given by Alfred Cooper, son of the animal painter, A. Cooper

81 'Shrine at the entrance of the courtyard of the Ducal Palace, Venice'. Water-colour, signed with monogram. Size: 11 × 8" – 27.9 × 20.2 cms. Exhibited: Birket Foster Centenary Loan Exhibition, Laing Art Gallery, 1925. Collection: Mrs Richard Talbot, great-grand-daughter of Charles Seely, MP, who commissioned 50 water-colours of Venice from Birket Foster, including this work.

82 'Pulpit in the Church of St Mark'. Water-colour, signed with monogram. Size: 8¼ × 12¼" - 21 × 31.1 cms. Exhibited: Birket Foster Centenary Exhibition, Laing Art Gallery, Newcastle upon Tyne, 1925.
Photograph: Moss Galleries, London.

RA. The idea was a novel one and seemed to give great pleasure to the party of friends who were asked to see it.' (From biographical details in possession of the Glasson family.)

Six complete sets of scenery, on 93 supports, were sold at Lot 53 at Christie's, 28 April 1894 - £52/10/-. These were as follows: Library scene from 'Fish out of Water' by Fred. Walker; 'Cool as Cucumber' - an interior by Birket Foster; 'Only a Halfpenny' - a hall, with staircase by Birket Foster; 'The Crooked Billet Inn' - cottage interior by Birket Foster; 'The Chimney Corner' - a chandler's parlour by Birket Foster; 'Our Wife' - Pomaret's shop at Amiens by Birket Foster.

Theatricals were to be a feature of Christmas at The Hill for eight consecutive years. Each performance was given for two nights and on one of these many of the villagers and all the employees of the Fosters received personal invitations to attend, which they did in enthusiastic numbers. Robert Dudley heads the cast list throughout, but new names appear over the years, e.g. Alfred Cooper, Margaret and Ellen Foster, with their brother, William, also Alice Foster, one of the daughters of Birket Foster's brother, John Harrison Foster. After 1878, there was a gap of six years and then a renewal, with Robert Dudley again at the head of the cast, with his son, the rather charmingly named Guildford Dudley (who had a genuine talent for acting) and Miss C.M. Chandler, one of the daughters of the local vicar. But one senses that the

old enthusiasm had gone and that Christmas at The Hill gradually became an altogether more staid celebration.

Birket Foster frequently spent some time in Brighton during the winter months and in 1873 his brother Dodshon and his sister Mary and her family were also there. In a letter written on 14 November he acknowledges the sum of £85 received from Robert Spence for two further drawings, which are recorded on the receipt as 'Black Gate, Newcastle' (£50) and 'A Street by Moonlight' (£35). Early in 1874 Birket Foster had been 'very busy with my pictures for the R.A. and the Watercolour and shall have a struggle to get them done'. There is rather a delightful fatherly reference to his daughters in that year, but still the letters to Robert Spence have a main theme of constant preoccupation with work. Margaret and Ellen must then have been either staying with the Spences or other relations in North Shields - 'I hope you are all well and that Meggie and Ellen are not being a nuisance in the district. We have good weather now and am enjoying it. I had a grand trip to Italy and worked very hard. I am now busy working on my sketches' (25 July 1874).

The mention here by Birket Foster of his trip to Italy is of particular significance, as it was connected with the largest single commission that he ever received. Some years previously, he had agreed to execute 50 watercolours of Venice (for a fee of £5,000) to the commission of Charles Seely, a wealthy Lincoln corn merchant, who was Member of Parliament for that city. Charles Seely had been used to buying pictures from Agnew's and it appears that he was so struck with one of Birket Foster's Venetian water-colours that had been handled by the firm that he decided to give the artist this exceptionally large private commission. The Venetian subjects in the Seely series are very far removed in style from the early vignettes of forest and field. It is perhaps the absence of living greenery that

136

makes it seem that Birket Foster must always be not quite in his element in such scenes. These water-colours show marble columns on massive, intricately decorated façades and minutely observed frescoes, the precise curve of gondolas and bridges, tall, straight lines of bell towers and complicated mosaic patterns in pavements. The results can have a look of a stage set with beautifully arranged tableaux placed against a static background. Some of the architectural detail has been wrought with such absolute concentration on accuracy that the effect suggests that some of the buildings may have been painted from photographs, but with the general activity and figures based on sketches which Birket Foster did on the spot. These water-colours are pictures of places and give the impression that the artist was very intelligently interested in the detail and otherness of the scene, but was not moved by it as he would have been by a cottage nestling in a field of elm trees.

The work entailed visits by Birket Foster to Italy almost every year from about 1871, but in compiling an outline of his tours abroad, Birket Foster himself did not seem quite certain of just how many times he had been to Venice in the course of the execution of these 50 water-colours. It should be noted that in a letter to Robert Spence, dated 11 December 1876, he writes: '... I am nearly completing my set of 50 Venice drawings ...' and on 29 January 1877: '... I am very busy now finishing Venice', which gives a near reference for the final date of the commission. It has to be remembered that this had to be worked in with all the other projects that Birket Foster had in hand. These Venetian studies had a definite influence on the general style of Birket Foster. He was induced to show a mass of small figures to represent crowd scenes in relation to the size of the architecture, and began to introduce these into his other compositions which were leading towards a much more topographical presentation of subject. (For further information on the Seely collection, see Appendix 4, pp. 200-1.)

Birket Foster was certainly in Italy again in 1875. He was accompanied by his second son, William, and his friend, Robert Dudley. It was on this trip that Birket Foster had yet another serious carriage accident, an event to which he seemed to be rather prone. It is recorded in the family memoirs:

'They crossed to Menaggio and took a carriage towards Lugano being told to change into one of the carriages returning after taking travellers to the lake, as it would be a better one. At a little village at the top of the climb out of Menaggio a return carriage was met and a change effected. A few minutes afterwards on beginning the descent, the driver, who was drunk (his pour boire had been too generous) did not put on the brake properly, the pace became too fast, the horses fell, scrambled up again and ran away. A fearful minute or two down horrid zig-zags with a high wall on one side and a deep drop onto the vine stakes on the other. A hopelessly sharp turn on ahead came in sight and just before it there was a crash. The carriage was smashed to pieces and Birket Foster and his party were thrown violently into the road. Birket Foster and Robert Dudley were cut about the face and knees, but Willie Foster fell sitting on his bowler hat which had tumbled off. As it was a good one it made an excellent buffer but the first thing that Birket Foster saw on pulling himself together was the driver, all apologies, bowing to him with B.F.'s hat which he had already appropriated.'

It is not surprising that after this episode all three men were ordered a week's rest by an English doctor who was staying nearby. However, one can sense from the relating of the story how it was subsequently to become a much-told amusing incident in the family, even if it could have led to premature obituary notices for Birket Foster.

Notes: Chapter Fourteen
1 All extracts in this chapter from letters to Robert Spence are published by permission of Newcastle upon Tyne City Libraries.
2 Extract from material supplied by Birket Foster to the Royal Berlin Academy reproduced by permission of Prof. Walter Huder, Archiv der Preussischen Akademie der Künste, Berlin.
3 Letters and information with reference to Chiddingfold Church by permission of the Guildford Muniment Room, Castle Arch, Guildford and information from local accounts by permission of the Vicar and Churchwardens of St Mary's, Chiddingfold.
4 The Witley Parish Magazine for January 1891 notes: 'Mrs

Birket Foster has kindly offered to give the Sunday School their treat this year. The form it will take is a secret; the secret will probably be revealed on the evening of January 9th' – the event turned out to be a feast in the schoolroom, duly described in the February issue. Information from the Guildford Muniment Room.
5 Birket Foster designed a title page for *Middlemarch*; the original drawing was sold at Christie's on 9 February 1923.
6 Information with reference to the house on Black Potts Ait from C.A.W. Jones, Divisional Reference Librarian, N.E. Berks.

15

Death of Fred. Walker, commissions for Robert Spence and the publication of *Brittany*

In the summer of 1875, Birket Foster and his family were staying at the White Hart at Windsor and it was from there that he sent a letter to his old friend Edmund Evans, very much in the way that one might write to an obliging brother:

> 'The White Hart, Windsor
> Sat. 17th. July 1875.
>
> My dear Ned,
>
> Will you kindly send by Monday evening's post 4 five pound notes for the enclosed cheque addressed in a registered letter to me at the Randolph Hotel, Oxford. We are going to extend our tour as we have been so unfortunate in our weather so far – and I shall want more funds – I am sorry to be so troublesome but I am sure you won't mind.
>
> In spite of the wet we are enjoying ourselves very much. We will give you a detailed acct. when we get home.
>
> Hoping you are all well
> Believe me yours,
> Birket Foster.'[1]

They had returned home by 29 July and Birket Foster gives Robert Spence some details of this holiday in the following letter, which has a sad postscript:

> 'The Hill, Witley
> 29th July 1875.
>
> Dear Robt.,
>
> I send a cheque for my premium. We have just returned from a driving trip – we have had some rain, but some fine weather. We went to Selborne, Basingstoke, Old Basing, Stratfield Saye, Eversley, where poor Kingsley is buried – Bramshill House (a splendid specimen) – then on to Windsor from there to Wallingford & Oxford & from there to Banbury and Stratford on Avon – back by Chipping Norton and Woodstock – Oxford again and then to Reading and Farnham home. There is a good deal of the picturesque left in England yet.
>
> Hoping you are all well. With love from us all.
> Your affec. bro.,
> Birket Foster
> I feel the loss of my dear friend Fred. Walker very much.'[2]

Frederick Walker had been ill with tuberculosis for some time, but had died rather suddenly on 4 June 1875, at the age of 35, while on holiday in Scotland. *The Times*

obituary wrote of 'Frederick Walker, ARA, a young painter of rare genius, cut off prematurely in the springtime of his powers'. Although he was 15 years younger than Birket Foster, one senses the depth of the bond between these two artists, who shared the same gentle nature and quiet love of beauty in the countryside and in painting. A portrait plaque to the memory of Frederick Walker was erected in the church at Cookham-on-Thames, where he is buried.

At the end of 1875, Birket Foster was attempting to fulfil yet another commission for Robert Spence. A less conscientious man would probably have worked up the subjects entirely from photographs, but Birket Foster had to see the exact locations for himself. It is totally unfair to equate the work of this artist only with repetitions of composite subjects e.g. children in flowery fields, cottagers in their gardens etc., because there are so many varied examples of work that is topographically exact and produced only once to a specific commission or during the course of a visit to a scene that took his eye. He wrote to Robert Spence:

> '28 Marine Parade, Brighton
> Nov. 1st 1875.
>
> My dear Robert,
>
> Your letter has been forwarded to me here & there has been unfortunately some delay in answering. Nothing (but ill health) shall stand in the way of my doing the sketches of Croydon for you. I have thought very much of you in your trouble. I have thought of writing but there is nothing one can say – but I have thought much of you and felt much for you. I am suffering from a bad cold now, but in a day or two before the foliage is gone I will go to Croydon and do my best.
>
> With dear love to you both,
> I am your affec. brother,
> Birket Foster.'

The trouble that Birket Foster mentions in this letter was the death at the age of 32 of Sarah Thompson, eldest married daughter of Robert Spence. A fortnight later he again writes from Brighton:

> '28 Marine Parade, Brighton.
> 15th November 1875.
>
> My dear Robert,
>
> I went over to Croydon unfortunately before I recd. your second letter & missed I fear the point you suggest over the bridge – but got into the field close by & I send

a sketch of what might be done with it from there &
also another sketch (very rough) of the Park & trees &
a pencil scribble of the view outside the churchyard just
where the road branches off to the old [?] Croydon
station – the subject would have to be a tall one like the
sketch to get in the spire.

I fancy I could make a good drawing of Croydon like
the more finished sketch if that was liked but I leave it
entirely to you of course – I could also finish the porch
sketch if you like. Write me what you think and send
the sketches back, unless you like to keep the general
view (little as it is). I thought it better to send them as
I shall know better what I am about when I hear from
you. A terrible day here yesterday. Sea very grand.
    With love
        Your affec. bro.
            Birket Foster.'

83 'Blackberries'. Water-colour, signed with monogram
(right). Size: $7\frac{1}{8} \times 5\frac{1}{2}''$ – 18.1 × 14 cms.
*Collection: Merseyside County Council, Walker Art Gallery,
Liverpool.*

'From The Hill
Decr. 16th 1875

My dear Robert,
    I have completed the 3 small drawings & as I thought
you might like to have them I ordered the frames which
are to be ready on Saturday – so you may look for
the case about Monday. May I leave the other one (the
large one) till after the Exhibitions have taken in as I
have so very much to do – things long promised. If I
may I will contrive to see Croydon again which will be
an advantage. I hope you will like those I now send. I
told Foord and Dickinson to put the frames down to

139

your account as you desired – my charge for the three will be £100. I mention this as I know you will want to know & it saves letter writing – I would rather make a drawing than write a letter.

With love from us all,
Yours affec. brother,
Birket Foster.
We returned on Monday from Brighton – the country is very nice but very cold after a warm town.'

It is interesting to note the details of these pictures in a receipt which Birket Foster sent on 22 December 1875: 'Recd. of Robert Spence the sum of one hundred pounds for three Water Colour drawings of "General view of Croydon – sunset" – "St Peters, Church from road to South Croydon railway" & "The Porch and churchyard, St Peters, Croydon".'

Early 1876 finds Birket Foster deciding to finish the commission for Robert Spence, rather than wait until after the spring exhibitions ('I am doing your other Croydon as it seems a shame to keep you waiting so long – I shall be able to do it by the end of next week I hope' – 28 January 1876).

A few days later, Birket Foster writes:

'I have sent the drawing to Foord and Dickinson and it will be put in its frame and sent to you on Monday or Tuesday morning. The price will be £70. I made the drawing larger than your size as I thought it would be better. I hope it will arrive safely and that you will like it ... Threatening snow which I don't like as it spoils the light for painting.'

The receipt for payment for this picture describes it as Croydon (rainbow) and is dated 11 February 1876. The accompanying letter has a note of relief:

'I am much obliged to you for the cheque for which I give a receipt on the other side. I was in London for two days when your letter came so I am late in replying. I have just received your second and am so pleased to find you like the drawing. I can assure you I had the greatest pleasure in doing them all for you ...'

As well as always being invited to The Hill for Christmas, there was another visit by Charles Keene that had become part of the Foster family tradition. On 23 April 1875, Keene wrote to his friend Joseph Crawhall of Newcastle (who supplied many of the ideas for his *Punch* drawings and of Crawhall's Ropery):

'... I went down to Witley on the 12th, purposely to hear the nightingales; they have arrived for the last four years on the 13th, at about 11pm. This year they had not come on the 15th! and I had to come to town the next morning – a backwardness unknown to the oldest inhabitant ...'[3]

In all the years that Birket Foster was at Witley, Charles Keene always tried to be there in order to hear the first nightingales. But it was in 1876 while Charles Keene was on holiday in France that the lease of Tigbourne Cottage expired and Birket Foster no longer held the main tenancy. The owner placed the property on the market and this was bought by W.H. Hammond Jones, a minor artist, who had shared the cottage with Keene at intervals. Keene was decidedly upset and felt that a deal had been done behind his back, with the result that he never set foot in Tigbourne Cottage again, but continued to visit The Hill and the

home of his friend J.M. Stewart, a retired bank official, who lived in Witley.

Sometimes it seems that Birket Foster could have spared himself unnecessary work. In a postscript to his usual summer letter to Robert Spence, enclosing the insurance premium, he notes: 'I have undertaken to furnish a drawing for the "Pictorial Europe" of the Bass Rock so I shall be running past you some time in August' (25 July 1876).

Birket Foster could have made a very good living by producing nothing but repeaters and one has to admire his sustained enthusiasm for new subjects and projects. On 11 December 1876, he was once again in Brighton and wrote to Robert Spence from:

'5 Royal Crescent,
My dear Robert,
I wish to ask if you will kindly help me in a small matter which has been on my mind for some time – I am nearly completing my set of 50 Venice drawings and am desirous of doing if all be well a series of 25 of the Thames from its source to the sea – and also a set of 12 of the Tyne – I am ashamed to say that I know nothing of the source of my native river & this brings me to the subject of my letter. Can you give me any information as to the most paintable subjects high up – I don't mean the North Tyne, but the Tyne proper – I suppose the North Tyne is not the river proper. If I recollect the river goes on higher up than Hexham – but where it comes from – or whether the scenery is interesting – I am quite ignorant.

I will give a list of the subjects I want to do and leave 3 blank spaces to be filled in – and I know no one better to suggest than you.'

At this point, Birket Foster has listed the following as already in his sketch books: Tynemouth, Shields, Newcastle, Vale of Tyne, Prudhoe, Ovingham, Bywell, Dilston, Hexham. He concludes the letter with a postscript: 'I fear I am bothering you, but I know you can help me. I hope to make the sketches this summer. Haydon Bridge is surely on the Tyne, though I don't fancy it is very drawable.' Obviously, Robert Spence must have done his best to help and Birket Foster is still concerned with the Tyne project when he sends his customary January letter:

'The Hill, Witley,
Jan 29th 1877.
My dear Robert,
I enclose premium as usual. I am really quite ashamed I have not answered your kind letter sooner. I am very much obliged – the best thing will be to have a talk & I will come and see you some evening when I am up North to make the sketches. I have someone after the Thames set, but I have not mentioned the Tyne series to anyone so that when they are done they will be for sale – as I don't suppose anyone will see them before they are completed.

I am very busy now finishing Venice & doing a picture for the R A which I hope I may be able to complete – but the days don't seem as long as they used. I don't exactly know when I shall get to the North, but it will be some time in the summer as I have to do a drawing at Rokeby for Mr Phillips Joddrel an old buck who has boyish reminiscences of the place. I promised to do this for him in the summer so I shall do some of my Tyne sketches at the same time.

84 Two chromolithographs from a series executed by Thomas Kell and published by McQueen in 1874. Size: Each vignette 4 × 3″ – 10.1 × 7.6 cms.
Collection: Jan Reynolds.

We had a visit the other day from Anthony Trollope who is a good talker – he was delighted with my books and wants to show me his. Witley is really getting a very important little village. Mr and Mrs Lewis (Geo. Eliot) have taken the house next to John – bought it in fact and are going to add to it. We like Sir Henry and Lady Holland very much & they have such nice people down – Trollope was staying with them. Hook came over to see us the other day and was very fresh and lively – but I've filled my paper.

With love to you all, your affec. bro.

Birket Foster.

Meggie was 21 on Saty. Time is getting on.'

On 24 July 1877, Birket Foster wrote: '... I am off on Monday into Brittany to get a subject that I know about ...' This would be for illustration in *Brittany: A Series of Thirty-five sketches by Birket Foster*, published by the artist, The Hill, Witley, Surrey, 1878. In his Preface, Birket Foster explained:

'I have been induced to publish this series of sketches in the hope that it may be acceptable as the exact reproduction of my drawings made during a recent tour in Brittany.

A prepared paper was used and Messrs Maclure and Macdonald by their delicate process transferred the sketches to stone, so that the pictures in the volume may be said to have been printed from the actual drawings. Brittany is so well known, and so much has been written about it, that I have thought it enough simply to give the subject of each picture. They were not drawn with a view to publication, but were merely the jottings of a rambler in some of the picturesque old towns of that picturesque country.'

This large and handsome book (which weighs very

nearly half a stone!) is bound in thick boards and beige cloth cover, with title and the Birket Foster device blocked in gold. The gold-edged pages are sewn and measure $10\frac{1}{2} \times 15$″. The paper is of a smooth and weighty quality, tinted cream, which provides an excellent foil for the sepia printing of the text and the sepia and neutral tones of the illustrations. The plates are not uniform in size, but are presented on a border (approximately 1″ wide) printed in a very pale grey/beige tone to form a mount. Each illustration has a short descriptive text on the facing page, in which the initial letter is illuminated in a square setting. The style of these decorated letters and the general design of the book point to this having been the work of the Chiswick Press, a name synonymous with good typography and printing during this period.

'Dedicated without permission to my travelling companions Captain Charles G. Nelson, RN and Robert Dudley, Esq.'[4] Birket Foster makes this pleasant little nod towards his friends, but the accompanying notes give an impression of Birket Foster wandering about alone with his sketch book. Some of the comments are short, but are written very much from the personal experience of Birket Foster, with only occasional glances at the standard guide books of the region. He shows himself particularly fascinated by the varying styles in local costume and in Pont l'Abbé he was very interested in the 'Egyptian' character of the head-dresses and gold embroidery, commenting: 'The effect is very splendid, but the women generally have very clumsy figures.' This may have been so, but Birket Foster represents their *faces* with exactly the same delicately

85 'In the church of St Melaine I found this poor woman fast asleep; so took the opportunity which her repose afforded of making the accompanying sketch'. Illustration no. 6 'St Melaine, Morlaix' from *Brittany: A series of Thirty-five sketches by Birket Foster* – published by the artist 1878. Lithograph by Maclure and Macdonald. Size: $4\frac{7}{8} \times 5''$ – 12.4 × 12.7 cms.

86 'The wooden sabot is almost universally worn by the poor people. They put straw into them to prevent them hurting the feet... The background of this sketch is the Place du Guesclin.'

Plate 32 'A Sabot Stall, Dinan' from *Brittany: A series of Thirty-five sketches by Birket Foster*. Size: $6 \times 4\frac{1}{2}''$ – 15.2 × 11.4 cms.

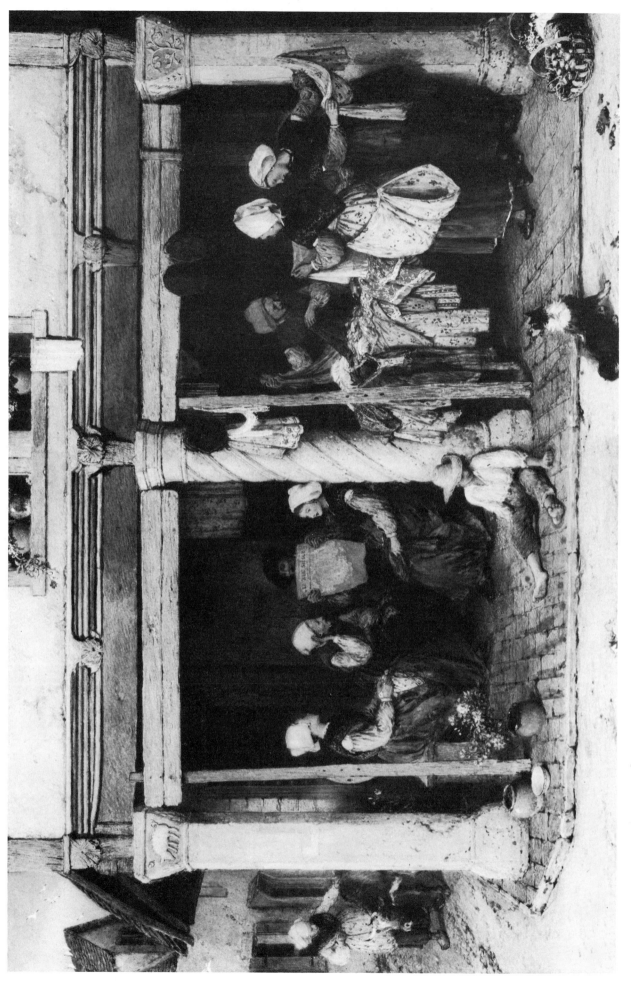

pert-nosed and rosebud-mouthed characteristics that are repeated again and again in his work. Jeanne, a waiting maid at the Hôtel des Voyageurs, Morlaix, stood for a sketch showing the costume of the area. The whole attitude of this figure cleverly suggests a concentration on keeping still and trying not to drop the large and knobbly gourd that she is holding out on a plate. But Birket Foster has not observed her Breton peasant face or any individual characteristics, but produces yet again a pretty version of the one that he always drew (see Birmingham City Art Gallery, p. 207). The figure of the sleeping woman (Ill. 85) has been selected for the skill with which Birket Foster has caught the essential repose of the subject and the fact that we are not distracted by one of his perky little faces. It is odd that Birket Foster should have been weak on this point, because he had such a genuine interest in people. His description of an old woman in Morlaix is full of keen and kindly observation:

'From my window I looked into the wool-shop opposite, which is the subject of my sketch. The old lady sat all day knitting. Numbers of people seemed to go in and gossip with her, but all the time I was there I never saw anyone make a purchase. Every morning at six o'clock, the large pincushion, the jersey, the little coloured shirt, and the ribands, were hung up, and at the same hour in the evening taken down; and I believe, if you went there now, you would find them just as they are drawn. There were five cats always in attendance; I have only shown four, as it really seemed too absurd. I may say, that cats are a speciality in the Grande Rue.'

The dark interior of the wool-shop which makes up large area of 'In the Grande Rue, Morlaix' does not present a very suitable subject for photographic reproduction, but one regrets not being able to show the smiling tabby cat in the foreground, so lovingly observed, even to the pads on the underside of its relaxed paws. Birket Foster understood cats. The subjects in this book also include a mercer's shop in Vitre, eight studies in Morlaix, views in Quimper, including the Butter Market and the fountain of Drennec (illustrated *Art and Antiques*, 1981). Pont l'Abbé was visited and Dinan, including a shrine in the Cathedral of St

Sauveur and a Sabot stall (Ill. 86). The final illustrations are in St Malo, finishing on the ramparts of that town.

Godfrey N. Brown (Professor Emeritus of Education in the University of Keele) was so charmed by the illustrations in *Brittany* that in 1977 he and his family decided that they would follow the path of the artist to see how much had changed since Birket Foster had made his sketching trip.

'Now I know that Birket Foster's Brittany is still there. It has changed of course, but its fundamental physiognomy is recognisable still. It is aspects of peasant life and dress that have changed the most but they have not entirely disappeared. We stayed at a farm where the farmer's wife still wore the sabots which so often appear in Birket Foster's Breton sketches. We still saw the beautiful lace coifs worn by the women of Brittany which he sketched so lovingly.'[5]

The general impression given by the illustrations in *Brittany* is most attractive, with a subtle and fluid use of line and an engaging and informative choice of subject, but the book was not a commercial success. This was almost certainly due to the fact that Birket Foster was not sufficiently versed in the methods necessary for book promotion. On 6 August 1878, he wrote to his cousin:

'My dear Robert,
    I am glad you have got the Brittany and think you will like it. I am much obliged for the £5. 5. 0. in payment. Fanny, Myles, Willie and I are off for a fortnights ramble into Derbyshire, Shrewsbury, Bridgenorth, Ludlow, Worcester, Hereford and Gloucester then to North Devon if we have time. I have not been away for a year and I feel very worn and tired and am looking forward to the change.
    I am very glad to have an improved acct. of Sarah. Give my very dear love to her.
        Yours very affecly.
            Birket Foster.
If you hear of anyone wishing to have a "Brittany" I have some left.'

Notes: Chapter Fifteen

1 Published by permission of the University of California (Department of Special Collections), Los Angeles, USA.
2 All letters in this chapter from Birket Foster to Robert Spence are reproduced by permission of Newcastle upon Tyne City Libraries.
3 From *The Life and Letters of Charles Samuel Keene* by G.S. Layard, Sampson Low, 1892.

4 Captain C.G. Nelson, RN, was a large, jolly-looking man, who is pictured in the William Foster albums. He had been Captain of the *Galatea* during a visit by Edward VII (then Prince of Wales) to Australia.
5 From 'Small Start' by G.N. Brown, published in *Art and Antiques*, 1981.

87 'A Shop at Dol'. Water-colour, signed with monogram (left). Almost as Plate 25 in *Brittany*. Birket Foster commented: '... the houses are supported on massive columns of stone, very curiously carved, between which wares are displayed. The shop in the sketch is a very good specimen.' Note: it still exists. *Photograph: Frost and Reed Ltd, London.*

16
The children of Birket Foster

Edmund Evans was a close friend of John Greenaway, whom we have seen was an assistant engraver during his apprenticeship with Ebenezer Landells. John Greenaway's daughter, Kate, proved to be a talented artist and it was after she had already illustrated several books that her father suggested that she should approach Edmund Evans with her latest drawings. She had made a series of illustrations for her own verses and these were at once recognised for their potential by Evans. He bought the drawings and arranged with Routledge to print these as a children's book, with the title *Under the Window*. This appeared in 1879 and was an instant success (eventually selling 70,000 copies in England alone) and establishing Kate Greenaway as an immensely popular illustrator, whose drawings of quaint and pretty children in high waisted frocks remain in publication today. Edmund Evans was now 53 and he and his wife, Polly, were still living at Leybourne, Witley. Their somewhat unlikely marriage had turned out most happily and they had three daughters and two sons – Ada, Lily, Henrietta, Wilfred and Herbert. Of their daughters, it was Lily who was a particularly characterful child, not in the least pretty, but keenly intelligent and lively. She was a special favourite with Kate Greenaway and some charming letters from this artist to Lily Evans were published in *Kate Greenaway* by Spielmann and Layard in 1905. Polly Evans also contributed to this book. Kate Greenaway dedicated *Mother Goose* (1881) to 'Lily and Eddie' (her nephew) – 'the two children she loved most in the world'.

Over the next few years the engraving and printing of books illustrated by Kate Greenaway was one of the main preoccupations of Edmund Evans. In 1880, *Kate Greenaway's Birthday Book for Children* was extremely successful and the following year saw the publication of *A Day in a Child's Life*[1] with music by Myles Birket Foster, FRAM, the eldest son of Birket Foster. This was also very popular and sold at least 25,000 copies. The combination of the art of Kate Greenaway and the ambience of the name of her collaborator must have been an almost foolproof recipe for commercial success, but Myles Birket Foster (1851–1922) was a musician who also achieved a very creditable position in his own right.

'27th Oct. 1880

'My dear Robert,

Myles' address is 28 Notting Hill Square. It is very kind of you to think of him – dear fellow I'm so glad that he is going to get married – it will be good for him in every way, but until he had a reasonable prospect it was wise to wait I think. We are having lovely weather and am enjoying having them all together very much. I am suffering just now from a rheumatic affliction in the scalp which is troubling me and I'm in the Doctor's hands. I've had it for more than two months but it is difficult to move.

With love from us all,
    Yours affec. bro.
        Birket Foster.'[2]

Myles Birket Foster had been articled for two years to Hamilton Clarke and studied at the Royal Academy of Music under Sullivan, Prout and others. He held several positions as organist and choirmaster, before achieving the 'reasonable prospect' which Birket Foster refers to in this letter, which was the appointment of Organist to the Foundling Hospital, London (now known as the Thomas Coram Foundation for Children, after the original founder). Coram, who was a friend of Hogarth, had established the Foundling Hospital in 1739 as a refuge for destitute children and this had gradually developed into an establishment with an exceptional musical tradition, so that it became fashionable to hear performances by the Foundlings in their Chapel. This was a very fine building, in which the original organ had been presented by George Frederick Handel, who also gave a manuscript copy of 'The Messiah' to the Foundling Hospital, where the work was frequently performed.

The minute books of the Foundling Hospital include an interesting entry for 1 January 1880, in which Dr John Stainer (composer of the famous 'Crucifixion') makes an obvious attempt to influence the Committee in favour of several more established musicians for this very prestigious position of organist and choirmaster, while acknowledging the abilities of Myles Birket Foster and several others. ('All shew *great* natural talent and are men of remarkable promise. But it will be for the Committee to decide how far it is wise or fair to older and tried musicians to pass them over in order to give fair youth a chance of eminence.')[3] But this is exactly what the Committee did and Myles Birket Foster was elected with a large majority over all other candidates. It was a good choice and Myles

88 Colour plate from *British Birds in their Haunts* by C. A. Johns, published by Routledge in 1909 and illustrated throughout by William Foster, second son of Birket Foster. Size: $8\frac{1}{2} \times 5\frac{1}{4}''$ – 21.6 × 13.3 cms.
Collection: Mrs L. M. Glasson.

Blackbirds Nest and Eggs
Blackbird, 14th day.

Just Hatched.   6th Day.
Day after.   9th Day.
4th Day.   11th Day.

[face p. 8.

Birket Foster was to hold the position with distinction and flair, showing a special understanding of the needs and abilities of the young people with whom he was involved. In later years he was a senior examiner for Trinity College of Music, London and travelled a great deal in this capacity.

Myles Birket Foster composed a Symphony in F Sharp Minor ('Isle of Aran') as well as overtures, string quartets, piano trios and music for children. An example of the latter is *The Children's Christmas* - a collection of verses by his cousin, Robert Spence Watson, LLD, which he set to music. As might be expected he wrote a considerable amount of church music and this was popular in its day. *Hymns Ancient and Modern* (revised version) includes two tunes by Myles Birket Foster: no. 305 'Soldiers of the Cross, arise!' and no. 306 'Lift up your heads, ye gates of brass'. Myles Birket Foster also wrote a *History of the Philharmonic Society*, published in 1913. (See also *Grove's Dictionary of Music and Musicians*, Vol. 3, p. 456, 5th ed.)

Myles Birket Foster, FRAM, was married in 1881 to Christine Lorimer. Their first child was born in 1884 and was named Myles Birket Foster. There were four sons and two daughters of the marriage and the third son, Robert Spence Foster, carried the family tradition to a fifth generation by naming his elder son Myles Birket Foster. It is John Foster, brother of the latter who has supplied material as shown on p. 21.

It was William Frederick Foster (1853-1924), the second son of Birket Foster, who was to follow in his footsteps and become a painter and illustrator, after studying at Heatherley's School of Art. *The Christian Year* (Routledge, 1878) contained 186 small illustrations by Foster of flowers, etc. and frontispiece, all engraved and printed by Evans in four colours. *The Floral Birthday Book* an undated publication from Routledge contained 368 illustrations by William Foster, engraved and printed in from four to six colours by Edmund Evans. Also undated was *The Bible Emblem Anniversary Book*, published by Routledge, with about 366 illustrations by William Foster, again engraved and printed in colour by Evans.

William Foster was a frequent illustrator for Ernest Nister's children's books, including such titles as *The Model Menagerie*, *Very Funny* and *Four Footed Friends*. Illustrations by William Foster from the last two titles appeared in 'A Victorian Artistic Haven' (*Country Life*, 4 December 1975). Pauline Flick, the writer of this article, has made a special study of William Foster as an illustrator and is of the opinion that many of his charming cats are indistinguishable from those of the more famous Louis Wain. Of particular interest is a children's book entitled *Keeper Jacko* which William Foster both wrote and illustrated. His work is signed either W. Foster or with initials and would not be mistaken for that of his father.

He was also a painter of landscapes, still life, interiors and genre, but his most academic contribution was undoubtedly in the role of ornithologist. The grounds of The Hill and the woods in and around Witley were ideal for his study of birds and it was here that William Foster placed innumerable nesting boxes in order to encourage the various species that he wished to observe at close quarters. Photographs in possession of Sarah Glasson include pictures of a smiling Willie Foster dissecting and mounting dead specimens, in company with his great friend, Bryan Hook, son of James Hook, RA. William Foster, in recognition of his work as an ornithologist, was elected a Fellow of The Zoological Society of London in

1895. The detailed knowledge displayed in the bird studies of this artist make these some of the finest examples of his work. The Zoological Society is in possession of several volumes in which this particular talent is illustrated. Some of his most minutely observed work was for *British Birds in their Haunts* by C.A. Johns (published in 1909 by George Routledge) (Ill. 88). This book was illustrated with 64 colour plates by William Foster, which comprised a total of 256 individual studies. The illustration shown has been selected for the genuine and tender quality of observation which the artist has brought to his paintings of the young bird's development. And is there perhaps some unconscious influence from William Hunt about the nest? *British Birds in their Haunts* was to become a classic reference and went into many editions. William Foster exhibited with the Institute of Painters in Water-colours and the Society of British Artists and showed 25 works at the Royal Academy between 1872 and 1894, including an etching of the staircase at The Hill.

There is an entertaining reference to William Foster in *The Life of Sir William Quiller Orchardson, RA* by his daughter Hilda Orchardson Gray. She recalled:

'28 February 1893 - my Father, my Mother and I were staying with the Alec Stevensons at Weybridge and a son of Mr Birket Foster came to dinner. During the evening a discussion on eyes occurred and my father expressed his opinion, as usual, that the "flashing" eyes and the "glittering" eyes of novelists was nonsense as eyes can neither flash nor glitter and that the whole expression of the human eye is due to the movements of the eyelids. Mr Willie Birket Foster (*sic*) there-upon produced some drawings he had made. On one piece of paper he had simply drawn the iris and pupil of an eye; on other pieces he had drawn eyelids of different kinds, each with a hole in the paper in the place where the iris should have been. These he superimposed in turn on the one iris-and-pupil drawing, thus producing a laughing eye, an angry eye and so on, according to the eyelid, the iris, of course, being the same in each case. This was considered by the company in general, and my father in particular, conclusive proof that eyes in themselves express nothing.'

Maybe so, but how fortunate that Willie Foster should just happen to have about him this set of drawings all ready to show his fellow guests. Did he always take them to dinner parties? The eyes of Willie himself are full of fun and one strongly suspects that it was he who was the originator of the entire conversation in order to have the opportunity to produce this amusing little diversion.

William Foster comes across as a particularly attractive personality - handsome and humorous, kind and compassionate. One can picture him in his Norfolk jacket bicycling through the Surrey lanes on a tour of the nest boxes. ('Willie had a tumble off his cycle into a ditch *full* of water - but is no worse', letter from Birket Foster to Edmund Evans, 1898.) William Foster was then well over 40, but still living with his father and stepmother. Fanny Foster may have had a difficult side to her character, but photographs of her with William suggest a very happy companionship between these two people who were nearer in generation than Fanny was to her husband. William Foster was a talented and enthusiastic photographer and was to compile several albums of photographs of The Hill, later including one for his widowed stepmother, with an inscription inside in the form of a photographic montage

'To F.F. from W. and M.F.'. The illustrations in this book include examples of these photographs which so well evoke the atmosphere of the period and life at The Hill.

William Foster was 51 before he eventually married. The wedding was reported in *The Court Journal* (29 October 1904). His bride was Mary Watson, daughter of W. Watson, MRCS of Lancaster. Mary was a niece of Fanny Foster and can be seen in family album photographs with her aunt. It is sometimes said that William married his cousin, but although she was related to him in the degree that the Foster and Watson families were undoubtedly linked, she was actually his step-cousin. The wedding took place at St Peter's Church, Kensington Park Road, London, and was obviously a very fashionable affair in which the bride was given away by her cousin, Lancelot Sanderson, KC. There were no children of the marriage. After the death of William Foster in 1924, a number of his works and those of Birket Foster came onto the market, followed by more such family-owned items in 1946, after the death of Mary Foster (see Henry E. Huntington Library and Art Gallery, San Marino, p. 213).

Birket Foster is referring to his youngest son, Henry, in a letter written from 51 Eversfield Place, Hastings on 10 February 1874.

'My dear Robert,
    I never wrote to thank you for your kind note about Harry – but have been rather expecting a line from him to tell us when he is off. The weather just today is bitter cold, but we have had some delightfully warm days since we came. I think it is a capital chance for Harry to see about him a bit and I hope it will do him good. I am very busy with my pictures for the R. A. and Water Colour & shall have to struggle to get them done. The fishing boats here are delightful and the country round is all that an artist could desire.
    Thanking you again for all your kindness to Harry – With our dear love,
        I am your affec. bro.
        Birket Foster.'

Henry Foster (1854-1928) did not follow his brothers into a career in the arts, but became a qualified engineer, studying for his articles and training mostly in Newcastle, where he was eventually to settle. Birket Foster always sounds a little anxious about Harry and his letters indicate that he felt very much at a loss, with regard to the world outside his own sphere. Two years later he commented in a letter to Robert Spence (25 July 1876):

'Harry is in the North again as the work at Chatham was not ready. I fancy it would be better for him to see a little more work & to go into other works as he is very inexperienced to go in for anything on his own yet. I am very much obliged for the kind interest you have taken in him'.

                                    'Jan 27th 1879
My dear Robert,
    I have been intending to write you a line for a long time but things come in the way and one doesn't do what one ought.
    I hope you keep nicely. I can indeed imagine what the terrible blank is – and I have felt very much indeed for you – I'm sure you know that – and I shrink so from stirring up so great a sorrow by anything I say.[4]
    Fanny has a bad cold and cough or else the rest are well.

We enjoyed having Harry at Xmas very much. I think he returned better for the change.
    With love from us all,
        Believe me your affec. bro. etc.'

The end of 1879 found Birket Foster once again very anxious about the future of his youngest son. In a letter to Robert Spence, dated 6 November, he writes:

'Harry writes me that a partnership has been suggested [word is very much smudged] to him, requiring for me far too much capital. I thought I would write you as you may be under some wrong impression as to my means. I have made as a rule a good income for an artist by very hard work, but with one pair of hands it is difficult to do more than meet comfortably the many expenses which are constantly occurring. I have to provide against ill health and the precarious state of the profession & I could not afford to let Harry have more than £2000 – and that would be a pinch at least at present. Are you quite sure that he is fit to take such a partnership supposing all is well? He is a good lad but I fancy the responsibility of a thing of that sort would be very great and that something much smaller would be better suited – but you know about these things far better than I & I must ask your advice. I know so little about these things that they trouble me grievously.
    You will forgive me writing all this but I wanted you to know and ask you to tell me what is best to be done.
        With love from us all, etc.'

Another letter to Robert Spence followed only two days later:

'Just a line to thank you very much indeed for all the trouble and interest you take on Harry's acct. I am greatly relieved by your kind letter this morning – I am sure it was too much of an affair ...'

Birket Foster may have shown a certain amount of fluster about the practicalities of engineering, but he was recalled by his youngest son as a very punctual man, who liked to see this in others. An anecdote related by a daughter of Henry Foster shows that his father had a very charming and generous way of making a point. It is told that a certain lady guest had been persistently late for breakfast, while staying at The Hill and one morning came down to find on her plate a dainty gold watch, which Birket Foster had presented as a timely reminder!

Charles Keene was always very good with young people and was a great favourite with the Foster family. He wrote to Joseph Crawhall of a short holiday with Birket Foster at The Hill in 1878 ('... the only drawback was the absence of his two charming daughters ...'). In his correspondence we learn of him helping Willie Foster with the painting of some pottery ware, commending Myles Foster to others for his qualities as a musician and humorist and taking a kind interest in the doings of Harry.

In July 1880, Keene told Joseph Crawhall that he had been spending a few days at Witley, while Harry Foster was there. He continues: 'How do you like him? We all think him a very jolly youngster. He talks of getting up a lawn tennis ground somewhere in Newcastle.'[5]

In 1883, Henry Foster cemented his Newcastle connection by marrying Ethel Clapham, who was his first cousin, once removed, on his mother's side of the family: i.e. his aunt Sarah (née Spence) had married Joseph Watson in 1835; one of their seven daughters, Esther Mary, married

89 '**Children with a Donkey**'. Water-colour - the pose of the boy on the donkey is directly modelled from a photograph of Birket Foster's youngest son, Henry. The Foster children had a pet donkey for several years. Size: 9½ × 13″ - 24.2 × 33 cms.
Collection: National Gallery of Scotland, Edinburgh.

90 '**The Convalescent**' - from a water-colour commissioned by *The Art Journal*, 1873. Engraved by C. Cousen. Size: 6¾ × 10″ - 17.1 × 25.4 cms.
Collection: Sheffield City Polytechnic.

Henry Clapham in 1859 and it was their daughter, Ethel, whom Harry Foster married. They were to have two sons and three daughters, including Henry Clapham Foster, who is shown in the Glasson album as a charming baby, happily sucking a fir cone in the garden of The Hill. He was later to become a Canon of the Church of England, a turn of events which did not meet with the approval of some of the Foster connections, who still adhered strongly to the Society of Friends, but Henry Clapham Foster was a man who inherited the kindly presence and humorous outlook of his grandfather and was to prove an exceptionally popular cleric.

On 11 October 1880, Birket Foster wrote to Robert Spence, concerning his elder daughter, Margaret Ann (1856-1923):

'... You have I daresay heard of Meggie's engagement to a son of Broderick Dale. I hope they are respectable people. I hear they are. I remember his Father and Mother staying a day or two at my father's house on their wedding tour, but I have not seen them since to my knowledge.

If there is anything wrong in it let me know. I love her very dearly and only desire her happiness. It is a serious matter but all the people I have seen who know the young man speak well of him & I thought him an open candid fellow when he came to see us (all this between ourselves). Harry is up in town with a job which is rather an anxious one for him, but I believe he will carry it through satisfactorily.

We enjoyed our trip to Wales very much indeed – South Wales I was disappointed with – beautiful places enough in their way but fashionable & unpaintable, but North Wales delightful – I had not been there for 25 years, but was charmed and hope to see it again, I worked very hard...'

On 19 July 1881, Charles Keene wrote to Crawhall, whose daughter had recently been married:

'How did you like putting on the yellow waistcoat? [a yellow waistcoat seems to have been the proper costume of the "heavy father" on the stage, when he gave his blessing.] We insist on Birket Foster donning this symbolic article when his daughter is married next month. He dreads it hugely...'[5]

John Broderick Dale was a banker of County Durham and South Shields and it was his eldest son, John Henry Dale, whom Margaret Ann Foster married on 25 August 1881. Very sadly, her husband contracted tuberculosis and died in 1892. They had been a happy and devoted couple and it was perhaps rather to her own surprise and certainly that of her family that Margaret Dale married Henri Etienne Adrien Stadnitski, a bachelor, in Witley Church on 18 July 1893. Margaret had met Stadnitski (who was, in fact, a Polish Count, although he did not use the title) while in Geneva with John Dale for his medical treatment. After their marriage the Stadnitskis lived abroad for many years, during the lifetime of his extremely demanding mother, but eventually retired to the suburban Englishness of Mitcham in Surrey. There were no children of either marriage.

Ellen (1857-1946), the younger daughter of Birket Foster, also met her husband in Geneva, while visiting her sister there. She fell very much in love with Lancelot Thompson Glasson, a law student, who was the third son of Thomas Glasson of the Penrith brewing firm. It seemed a very suitable alliance, but Birket and Fanny Foster were at first opposed to the match, as Lancelot also had tuberculosis, but Ellen was determined and they were married on 22 December 1886. It was certainly much due to the devotion of Ellen that her husband eventually regained his health and was able to take up his career, qualifying as a barrister in 1889 and also serving for many years on the board of M.B. Foster and Sons, of which he became chairman in 1905. Ellen and Lancelot Glasson had three children: Margaret Ellen Glasson (1891-1981); Lancelot Myles Glasson (1894-1959); and Sarah Gertrude Ann Glasson (1897-) whose invaluable contributions to this book have already been gratefully recorded.

A genealogical table showing the children of Birket Foster and some of their descendants, as well as other family information, can be found in *Robert and Mary Spence of North Shields* – compiled by Philip Spence (Newcastle upon Tyne: Reid and Co. 1939). Philip Spence was a grandson of Robert Spence, the cousin and brother-in-law of Birket Foster. See also *The Descendants of John Backhouse* (Yeoman, of Moss Side, Near Yealand Redman, Lancashire. Compiled by Joseph Foster and privately printed at the Chiswick Press, 1894). The section 'Foster, formerly Forster of County Durham' contains genealogical tables and photographs of Birket Foster and his four brothers (p. 45) and also of his parents and some other relations.

Notes : Chapter Sixteen

1 For further information on *A Day in a Child's Life* see letter from Myles Birket Foster, FRAM. as published in *Kate Greenaway* by M. H. Spielmann and G. S. Layard, 1905, p. 101.
2 All extracts in this chapter from letters to Robert Spence are published by permission of Newcastle upon Tyne City Libraries.
3 Information from C. P. Masters, Director and Secretary, Thomas Coram Foundation for Children, 40 Brunswick Square, London WC1. See also *The History of the Foundling Hospital* by R. H. Nichols and F. A. Wray, Oxford University Press, 1935.
4 The bereavement mentioned in this letter was the death of Sarah - née Hagen - wife of Robert Spence.
5 From *The Life and Letters of Charles Samuel Keene* by G. S. Layard, Sampson Low, 1892.

17

Fakes, identification of period, and prices

On 31 January 1880, Birket Foster wrote a letter to Robert Spence, which contains information of particular interest. Spence had obviously asked his advice about a doubtful work and Birket Foster replied:

'I cannot of course say without seeing it whether the drawing is mine or not. There is a subject which might bear that title that was Chromolithographed years ago. The forgeries are generally selected from the published prints. I should not advise anyone to buy it that was not very confident of his judgement. I am constantly having pictures for recognition – all forgeries. One man the other day gave 150 gns. for a little oil picture sold to him as mine – it was a copy of a small drawing which has been forged several times. . . .'[1]

In 1906, M. H. Spielmann was to note that Birket Foster was perhaps the most frequently forged artist of his day and that the practice still continued. These fakes became so numerous in the lifetime of Birket Foster that he was forced to charge a small fee for giving an opinion on work that was brought to him for identification, in order to keep some limit on these continual requests.

It is interesting to speculate as to just why it was that Birket Foster was so much faked. What special facet or property of his work induced this? The question can be viewed from rather opposite points. Either his work was so everyday and so unclassical in construction that it seemed that anyone might copy it, or it had a definite style which careful analysis might be able to reproduce. The sheer demand for his work was certainly the main reason for the fakes and reflects well on the popularity of the originals, but there must be more to it than this. Perhaps it was that Birket Foster became a household name in the homes of the middle class and at one time there was what can only be called an insatiable craze for his pictures. Most of the copies faithfully reproduce the actual theme of the original and in his particular selection and arrangement of subjects Birket Foster had struck an individual line that was not being produced by any other artist of his day. The actual niceties of execution were not within the grasp of many of those who only wished to have on their walls a picture that at least appeared to be by Birket Foster. The artist himself was a man of gentle and unpretentious ways, who is thought to have known very well the source of some of these commercially inspired copies, but would never consider making any kind of fuss, even after the registration of his monogram as a trade mark had failed to stop the infringement of his copyright. It was tiresome to have

to keep giving his opinion as to whether work was or was not by his hand, but Birket Foster accepted this with quiet resignation. And so, the fakes flourished.

The subject of forged works purporting to be from the hand of Birket Foster is a slightly delicate area, as individuals or museums do not always wish to fear the worst of works in their possession and the discussion of specific items is not always possible. It is also an undoubted fact that the presence of fakes led at one time to a spate of rejections of work said to be by Birket Foster, even if it sometimes later proved to be perfectly right. Some dealers were nervous of the name of Birket Foster and the art market became very touchy about this artist and prices actually showed a decline, but recent years have brought a more knowledgeable understanding of his technique and the area in which to look for faked work.

As stated by Birket Foster, fakes were nearly always derived from colour prints after his work and sometimes from the black-and-white engravings. I am most grateful to the Herbert Art Gallery, Coventry for allowing me to illustrate an example which was donated in 1945 as the work of Birket Foster, but has now been withdrawn as such (Ill. 91). It was presented as one of a group of works by various artists but had never been exhibited by the museum, who quite rightly considered it a poor example and have now accepted my opinion as to the spurious nature of the work. It is undoubtedly a copy of a print and almost certainly from a series published by S. Hildesheimer and Co. These were true to the outline of Birket Foster's original composition, but the essential brushwork was not correctly suggested and the modelling of the figures did not reproduce the taut detail of the Birket Foster style. In this water-colour the colouring is harsh and unatmospheric and lacks the blending of tones to be found in a genuine work. Note the treatment of the limbs and the faces, the stiffness of the drapery and the disproportionate sheep in a fuzzy under-painted background. A comparison with any of the other illustrations in this book will point up the fact that the faces in this example are totally without the characteristic modelling that is so typical of Birket Foster. There is no real knowledge of line and form behind the brush strokes in this water-colour drawing and the results are exactly what one would expect if someone was working from a reproduction – and the faces are strongly influenced by those portrayed in the Hildesheimer prints. The registration of Birket Foster's monogram had practically no effect, as this was so easily forged, although such additions may not always have been done at

91 This water-colour is *not* by Birket Foster, but is illustrated as an example of a faked or copied work. Formerly attributed to his name, but now accepted as spurious (see p. 153). The author is grateful to the Herbert Art Gallery, Coventry, for permission to reproduce this work, which is not representative of their general collection.

the time of the execution of the work. It is perfectly possible for a legitimate copy to have been made by a well-brought-up young lady in her painting class, which many years later could have come into the hands of those who merely had to add the appropriate initials to pass the work off as that of Birket Foster.

Most of the fakes are indeed straight copies from prints and do not even have the subtlety of work imitating that of Foster or in his style. In most cases it is possible to go back to the chromolithograph or the engraving from which the copy was derived with almost painstaking repetition of compositional detail. A form of semi-fake can be met with in chromolithographs of work by Birket Foster onto which have been applied touches of water-colour paint. These have been known to deceive even those who have lived with such an example for years in the belief that the work was an original water-colour. If it is framed, take a suspect piece to the light and look sideways across the surface. Any added pigment will then be revealed against the tell-tale smoothness of the surface of the print. If unframed, there can be no deception. It should be pointed out that collectors should not instantly conclude that a work is a fake because it depicts a subject which has been chromo-lithographed. Birket Foster had first to produce the originals. It was often popular themes of which there are several water-colour versions that were ultimately made into colour prints. Difficulty can arise from the fact that certain sketches by Birket Foster were 'faked up' after his death and made to appear more finished, usually with the addition of extra colour and perhaps a few figures in his later style, but the extraneous nature of these workings should be discerned by the trained eye.

There is no space to show more than one forgery in this book, but I can give further illustration by relating details of another example of a different type. This large, mono-grammed water-colour drawing has been in possession of the same family for many years after having been purchased about 1913 by a professional man in the provinces who was sold it as the work of Birket Foster. On first seeing a small transparency of this water-colour I felt it likely that it was indeed by Birket Foster, as the composition was exactly in his style. I noticed that the subject was based on a *reverse* of the engraving in *The Illustrated London News* with the title 'Gathering Mistletoe' (Ill. 13). All the same elements were there, but the main theme had been translated into gathering holly, with some slight alterations to the basic poses of the figures and the addition of a child in a wheelbarrow in the right foreground. Birket Foster, if working up a water-colour from the *original sketch* for 'Gathering Mistletoe' would obviously produce a result that was in reverse of the engraving. All appeared sound in theory until I had an opportunity to examine this particular water-colour drawing. It proved to be a pleasantly competent piece of work, but was *not* by Birket Foster, for the following reasons: It was crisper in execution than the illustrated example of a fake, but the lack of stipple gave immediate cause for doubt. Nowhere on any surface of the drawing had the paint been applied in the manner so well illustrated in 'The Harrow', on which the stiff application of a very dry medium has actually chipped off the paper. The surface of the holly drawing was too bland and lacked the essential tautness of touch which characterizes the work of Birket Foster. It was not dainty enough. Copyists used one stroke whereas Birket Foster would have touched the paper twice with a finer brush to produce the same line, not an effect of fuss or over-working, but to give an impression of definition and infinite care. Copied work often fails over the modelling of the *boots*, so characteristic of the footwear of women and children in the work of Birket Foster. Fakes often seem to have been painted by an artist who has never actually looked at a boot and in attempting to copy these all the essential sturdiness can be lost. In this copy it was noticeable that some of the holly had more the appearance of bunches of grapes than the precise arrangement of leaf and berry that one expects from Birket Foster who was usually very sound on botanical detail.

Christie's were subsequently consulted for a market valuation and, in confirming my opinion, it was thought

that a possible price at auction of about £150 might be expected for this water-colour, which if it had been an original Birket Foster would have fetched a very much higher figure. The translation of the main subject from gathering mistletoe to picking holly was a pointer to the fact that a genuine version by Birket Foster almost certainly must exist, as it seemed highly unlikely that a faker would have had the subtlety to produce a piece using the basic elements of a reverse of the much smaller *Illustrated London News* engraving and still retain all the essential characteristics of style. Some time later, another water-colour of 'The Holly Gatherers' was brought to my notice and it was at once obvious that this must be the original Birket Foster. It was almost the same size and identical in composition, but had that extra control about the brush work and the general handling of the medium, as if the entire work had been brought into sharper focus, holly berries, boots and all.[2]

It is not easy to give a clear point-by-point description of how to know the difference between a genuine Birket Foster and a fake, as so much of this has to be done by an instinctive recognition of the copied line and comes from practised study. If in doubt, take advice. The art market is not now flooded with Birket Foster fakes, as dealers and auction houses are much more selective, and the average collector has no cause to be wary of the name of this artist.

Birket Foster rarely dated his work, but there are several basic pointers which can help to ascertain the general period of a water-colour drawing by this artist. Very early examples are often signed 'B. Foster' as in the style employed for the black-and-white engravings, but the characteristic monogram was also present from the start of exhibits with the Society of Painters in Water-colours. It is no real pointer to date, as Birket Foster sometimes added this to early sketches before selling these at a later period.

The hallmarks of style associated with his work throughout the 1860s were quickly established with very little transitional experiment. 'The Milkmaid' (Ill. 40) has been much reproduced, both in colour and black-and-white. Dated 1860, this example shows Birket Foster working in a most minutely detailed manner, as if to exhibit every leaf and thorn, a method that must have taken hours of working time. 'The Sheep Fold' (Ill. 43) is very much in the same period of about 1860-5. 'The Harrow' (Colour Ill. A) illustrates a fine example of this period. The group of children, two of them with their hair in snoods and the small boy with his round hat, all belong very much to the first or very early middle phase of his water-colour style, as does the relationship of the size of the figures to the general composition. 'Rottingdean, near Brighton' (Colour Ill. B) is dated 1865 and shows a slight transition from the early minute treatment. By this time, the demand for the water-colours of Birket Foster was such that he could not have fulfilled his commissions if he had continued to employ such a microscopic technique, hatching in every line, as if for the engraver's tool. He began to plan his compositions differently, so that in 'A Peep at the Hounds' (Colour Ill. C) dated about 1870, there is still a beautiful crisp finish about the main subject matter, in contrast to the more fluent presentation of the sky, but the wild rose bushes, lattice fence, leaves, etc. are more lightly suggested than the absolute delineation of 'The Sheep Fold' and 'The Milkmaid'. The colouring of both these two early water-colours has a certain sharpness or acidity about the greens, which was to be softened and

155

92 'A Pedlar'. Water-colour, signed with monogram (right). Size: $17\frac{1}{2} \times 26\frac{3}{4}$" – 44.4×67.9 cms. *Collection: Ulster Museum, Belfast.*

93 'The Story Book'. Water-colour, signed with monogram (left). Size: $11\frac{1}{4} \times 15\frac{1}{4}$" – 28.7×38.7 cms. *Photograph: Frost and Reed Ltd, London.*

THE P. L. A. MONTHLY
June 1934

GREENWICH AS A PAINTER SAW IT
A BIRKET FOSTER PICTURE OF 1878

THIS COVER PICTURE MAKES AN INTERESTING CONTRAST WITH THAT USED LAST MONTH, A PHOTOGRAPH TAKEN FROM THE FORESHORE OF PORT OF LONDON WHARF, ON THE NORTH BANK. THAT SHOWN HERE IS FROM A WATER COLOUR BY THE LATE BIRKET FOSTER WHICH HE PAINTED SPECIALLY FOR THE PARIS UNIVERSAL EXHIBITION OF 1878. IN THE FOREGROUND IS A STRETCH OF FORESHORE WHERE STILL IS TO BE SEEN A MISCELLANEOUS COLLECTION OF SMALL CRAFT IN FRONT OF BOAT-REPAIRING SHEDS AND THE OLD BUILDING WHICH IS THE HEAD-QUARTERS OF THE CURLEW ROWING CLUB. ONE OF THE CRAFT SHOWN IS A BAWLEY. THE DOMES AND BUILDINGS OF THE ROYAL NAVAL COLLEGE CLEARLY MARK THEMSELVES OUT, WITH A SAILING-SHIP AND A COUPLE OF TUGS IN THE STREAM OPPOSITE. FIFTY YEARS AGO GREENWICH WAS STILL THE HOME PORT OF A NUMBER OF FISHING BOATS. IT IS NOTICEABLE THAT THE ARTIST HAS NOT INCLUDED ONE STEAMSHIP IN HIS PAINTING. THIS WATER COLOUR WAS SOLD AT CHRISTIE'S IN MAY, 1924, FOR 1,850 GUINEAS. IT WAS PURCHASED BY MESSRS. VICARS BROTHERS, LTD., 12, OLD BOND STREET, LONDON, W.I, LAST NOVEMBER, AND IS NOW REPRODUCED BY KIND PERMISSION OF THE PRESENT OWNER, WHO BOUGHT IT FROM THE FIRM NAMED.

mellowed as Birket Foster progressed in his entirely personal explorations of the use of the water-colour medium. It is this type of subject, showing children in a generalised countryside setting that is most typical of earlier work, but as his career proceeded so there was an introduction of more specifically topographical themes. The 'Polly Brown' figure had disappeared by about the end of the 1860s and in the next decade there was introduced the frequent figure of a girl with carroty-red, medium-length hair (almost unkempt) which is held back with a narrow band, instead of the snood hairnets of the earlier period. The presence of this girl or one shown with a looped-up skirt and often a sort of tunic blouse, with her arms akimbo above her head or held at her waist, is a certain pointer to later work. Figures with these characteristics commenced about 1875 and the red-haired girl with her tucked-up skirt was to achieve a kind of endearing monotony, as a characteristic entirely individual to the Birket Foster style. 'The Stepping Stones' (Colour Ill. D) is an exceptionally fine piece of later work (almost certainly dated about 1880) and includes inevitably this girl in one of her endlessly repeated poses.

Another facet of later style is typified in an example such as 'A View of King's College, Cambridge' (Ill. 99) in which the geographical location is the essential subject of the piece and the *tiny* detailed figures are more in the nature of grace notes. The main theme of these topographical works is broader in treatment than earlier work, although in all cases the little figures continue to be executed with deft touches of extremely dry colour, but in some late examples these are rather scattered about the composition and not fully integrated with the whole. It is in this area that Birket Foster had his near failures. There are almost no really weak examples from this artist, but in the period about 1875-92 some pieces (often specifically topographical) are less crisp in execution, dotted with repetitive figures and not equal to earlier work. But it should be noted that after his semi-retirement (1893) his water-colours began to show a new quality of observation, a kind of serenity, as Birket Foster then painted only as he wished and not under the demand of the dealers. 'The Ferry, Walberswick' (Ill. 106) is such an example.

In 1882, L. & W. Vokins, the London fine art dealers, staged a Loan Exhibition of 118 examples of the work of Birket Foster. *The Times* commented:

'... he was practically the inventor of a style, which consisted at first of minute execution with the finest point, and with the use of body colour carried it to such an extent which when he first practised it was quite new. But as this method obviously led him away from the qualities of breadth, rich in tone of colour, and translucent effect of light, which belong to pure watercolour, he soon became sensible of it and gradually departed from the aim at excessive detail and employed a broader touch and worked upon a larger scale. But he still maintains the principle of his style, and although enlarging it somewhat in the direction of obtaining greater breadth and general harmony, as in his latest works, he has never lost an atom of his individuality or swerved from his original view, however opposed it might be considered to be to what is called legitimate in

water-colour art. It is this decided character that gives the greatest interest to Birket Foster's work ...'(as quoted by Marcus Huish, *The Art Journal* 1890. See also *The Magazine of Art*, 1882, p. xxii).

That a dealer of the stature of Vokins was prepared to mount an exhibition of the work of Birket Foster at this stage in his career indicates that here was a painter who had weathered a period of exceptional change in art, although the general academic climate was now against him. During the preceding decade the French Impressionists had exerted a far-reaching influence on style and by 1882 they were already holding their penultimate exhibition. Some of the critics liked to be modish and dismiss Birket Foster as old-fashioned in theme and much too neat in style, but there was still a strong following for his work among the public and the dealers knew this. *The Art Journal* remained loyal, although aware of current trends, as in a review of the 1885 Water-colour Society exhibition:

'Mr Birket Foster's "Dipping Place" is in some respects the most important picture in the room; the rich tone of the background keeping down the effect which the minute finish of the work might produce on those who prefer hasty and general effects.'

The figure in the foreground of a girl with a jug was very similar to that shown in the etching from *The Hamlet* (Ill. 36) and the water-colour was closely based on that with the same title in '*Pictures of English Landscape*' – an absolute proof that Birket Foster was using these pieces as subjects over 20 years after publication of the engravings. 'The Dipping Place' has been reproduced by the Medici Society.

The Art Journal commented on the 1886 exhibition: 'Mr Foster is quite himself, but little more, in the large drawing that occupies the place of honour' (not specified). All the communications to Birket Foster from the Royal Society of Painters in Water-colours with reference to his sales have been preserved for the years 1887-1898. This was the twilight of his career, but Birket Foster was still able to sell a large proportion of his exhibits on Private View days, e.g. nos. 18, 102, 159, 171, 338 in 1887 and nos. 163, 222, 318, 322, 334, 336 in 1888, with other exhibits sold later (see catalogue for titles). The *average* price of these exhibits was about £47/5/-, but in the summer of 1890 'The Arrival of the Hop Pickers, Farnham' (Ill. 103) was marked at £500. This and 'A Surrey Lane' – £63 – were both sold at the Private View to individual collectors, but in the Winter Exhibition of that year, one notes that the dealer T. Richardson of Piccadilly had marched into the Private View and purchased seven out of the ten works exhibited by Birket Foster (total price: £325/10/-). On 28 November 1892, Birket Foster was informed that his exhibit no. 147 - 'Bridge on the Cluny' had been sold for £63 to a buyer who rather charmingly gave his address as The Bank of England. The uniform excellence of the quality of work produced by Birket Foster makes one question exactly what criteria he set in pricing his pictures. A little scrap of paper in his handwriting suggests that he may have charged roughly by the inch! e.g. $7 \times 5'' = £36/15/-$; $11 \times 8'' = £65$; $16\frac{1}{2} \times 13\frac{3}{4}'' = £150$; $26\frac{1}{2} \times 17'' = £300$, etc.

In 1894, the owner of Wargrave Manor in Berkshire purchased no less than seven works by Birket Foster on Private View day (£324) and in the following year it is

94 Reproduced from *The Port of London Authority Monthly*, June 1934.
Greenwich Libraries: Local History Collection.

95 '**The Ferry Boat**'. This water-colour is very similar to the engraving of the same title in *Pictures of English Landscape*. In this case, Birket Foster has slightly changed the foreground introductions. Signed with monogram (left).
Photograph: Christie's.

pleasant to note that it was Edgar Horne, the new owner of The Hill, who bought 'A Little Courtyard in the Alhambra' (£36/10/-) which would enable this to hang in the former home of the artist. In 1896, as well as other sales, 'Ichrachan, Taynuilt' was purchased for £100 and in 1897 'Wild Flowers' for £150, with nine out of his total of ten exhibits also being sold. The last sales of work by Birket Foster exhibited with the Society are recorded on 15 December 1898 for 'The Pet Lamb' and 'Roy Bridge,

Inverness-shire' which were bought by a private collector for £89/5/-.

Towards the end of his career, Birket Foster was asked by the Royal Academy of Berlin to submit a list of his most important works and he replied: 'The above are some of the principal drawings made, but as many of them were sold to dealers I don't know who the present owners are.' Some of the subjects on this list have already been discussed, but Birket Foster named the following: 'On the shore, Bonchurch, Isle of Wight' – 1862; 'On the beach, Hastings' – 1865; 'The Convalescent' – 1868 (which Birket Foster notes was bought by An American); 'The Meet' – 1869; 'The Weald of Surrey' – 1870. The last two works were to form part of a major collection of the water-colours of Birket Foster in possession of Barnet Lewis, a wealthy

art collector. Both these pieces and 44 others from this source were illustrated in the 1906 biography. A collection of no less than 118 Birket Fosters was to be sold by the executors of Barnet Lewis (as part of a sale of his large general collection) at Christie's in February/March, 1930. The lots included 'Passing the Flock' exhibited at the Franco-British Exhibition in 1906 and 'The Dipping Place'.

Birket Foster continues his list with 'Lancaster' – 1871 – bought by his brother J. H. Foster; 'A fruiterer's shop' – 1873 (see *Water-colour Painting in Great Britain* by Martin Hardie, p. 111, B. T. Batsford); he also names 'A Fish Stall, Venice' – 1875 and 'Study of the Sea' – 1876; followed by 'A New Purchase' – 1878. He lists 'The Falls of Tummel' for 1879, purchased by Edmund Evans and

96 'The Village Churchyard'. Signed with monogram (right). This water-colour is almost identical to the engraving of the same title in *Pictures of English Landscape*, but without the figure or cattle. When the engraving later appeared in a reprint edition entitled *Pictures of Rustic Landscape* it was used to illustrate a piece on Selborne Church by Gilbert White. Birket Foster refuted this in a letter: '... this has nothing to do with Selborne ...' Size: $30\frac{1}{2} \times 26\frac{1}{2}''$ – 77.4 × 67.5 cms.
Photograph: Christie's.

'Greenwich' which he also dates as 1879 and was also bought by Edmund Evans. (Note: It seems that Birket Foster must have mistaken the date of this piece as the University of California holds a receipt dated 10 April 1878, which Birket Foster sent to Evans for £400 in payment for 'On the Thames, Greenwich' – almost certainly

161

as Ill. 94.) 'West Portal of Rheims Cathedral' is noted for 1880 (bought by a Mr C. Roberts) and 'Highland Scene, near Dalmally' – 1885 – bought by J. H. Foster, who also bought 'In the Market Place, Verona' – 1888. 'Arrival of the Hop Pickers at Farnham' – 1890 (Ill. 103) was sold to W. J. Joicey and has already been noted as priced at £500. J. H. Foster bought 'Ben Nevis' – 1891 (see *Water-Colour Painting in Great Britain*) and 'Loch Maree' – 1892. Foster concludes this list with 'The Footpath by the Water Lane' – 1892. Four of the water-colours bought by J. H. Foster were later sold at Christie's in 1906. (See p. 188 for further details.)

Water-colours by Birket Foster, in spite of fluctuations of fashion in art and interior design, have always been capable of bringing good prices, even in wartime England. In September 1943, pictures and water-colours from the collection of the late Colonel Sir William Thomlinson were sold at Christie's. *The Times* commented, under the headline 'High Prices for Birket Foster drawings':

'... This success was all the more remarkable owing to the fact that 45 water-colour drawings by him, ranging in size from mere vignettes to such a work as "Near Dalmally, Argyllshire", measuring $29\frac{1}{2} \times 42\frac{1}{2}''$, were offered – the general feeling being that such a number of works would be a severe test, even for his undoubted popularity.

The sale of the Thomlinson property (17 September 1943), consisting of 144 lots, brought a total of £20,600. Of this sum the 45 Birket Foster drawings made £11,798-17s. The more notable of these included "A Summer Landscape: Children playing on a fallen tree," which made £945; "Water-Lilies: two boys in a punt gathering a water-lily with a girl seated on a bank" £861; "The Sheep Fold" £840 [almost certainly Ill. 43]; "Windsor Lock, with the castle seen in the background" £819; "The Ferry: Sunset" £777; "Near Dalmally, Argyllshire" £714 [this cost £577 10/- in 1906]; "The Cottage Door: three children, one peeling an apple, another standing holding a broom" £504; "A

Woodland Scene: a girl with ducks near a pond" £441; "Gathering Lilac" £420 ...'

It is possible that these prices may have been slightly influenced by reason of a story that had got about that a mass of Birket Foster originals had been lost in the London blitz of 1940. The Foster connections have not heard of this and the probability is that it was not true, but may have evolved from the fact that all the Birket Foster blocks for *The Illustrated London News* had been destroyed – and M. B. Foster and Sons had been badly bombed.

It was after the war that a certain touchiness about the work of Birket Foster depressed the market for a while, owing to an exaggerated reaction to the possibility of fakes, but this was a passing phase. Many of the fakes have been identified and eliminated and a generally higher standard of expertise has now produced an excellent market for the work of Birket Foster, which must be sustained.[3] Any collector who buys a Birket Foster is indeed acquiring a unique item, as his style was so very much his own. He may have repeated themes, but he was an artist who took a real joy in his work and this has generated a special kind of integrity about his pictures.

A large water-colour of a haymaking scene reached the exceptionally high figure of £15,500 at Sotheby's in 1980, but a more usual range is represented by £9,000 for 'The Ferry' (Ill. 95) at Christie's in 1981 and also £9,000 for 'The Sheep Fold' (Ill. 43) in 1982. In the same sale 'The Village Churchyard (Ill. 96) fetched £8,500 and a later more topographical piece with the title 'Ichrachan, Taynuilt' (see p. 160) was sold for £2,400. 'A Peep at the Hounds' (Colour Ill. C) which was sold at Christie's for 280 gns in 1959 achieved £4,800 when the work reappeared there in 1982. Good examples can be estimated at anything between £4,500-£10,000 plus, with slighter or rather later pieces more in the region of £1,000-£4,000, depending on condition and the general appeal of the subject. The highest prices are still most likely to be made for genre scenes with typical introductions of women and children in a picturesque country landscape.

Notes : Chapter Seventeen
1 Published by permission of Newcastle upon Tyne City Libraries.
2 The faked work remains in the original private ownership. Since this part of the text was written, the Medici Society has issued a reproduction of the genuine work as a Christmas Card (ref. A-U27).
3 Bénézit – *Dictionnaire des Peintres, Sculpteurs, etc.* Vol. 4, p 452-3 gives some representative prices from 1861 to 1947.

18

Final years at The Hill and the move to Weybridge

'To Birket Foster, Esquire
My dear Foster,

A 'Dedication' – although considered now-a-days a somewhat antiquated formality, a sort of ceremonious bow on the part of an author – has like many other old-world fashions, a significance of cordial regard and friendliness. Such at least are the feelings I desire to express in dedicating to you this book.

Very sincerely yours,
Robert Dudley.'

This printed dedication appeared in *Monthly Maxims* ('Rhymes and Reasons to suit the Seasons and Pictures New to suit them Too') by Robert Dudley, which was published in 1882 by De La Rue and Co. with a great deal of advance publicity and advertising, but in spite of being a good quality production with competent illustrations, it was thought by *The Art Journal* to be a disappointment:

'... what possible good can such a publication serve? Mr. Dudley's drawing is exceptionally good, but his comicalities fail to raise a laugh, and as in turning each page a fresh instance of his power as an artist is seen, our annoyance is only increased that so much time and trouble have been thrown away....'

No doubt copies of this book would be liberally distributed as presents by both the Dudley and Foster families.[1] Illustration 97 shows Birket and Fanny Foster with the Dudleys and some of their family and other guests on Christmas Day 1882. The little dachshund that Willie Foster is holding was called 'Punch' and had been a gift to the Fosters from Charles Keene. 'Punch' was one of the puppies of 'Frau', his own much-loved dog, who frequently appeared in his work. Another puppy went to Robert Dudley and was named 'Bismarck'. The very last drawing that Charles Keene was ever to make was of 'Frau' in October 1891, just after her death at the age of 16 – a beautiful and infinitely touching study. 'Punch' and a little West Highland terrier called 'Sandy' often appear in the Foster family albums and frequently with Fanny Foster, who was particularly fond of these dogs.

These Christmas photographs give a happy glimpse of the house party out on the terrace in the winter sunshine or grouped on the steps, while Willie Foster manipulates his camera and carefully records the exposure times – 10 seconds for the group illustrated, which makes it hardly surprising that some of them look a mite solemn or strained. The gathering at The Hill in 1882, included Myles and his wife Christine, Harry and his fiancée Ethel,

Willie and Ellen, who were unmarried and still living at home, Charles Keene, Robert Dudley and his wife and two sons, with Bryan Hook (son of James Hook RA) and two other male guests. But, in spite of the renowned hospitality at The Hill, it happened that on the day that Birket Foster was to receive his most illustrious visitor he was quite alone in the house, except for the servants. This event must have taken place between about 1880 and 1884.

Princess Louise, Duchess of Argyll, fourth daughter of Queen Victoria, had a very genuine talent for painting and drawing and an intelligent interest in the work of artists of the period.[2] She admired the style of Birket Foster and while staying near Witley she decided that she would pay him a visit at The Hill. Thus, one afternoon, while Fanny Foster and Ellen were out for a drive in the carriage, a message was received that Her Royal Highness Princess Louise would shortly be passing and would like to call if convenient. Birket Foster was a shy man and was as much flustered as the servant who had taken the message. He was appalled at the thought of entertaining a Princess with hardly any warning and without his wife and daughter to support him, but it was too late to pretend to be ill or out. In later years, Ellen would tell and re-tell this highly amusing story to her children, as her daughter Sarah Glasson relates:

'... in a little while he heard sounds that sent him scurrying out into the hall and he was in time to meet the Princess at the door. She was staying with friends a short distance away and had ridden over, unattended, on her horse, which was tethered outside. Birket Foster bowed, shook hands and got out at least some of his hastily prepared speech of welcome and then proposed that they should go to his studio so that he could show the Princess some of his work. She readily agreed and he led her to the big studio with its magnificent screen designed by Burne-Jones. This created a diversion as she had to have the eight panels of the life of St Frideswide explained to her while she admired the work. Later, they discussed art and artists and Birket Foster found to his pleasure that after all it was not difficult to talk to a Princess with like tastes and interests and that, in fact, he was enjoying himself.

All too soon she rose to depart and Birket was escorting her across the hall, when he was suddenly overtaken with a terrible thought. She had ridden over unattended and he would have to perform the duties of a groom! Complete panic. He couldn't do it! He didn't know how to and would surely, either not get her up,

163

97 At The Hill: Christmas Day 1882. Back row: Charles Keene, Guildford Dudley, Henry Foster, Birket Foster, Robert Dudley. Seated: William Foster (with 'Punch'), Mrs Robert Dudley, Frances Foster and Ambrose Dudley. From an album in possession of Sarah G. A. Glasson.

or, worse still, throw her right over the horse's back onto the ground! Murmuring something about another sketch which he simply *must* show her, he left her in the hall and fled back to the studio. He had a moment or two of breathing space, then collecting a little drawing he returned very cautiously to the hall. There was no sign of the Princess and then, to quote the end of the story which never varied – I don't know what happened, but when I went out she was *ON!*'

Ellen Glasson told her children that when she and Fanny Foster returned from their drive, they found Birket Foster rather pleased with himself and confident that the visit had gone well. One can be very certain that indeed it had. Princess Louise must have found the company of Birket Foster a refreshing change. His shy, plain Quaker courtesy and gentle humour would be very different from the obsequious and totally insincere attitudes she would so often have had to endure.

On 13 April 1883, Charles Keene, by now in failing health, wrote to a friend: '. . . I ought to have been down in Surrey last night to hear the nightingales come. Birket Foster has gone to Spain, Tangier, etc. for six weeks.'

Birket Foster and Willie Foster were accompanied on

this trip by Robert Dudley. They sailed on 2 April by P & O liner to Gibraltar. A rather nice touch is to be found in the fact that at this time M. B. Foster and Sons were supplying large quantities of beer to all the major passenger shipping lines, including this one. It would no doubt amuse Birket Foster, although it is unlikely that any of the other passengers were aware of the connection between their bottle of 'Bugle Brand' and the famous artist travelling on board.

Owing to bad weather, the party was delayed for a week in Gibraltar and unable to cross to Tangier, but appears to have been very hospitably entertained by the Governor during this interval. Descriptions of journeys often make very dull reading, but can be useful in helping to date examples of work that result. H. M. Cundall gives details of this trip as follows:

'Eventually they were able to cross in a tug-boat, and they put up at Broussaud's Hotel, just outside the town, beyond the camel market. Here the party remained for some time making many sketches, the bright colours of the barbaric costumes affording many subjects for Birket Foster's pencil. On their return to Gibraltar they took a steamboat to Cadiz, and from there they went by train to Seville, where a stay of some days was made. Thence to Granada to see the Alhambra. Here Birket Foster made many sketches, and on one day he climbed up the building to copy some Moorish ornament, but he was obliged to abandon it, saying he thought the Moresque patterns must have been the invention of the devil. Robert Dudley states that this was the only oc-

casion on which he ever saw him fail to accomplish a task he had set himself to do with his pencil. From Granada the party proceeded to Cordova, thence to Madrid; afterwards to Avila and Burgos. From the latter town Birket Foster wrote the following letter, on 26 May 1883, to his son Myles:

"We have had a most delightful trip. I say *have* for we are coming home at full speed. Granada is perfect. The Alhambra, the woods full of Nightingales, the glor-

98 'A Window in the Alhambra, near Granada'. Watercolour signed with monogram (left). Birket Foster visited Spain in 1883. Size: 13½ × 10½" - 34.2 × 26.7 cms. *Photograph: Christie's.*

ious background of snow mountains, a good hotel and nice people make a thing not to be forgotten. Tangier was another delight. Moors, Arabs, Jews, camels, mosques - no mosquitos - and a good hotel with Arab

165

99 **'A View of King's College, Cambridge from King's Parade'**. Water-colour, signed with monogram (left). Size: 3¾ × 5½″ – 9.5 × 14 cms. Reproduced as Plate 4 in *Some Places of Note in England* – a series of lithographs from water-colours by Birket Foster, 1888.
Photograph: The Leger Galleries, London.

waiters, the hotel being the only European thing in the place. The music was awful. We went to a cafe to hear Moorish songs and did not get over it for days. Gib. was nice, and the Governor, Sir John Adye, and his family also. Seville was wet, and in consequence we did not see much life, but we went to a cafe and saw gypsies doing fandangos and singing awful ditties – so long that Dudley said he was sure it was the 199th Psalm.

"After Seville came Granada, then Cordova with its fine mosque. A magnificent looking organ at Seville, but very brassy; singing nothing much – beautiful mantillas etc. Cordova organ very fine and well played. From Cordova to Madrid – a Spanish Paris. On Sunday we went to a bull fight. The King and Queen were there. Oh, my goodness, of all the beastly exhibitions of cruelty! There was such a squash of humanity I couldn't get out, or I shouldn't have been there long. One light-coloured bull went at horse and man and buried and wriggled his horns in the inside of the horse, emerging with a head bright crimson, the entire inside of the horse hanging down to the ground, and yet the poor thing stood a minute before it toppled over dead. There are men to stop up holes with wadding – but, o, never again, as long as I live. From Madrid we went to Toledo, a charming old place. Inn of a very primitive character. After dinner we sat in the old courtyard amongst the diligences. The landlord and his wife also, while the chambermaids danced to the guitars of two blind men

for the amusement of the guests. Even the stout landlady danced (castanets of course) a real bit of old Spanish. Organ at Toledo and singing very fine. Back to Madrid to see the Corpus Christi fete. Magnificent procession. Madrid to Burgos, almost the best of all. We leave tomorrow for San Sebastian and so into France."'

Cundall concludes:

'From Burgos the travellers crossed over the Santillaos range of mountains to San Sebastian and Fonturabia; then over the Bidassoa into France, stopping a short time enroute at St Jean de Luz and Biarritz and then home by way of Bordeaux and Paris after an absence of two months.'

It is fortunate that there exists a note in Birket Foster's handwriting of a list of finished water-colours that resulted from this expedition to Spain, as follows: Moor's Market, Gibraltar; Gibraltar; Garden, Little Mosque; Sierra Nevada from Alhambra; Doorway, Little Mosque; Seville Square; Seville Market; Patio; Alhambra from the Generaliffe; Lady's Bower; Cadiz; Toledo; Little Courtyard, Alhambra; Fonturabia; Avila, Market Place; Burgos; Fountain, Seville; Seville with the river; Cordova; Court of Oranges, Cordova; Gateway, Granada (upright); Well, Granada; Market, Toledo.

Birket Foster had these 23 examples priced for a total of £1,090 with figures varying between £35 and £60.

In a letter to Polly Evans (née Brown) written from Bellagio, Lake Como on 15 May 1887, Birket Foster writes: '... we are having very cold weather here at the Lakes. I hope it won't last as we have had a good roasting at Naples and Sorrento. I suppose we shall (remain?) for a few days more and then move on to L. Maggiore...'[3] This long tour included the South of France, Venice,

Rome, Florence and Naples. While sketching in Florence, he was suddenly arrested by the police and marched off, for some reason which he never understood, but no doubt the unsuspecting Birket Foster had infringed some petty regulation and he was soon released and much amused by the incident.

A book with a similar format to *Brittany* was published by Dowdeswell and Dowdeswell in 1888. This was *Some Places of Note in England*, a series of 25 drawings by Birket Foster, with short descriptions by the artist. The Preface states:

'In giving a description of the Illustrations to these Places of Note In England, I have simply mentioned what it is that makes them celebrated. The facts have been borrowed from what I believe to be the most reliable sources.

The Drawings have been transferred to stone, and very carefully printed by Messrs Maclure and Company.'

It is important to note the significance of this last sentence, i.e. Birket Foster did not make the drawings on a prepared paper (as for *Brittany*). The resulting lithographs show very obviously the vital difference between the two books. The illustrations in *Some Places of Note in England* have lost much of the life of the original drawings and the general effect of these sepia engravings is rather automatic. This large volume is handsomely bound in a blue cloth cover and leather spine with pages only fractionally smaller than those of *Brittany* ($14\frac{1}{2} \times 10\frac{1}{2}''$). The plates are of a uniform size ($4 \times 5\frac{3}{4}''$ – with a slightly tinted indentation of the paper to give a total presentation of $6\frac{1}{4} \times 8''$). The book was designed and printed by the Chiswick Press and contains typical decorations in the style of this firm.

The illustrations are based on sketches and drawings

100 'Bridge Street Row East, Chester' – as seen from no. 23. Buildings opposite now demolished. Water-colour with body colour over pencil, signed with monogram (right). Size: $4\frac{3}{4} \times 6''$ – 12 × 15.2 cms. Reproduced: Plate 7 in *Some Places of Note in England* – a series of lithographs from the water-colours of Birket Foster, published in 1888.
Photograph: Sotheby's.

from a wide span of years. 'Bamboro' Castle' was from a sketch made during the visit to the Farne Islands in 1848. Birket Foster introduces some slight personal interest into his commentary by telling us this, but, in general, the descriptions are pure guide book and very dull. Warwick Castle, we are told, is a view 'taken from the bridge', but a nice touch is added to the illustration by the introduction of an interesting little detail in the riverside meadows. On very close inspection, this proves to be a rotund gentleman, seated at an easel, with brushes to hand and a small girl sprawled on the grass beside him.

'Cambridge' and 'Chester' (here Ills. 99, 100) show original water-colours which were later reproduced in *Some Places of Note in England*. Both these works are full of interesting topographical detail and this has been faithfully reproduced in the lithographs, but with a subtle smoothing of the original treatment – and the unexplained addition of an 'S' to Geeson in the Chester piece. The full list of subjects is as follows: Bamborough Castle, Northumberland; Berkeley Castle, Gloucestershire; Bolton Priory; Cambridge; Canterbury; Carisbrooke; Chester; Eton College; Haddon Hall; Hampton Court; Hastings; Knaresborough, Yorkshire; Lambeth Palace; Oxford; Richmond-on-Thames; Stratford-on-Avon; Tewkesbury; The Tower of London; Tilbury Fort; Warwick; Westminster; Winchester; Windsor; Woodstock; York.

Some Places of Note in England provides a helpful refer-

167

ence to the locations used as subjects by Birket Foster, but it does not bring forward the spirit of the originals in the manner of *Brittany*. These volumes can be found in very good condition, as the paper is not easily subject to foxing.

In 1890, Marcus Huish, Editor of *The Art Journal*, proposed to write a long article on Birket Foster, which was to form the Christmas Supplement for that year. One of the most interesting aspects of his article is that he went down to Surrey to interview Birket Foster and in his description of the journey we have a nice evocation of an England that was still under the reign of Victoria, but had all the atmosphere of the approaching Edwardian era.

'The South-Western line retains for a longer distance perhaps than any other its hideous metroplitan character. The country betters some time before Godalming is reached, but it is after passing that picturesque town that West Surrey dons its forest garb; then it is that above the sandy embankment, tipped with heather and bright with broom, one enjoys that always delightful sensation of peering down the dim arcades formed by innumerable pines, whose resiny odour penetrates even the stuffy railway compartment.

As the train deposits us at the little station of Witley, we find ourselves in a garden, and the scent of the pine wood is exchanged for that of roses, hundreds of which, the product of a single root, line the platform from end to end. Traversing a short pathway, we arrive at a wicket gate, which opens into a wood, and we are on Mr Foster's soil, and at the base of a steepish ascent, upon which stands his residence 'The Hill'. The shelter of the wood is presently exchanged for that of an avenue of deftly woven filbert-trees, diverging paths from which open up vistas of a sundial garden, a mass of roses, poppies, campanulas, corn and sunflowers, a lakelet white with water-lilies, and well-stocked strawberry beds.'

Marcus Huish then follows with a description of the site of The Hill, as quoted on p. 89 and after extolling the beauties of the house ('... decked by flowers which depend from the windows and over its sides and roof ...') he continues:

'Leaving a game of bowls in which he had been successfully combating against his son and a young student of the Royal Academy (who is supposed to be hard at work painting an old graveyard near by, the competitive subject for the Turner Gold Medal) our host hastens up the lawn to greet us. Tall and erect, no one would credit that he is over sixty years of age, whilst his open countenance and hearty welcome quite belie the somewhat stern appearance in which his portraits always clothe him, and which is present even when the photographer is, as in the case of the one taken for us, a member of his family and the locale is his own garden. One is at once assured of a welcome at Witley, and having long heard of the treasures which The Hill contains, but a few moments elapse before a movement is irresistably made towards the house, and one's back is turned on the delights of the garden.

As Mr Foster hastens to tell us, in a somewhat deprecatory tone of voice, and as if to reconcile one to

101 The Hill: photographed by William Foster about 1890. Fanny Foster on the terrace with 'Sandie'. Below: the carriage drive entrance.

shortcomings, he has practically been his own architect. There is little need for him to mention this, for the house and its contents testify to that best quality, when the designer is an artist - individuality.'

Birket Foster had now been at The Hill for 27 years, and Huish delighted in all that he saw of the house and garden, which had matured with its designer and must then have been at about the highest point of its charm, although the career of Birket Foster was fading with the Victorian era and with it were passing so many of those who had been an essential part of it. The friendship between Birket Foster and Charles Keene finally came to an end in 1891. Keene had written to Joseph Crawhall on 16 December 1889:

'I've had an invitation to Birket Foster's for Christmas, but since I have been an invalid have got to be partial to my own bed and fireside, but I shall try and pluck up courage to go. I'll advise you in time; at present I'm enjoying a convalescent immunity from pain, and feel braver - have been recommended the juice of lemons without sugar and begin to believe in it ...'

There is something very touching about this glimpse of the now fatally ill Charles Keene, struggling to summon up the strength to join once again the festivities at The Hill, where his presence had become a traditional part of Christmas. Charles Keene, amusing talker and kindly listener, musicianly singer and gentle, original personality, so much loved by all the Foster family, was never to see The Hill again, although he lingered for just over another year, until his death on 4 January 1891.

In his *Art Journal* article, Marcus Huish provides an interesting comment on the fact that by this time books illustrated by Birket Foster were out of popular favour, as the tide of social change swept in an entirely different style of life and art.

'We see them marked in the second-hand booksellers catalogues at six, five, nay even three shillings a piece and pass them by, although in the majority of instances, independently of the illustrations, they are admirably printed editions of standard authors. When Art is so much a matter of fashion it is hopeless to forecast, and foolish to do so in print, but yet I have no hesitation in saying that the time cannot be far distant when the turn of the wheel will bring again a more accurate appreciation of these admirable specimens of true woodcutters' art, and that in their *first* editions, where alone the blocks are seen to their best advantage, they will be sought for and bought up at very different prices from those for which they are now offered.'

This prophecy took some time to fulfil, but nearly one hundred years later it has been totally justified and the quality and charm of these finely crafted illustrations is reflected in current prices for any book illustrated by Birket Foster. It is strange that circumstances should have prevented Birket Foster from providing illustrations for a book of poems by Lord Tennyson, but we note from an incidental mention by Huish that the Poet Laureate lived quite near to The Hill and the two men did indeed become friends in their later years, although their last meeting was at Freshwater, Isle of Wight, where Birket Foster was staying and Tennyson had a house. During this visit Birket Foster frequently went for walks with Tennyson in the grounds of his home and this was obviously a great enjoy-

102 The Hill: the grounds (about 1890). From photographs by William Foster in possession of Sarah G. A. Glasson.

ment for both men. Tennyson would conduct spirited discussions on a wide variety of subjects, although he was very much an invalid and had a nurse in constant attendance. Even so, the burly Birket Foster felt that the poet was strong enough to walk him off his legs, but Tennyson would pause now and then and recite passages from his own poems to suit the scenery or the conversation – and then set off again at a great pace!

On one occasion, he showed Birket Foster a large cedar-wood box of cigars with a facsimile of his signature in gold wire on the lid and remarked: 'This is the sort of thing that they send me from America, but what's the good of them? I don't smoke cigars.' His son, Hallam Tennyson, promptly volunteered to make sure that they were not wasted.[4] *

A most poignant letter was written by Birket Foster on 8 October 1892 to his brother, who then lived in Newcastle:

'My dear Robt.,

I was very pleased to get your letter this evening – I have just arrived at home from Scotland.

It was a great blow to me the death of Lord Tennyson – I was to have sent him a very fine Photograph of himself which Cundall took many years ago – the one he liked best and which he hadn't got. Willie copied it with his camera & I promised to send the original to Lord T. There seemed no hurry and as we were leaving for Scotland it got deferred. Now I can only send it to his son or Lady Tennyson with my tears.

The old Poet's words to me on the last walk we had together are significant. "Does it ever strike you, as a landscape painter, that going through an avenue of trees into the light beyond is like passing through the grave into Eternity." We were then going through a dark mass of trees with bright sunshine beyond. It is a great loss to me for I was getting very intimate with him. At parting when I said how much I had enjoyed my walks with him he said I'm very sorry you are going – come and see me at Aldworth.

In passing down Regent St. today I saw shops full of the wreaths to be placed on his tomb. I should have liked to have been present but I arrived too late to get a ticket for the Abbey.

I met Myles Meggie and Christine in Scotland and he told me how he wanted to leave the Foundling as he has so much work to do he finds the 3 days a week too great a hole in his time. Fanny and Willie are at Sedbergh for a few days – My Exhibition work compelled me to return as I have much to do.

With dear love to you both,
    I am your affec. bro.
    Birket Foster.'[5]

In 1893, Birket Foster became seriously ill with what were probably the first symptoms of his last illness. Considering the number of times in his working career that he had shaped a paintbrush between his lips, one is given to speculate (as his family did) as to whether a cumulative effect of trace elements of poisonous pigment had been the initial cause of his fatal stomach complaint. Birket Foster was now 68 years old and times were changing. His work was still popular, but in a genre that was on the wane, as new fashions in art heralded the approach of a new century and an entirely different world. He was still in very comfortable financial circumstances, but the responsibility for the upkeep of a house and grounds of the size of The Hill was too much for an ailing man and it was decided that this should be sold. The event caused a spate of rumours that Birket Foster was either dying or financially ruined, so that a newspaper published the following: 'It may be interesting to our readers to know that Mr Birket Foster's reason for leaving Witley is a simple one. He is tired of the place and requires new pastures; that is all.'

The Hill was described in the press as 'A Surrey Eden' and was sold in 1893 for what was then considered to be the large sum of £10,000 to a Mr Edgar Horne, Chairman of the Prudential Assurance Company, who had always very much admired the style of The Hill and wished to maintain it in the spirit of the original conception of Birket Foster. Edgar Horne was also of Quaker descent and was a grandson of Richard Alderson, who had been one of the principal members of the Brigflats Meeting of the Society of Friends, in company with Robert Foster, grandfather of Birket.

Birket Foster left The Hill on 25 June 1894. The Glasson family have in their possession a cutting from an unnamed newspaper (obviously from a northern provincial source) which states:

'The "Daily News" kills a great artist today. The gloomy deed is connected with the picture sale at Christie's on Saturday [i.e. 28 April 1894]. One reads that "pictures are still good investments, even in these hard times. At Saturday's sale at Messrs Christie and Manson's two collections were disposed of, and one alone, the late Mr Birket Foster's, fetched £6,291". In noticing the exhibition of the old Water-colour Society the other day I spoke of the freshness and vigour of Mr Birket Foster's drawings. I may now add that they were all sold immediately on the opening of the exhibition. Mr Birket Foster is by no means dead, though I regret to say that he is in ill-health. This, in fact, is the reason for the sale of some of his pictures at Christies on Saturday.[6] Mr Birket Foster is breaking up his house at Witley, which is on the borders of Surrey and Sussex. He has lived there in a kind of princely state for a great number of years. Witley is a lovely countryside, with abundance of those quaint thatched cottages with which Birket Foster has made us familiar, and is near to Haslemere, which has of late years become a colony of artists and literary men. I wonder if this eminent artist is coming back to the North. He belongs to North Shields as I need not remind you. He is a member of the somewhat complex family to which the Spences, the Spence Watsons and the Corders belong. His ancestry would be found, I believe, in the little Quaker burying ground at North Shields.'

Ancestral ties did not take Birket Foster back to the North, but he was to remain in his beloved Surrey, where he and Fanny (and William) made their new home in Weybridge. Here they lived at Braeside, which was the last house in the road that is now known as Hanger Hill, but was then Station Road. Braeside was on the edge of and opposite to the Heath and it was as Braeside, The Heath, that the house was known. It was obviously much smaller than The Hill, but was by no means a pokey substitute, as it stood in an acre of ground and was large enough to be converted into an hotel in later years.[6]

It must have been a sad wrench for Birket Foster to sell almost his entire collection of pictures, although obviously he would no longer be able to house these, but his choice of those to retain is perhaps a little unexpected, particularly in regard to the Hunts. Eight of these were sold, including the specially commissioned pieces. Only 'Hastings Castle' (dark battlements in a horizontal composition) and a very dismal and very dead 'Hare and Partridge' were kept. Surely these cannot have been Birket Foster's favourites? One would have so much more expected him to have chosen one of the flower or nest pieces. Turner's 'Lake of Geneva' appears to have been kept, with 'Sunset' by Samuel Palmer and Fred. Walker's Venetian palace with Orchardson standing in a window, although the gentle 'Chaplain's Daughter' was sold, but not the study of Ellen Foster. 'The Hhareem' by J. F. Lewis was put up as lot 25, but was bought in at £183/10/- (and would not finally leave ownership of the Foster family until 1921 when it was sold at Christie's for 125 gns.). One of the known favourites in Birket Foster's collection was a charming little study by Edouard Frère, showing a small girl warming her hands by a stove. Birket Foster had a special affection for this piece and it was not included in the 1894 sale.

103 'The Arrival of Hop Pickers, Farnham'. Water-colour, signed with monogram (left). Exhibited no. 63 at the Royal Society of Painters in Water-colours, 1890. Sold at the private view for £500. Size: 29 × 42″ – 73.6 × 106.6 cms.
Photograph: Frost and Reed Ltd, London.

Notes : Chapter Eighteen

1 A copy of *Monthly Maxims* in possession of Prof. G. N. Brown has written on the fly leaf in Birket Foster's hand: 'To Capt. and Mrs Nelson/On their Silver wedding/With best wishes from Fanny Foster and Birket Foster/Jan 7th 1883.'

2 Birket Foster (at some date in the early 1870s) is known to have made a donation of five monogrammed water-colours of Hastings to the Duchess of Argyll for sale at a charity bazaar under her patronage. In 1886 he received a very admiring letter from the subsequent purchaser, who wished to be assured that the 'Beautiful Pictures were indeed painted by a Gentleman so distinguished as Birket Foster, RA' (*sic*).

3 Letter to Polly Evans published by permission of the University of California, Los Angeles, Special Collections Department.

4 Information from the Glasson family.

5 Published by permission of Andrew J. Ashton, Keeper of Art, Bury Museum – from his private collection. Formerly in the collection of Percy Corder and exhibited item no. 164, Special Loan Exhibition – Birket Foster Centenary, Laing Gallery, Newcastle upon Tyne, 1925.

6 See appendix for further details of the 1894 Christie's sale of pictures in the collection of Birket Foster.

7 Braeside Hotel, Hanger Hill, Weybridge was demolished in the early 1970s and Conniston Court, a block of flats, now stands on the site.

19
The Last Years

On Christmas Eve, 1894, Birket Foster replied to a letter from Mrs Ruth Church (née Dale) who was a sister of his eldest daughter's first husband. Photographs of Ruth Church appear in the family album – a plumply jolly young woman, with a humorous expression, behind a pair of rather unbecoming pince-nez. At the top of his letter, Birket Foster has drawn a little robin, within a roughly suggested square.

> 'My dear Ruthie,
> It was kind of you to remember me and I shall value the little stamp case more than I can tell you. I have been bad with bronchitis almost ever since your little visit to us & have never been out of the house – so you must kindly accept a *home-made* Xmas card with my love and best wishes for as much happiness as is good for you. We half hope Ellen and Lance will come to us tomorrow, if not we shall be alone.
> We enjoyed Edith's visit to us greatly. Last week we had Mr Dudley to lunch one day & Alfred and Lizzie Cooper & Mr and Mrs Evans another.
> I am getting on with my Pardon Procession – I hope it may turn out well – We have very little news. I suppose you are busy receiving and visiting and letter writing. Remember me very kindly with best wishes to Mr Church and Miss Beale - & with love to yourself.
> I am very affect.ly yours,
> Birket Foster.
> The Stevensons were in yesterday.'[1]

Some years ago, Professor G.N. Brown (now of the Betley Court Gallery) bought this letter in a second-hand shop. It had been framed to show the robin sketch (with part of the letter also visible) and with the item intact. With the exception of Mr Church and Miss Beale, the people mentioned in this letter have already appeared in this book. Birket Foster must have been full of memories of past Christmasses at The Hill, as he told Ruth Church of old friends, of Polly and her sister Lizzie and of Robert Dudley, who had been such a stalwart organiser of the amateur theatricals. Many of the people who had been at these lively gatherings were now dead and the Foster sons and daughters were gone from home and had family commitments of their own, with the exception of Willie Foster, who was still living at Braeside, but may have been spending Christmas with the Hooks. One senses a quiet nostalgia in this letter. But, in spite of age and infirmity, Birket Foster was still working and still deriving interest and pleasure from this, although he had spent over 30 years as

a water-colourist and nearly half a century as an independent artist. In the autumn of 1894, he had written to Edmund Evans from 1 Cumberland Terrace, Southwold, Suffolk (a favourite haunt of Charles Keene). He commented: '...it has been very stormy weather cold with heavy showers here, but this is a delightful place. I have done a good deal out of doors and enjoyed it very much ....' 'The Ferry, Walberswick' (Ill. 106) is linked with this visit and has that subtle quality of renewed delight in his work that is shown in many of these very late examples. 'The Pardon Procession' that he mentions in the letter to Ruth Church was based on a sketch which was used in the illustration of *Brittany* – showing young girls in white, walking through the streets of Quimper, holding banners and an image of the Virgin. This particular work was rather long in being completed and for reasons which are amusingly recorded in the family biographical notes:

> 'B.F. was etching and Mr Heygate [a friend of William] while smoking and prowling about found a large unfinished water-colour drawing of a Pardon Procession in which a group of girls were carrying a draped stand with nothing on it. He asked why it was not finished and B.F. replied: "It is all Willie's fault. I've asked him dozens of times when he has gone to London to bring me a Virgin Mary and he has not done it!" B.F. did not know the correct colours of the robes of the BVM but eventually got all further information from Father MacDaniel at Weybridge...'

Birket Foster exhibited this picture with the Royal Society of Painters in Water-colours in 1895.

In 1874, Birket Foster had been invited to become an honorary member of the Royal Berlin Academy. He enjoyed this recognition, although he did not exhibit very frequently. On 2 February 1895, he wrote to Mrs Stevenson, who would be of the chemical manufacturing family in North Shields, who also had a house in Weybridge,

> 'Dear Mrs Stevenson,
> Mrs Foster tells me you are a German scholar. If so I am going to ask you to do me a great favour & translate the enclosed or at any rate give me the drift of it. They will write to me in German & I generally put them in the fire, but as I am a member and this from the envelope seems urgent & important I must somehow get it translated – Perhaps it is only to wish me a happy new year – or it may be they wish to turn me out of the Academy for not exhibiting.

Poor Mrs Foster is in bed with Bronchitis – and is very poorly. Dr Sealy has her in hand and I hope she will soon be up again. The weather is against it rather.
I hope you are keeping alright.
With love from us all, I am very sincerely yours,
Birket Foster.
I think Willie is beginning a bad cold.'[2]

In fact, the letter from the Royal Berlin Academy was to congratulate Birket Foster on his seventieth birthday! This was due to fall on 4 February 1895 and once the purport of the letter was revealed he was greatly touched by the gesture and one is left to wonder if any of the British exhibiting bodies had the civility and kindness to mark the occasion in a similar manner, or in such fulsome terms:

'... what you have accomplished in your rich and fruit-ful life for the advancement of art will outlive the memory of man. For the faithful rendering of all that is beautiful and noble may there be allotted to you a sunny and long life's evening with undiminished power of work. ...'

Edmund Evans, his friend for over 50 years, had not forgotten. On 22 February 1895, Birket Foster wrote to him:

'My dear Ned,
I wish you many happy returns of your birthday. Thank you very much for remembering mine and for your good wishes. I fear it is a bad time for picture selling – but Woods is rather apt to depress you before the sale so that you may be pleased with the result. Willie went to McLeans to see our St George and the Dragon series – which he has bought and is going to publish as Photogravure and engraving mixed. W. says they look simply splendid. They have been varnished slightly which brings out the colour just as it was when they were painted – we really ought to have made more out of them.'

At this point in the letter, the paragraph which follows has been cut out on the instructions of Birket Foster, who has written 'burn this' in the margin. As a result we are not able to discover what had displeased him about the sale of the seven panels by Burne-Jones that had been in the dining-room at The Hill. When these were auctioned at Christie's (28 April 1894) the complete set had been bought by Agnew for £2,100, which would seem to be a satisfactory price for the period, but no doubt Birket Foster had got wind of a much larger sum later being obtained by this dealer. There appears to have been no mention at this time of the part played by Charles Fairfax Murray in the execution of the 'St George and the Dragon' series, but Burne-Jones did some re-painting of all seven panels before these were exhibited at Gooden's Gallery, Pall Mall, London in January 1896. In August 1897 these paintings gained a gold medal for Burne-Jones at the Munich International Exhibition. The remaining portion of the letter concludes:

'... plate is progressing.
With love from us all,
Yours affec.
Birket Foster.'[3]

Edmund Evans must have been working on an engraving for a print after the work of Birket Foster in order to publish this as an individual issue. Foster writes again on 10 March 1895:

'Dear Ned,
I am sorry I have been so long in touching the proof, but I have had much to do of one sort or another. You have done much good work on the plate but there is much to accomplish before it is presentable.'

Birket Foster then goes into detailed instructions as to the corrections required ('... I have reduced the light on the birch tree a little – get the jug into tone – it looks like rock work ... the girl's white bodice should have all the folds and markings very delicate ...', etc.). In a further letter, he comments: 'I hope you will be able to dispose of it, but I fancy the etching business has been rather over-done.'

Birket Foster had himself undertaken a few etchings in the previous decade or so, but probably with little real enthusiasm. In 1880, he had agreed to the request of H. M. Cundall that he should produce an illustration for *The Etcher*. In April of that year he wrote:

'Dear Mr Cundall,
I have tried my hand at an etching, but it is so long since I did anything of that kind, I am rather diffident about sending it to you. I had intended throwing it on one side and trying again, but my painting engagements are so increasing that I fear I shall not have time to do anything more at present, but if you think it will suit you, all well and good. The printer will be able to do more for it I daresay than you see in this proof.
Believe me, yours sincerely, etc.'[4]

The etching on copper was entitled 'Sheep Feeding' and appears to have taken Birket Foster back to an influence from Bewick. This rather dull illustration was nevertheless successful and stimulated interest in obtaining more such work from Birket Foster. In the following year *The Art Journal* published a Foster etching of 'The Old Mill' and 'The Little Shepherds' in 1890. Birket Foster also etched 'The Wandering Minstrel' in 1881 (published by Dowdeswell) and 'Crossing the Brook' in 1883 (published by A. Tooth). An etching of Fred. Walker's 'Driving Geese, Cookham' was published in 1888 by McLure and McLean and 'Home Sweet Home' by the Fine Art Society in 1891. These late etchings have to be regarded as more of a novelty than part of the serious work of Birket Foster. Most were executed at the request of publishers with whom he had long been associated and who would be fully aware of the commercial possibilities of any etching to which the name of Birket Foster was attached.

On 28 May 1895, Birket Foster wrote to the elder son of Edmund Evans, who was in partnership with his father:

'Dear Wilfred,
You are welcome to engrave my portrait for the book if Mr Nimmo is anxious to have it done.
Your affec. uncle.'

(– a familiar form of address by which Birket Foster would be known to the children of Edmund Evans). The book to which Birket Foster refers was *Pictures of Rustic Landscape* with passages in prose and verse selected by John David-son, author of *Ballads and Songs* – with portrait and 30 engravings (published by John C. Nimmo, London, 1896). The book was printed by the firm of Edmund Evans and was merely an attempt by a publisher to capitalise on the

success of *Pictures of English Landscape*. The illustrations are printed from the Dalziel blocks, but the book does not have the essential feel of the original editions. The text is *not* an improvement on that of Tom Taylor, who was at least aiming to 'illustrate' the Birket Foster subjects. *Pictures of Rustic Landscape* contains a very ill-assorted anthology. On 18 June 1895, Birket Foster replied to a query from Wilfred Evans: 'None of the drawings in the English Landscape book are localities. The enclosed has nothing to do with Selborne.'

'The Village Church' had been used to illustrate a piece on Selborne Church by Gilbert White! The fact that Birket Foster says that his drawing is nothing of the kind

104 'Wandering Minstrels'. Water-colour, signed with monogram (left). Size: 25 × 20½" – 63.5 × 52 cms. Exhibited: Birket Foster Centenary Exhibition, Laing Art Gallery, 1925.
Collection: Burnley Borough Council, Towneley Hall Art Gallery and Museum.

is typical of the inevitable topographical confusion that must result from this hotch-potch of only vaguely related text, as used in conjunction with the Birket Foster illustrations. In the same way, an academic discussion by Izaak Walton is totally out of keeping with Birket Foster's drawing of 'The Little Anglers', although one concedes that 'The Miller's Daughter' by Tennyson does have a certain relevance to 'The Water Mill'.

105 'A Highland Burn'. Water-colour, signed Birket Foster. Must be dated about 1893. Size: $8\frac{1}{4} \times 5\frac{1}{2}''$ – 21 × 14 cms.

Reproduced by Gracious Permission of Her Majesty the Queen. Photograph: Royal Library, Windsor Castle.

In a letter of 26 June 1895, Birket Foster wrote to Wilfred Evans with a somewhat weary attitude to the whole project:

'I don't think you need alter the background – It is rather a plaster, but I fear we might make it worse instead of better.

The portrait is I suppose as good as these things generally are.

Yours affec.ly,
Birket Foster.'

The portrait was engraved from the photograph (Ill. 109) and appears to be a competent piece of work, in spite of Birket Foster's rather quaint reference to its being 'a plaster'. *Pictures of Rustic Landscape* can never be in the same category as *Pictures of English Landscape*, but the book does provide an opportunity for the collector to acquire reprints of all the illustrations from the latter, in a volume that is less likely to be in a collapsed condition than many of the original editions. *Pictures of Rustic Landscape* has a sewn binding and is in heavy boards and green cloth cover, with gold-blocked titles and page edges. This book should not be confused with *Pictures of English Rustic Life* – a piece of book-making by the Dalziels, which was published by Routledge in 1882. This had originally been intended as a companion volume for *Pictures of English Landscape* and all the drawings were to have been after the work of Fred. Walker, but in the event only eleven were finished and *Pictures of English Rustic Life* eventually came out after the publication of the 1881 edition of *Pictures of English Landscape*. The former does not contain work by Birket Foster. The variations of similar titles can be very confusing, but it should be noted that *In Rustic England* published by Hodder and Stoughton in 1906 contains 25 attractive colour plates from the Rowney and McQueen prints of work by Birket Foster.

As Birket Foster was writing to Edmund Evans on 9 February 1896, it was 55 years since they had first met. Birket was probably remembering the old days when two youths wandered about the wharves of London, looking for picturesque 'bits' to sketch, unconcerned with time or weather. He was never to grow crabby or complaining in his old age, but his letters have an inevitable nostalgia.

'Braeside,
The Heath, Weybridge, Surrey.
My dear Ned,
I was so pleased to get your letter thank you very much for your good wishes. I am such a bad letter writer that I will wish you many happy returns of the 23rd. which I believe is your day now. We are getting old but with care I hope we may both of us have a few more years to enjoy *this* beautiful world, I have managed with the greatest care to escape as yet getting cold, but it is not *summer* yet. I enjoy my work I think more than ever but of course I don't do as much as I used to – I take my time about it. I went to town on Thursday last. I hadn't been in London for ages – it was a risk but I have not suffered for it. I went to attend our meeting for electing members and associates. Allen the Scotch painter and Arthur Hopkins were made members and we elected Miss Butler a charming painter of cattle and a Mr Hopwood a very *strong* figure man whose work I never saw before – Swan ARA rebuked and Lockhart who forfeited his associateship for not exhibiting as associates.'

The references in this slightly confusing account of a meeting of the Royal Society of Painters in Water-colours are to Robert Weir Allen (1852–1942) and Arthur Hopkins (1848–1930) – the latter painted country scenes in the style of Helen Allingham; Mildred Anne Butler (1858–1941); Henry Silkstone Hopwood (1860–1914); John Macallan Swan (1847–1910); and William Ewart Lockhart (1846–1900). Birket Foster continues:

'Herkomer told me that he had been *enlarging* several of my Pictures of English Landscape to illustrate a lecture on composition – I said to him that I thought composition was ignored nowadays and he said "Ah! it is coming back again".'

Hubert Herkomer, RA, acted as President of the Royal Society of Painters in Water-colours throughout 1896 and until 1898, owing to the illness of Sir John Gilbert. He threw himself into the work with rather embarrassing energy and effected many changes in the rules of the Society. He was knighted in 1907, but always preferred to be known as 'Professor', having held the Slade Chair in Fine Art at Oxford, but the lecture here referred to would no doubt be given before students at his own school in Bushey, Hertfordshire.

There is something rather touching about the now infirm Birket Foster making a determined effort to attend yet another election meeting of the society of which he had been a member for over 36 years. He had never been a man to pontificate about painting and always gives an impression of being very modest about his own success, but his devotion to art was deeply felt. We can sense this in a letter that was published in conjunction with one from H.S. Marks, RA, with reference to the proposed donation of an art gallery in the East End of London. The letter is headed: 'Birket Foster, R.I. [sic] on the Influence of Art for Good' and is dated 15 February 1896:

'Dear Sir,
Canon Barnett's proposal that East London should have a building comprising an art gallery meets with my warm approval.

The elevated effect of Art upon the lives and characters of those who are brought under its influence cannot, I think, be over estimated. That this is so amongst the cultured and educated needs no argument. But beyond this I believe that human nature does not differ widely in its capability of being led to see and appreciate the beautiful, and the sight and appreciation of that beauty is, of necessity, ennobling and refining.

In the hard lives of the poor of East London there is, perhaps, nothing that works more powerfully for evil than the absence of the beautiful and the ideal in life, and there is in Art a moral force powerful in combatting this evil.

If an art gallery be established in your midst where the people of East London will have opportunities of seeing the works of our best artists, the influence of this will not be without its effect for good.

I am, Dear Sir,
Faithfully Yours,
Birket Foster'

(from a newspaper cutting in the possession of the Glasson family – not named.)

Birket Foster concluded his letter to Edmund Evans on a sad note:

'Witley seems in a very deserted condition – I hope you

106 'The Ferry, Walberswick'. Water-colour, signed with monogram (left). Probably dated about 1894. Size: 9½ × 13½″ – 24.1 × 34.2 cms.
Collection: Miss P. Jephcott. Photograph: Richard and Georgina Ivor.

107 'On Guildford Common'. Water-colour, signed with monogram (left). Size: 5⅞ × 8¾″ – 14.9 × 22.3 cms.
Collection: Metropolitan Borough of Rochdale, Rochdale Art Gallery and Museum.

180

will be successful as to the sale of your house. Julia writes me that they have let their house to Lord William Seymour.

I fancy M.B. Fosters will come all right now that it is reorganised. I hope so.

With love to you all from us all,
I am affectionately yours,
Birket Foster.'

The general tone of an article in *Commerce* (10 June 1896) is set by the title 'Beer Sellers and Beer Cellars', but in spite of a heavily jokey style (under the pseudonym 'Lesser Columbus') this 36-page, illustrated piece gives a very detailed and informative account of the firm of M.B. Foster and Sons. Birket Foster, in his letter to Edmund Evans, would appear to have some anxiety about the firm, although it is difficult to see a reason for this, unless it was in connection with a recent appointment of some new directors. M.B. Foster and Sons had become a limited company in 1890 and its operations now formed a major industrial complex, which occupied two vast sites in London and Woolwich, with private railway sidings and a jetty to accommodate the shipping side of the business. M.B. Foster and Sons were now the largest firm of bottlers in the world[5] – a far cry from the day when young Robert Foster hid a bottle of home-brewed beer under a stone in a stream to keep it cool. (See also p. 188.)

On 21 February 1897, just after his seventy-second birthday, Birket Foster wrote to Edmund Evans:

'... We are growing old, but I am thankful to say that I enjoy life still and love my work. I went to a meeting of the Old Society on Thursday to elect associates, but no one was deemed quite up to the mark and no election took place. T. Hope McLachlan our neighbour here was the nearest and I think it was shameful that he did not get in as his drawings were very good – fine – I hope he will succeed next time.'

The romantic and moody landscapes of T.H. McLachlan, ROI, may have appealed to Birket Foster, but they were never to obtain acceptance for the artist as an Associate of the Royal Society of Painters in Water-colours. Birket Foster continues his letter with comments on some of his fellow members: 'Sir Ed. Burne-Jones is a good deal aged – and Marks looks very tottery . . .' Both painters were younger than Birket Foster, but both were to die within the next 18 months. Not so the remarkable grand old man of the Society who was 'Wm. Callow looking quite young at 90 or very near it . . .' In fact, Callow was $84\frac{1}{2}$, but had another ten active years to live. One likes to think that his cheerful longevity was a comfort to Birket Foster, who was undoubtedly feeling the loss of so many of his contemporaries and his own advancing years. He adds: 'This is a glorious day and makes one feel to want to be out working but it won't do yet . . . Racquet Court to be demolished!! What changes are taking place. . . .' In May 1896, the Racquet Court business of Edmund Evans was formally transferred to his sons, Wilfred and Herbert Evans, and the family tradition was later carried on by his grandson, Rex Evans. The firm was amalgamated with W.P. Griffith in 1953, but finally ceased to trade in the late 1960s.

The letter from Birket Foster continues:

'Mrs Allingham had lunch with me in town before the meeting of the RWS and told me she saw you at Hampstead, Leighton and Watts are fine in their different ways.

I hope you have quite got over the effects of your chill – you'll have to take care. Lance occasionally comes over to see us. Ellen seems to have got over her trouble pretty well, but Peggie has been poorly. Willie and I voted for our Conservative Member on Thursday – it was a very quiet affair.

We have very little news that would interest you as you don't know the people here – it is a very chatty neighbourly place and we like it very much.

With love from us all to you and yours,
Best wishes for the 23rd.,
I am affectionately yours,
Birket Foster.'

Birket Foster is here referring to Helen Allingham, RWS (1848–1928). As Miss Helen Paterson she had married in 1874 William Allingham, the Irish poet, and was elected an Associate of the Water-colour Society in the following year, but did not attain full membership until 1890. Ruskin much admired her representations of 'the gesture, character and humour of charming children in country landscapes' – a description which has an obvious link with the style of Birket Foster. Helen Allingham herself felt that the two artists who had most influenced her were Frederick Walker (for her figures) and Birket Foster. A similarity between her subjects and those of the latter is strengthened by the fact that Mrs Allingham also had a home in Witley and drew on the same Surrey landscape for her popular cottage garden scenes. Many of these were executed on the spot (unlike the mainly studio productions of Birket Foster) and show a broader technique than that of Foster, with less definition of line and tone. It had been somewhat unkindly hinted that without Birket Foster there would have been no Helen Allingham, but he would have none of this and always refuted the suggestion and credited this talented painter with her own style, which he considered had 'much more modernity in it than mine'.[6]

In the following year, again on 21 February, Birket Foster wrote to Edmund Evans: '. . . you speak of Hastings. They are spoiling every place. We have just lived in time.' In the same letter Birket Foster mentioned various exhibitions which he had attended:

'I wish you could have seen the Gilberts – they were really magnificent. The Millais collection is really a wonderful one man show though one was familiar with most of them – they seemed to have improved. He was indeed a great painter. The New Gallery is interesting but I confess I don't care for the Rossettis – I thought he was better than what is shown. Freddy's 'Plough' looks fine and I was interested in seeing Millais' [?] celebrated 'Chess Players' which was painted in an hour or two – and fetched some thousands of pounds once at Christies. I am glad to hear you like working a bit. It is a great solace. I see K.G. [Kate Greenaway] has an exhibition at the Fine Art Soc., well spoken of in The Times today. Tennyson's Life is as you say a treat – Walker's Life is I think well done – there was not much material to work upon.

I have got a bit of a cold just come on but I don't think it is anything – Fanny is only ailing she is like a weather glass up and down. Fine clear weather *well* – mild muggy weather very bad. We hope to get away to Torquay at the end of March which I shall enjoy. I am hard at work completing 40 drawings of Scotland for Tooth who will exhibit them.

Willie had a tumble off his cycle into a ditch *full* of water - but is no worse. With love to you all and best wishes your birthday.

I am affectionately yours,
Birket Foster.'

The friendship with Edmund Evans runs like a happy thread throughout his life and it is from the words of the latter that we have a harrowing account of the last illness of Birket Foster. On 28 February 1899, Edmund Evans, in a letter to an acquaintance, wrote:

'. . . You will be sorry to hear that my old friend Birket Foster has been very ill in the last 8 to 10 weeks - quite lost his appetite and a fortnight ago he had a fearful haemorrhage from the stomach. He fainted from the loss of blood and on recovering bade his family goodbye, but he still keeps in the same state, so we can but hope, as where there is life there is hope. Yet I fear his earthly life is over. . . .'

Birket Foster died on 27 March 1899. Edmund Evans was to write:

'I feel lonely this morning, for I went to Fernside and found Willie Foster there, talking with his uncle about the funeral of Birket, who died on Monday evening after three attacks of haemorrhage following sharp after each other. Another link of my chain of life gone, I cannot help feeling the loss, for I have known him since I was fifteen. He came to Landells in his sixteenth year and we took to each other at once . . .'[7]

The national press mourned Birket Foster in many lengthy obituaries, including *The Times* which commented on 29 March 1899:

'. . . It was only last autumn that we noticed a whole series of drawings of Scotland which had occupied him during two or three previous summers and which were exhibited with success in London. . . . It is remarkable that up to the very end, even in days when modern English art was passing through a period of great depression, and when many more powerful artists found their work quite unsaleable, Mr Birket Foster's drawings always sold . . .'

The above is part of a long tribute. As will be realised, most of the obituaries contained a repetition of biographical information which has already been discussed and for that reason it is not proposed to give any in full detail. Praise for Birket Foster was universal, but a Special Memoir in the *Daily Chronicle* brought out one of the more subjective and thoughtfully reasoned assessments:

'. . . His death breaks another link in the chain of British Art, or rather of British Illustration, for Birket Foster, with his seventy-four years of working life, takes us back to the very beginning almost of wood engraving. It was Foster who carried on the tradition of Harvey, just as Harvey carried out the teachings of Bewick. We know perfectly well that Birket Foster, the friend of Keene, the friend of everybody, is at the present moment more thought of in the sale-rooms and in the picture galleries for his water-colours than for his black-and-white. Yet these water-colours are, and always were, tinted versions of his illustrations. But there was a time - years before the vaunted sixties - and even after, too - when this contemporary of Palmer and the

108 Edmund Evans, photographed at The Hill by William Foster in 1886.

Linnells upheld, with John Gilbert, for a long time the dignity and honour of illustrations in England.

There was a time when the work of artists like John Gilbert and Birket Foster was welcomed in *The Illustrated London News* when the proprietors and editors of such papers could appreciate the fact that it was artists like Gilbert in figure work and Birket Foster in landscape who brought them their circulation; today, the kodak and the comic print are all-sufficient to the public to whom most illustrated newspapers appeal. It is still a pleasure to turn over those old pages of *The Illustrated London News*, but we wonder who in the future will ever turn over the greater number of illustrated publications of today, except in curious, quaint wonderment at our degeneracy. For Birket Foster added to this paper, and to many books, a quiet beauty that was all his own. We do not mean to say that Birket Foster is to be placed with Samuel Palmer or J.W. North at their best. But there is a niche for him in the Temple of Fame, and he is one of those men who, in Illustration, have made a very great mark on the age.'

In 1874, Birket Foster had written in his biographical notes for the Royal Berlin Academy: 'Mine has been a very uneventful life, but one which my art has made very pleasant to me.' After his death, these words had a poignant echo in the tributes of others. *The Daily Chronicle* continued:

'His life was quiet, serene and beautiful and so was his art. On his death, those who knew him will mourn the loss of a constant friend, and those who did not know him, but his work, must admit that a very serious and

From a photograph by Messrs. C. E. Fry & Son.

conscientious artist has been taken from us. He did not outlive his fame; far from it; it is greater perhaps now than it ever was . But it is rather strange that the man who encouraged Keene to go on, who helped Fred Walker to fame, who predicted the greatness of Pinwell, should have survived them all ...'

Obituaries appeared in all the national daily newspapers, including the *Morning Post*, which published an exceptionally long piece, in which it was regretted that Birket Foster had virtually barred himself from almost certain election as an RA by giving up oil painting, and the *Daily Graphic* with the following opinion of his work:

'His style of careful stippled workmanship appears rather niggling by the side of the broad way of painting landscape which artists affect today; but, if his pictures had their limitations, and if the method of all was very much the method of one, yet within their limitations, they were carefully done and finely finished, they were never slovenly, but always conscientious and they were the sort of art that people could understand ...'

On 1 April 1899, the *Surrey Advertiser and County Times* published a long tribute:

'By the death of Mr Birket Foster, which took place at Braeside, Weybridge on Monday evening at the ripe age of 74, England lost her most popular water-colour painter and one who was well known in Surrey, not only through his works, but because for the last 37 or 38 years he has made his home in our beautiful county.'

This piece contained the rather quaint statement (which was a direct quote from *The Times*) that the décor of The

Hill had included paintings by Burne-Jones made at a period when this artist was 'admired by a few eccentrics, but by no others' – an opinion that could have been more tactfully expressed.

The Surrey Advertiser also noted: 'During the 30 years that he remained at Witley, Mr Birket Foster devoted himself assiduously to his art and took little interest in local matters. Occasionally however he lent the use of his grounds for garden parties and other gatherings for charitable purposes. ...'[8] This is a rather unfair comment, as we know that Birket Foster cared deeply about Witley and took the keenest interest in the preservation of its beauty, but was not one to become president of local societies or serve on committees, which would be the kind of participation that was understood by the local press.

It was to Witley that Birket Foster finally returned. On his coffin were daffodils and primroses, the simple country flowers that he loved so much. The funeral was on the day before Easter Sunday and a great many people attended the service in the Parish Church, including a strong representation from the Royal Society of Painters in Watercolours. Afterwards, Edmund Evans wrote in his diary:

'April 1 – Birket Foster buried at Witley today, one year older than I ... Pleasant are the recollections of friendship with my old friend ...'[9]

The Dalziel Brothers provide a final tribute:

'Birket Foster was a genuine man; kind and generous to a degree in all ways of life. He stands as one of England's most popular landscape draughtsmen and as a painter in water-colour of great distinction.'

Notes: Chapter Nineteen

1 Letter to Ruth Dale published by permission of Professor G.N. Brown of the Betley Court Gallery near Crewe.
2 Letter to Mrs Stevenson published by permission of Sarah G.A. Glasson, granddaughter of Birket Foster.
3 All extracts from letters to Edmund Evans and Wilfred Evans in this chapter are published by permission of the University of California (Department of Special Collections), Los Angeles, USA.
4 From *Birket Foster*, H. M. Cundall, A. & C. Black 1906.
5 Information from *Commerce* and other sources supplied by the Local History Room, Marylebone Library, London W1.

6 See page 85 of *Happy England* as painted by Helen Allingham with memoirs and descriptions by M. Huish-Adam and Charles Black, 1903.
7 From *The Reminiscences of Edmund Evans: Wood Engraver and Colour Printer*, introduction by Ruari McLean, Oxford University Press, 1967.
8 Obituary from the *Surrey Advertiser and County Times* supplied by the County Library, Guildford, and others from a folio of newspaper cuttings in possession of William Glasson.
9 From *The Reminiscences of Edmund Evans*.

109 Birket Foster in old age, photographed about 1890. Copies of the original photograph are in possession of descendants, but this illustration is from the frontispiece of *Birket Foster* by H. M. Cundall, 1906, in order to reproduce an unfaded print and the facsimile signature.
Collection: Paul Rich.

20

Some events after the death of Birket Foster

The legal terminology of the will of Birket Foster (dated 31 May 1895) covers four pages of typescript and refers mainly to provision for his widow and children, but without specific mention of works of art, etc. which might have been of general interest. The gross value of his personal estate was first proved on 6 June 1899 at thirty thousand, five hundred and thirty seven pounds, twelve shillings and fourpence. A sale of most of the remaining works of Birket Foster was held at Christie's on 26-7 June 1899 (see appendix p. 201) and the 272 lots raised £5,324/16/6d. The estate of Birket Foster was consequently resworn in December of that year for an increased final total of £35,323/14/4d – a not inconsiderable sum which represents much more in terms of the monetary values of today. This sum is a pointer to the financial success that Birket Foster had achieved by means of his work, after taking into account some inherited money and the many expenses of a generous family man who had for years been responsible for the upkeep of a large establishment.

After the death of Birket Foster, his widow went to live at Newlands, Petworth, Sussex (also the address of William Foster until his marriage in 1904). Frances Foster was good to her step-grandchildren and Dorothy, daughter of Henry, well remembers staying with Fanny at Petworth and being taken to see The Hill and told about the days when it was the home of the Foster family. Frances Foster died in 1921, aged 80, after which there was a further sale of Oriental porcelain from the collection of Birket Foster (Christie's, 1 December 1921, lots 1-25) and further work by Birket Foster and by artists whose pictures he had owned (Christie's, 2 December 1921).

Edmund Evans died at Ventnor, Isle of Wight, in August 1905, at the age of 80. Leybourne, his former home at Witley is still standing and occupied as a private house.

Edgar Horne had introduced some further stained glass windows into the Hill. The Catalogue of designs by William Morris and Co. record the following –
1 8 April 1896 – A single light, with the subject 'Flora' (Burne-Jones 434) painted by Veal with border drawn by Dearle and painted by Wren, quarries by Wren. (Present whereabouts unknown.)
2 January 1897 – 'St Cecilia' – painted stained glass panel by Walters, with quarries by Wren and scroll drawn and lettered by Campfield and painted by Wren. (The second item is now in the William Morris Gallery, Walthamstow. Reference no. C76.)

In 1906, The Hill passed into the ownership of S.B. Boyd-Richardson, who was a grandson of the Hornes, but by 1939 the house (now known as Witley Court) was in the possession of Pinchin and Johnson, paint manufacturers, who had evacuated their London firm to the premises, which they used throughout the war for business purposes. In 1952, The Hill (or Witley Court) was sold for demolition and a new house was built in its place (utilising the old foundations) with five additional houses in the grounds of the Hill. Those interested in the conservation of Victorian buildings should not be too distressed. Birket Foster had been virtually his own architect and could not be expected to understand the technicalities of stresses and strains or the durability of building materials. By 1952, the house was in a sadly dilapidated condition and riddled with dry rot and woodworm. The stained glass was sold as demolition progressed and it was Lancelot Glasson, grandson of Birket Foster, who purchased the 'St Cecilia' panel and subsequently sold this to the William Morris Gallery, while retaining certain items that were more suitable for family ownership and had actually been in the house during the time of Birket Foster, e.g. 'The Seasons' and the madrigal panels. Other stained glass and some tile panels went to the Victoria and Albert Museum and the William Morris Gallery (as described and illustrated). It was only possible to save a small fraction of the woodwork, e.g. the linenfold panelling was restored and utilised in the hall of the present Witley Court and carved motives from a ceiling are incorporated in the balustrading of the staircase.

Lancelot Myles Glasson (1894-1959) was a talented figure and portrait painter, whose descent from Birket Foster is not widely known, owing to the fact that he preferred to make his way as an artist in his own right. Captain Lancelot Glasson, MC, was severely wounded in the First World War and had a leg amputated, with the result that he was to suffer pain and discomfort for the rest of his life. His decision to become an artist was taken after the war, when he studied at Heatherley's Art School and the Royal Academy Schools. Lancelot Glasson worked mainly in oils and exhibited at the Paris Salon and the Royal Academy (see appendix p. 200). His most celebrated painting was 'The Young Rower', which was exhibited at the Royal Academy in 1932 and attracted immediate attention. In that year the 'Modern Room' was revived as a feature of the exhibition and *The Sunday Times* (1 May 1932) was to comment:

'The contents of this are anything but dull, and it includes at least one painting of outstanding merit by a little known artist. This is Mr Lancelot M. Glasson's picture "The Young Rower" (669) which depicts a charming young oarswoman kneeling to pull up her sock. The figure is delightfully placed on the canvas, the Degas-like pose being full of grace and satisfying in design. The form is well and firmly drawn, the modelling just without being exaggerated, and the colouring is pleasant and adequate. It has many merits, but what is the most important is that it has something very few other exhibits possess, sheer compelling beauty. It is a work to which we can return again and again with joy; if there should be any "Picture of the Year" this summer, it is likely to be Mr Glasson's "Young Rower".'

One might not realise from the remarks of Frank Rutter of *The Sunday Times* that this refreshing and unusual piece of painting was a nude study. The setting is a locker-room and the model has on serviceable navy shorts and kneels to pull up her woolly socks, but has not yet put on her rowing vest. As predicted, this painting did indeed become 'Picture of the Year' by popular press acclaim and Lancelot Glasson was both amused and surprised to find himself besieged to give interviews, which included some that were aimed at a readership not much concerned with the finer points of art.

'Miss 1932's Poise – Why Art Critics Chose "The Rowing Girl"' (sic) was headlined in *The News Chronicle*, with the typical slight inaccuracy of the popular press, which carried an interview which was almost certainly a much edited version of what the artist actually said, even if true to the spirit of his remarks. This newspaper stated:

'The picture of "The Rowing Girl" by Mr Lancelot Glasson, which the News Chronicle art critic chose as the picture of this year's Royal Academy, was painted in his studio from studies made on the banks of the Thames.

"Perhaps the reason why my picture has attracted so much notice", Mr Glasson told the News-Chronicle last night, "is that I appear to have been struck by a new idea. The athletic river girl has not been done before. After all, it is the healthy girl that the artist admires today, not the sloping shouldered type of 60 or 70 years ago. The rowing girl has health and poise." Mr Glasson, who was educated at Marlborough and studied at the Royal Academy Schools, has been exhibiting at the Royal Academy for about six years. Still in his thirties, he served with the Royal Fusiliers during the war.'

On 6 May 1932, the Blackpool municipal art gallery telephoned an offer for 'The Young Rower', but this had just been sold privately for £120, which seems a very modest sum. The painting is now in the Rochdale Art Gallery and has recently been seen in loan exhibitions (e.g. the Hayward Gallery's 'The Thirties' and the Greater Manchester Council's 'Face to Face' Exhibition at the Stockport Art Gallery 1981). Glasson also successfully painted commissioned portraits, but without much personal inclination, and it was the need for more financial security that led him to join the family firm of M.B. Foster and Sons. He was a man of foresight and business ability and was subsequently to become one of the chief organisers of British camouflage projects in the Second World War. He enlisted the help of fellow artists and his expertise was such that he was a member of the British ARP Mission to Moscow in 1941.

In 1945, he returned to M.B. Foster and Sons and continued to carry on this family tradition, but his painting was only intermittent. After a long interval, his enthusiasm returned and 'Sarah', his exhibit shown at the Royal Academy in 1949, was another conspicuous success for a talented painter, whose work is indeed deserving of individual recognition, although it must now attract an additional interest as that of a grandson of Birket Foster.

M.B. Foster and Sons celebrated its centenary in 1929, by which time Lancelot Glasson was Chairman of the firm. *The Story of M.B. Foster and Sons Ltd – Bottling Beers for A Hundred Years* was the title of a commemorative pamphlet, which outlined the history of 'The Greatest Bottlers of Bass and Guinness in the World' – the output was now exceeding $41\frac{1}{2}$ million bottles per year. The delivery side of the firm was extensively motorised, with a fleet of lorries and vans, but some of the traditional dray horses were still proudly retained. M.B. Foster and Sons was badly bombed in the Second World War and was subsequently affected by the fact that it became the general practice for breweries to bottle their own beer. In 1957, there was a merger with Probyns, another bottling concern, and the whole is now merged with Young's Brewery, Wandsworth, which was visited by Her Majesty the Queen in 1981, when she greatly admired the fine dray horses still used by the firm.

The Royal Society of Painters in Water-colours, as part of the Winter Exhibition of 1899, placed a small loan collection of work by Birket Foster (and the very minor George Henry Andrews) on display on a long screen in the middle of the gallery. The exhibition was uncatalogued and appears to have been a rather unsystematic and perfunctory tribute to two lately deceased members of the society.

'The late Mr Birket Foster's work is known to everybody. There was a time when it was over-rated. It is now unduly decried because the greatest virtue that he had – the virtue of elaborate, perfect composition – is unduly at a discount, and there is little disposition nowadays to forgive smallness of handling and the deliberate attainment of the pretty ...'

The reaction of the above critic (newspaper unknown) points up the manner in which fashionable opinion was embracing all that was new in art to the detriment of the Birket Foster style. ('And these, though appealing little to the most modern taste, are not in truth to be despised. He saw an England clean and dainty, swept and garnished; and that is what he painted.') So wrote the art critic, damning with faint praise, but in fact the work of Birket Foster was never to fall into the total eclipse that was the fate of so many once highly popular Victorian artists. In 1902, 'A Village Ale House' made 480 gns and 'Hounds in Full Cry' 460 gns (over four times as much as was obtained in the same sale for a good vignette by J.M.W. Turner). In the following year, Christie's sold 'Gathering Elderberries' for 380 gns; 'Going to Market' for 250 gns; 'Evening on the Yare' for 280 gns and 'Birds Nesting' for 175 gns. *The Daily News* 26 March 1906, is informative:

'Belonging to the late Mr John H. Foster, Fernside, Witley, were four water-colours by his kinsman, Birket Foster, who died in 1899. "Loch Maree" – $30\frac{1}{2} \times 36\frac{1}{2}''$ – brought 530 gns; "In the market place, Verona" – $27 \times 40''$ – 470 gns; "Ben Nevis" – $29 \times 46\frac{1}{2}''$ – seen at the Guildhall in 1896, 460 gns; and "A Highland Scene, near Dalmally" – $30 \times 43''$ – 550 gns. At the Boulton sale four years ago Birket Foster's "Village Alehouse" – 18 × 28″ – brought 480 gns.; as long ago as 1865 his "Donkey Ride" – 13 × 27½″ – fetched 399 gns; and within the last few years a drawing has brought about 700 gns.' (from report of a sale at Christie's).

It was also in this year that in *The Daily Graphic*, 26 December 1906, M.H. Spielmann (author of *A History of Punch* and *Kate Greenaway*) reviewed at length *Birket Foster, RWS* by H.M. Cundall and *In Rustic England* by A.B. Daryll. Extracts from his comments provide an informed evaluation of Birket Foster.

'There can be no doubt that the work of Birket Foster has always appealed with special and alluring force to the taste of the British public; and if Mr Cundall goes a little too far in claiming for it a popularity greater than is enjoyed by that of any other painter, it was true in a sense when the rage for it was at its height. ... What was the reason for this prodigious favour? It was that Birket Foster produced something new – he was a *tête d'école*, who was to show the way later on to Mrs Allingham, Kate Greenaway and others, and for facility and easy mastery of his subject and materials was never approached by any other of his followers or rivals. It was because he was intensely English in his view of art and life and Nature; because his pretty gracefulness was inherent in everything he did; because he was as faithful to children for his figure interest as was Edouard Frère, but always to charming, unaffected peasant children, who formed themselves inevitably into graceful well-composed groups, naturally and easily, and unconscious of being watched and because his colour was always gay, his weather always, or nearly always bright, his humour always good, his drawing always incisive, his poetic outlook quite intelligibly idealistic, his landscapes and distances stretching to the horizon as pretty and pleasing as in comic operas, yet sound, charmingly seen, and wonderfully realised, and good, too, as art – as amiable, honest, skilful and light-hearted as dear, big, warm-hearted Birket Foster himself. ... He will always be remembered as a very charming personality, a very personal water-colourist, whose tenderness of vision and delicacy of touch tickle and delight the eye of the public of taste, while he himself by reason of his own sweet nature and kindly outlook on life, has entered into the heart of the picture-loving public, and will be cher-

ished there as an artist, as he is cherished as a man in the memory of his friends.'

On 3 February 1925, *The Daily Telegraph* noted:

'To-morrow marks the centenary of the birth of Myles Birket Foster, but it is doubtful whether any special preparations have been made to celebrate it, and, as it happens, there does not appear to be a Birket Foster water-colour drawing in Friday's sale at Christie's. This is somewhat remarkable when the long chain of his works at auction is remembered, especially since his death nearly twenty six years ago. As the painter of the simple unforced lyric of the country lane he still stands secure in market appreciation, despite all forms of criticism. But this auction success is not the manufactured enthusiasm of the dealers. These perspicacious men leave it to the public to name their favourites. . .'

There is an element about the work of this artist that will always attract the eye and the heart. A few years ago, a visitor to Witley church-yard asked the Vicar where she could find the grave of Birket Foster, as she wished to give thanks to his memory. It transpired that some time before while rummaging in a junk shop she had been instantly charmed by a little water-colour, even though this was in a very grubby state and priced at only £2. After taking it home she cleaned it up with an india rubber and sensed that there was real quality about this attractive picture of a girl with a wild rose in her hand. The work was identified as that of Birket Foster by one of the London auction houses, where it was subsequently sold for about £850 – a sum which enabled the Witley visitor to buy the car that was so greatly needed to take out a disabled relation. The kindly nature of Birket Foster would indeed have been touched if he could have known of this charming gesture at his graveside.

In the 1925 assessment *The Daily Telegraph* continued: 'The late Hazell Vicars used to say that he had seen three booms and three falls in Birket Foster's market career, adding "I now believe that he is as permanent as the Bank of England . . ."'

Over half a century has passed since this opinion was expressed and the years have only served to prove the enduring qualities of the work of this artist in market value and in the affection of the public. His gentle evocations of the countryside have made the name of Birket Foster stand for ever as part of the English heritage.

Appendixes

APPENDIX 1

List of books containing illustrations by Birket Foster

* denotes illustrated entirely
by Birket Foster.

Ireland: Its Scenery and Character – compiled by Mr and
Mrs Samuel Carter Hall
How and Parsons, 1841. See pp. 14–15

Richmond and Other Poems – by Charles Ellis
Madden and Malcolm, 1845. See p. 15

**The Country Year Book* (four parts) – text by Thomas
Miller
(*Boys' Spring Book*, etc. See pp. 20–1)
Chapman and Hall, 1847

The Female Worker to the Poor
Seeley Jackson, 1848

A Picturesque Tour of the River Thames – by J. F. Murray
Henry Bohn, 1849

The Poetical Works of H. W. Longfellow
Bohn's Illustrated Library, 1849

The Pilgrims of the Rhine – by Sir E. B. Lytton
Chapman and Hall, 1850 (only one illustration by Birket
Foster)

Evangeline: A Tale of Acadie – by H. W. Longfellow
David Bogue, 1850. See pp. 32, 35–7. Also Ills. 17 and
18

**The Year Book of the Country* or *The Field Forest and
Fireside* – by William Howitt
Henry Colburn, 1850. See p. 40. Also Ill. 22

**Original Poems for my Children* – by Thomas Miller
David Bogue, 1850

**The Moorland Cottage* – by 'The author of Mary Barton'
– i.e. Mrs Gaskell
Chapman and Hall, 1850. See p. 40. Also Ill. 21

**The Illustrated Book of Songs for Children* – from a Ger-
man text
Orr and Co, 1851. See p. 32

**Christmas with the Poets* – compiled and engraved by
Henry Vizetelly (two tone)
David Bogue, 1851. See pp. 42–4. Also Ill. 23

Voices of the Night, the Seaside and The Fireside – by H. W.
Longfellow
David Bogue, 1851. Includes 44 by Birket Foster

**The Poetical Works and Remains of Henry Kirk White*
George Routledge and Co, 1851. See p. 47

The Poetical Works of Oliver Goldsmith
Cundall and Addey, 1851. See p. 63

Longfellow's Poetical Works (– this volume includes 'Voices
of the Night', 'The Golden Legend' and 'Evangeline',
with a total of 81 illustrations by Birket Foster; remaining 35 by Jane Benham and John Gilbert)
David Bogue, 1852

**The Story of Mont Blanc* – by Albert Smith
David Bogue, 1852

A Month in Constantinople – by Albert Smith
David Bogue, 1852. See p. 54

*Hyperion – by H. W. Longfellow
David Bogue, 1852. See Chapter Six. Also Ills. 24, 25

**A Visit to the Holy Land, Egypt and Italy* – by Ida Pfeiffer
(translated from the German by H. W. Dulcken)
Ingram, Cooke and Co., 1853. See p. 46

**Fern Leaves from Fanny's Portfolio* – by Miss G. P. Willis
Ingram, Cooke and Co, 1853. See pp. 46–7

A Picturesque Guide to the Trossachs
Adam and Charles Black, 1853. See p. 51

A Picturesque Guide to Scotland
Adam and Charles Black
Note: The first edition with this title can only be dated
circa 1842 and this obviously does not contain illustrations by Birket Foster. Editions with his illustrations
should be looked for after about 1853.

A Picturesque Guide through North and South Wales
Adam and Charles Black, c. 1850
The examples illustrated are from the 10th edition,
dated 1860. See Ill. 38

The Lady of the Lake – by Sir Walter Scott
Adam and Charles Black, 1853. See p. 51

Poetical Works of James Thomson
Routledge and Co., 1853

Poetry of the Year (only one illustration by Birket Foster)
George Bell, 1853. Includes 22 half-page chromolithographs, printed by Hanhart and Day pasted down onto
the type pages. The book was one of the first to use
colour prints in this manner and was designed by Birket
Foster's friend, Robert Dudley.

A Holiday Book for Christmas and the New Year
Ingram, Cooke and Co, 1853. '. . . Amusement for Winter evenings . . . profusely and superbly illustrated . . .
contains about 250 engravings of the highest order . . .
a most delightful Table Book for the Drawing Room.
£1-1s'– advertisement at the back of *Fern Leaves from
Fanny's Portfolio* – 1854 edition.

The Boyhood of Great Men – by J. G. Edgar
David Bogue, 1853

The Lay of the Last Minstrel – by Sir Walter Scott
Adam and Charles Black, 1854. See pp. 51-3. Ills. 26, 27

A Memento of the Trossachs, Loch Katrine, Loch Lomond, etc.
Adam and Charles Black, 1854. Repeats in small gift-book form illustrations in the Picturesque Guide.

Proverbial Philosophy – by Martin Tupper
Thomas Hatchard, 1854.

The Illustrated Byron
Published by Henry Vizetelly, 1854

An Elegy written in a Country Churchyard – by Thomas Gray
Published for Joseph Cundall by Sampson Low, 1854 Examples by Birket Foster include the famous opening line 'The curfew tolls the knell of parting day'. This illustration was engraved by J.W. Whymper and reproduced in *The Art Journal*, 1890, p. 6. See also City Art Gallery, Bristol, p. 208

The Poetical Works of Thomas Gray
Routledge and Co., 1854

*Little Ferns for Fanny's Little Friends – by Miss G.P. Willis
Nathaniel Cooke and Co., 1854. See p. 47

Footprints of Famous Men – by J.G. Edgar
W. Kent, 1854

Happy Days of Childhood – by Amy Meadows
Joseph Cundall, 1854. Small inexpensive anthology, with illustrations by Birket Foster and Harrison Weir.

The Blue Ribbon: A Story of the Last Century – by A.H. Drury
King and Son, 1854

The Golden Legend – by H.W. Longfellow
David Bogue, 1854. 35 by Birket Foster, others by Jane Benham

The Life of Nelson – by Robert Southey
David Bogue, 1854. See p. 206

*L'Allegro and Il Penseroso – by John Milton
David Bogue, 1855. See pp. 54-9. Also Ills. 28, 29

Marmion: A Tale of Flodden Field – by Sir Walter Scott
Adam and Charles Black, 1855. 45 illustrations by Birket Foster, others by John Gilbert

The Pleasures of Hope – by Thomas Campbell
Sampson Low and Co., 1855

The Clergyman's Daughter – by L. Richmond
Published by Seeley, 1855

*Matilda Lonsdale – by Charlotte Adams
Routledge and Co., 1855

The Poetical Works of Mark Akenside and John Dyer
Routledge and Co., 1855

The Poetical Works of William Cowper
Routledge and Co., 1855

*The Task – by William Cowper
James Nisbet and Co., 1855. See pp. 8-11 (*The Art Journal* Christmas Supplement, 1890)

*The Traveller – by Oliver Goldsmith
David Bogue, 1856. Thirty etchings on steel by Birket Foster

*Mia and Charlie – by Harriet Myrtle
David Bogue, 1856

*Sabbath Bells Chimed by the Poets
Bell and Daldy, 1856. See p. 59. Also Ill. 31

*The Rhine and its Picturesque Scenery – by Henry Mayhew
David Bogue, 1856. See p. 54. The engravings in this book are such as to render the subjects almost unrecognisable as the work of Birket Foster. The stiffly topographical subjects are engraved by T.A. Prior, B. Bradshaw, etc.

Poetical Works of George Herbert
James Nisbet and Co., 1856. See Ill. 30

Sacred Allegories – by Rev. W. Adams
Rivington and Co., 1856

Early Lessons – by Maria Edgeworth
Routledge and Co., 1856. Earlier editions from the same publisher *not* illustrated by Birket Foster.

Willy's Country Visit – by B. Goldfinch
London, 1856

Songs of the Brave: The Soldier's Dream and other Poems and Odes
Sampson Low and Co., 1856

*The Sabbath: Sabbath Walks and other Poems – by James Grahame
Nisbet and Co., 1857

Gertrude of Wyoming – by Thomas Campbell
Routledge and Co., 1857

The Lord of the Isles – by Sir Walter Scott
Adam and Charles Black, 1857. 37 illustrations by Birket Foster

*The Farmer's Boy – by R. Bloomfield
Sampson Low and Co., 1857

The Poetical Works of R. Bloomfield
Routledge and Co., 1857

The Poetical Works of Sir Walter Scott
Adam and Charles Black, 1857

The Rime of the Ancient Mariner – by Samuel Coleridge
Sampson Low and Co., 1857, but issued for Christmas 1856
Only two illustrations by Birket Foster. '... They [*The Athenaeum*] made a terrible mistake in the review of the Ancient Mariner—giving me the credit for Duncan's drawings. As perhaps you would see I was forced to write them a line. They are right with regard to the first illustration - "There was a ship" but the ice region and all the rest are Duncans ...' (letter from Birket Foster to Robert Spence, 7 December 1856)

Rhymes and Roundelayes in Praise of Country Life – edited by Joseph Cundall
David Bogue, 1857. Also published by Routledge in new format, 1875
A Birket Foster illustration from the 1857 edition is shown in *A Treatise on Wood Engraving* by Chatto and Jackson, 1861

The Poets of the Nineteenth Century – selected by R.A. Willmott
Routledge and Co., 1857. 15 by Birket Foster

Ministering Children: A Tale – by Marie L. Charlesworth
Seeley Jackson and Halliday, 1857

Dramatic Scenes and New Poems – by Barry Cornwall
Chapman and Hall, 1857. See p. 116. 14 by Birket Foster

*Aldershot and All About It – by Mrs Young
Routledge and Co., 1857. See p. 60

The Poems of William Bryant
Appleton, 1857; also published Griffin and Co., 1858
'Messrs D. Appleton of New York requested us to provide a set of illustrations to the Poetical Works of William Cullen Bryant. They wished for a large number by Birket Foster who was at that time at the very height of his popularity for black and white work.
'Out of something like one hundred pictures he gave us thirty six, all of which were beautiful examples; many

of them exquisite little vignettes.' – (*The Brothers Dalziel* 1901, B.T. Batsford reprint, 1978)

The Course of Time – by Robert Pollok
William Blackwood and Sons, 1857. See p. 60
This poem was first published in 1827 and had been through 20 editions in the succeeding 30 years, but it was said that Birket Foster felt that it was inevitable that he would be asked to illustrate this famous work, as the publishers searched about for books of poetry as vehicles for his drawings. The artists illustrating this volume included Tenniel and J.R. Clayton, with the Dalziels and Edmund Evans included in the engraving.

The Poetical Works of Edgar Allan Poe
Sampson Low and Co., 1858. 'Annabel Lee' – illustrated in *The Art Journal* – Christmas Supplement, p. 19

Comus – by John Milton
Routledge and Co., 1858

Lays of the Holy Land from Ancient and Modern Poets
James Nisbet and Co., 1858. A Birket Foster illustration from this book was reproduced in *A Treatise on Wood Engraving* by Chatto and Jackson, 1861.

The Select Poems and Songs of Robert Burns
Kent and Co., 1858. 'Banks of the Nith' by Birket Foster was reproduced in *A Treatise on Wood Engraving*

Prince of Peace or Lays of Bethlehem
Seeley and Co., 1858

*The Minstrel – by James Beattie
Routledge and Co., 1858. See also reprints of illustrations in *Beauties of English Landscape*, 1874

Home Affections Portrayed by the Poets – selected by Charles Mackay
Routledge and Co., 1858. 20 by Birket Foster and also examples by his future brother-in-law, J.D. Watson. 'Come awa', come awa'' – Thomas Pringle, illustration by Birket Foster, p. 141 in *The Brothers Dalziel* (reprinted B.T. Batsford 1978). See also *Beauties of English Landscape*, 1874

**Kavanagh: A Tale* – by H.W. Longfellow
Kent and Co., 1858. 38 illustrations by Birket Foster

Poetry and Pictures from Thomas Moore
Longman, Brown, Green and Co., 1858

*The Shipwreck – by William Falconer
Adam and Charles Black, 1858 – also published Bickers and Son, 1863

*The Grave – by Robert Blair
Adam and Charles Black, 1858

**Picturesque Guide to the English Lakes*
Adam and Charles Black, 1858. See p. 54

The Upper Rhine: The Scenery of its Banks and the Manners of its People – by H. Mayhew
Routledge and Co., 1858

**Birds, Bees and Blossoms* – by Thomas Miller
J. and C. Brown and Co., 1858. See pp. 60–1. Also Ill. 32
(Also issued in separate parts in coloured paper covers)

English Country Life – by Thomas Miller
Routledge and Co., 1858

Pastoral Poems – by William Wordsworth
Sampson Low and Co., 1858

Summer Time in the Country – selected by R.A. Willmott
Routledge and Co., 1858
The cover of this book is of special interest as it has an oval onlay printed in colours by Edmund Evans, after a drawing by Birket Foster. Illustrated in colour in *Victorian Publishers' Book Bindings* by Ruari McLean, 1974

The Seasons – by James Thomson
James Nisbet and Co., 1859. See p. 66. Also Ill. 32

The White Doe of Rylstone – by William Wordsworth
Longman, 1859 – also Bell and Daldy, 1867. Illustrated *The Art Journal*, 1890

Poems by William Wordsworth – edited by Rev. R.A. Willmott
Routledge and Co., 1859. 70 illustrations by Birket Foster, including 'Lines Written on Early Spring', reproduced, p. 145, *The Brothers Dalziel* (reprinted B.T. Batsford 1978); also 'Intimations of Immortality', p. 151, same volume.

Poetical Works of Thomas Gray
Sampson Low, 1859. 'A pretty little pocket edition this of the poems of one of the most popular English writers . . . a few illustrations from the fertile and truthful pencil of Mr. Birket Foster . . .' (*The Art Journal*, 1859)

**The Hamlet: An Ode written in Whichwood Forest* – by Thomas Warton
Sampson Low and Co., 1859
Illustrated with 14 etchings on copper by Birket Foster. See Ills. 35, 36

Favourite English Poems of the Last Two Centuries – edited by Joseph Cundall
Sampson Low and Co., 1859
'Illustrated with upwards of two hundred engravings on wood from drawings by the most eminent artists.'

The Poems of Oliver Goldsmith – edited by Rev. R.A. Willmott
Routledge and Co., 1859 – second edition in 1860 has additional engravings, also 1877 and later. See pp. 64–5. Also Ill. 37

A Country Book – by William Howitt
Routledge and Co., 1859

The Merrie Days of England – by Edward McDermott
Kent and Co, 1859 (only 4 examples by Birket Foster)

*Odes and Sonnets
Routledge and Co., 1859
All 63 illustrations in this book are by Birket Foster, with ornamental designs by John Sleigh, engraved and printed by the Brothers Dalziel. The title page was printed in two blues, green and pink and red by the Dalziels at their Camden Press. This title page and the credit page were an attempt to use wood engraving to give an effect of illumination. Ruari McLean states: 'Nothing else quite like them occurs in the whole century.'

The Deserted Cottage – by William Wordsworth
Routledge and Co., 1859

Poets of the West
Sampson Low and Co., 1859 – selection of American poems, reprinted 1860

Childe Harold's Pilgrimage – by Lord Byron
John Murray, 1860

The Tempest – by William Shakespeare
Bell and Daldy, 1860 (only five by Birket Foster)

The Merchant of Venice – by William Shakespeare
Sampson Low and Co., 1860 (only five)

**Common Wayside Flowers* – by Thomas Miller
Routledge and Co., 1860. See p. 65

The Poetical Works of James Montgomery
Routledge and Co., 1860
In the 39 illustrations by Birket Foster he is not too happy in the depiction of Chinese pagodas, etc. in 'A Voyage Round the World', but is better in such poems as 'A Walk in the Spring'.

A Book of Favourite Modern Ballads – edited by Joseph Cundall
W. Kent and Co., 1860. See pp. 65-6
This edition in black and grey, with decorations and borders printed in gold, all engraved by Edmund Evans. Reissued *c.* 1865 by Ward, Lock and Tyler, printed in six colours. In this edition the examples by Birket Foster include the central illustrations for the frontispiece and title page, designed and ornamented by Albert Warren. (Reproduced facing p. 132 in *Victorian Book Design and Colour Printing* by Ruari McLean, 1963.) This title was also issued in two volumes (each containing half the book) as *Choice Pictures and Choice Poems* and *The Illustrated Poetical Gift Book* – undated.

Lalla Rookh – by Thomas Moore
Routledge and Co., 1860
Also contained in *Moore's Irish Melodies* with reprints from the 1858 edition of Moore – published by William Mackenzie (about 1912)

Songs for the Little Ones at Home
Published by Joseph Cundall, 1860 (and under the imprint of Sampson Low in 1863)
Sixteen colour illustrations by Birket Foster and J. Absolon, printed by E. Evans.

The Carewes – by Margaret Gillies
W. Kent and Co., 1860

The Scottish Reformation – by Dr Peter Lorrimer
C. Griffin, 1860.

Household Song: Collection of Lyrical Pieces
Kent and Co., 1861

**Birket Foster's Pictures of English Landscape*
Routledge and Co., issued for the 1862 Christmas season, but first dated copies 1863. See Chapter Nine; also Ills. 47-52

The illustrations in this most important book are listed in full, as follows. The artist's notes are those on a set of proofs in the possession of the British Museum.

1 *The Green Lane.* Birket Foster wrote on one of the proofs, with reference to the engraving: 'Very near perfection'. An almost identical water-colour version of the subject was illustrated as 'Lane near Dorking' (pl. XV) in Lancelot Glasson's article on Birket Foster, 'Old' Watercolour Society, Vol. XI, 1933. Also as 'The Green Lane' – water-colour presented to the Royal Society of Painters in Water-colours from the Nettlefold Bequest.

2 *Donkeys on the Heath.* (Ill. 47) Birket Foster wrote on a proof: 'I couldn't better this if I tried' – meaning that he had no suggestions to add to the result produced by the engraver.

3 *The Mill.* This shows a windmill as the main subject (right) with large expanse of detailed cloud effect, small cart and horse facing out of the composition (left). Birket Foster commented: 'Very nice. The sky wants toning [touching?] tone it very much and it will be very good.' This instruction on the proof is difficult to decipher, as some writing at the end of the mount is lost where it has been trimmed.

4 *The Little Anglers.* Group of children (right) in woodland setting, with stick propped on forked branch as fishing rod. Sheep (left) under trees.

5 *The Gleaners at the Stile.* Reproduced *The Art Journal* – Christmas Supplement, 1890 p. 3. Comment on proof: – 'This is very beautiful.' Composition shows three girls (centre) grouped round a stile, with seated dog. Densely wooded background, with trees and church glimpsed in the distance.

6 *The Old Chair Mender at the Cottage Door.* This is a very similar composition to Colour Ill. E. Birket Foster painted several versions of this subject. His instructions on the engraving proof read: 'The light brick work on the cottage wants seeing to. Be sure to touch the figures as I have done, the woman's head especially.' And underneath: 'It will be very nice with the touching.'

7 *The Farmyard.* (Ill. 48.) Birket Foster wrote on the right-hand side of the proof: 'The sky is very beautiful here. Keeping the crossline out of the horizon is a wonderful improvement'. And underneath: 'Very beautiful'.

8 *The Hayfield.* Harvesting scene with a hay cart in mid-distance, an evening sky and in the foreground three figures by a river, with a small boy poking a stick into the water.

9 *The Reapers.* Four figures reaping, trees right, foreground with brambles and pool, ricks in the far distance.

10 *Building the Hay Rick.* (See frontispiece)

11 *The Country Inn.* (Ill. 49) Loosely based on the reverse of an illustration for 'The Village Inn' by Oliver Goldsmith. This subject was repeated several times in water-colour versions.

12 *The Smithy.* Two horses (one being shod) outside a smithy, with a man in a doorway and children watching. Large tree (right), duck pond and wooden stocks in the foreground, cottages in distance. Small water-colour in the Tate Gallery is a direct version of this subject, but with the composition expanded to the right to include an extra figure in the later style.

13 *The Watering Place.* Three horses drinking in a river (one mounted by carter) with trees in the background. Birket Foster wrote, with reference to the top section of the trees: 'This part of the tree work is not at all good.' Referring to the top centre: 'This part is cut away and is lighter than the sky in parts—which is not like the drawing.' And, right hand side, below: 'Though parts are very nice, I like this the least of any I have seen.'

14 *Cows in the Pool.* Rather dark, showing five cows under an arched tree composition, with wooden gate and sheep meadow in the distance. The engraving did not please Birket Foster. He wrote on the proof: 'I dont much like the sky and the distant bit with the gate looks poor.' The final illustration shows obvious signs of this comment having been heeded, as there is some very fidgety hatching in this area.

15 *The Market Cart.* (Ill. 50) Birket Foster has pencilled across the proof: 'Much too dark'. The final illustration does not seem so, but may not have produced the effect of light that Foster had intended in the original drawing. There are probably more market cart water-colours than from any other subject in *Pictures of English Landscape*.

16 *The Wood Wain.* Horses harnessed to a cart loaded with felled logs, figures on tree trunks in the foreground, with densely wooded background.

17 *A Winter Piece.* Bare trees framing a snow-covered cottage, disproportionate robin on a branch in mid-composition, ducks huddled right foreground. This piece points forward to innumerable Christmas card imitations of this type of scene and is a much weaker drawing than the other illustrations.

18 *Old Cottages.* Birket Foster was of the opinion that this was 'too black – but very well engraved'. It shows a typical Birket Foster composition of a woman and a child outside

a thatched cottage (right) with beehives (left foreground), stile and sheep meadow in the distance.

19 *At the Cottage Door.* (Ill. 51)

20 *At the Brookside.* Rather dark woodland scene, with rabbit left foreground and bird flying across a very solid mid-distance. The instructions on the proof attempt to correct the faults: 'Please try to get the colour up where it is pencilled and reduce the black where whitened as it will make the effect of the cut quite right – be sure to get the colour up by the bird.' The *final* result is still a little weak in definition.

21 *Four Stages of the Stream, 1. The Dipping Place.* This is a version of an illustration to 'Sweet Highland Lass' by Wordsworth – see *Beauties of English Landscape*, 1874 p. 237. Several water-colour versions exist, including one reproduced in the Medici Masters Calendar for 1980 (Southgate Gallery, Wolverhampton), Birket Foster wrote on the engraving proof: 'Very Nice.' See. p. 159.

22 *Four Stages of the Stream, 2. The Stepping Stones.* Reproduced in *The Art Journal*, 1890, p. 7. Woman, girl and very small child crossing a stream by means of stepping stones, densely wooded background.

23 *Four Stages of the Stream, 3. The Lock.* Birket Foster has pencilled slanting lines across parts of the sky, with the slightly tetchy comment: 'I don't know what these bits of dirt mean – they must come away and the lines be made very thin.' The composition shows a woman and children (right) standing by a wooden lock gate. At left there is a light tree, against a darker, larger one. Birket Foster has indicated the former and commented: 'The tree foliage is far too light'. The result suggests that the final effect would still have been lighter than he intended. At least one water-colour version of this subject.

24 *Four Stages of the Stream, 4. The Mill.* Foreground area of river, with two figures on a wooden bridge and the main water mill subject placed right, with background almost filled with trees. This is a close version of the first illustration to 'The Deserted Village' as shown in colour in *The Poems of Oliver Goldsmith*, 1859.

25 *Under the Moonbeams.* Moonlit scene, showing sheep in a meadow across a composition of water and trees with moon glimpsed behind clouds. Instructions on the proof read: 'The tree stems are cut away too much'. Birket Foster has almost filled the area of the trunks with pencil marks and in the engraving the foreground and trees are very dark, as a contrast to the moonlit sky.

26 *At Sunset.* This riverside scene, with houses and distant poplars, has a suggestion of influence from the sunset paintings of George Augustus Williams. It is not one of the most successful of the *English Landscape* illustrations, as the central area is much too dark and unvaried in engraving line.

27 *The Village Churchyard.* Birket Foster rather charmingly pencilled on the proof: 'Very nice – the water would be better for a little knocking about.' Composition almost identical to water-colour (Ill. 96), but excluding the cattle and figure.

28 *The Ferry Boat.* Composition almost as Ill. 95.

29 *The Cottage on the Beach* (Ill. 52)

30 *At Sea and On Shore.* Moonlight fishing village scene, with cottages on a headland (right), boats and creels in foreground, ship with sails on horizon.

For reprints from *Pictures of English Landscape* see also *Pictures of Rustic Landscape* – published by John Nimmo,

1896. This shows the same series of illustrations, but with a different text. See pp. 176, 179. These two books should not be confused with *English Rustic Pictures* engraved by the Dalziels and published by Routledge in 1882. This does not contain work by Birket Foster. See below for *Beauties of English Landscape*.

Summer Scenes, published 1866; see same title, 1876.

*Poems of Thomas Hood

Moxon and Son, 1871 and 1872.

*Beauties of English Landscape

Routledge and Co., 1874. See vignette p. 18.

A compilation of 170 of the most successful engravings by Birket Foster that had appeared under the Routledge imprint. Engraved by the Dalziel Brothers, J. Cooper, Edmund Evans, H. Harral, etc. *Beauties of English Landscape* includes illustrations from 'The Minstrel' by James Beattie (1858), *Home Affections Portrayed by the Poets* (1858) and *Poems of William Wordsworth* (1859) and other volumes. In 1873, Birket Foster wrote to the Dalziels: '... I have no objection to Messrs. Routledge sending me a cheque for 50 guineas or to the first title Beauties of English Landscape by B.F. On second thoughts I don't like *Beauties* - try some other word...' (From *The Brothers Dalziel*, reprinted B.T. Batsford, 1978).

*Summer Scenes - by Birket Foster

George Bell and Sons, 1876

This book is sub-titled 'A series of photographs from some of his choicest water-colours'. The photographs are not reproductions, but actual sepia prints pasted onto the page and used to illustrate 'appropriate' selections from the works of Warton, Thomson, etc. The text for this edition was designed by the Chiswick Press and the book is an enlarged version of one published by Cundall and Flemming in 1866, which did not include this text. *Summer Scenes* contains 15 photographs (almost certainly the work of Joseph Cundall). These are of rather varied quality, but sometimes show a very good representation of the brush strokes of Birket Foster. A collection of Victorian photographs is always of interest and this book helps to date work executed before 1866. Whether all the illustrations are indeed from the choicest water-colours of the artist is a matter of opinion, but certainly some fine works are included, e.g. 'The Seaside Swing' (reproduced as 'The Swing' by the Medici Society - ref. no 100BD-S 184) is very much a companion piece to 'Rottingdean, near Brighton' (See Colour Ill. B)

*Brittany: A series of thirty-five sketches by Birket Foster.

Published by the artist from The Hill, Witley, Surrey, 1878. See pp. 141, 145. Also Ills. 85, 86

*Some Places of Note in England

A series of twenty-five sepia lithographs after the work of Birket Foster

Dowdeswell and Dowdeswell, 1888. See p. 167

*In Rustic England - by A.B. Daryll

Hodder and Stoughton, 1906

Twenty-five colour illustrations from previously published chromolithographs of water-colours by Birket Foster, including 'Peep at the Hounds' - Colour Ill. C

Myles Birket Foster - by M.B. Huish

J.S. Virtue

Bound copy of *The Art Journal* article with small additions

*Birket Foster - by H.M. Cundall

Adam and Charles Black, 1906

Portrait frontispiece Ill. 109

Book produced in ordinary and De Luxe edition. Sixteen of the 73 colour illustrations in this book were later reprinted in a slim volume (no text) entitled *The Water-colours of Birket Foster* (A. and C. Black, 1921).

The following minor titles contain illustrations by Birket Foster, but the reader should take it that these are merely reprints from blocks used for earlier volumes and not specifically commissioned for these books, listed alphabetically:

Aunt Mary's Sunday Picture Book
Beauties of Shakespeare
Boy's Picture Reading Book
Gleanings for the Drawing Room
Helen's Babies
Illustrated Poetical Album
Little Book about Country Life, A
Memorable Women
Mrs Routledge's Album for Children
Musing about Men
My Best Frock and other Tales
Nature's Mighty Wonders
Old English Ballads
Picturesque Europe
Routledge's Sunday Album for Children
Songs of the Seasons
Sunshine and Shadow
Thousand and One Gems of English Poetry
Tiger Lily and other Tales
Trial of Sir Jasper, The
Victoria Picture Reading Book, The
Young Lady's Picture Book, The

Sketches of Country Life (packet of twelve cards)
Published by the Religious Tract Society, 1877.

APPENDIX 2

Complete list of exhibits by Birket Foster with the Society of Painters in Water-colours – 1860-99

This list is as published from the catalogues of the Royal Society of Painters in Water-colours in 'Birket Foster' by Lancelot Glasson ('Old' Water-colour Society Vol. XI, 1933). The Society of Painters in Water-colours became the *Royal* Society . . . in 1881.

1860
30 Feeding the Ducks
208 View in Holmwood Common
236 Children Going to School
276 View on the River Mole

1861
7 Wark's Burn, Northumberland
192 Gleaners
212 Downhill
215 Cattle in the Stream
225 A Cottage
237 Burnham Beeches

1862
91 A Loch
246 The Bird's Nest
249 Fishing

257 The Little Nurse
263 Water-Lilies
289 The Dairy Bridge, Rokeby
292 On the shore, Bonchurch, Isle of Wight
319 A Fisherman's Cottage, Isle of Wight

Winter Exhibition
384 Edinburgh Castle
438 Studies of Skies
439 Studies of Skies

1863
145 The Ferry
226 A Village Maiden
228 Lane Scene, Hambledon
257 At Hambledon, Surrey
269 Hay Carts
272 Near Peterborough
275 Collier Unloading
284 Cottage at Chiddingfold
299 River Scene – evening

Winter exhibition
148 At Pinner; Lobster Pots; Brighton Boats; At Bonchurch; Ryde; Queensferry Rock; The Spring
157 Near Littlehampton; Marsden; Dunstanboro'; Newhaven; Firth of Forth; Queensferry; At Bonchurch
184 Craigmillar Castle; Dunblane; Craigmillar
318 A Tree-Stem; Preston, Sussex
368 Streatley; Richmond Park; The Ferry; Bamborough Castle
374 River Mole, ditto

1864
125 Flying a Kite
143 The Donkey Ride
158 River Scene
164 Cattle Drinking
271 Morning
279 Evening
288 Sunset
304 The Wooden Bridge
306 Sand Cart

Winter Exhibition
268 Hitchin Market Place; Near Streatley
291 Haslemere
371 Old Barn; On Hampstead Heath; Saltburn-on-Sea
374 Study of Ferns
379 Ingleton; Lucerne; Cottages at Hambledon
393 Near Dorking
424 Ben Lomond; Near Barnard Castle; Ben Venue
446 River Scene; A Barn Roof; Sheep; Cottages at Chiddingfold; Chiddingfold Church; The Mill

1865
12 On the Beach, Hastings
33 Primroses
242 The Shrimper
249 Expectations
281 The Lesson
295 The Bird's Nest
307 'To gather king-cups in the yellow mead/And prink their hair with daisies.'
314 The Swing

Winter Exhibition
385 A Frame containing four Studies of Village Children

1866
273 River Scene – Evening
321 Winterbourne – Bonchurch, Isle of Wight

Winter Exhibition
375 Cottagers
408 Trees
417 Skies

1867
 86 Bellagio, Lake of Como
150 The Old Breakwater
136 Old Shoreham Bridge
241 The Dead Jay
249 The Way Down the Cliff
263 York

Winter Exhibition
356 Rocks at Barnard Castle; Tees' High Force; Weir at Barnard Castle
373 At Marsden; Newbiggin by the sea

1868
218 The Mole, near Betchworth
231 The Convalescent
251 Snowdrops
279 The Donkey
289 The Little Chickens

Winter Exhibition
191 Study of Sea, Northumberland Coast
211 Study of Hay; Timber
384 A Lock, Stratford-on-Avon
390 The Peacock; The Rabbit Hutch
403 In the Wood
414 Beech-stem, Autumn

1869
 75 The Meet
240 A Breakwater
266 A Mill Pool
274 Village Children
291 A River Scene

Winter Exhibition
120 Grand Canal; Study of pots and a girl at a well, San Remo; House on the Grand Canal, Venice
123 Edinburgh Castle; Basket of Cowslips; Barrasford, North Tyne
174 Pangbourne
328 Autumn Studies
339 Richmond, Yorkshire
344 Loch Lomond; Creels; Cottage at Cullercoats
347 Haughton Castle, North Tyne
390 The Brook at Barrasford

1870
 12 The Weald of Surrey
 66 Burnham Beeches

Winter Exhibition
 48 The Greta at Rokeby
 79 Houses at Eton

168 Burnham Beeches
172 In the Woods at Burnham
297 Eton College
308 Beech Tree; Cottage Door
316 Eel Pots
345 Cottage at Bray
368 On the Thames, near Eton
377 Roses; Nasturtiums

1871
128 The Valley of the Tyne
199 Greta Bridge, Yorkshire
201 River Scene with Barges
209 On the Thames, near Eton
235 Rabbits
238 Hay Barges
243 River Scene, with Sheep
248 Old Walton Bridge, on the Thames
254 Cowslips

Winter Exhibition
 27 Stratford-on-Avon; Morcambe Bay; Dunstanboro'; The Thames, at Eton
162 The Falls of the Tummel
164 Edinburgh
180 Dead Gull; The Bass Rock
192 Newcastle from Gateshead Fell; Newcastle and the River Tyne
248 River Bank; The Punt
303 On the Garry
327 Cottage at Tarbet
337 Lancaster; Highland Cottage, Loch Tummel
344 Dunblane
381 Sunflowers; Nasturtiums

1872
 11 Haymakers
182 The Village Inn
265 St Michael's Mount

Winter Exhibition
 30 St Andrews
338 At Salisbury

1873
 10 Melrose, Dryburgh, Abbotsford
133 Bereft

Winter Exhibition
102 Turin
123 Study
171 Shoreham
293 At Verona
326 A Fruiterer's Shop
335 A Well at Hastings
354 Flowers
363 Study of Fish
370 A Pike

1874
 49 Lausanne, Lake of Geneva
 75 The Spring
226 The Return of the Life-boat
242 Antwerp
256 Bridge over the Moselle, Coblenz

Winter Exhibition
305 Calais, St Andrews and Rye
330 Studies of Fish
343 Cologne
352 In the Farmyard
357 On Lake Como

1875
102 A Cottage
109 Fish Stall at Venice
120 A Shrine - Venice
218 Alsatian Flower Girl

Winter Exhibition
105 Study of Sea
159 Woodland Scene
375 A Footbridge
385 A Pig Sty
444 On Hambledon Common

1876
59 A Donkey that Wouldn't Go
71 In the Market at Toulon
110 Exercising the Hounds
125 Fountain at Toulon

Winter Exhibition
352 Dunbar Castle

1877
32 The Capture of a 32-Pounder
172 A Chair Mender

Winter Exhibition
220 Market at Dinan; Women washing on the Loire
363 Loch Leven
375 In the Church of St Melaine, Morlaix, Brittany
386 On the Thames at Caversham
419 St Andrew's
448 Thames near Eton; On the Stour; Thames near Shiplake

1878
106 Venice
121 A New Purchase

Winter Exhibition
312 The Fountain at Drennec, Brittany
350 Rouen Cathedral
353 On the Common, Hambledon
373 A sketch at Haddon Hall
379 Fruit Stall near the Rialto, Venice
399 The Letter

1879
23 The Wandering Minstrels
141 The Falls of Tummel

Winter Exhibition
199 On the Coquet at Warkworth
216 The Thrum, on the Coquet, at Rothbury
321 A North Country Stile
337 Riverside, near Warkworth

1880
24 Venice, from the Giudecca

54 West Portal of Rheims Cathedral
109 The Corn Field

Winter Exhibition
232 Cattle in Water
234 On Hambledon Common
317 Stepping Stones
319 Bridge, near Dartmouth, Devon
324 Dittisham, on the Dart
327 Feeding the Geese
352 Stream at Beddgelert, North Wales
369 Shelling Peas
377 Cottage near Tenby

1881
9 Stepping Stones
15 An Old Water Mill

Winter Exhibition
158 St Gervaise, Falaise - Market Day
203 Falls of the Tummel, Perthshire
306 A Welsh Stile
323 Lyme Regis (two views)

1882
116 Turnberry Castle, Ayrshire - the early home of Robert Bruce
161 The Watering Place

Winter Exhibition
68 An Old Watermill
174 Fish and Fruit
183 Lancaster
313 The Brook
355 David Cox's Cottage, Betws-y-Coed

1883
143 A Surrey Landscape
281 Clovelly

Winter Exhibition
49 Cottage at Banavie, Inverness
110 Highland Bridge, Lochearnhead
163 Ben Nevis
381 The Angler
428 The Kingfisher

1884
9 A Lane near Dorking
65 Passing the Flock
232 A Windfall
244 An Itinerant Musician
252 Gypsies

Winter Exhibition
141 In the Western Highlands (3 drawings)
373 A Surrey Cottage

1885
91 The Dipping Place

Winter Exhibition
41 Ben Venue from Loch Achray
88 Highland Scene near Dalmally
300 A Highland Cottage

1886

5 The Hermitage Bridge, Dunkeld
114 Seville
257 Sandpits, Hambledon Common
286 Buttercups

Winter Exhibition

35 Girl at a Brook, Western Highlands
173 Loch Awe
311 A Highland Cottage
347 Bridge near Dalmally

1887

25 The Loch

Winter Exhibition

18 Autumn Leaves
102 Highland Cottage near Connel Ferry; in Canty Bay
118 'A Spanish Gypsy'
159 Cottage at Sidmouth
171 Flowers and Fruit (3 subjects)
234 Runswick; Crab and Lobster; The Old Pier
338 A Cottage
344 A Farm

1888

111 In the Market Place, Verona

Winter Exhibition

163 A Lace Maker
174 Abandoned; Study of Rocks, Gairloch
183 Study of Rocks and a Boat, Gairloch
222 Old Cottages, Hambledon; Sheep and Lambs
318 Crofters' Cottages, Gairloch
322 Sketch in Hambledon, Surrey
334 Cottage at Talladale, Loch Maree
336 A Cottage, Hambledon
372 Sketch at Gairloch

1889

211 Ruined Cottage at Gairloch
212 A Surrey Lane
214 Ben Venne and Ellen's Island, Loch Katrine
238 A Surrey Farm
244 A Cottage on Hambledon Common, Surrey
255 Cottages at Gairloch, Ross-shire
265 In the Cathedral of St Sauveur, Dinan, Brittany
269 Washing Place near Quimper, Brittany

Winter Exhibition

25 A Highland Village, Loch Alsh
42 Cottage near Balmacara
121 Collier unloading
132 Haytime
177 Harvest Time – Loch Duich
293 A Highland Barn – Balmacara
331 Oats – Balmacara
338 A Highland Cottage Loch Alsh
340 A Misty Day, Loch Alsh, Ross-shire
359 At Balmacara – Skye in the distance

1890

63 Arrival of Hop-pickers, Farnham (Ill. 103)
195 A Surrey Lane
215 Runswick, Yorkshire

Winter Exhibition

6 On the Rocks, Arisaig
49 The Island of Rum, from near Arisaig
74 A Crofter's Cottage, Western Highlands
82 Old Cottages, Near Arisaig
95 Waiting for the fishing boat, Arisaig
154 Cottage at Letterfern, Loch Duich
178 Highland Cottages, Arisaig
194 Goatfell from Brodick Bay, Arran
202 Harvest in the Highlands
336 Harvesting – near Arisaig – the Island of Skye in the distance

1891

104 A Knife Grinder
115 Ben Nevis
200 In a Garden at Sorrento

Winter Exhibition

149 Fisherman's Cottage, Gairloch
157 On the Shore, Gairloch
166 Rocks at Gairloch
179 Cottages at Gairloch
186 Near Loch Elvie
205 A Fisherman's Garden, Runswick
215 A Surrey Lane
358 The Sun-dial

1892

107 Loch Maree
- The footpath by the Water Lane
173 Oranges and Lemons, Mediterranean

Winter

130 A Highland Stream
147 Bridge over the Cluny, Braemar
154 A Highland Water Mill
185 On Hambledon Common
189 On the River Cluny, Braemar
303 Near Bonchurch, Isle of Wight
308 An Old Mill – near Braemar
320 A Girl at the Spring
341 Cottage, near Banavie
345 The Old Pier, St Andrews

1893

33 'To gather Kingcups in the yellow mead
And prink their hair with daisies.'
98 In Glencoe
128 Fast Castle – The Wolf's Crag of the Bride of Lammermoor
240 An Old Fiddler

Winter Exhibition

105 The Model
131 Near Braemar
161 At Calbourne, Isle of Wight
184 Barking Time
191 Under the Beech Tree
308 Fraser Bridge, Braemar
319 Cottages near Dalmally
336 Downey's Cottage, Braemar
342 Milton's Cottage, Chalfont St Giles
344 Cottage at Braemar

1894

16 A Cottage at Taynuilt
125 A Market at Seville
183 In a Wood, Witley
201 In a Garden at Sorrento
204 Fisherman's Cottage, North Berwick
205 Freshwater Bay
219 Near Freshwater, Isle of Wight
233 Cottage at Ballater
243 On Hambledon Common

Winter Exhibition

32 Cottage at Kimbolton
42 A Suffolk Well
96 The Stream at Wornditch, Kimbolton
188 'June' – in a cottage near a wood
194 The Old Pier at Walberswick
219 On the Beach, Southwold
323 A Windlass, Southwold
343 At Wornditch, Kimbolton
349 Walberswick, Suffolk

1895

88 Horning Ferry
103 Near Ballater
118 Procession on Pardon Day – Quimper, Brittany
205 A Little Courtyard in the Alhambra
209 At Walberswick, Suffolk

Winter Exhibition

52 Near Connel Ferry
64 An Orphan
150 Butterflies
165 The Village Tree
309 The Island of Mull from Oban
323 Cottages at Taynuilt
330 A Highland Cottage
340 Cottage near Connel Ferry

1896

11 Walberswick, Suffolk
12 In a Garden at the Alhambra
17 Ichrachan, Taynuilt
200 Girl at a Stream
201 On Hambledon Common
207 Waiting for the Ferry
211 Southwold from the Black Quay

Winter Exhibition

6 On the Canal, Weybridge
30 Highland Cottage, near Taynuilt
38 Burano, Venice
87 Loch Etive, from near Connel Ferry
91 A Farm, Connel Ferry
157 Ben Cruachan
327 Near Taynuilt
328 Roses

1897

13 Wild Flowers
209 Near Connel Ferry
220 Crofters' Cottages at Strath, Gairloch

Winter Exhibition

52 Traveller's Joy
62 The Alhambra

141 A Roadside Shrine near Genoa
239 A Rest by the Way
252 Haytime
261 A Stream
267 At Connel Ferry

1898

89 Ben Ledi from Callander

Winter Exhibition

61 On the River Spean
67 The Pet Lamb
75 Roy Bridge, Inverness-shire
83 Loch Etive
157 Highland Village, near Taynuilt
198 Old Cottages, Loch Etive
298 Cottages, near Taynuilt
304 Cottage, near Connel Ferry

1899

224 A Milkmaid, Arisaig

Spellings have been corrected in the case of obvious errors in the catalogue. These mistakes in the original source were often the result of a misreading of handwritten labels.

APPENDIX 3

List of exhibits with the Royal Academy of Arts

Year Exhibit
no.

1859 873 A Farm: Arundel Park in the distance (water-colour)
1869 829 A Surrey Lane
1870 474 Dunstanborough Castle
1871 298 The Thames near Eton
    512 The Bass Rock
1872 414 Over Sands
    511 The Ford
1873 122 In the Isle of Wight
    973 A Pedlar
1874 535 A Lifeboat: the return from the wreck
1875 123 On the River Mole
    159 Evening
('I am just diving into two oil pictures for the R.A. I don't know whether I shall get them finished, but I hope so . . .' – letter to Robert Spence, 27 January 1875)
1876 1319 A Peep at the Hounds
1877 633 A Brook
1881 1220 The Wandering Minstrel (etching)
A hopeful correspondent once wrote to Birket Foster, as follows:
'Dear Sir, If your picture in the Royal Academy is for sale kindly quote *bottom* price for it, yours obediently, etc.'

List of Exhibits by William Foster with the Royal Academy of Arts
1872 474 Still Life
1873 62 'The moping heron, motionless and stiff, etc.'
1874 971 Startled Teal
    992 Leadenhall Market
1877 621 The Vain Jackdaw
    1253 The Gate House, Sandwich

1879   666 A Sussex Farmyard
        1281 Venice
1880   1294 Amble Harbour, Northumberland – etching
        1298 At Hastings – etching
1882   1239 At Dartmouth – etching
        1316 Staircase, The Hill, Witley – etching
1883   438 Gypsies
1884   393 'Welcome the friendly banks, refreshing seat, etc.'
1885   793 Seed Potatoes
1886   99   At the World's Mercy
        671 Blowing Birds' Eggs
1888   1075 'They're off'
1890   969 Feeding the Puppies
        970 'Who goes there?'
        1196 A Summer's Day
1891   1106 'What's that?'
1892   1077 Cosford Mill
1893   1009 Thieves in the Corn
1894   952 The Cluny from Braemar

Exhibits by Lancelot Myles Glasson (grandson of Birket Foster) with the Royal Academy of Arts

1928   204 The Bather
1929   127 Repose
1930   440 Venus Waking
1931   296 Déjeuner sur l'herbe
1932   669 The Young Rower
1933   346 The Four
1934   80   Dacre Castle
        373 The Swimmer
1935   214 The Sun-Bathers
1936   109 The Runners
        757 Arabella Unpacks
1938   470 Arabella Resting
1949   425 Sarah

APPENDIX 4

Special Loan Exhibition of Pictures of the British School in Oils and Water-colours – Museum and Art Gallery, Nottingham Castle, 1896

Exhibits of work by Birket Foster, as follows:
109 Warks Burn, Northumberland
110 Lancaster
111 Bridge near Dalmally, Perthshire
112 Children on the Seashore (see Whitworth Art Gallery p. 210)
113 Sandhills, Surrey
114 Durham Cathedral and the River Wear
115 On the Thames at Eton
     On the Stour, Dedham
     On the Thames at Shiplake
116 Saumur, France

Charles Seely, M.P. would never allow his collection of Birket Foster water-colours to be exhibited (rather to the regret of the artist). But, the pictures were inherited by his son, Colonel Sir Charles Seely, Bart., a wealthy colliery owner and M.P. for Nottingham. He was to allow 44 of these Venetian scenes to be shown in this exhibition, as follows:
65 Baldacchino in St Mark's (89)
66 Canal San Giuseppe (64)

67 Portico and Steps of Santa Maria della Salute (69)
68 In the Vestibule, St Mark's (62)
69 The Dolphin Bridge, Grand Canal (95)
70 Church of St Simone and St Judi (88)
71 A Shop in Rio dell' Orto (65)
72 Ponti del Panada (*sic*) (58)
73 Canale del Mori (studio of the painter Tintoretto to the right) (92)
74 Sotto Portico dei Sante (98)
75 Pulpit in the Church of St Mark (72) (Ill. 82)
76 Entrance to the Ducal Palace (70)
77 The Rialto (87)
78 Venice from the Steps of San Giorgio (71)
79 Santa Maria Salute from the Giudecca (90)
80 Burano (81)
81 Gondola Landing Place, Grand Canal (84)
82 Steps at the Rialto (68)
83 Canale Dell' Ospitale, with part of the Scuola di S. Marco (57)
84 The Lion Column – St Giorgio in the distance (93)
85 The Approach to Venice by Railway (96)
86 The end of the Riva Degli Schiavoni (67)
87 Palazzo Viccietti Rio del Fara (74)
88 Archway to Court La Tratta Osstate di Cordevia (73)
89 A Well in the Court of the Orologio (82)
90 The Grand Canal (59)
91 A Well in the Courtyard of the Ducal Palace (91)
92 Feeding the Pigeons, Place San Marco (97)
93 Calle Prima Due Corti (60)
94 A fruit shop, Rialto Market (76)
95 A fish shop, Rialto Market (75)
96 A Shrine in the Courtyard of the Ducal Palace (55). (Ill. 81)
97 The Rialto (80)
98 The Church of the Presentazione and San Giorgio from the Giudecca (86)
99 The steps of the public gardens (79)
100 Murano (77)
101 Shrine near the Ducal Palace (94)
102 Venice from near the Lido (56)
103 Fishing boats, San Giorgio (78)
104 The Bridge of Sighs (66)
105 The Library of the Piazzetta (63)
106 Chiesa Dei Gesuati, Giudecca (61)
107 Strada Nuova dei Giardini (83)
108 The Church of San Barnabas Apostolo (85)

The numbers in brackets denote those used when the above works from the Seely Collection were exhibited in the *Special Loan Exhibition of Works by Birket Foster*, which was held at the Laing Art Gallery and Museum in 1925. A few of these water-colours appeared in the inaugural exhibition of the Laing in 1904, but the collection had not otherwise been exhibited since 1896. By 1925 the works were in the possession of Lieutenant-Colonel Frank Seely. In later years, an idea has grown up that the Seely Collection of Venetian water-colours was still intact, but not available for loan or public exhibition, but this is not correct. Sir Charles Seely died in 1915 and already the collection was not quite complete, as certain examples had been given to other members of the family, who subsequently sold them. In 1928, the pictures were stored at Nottingham Castle for a while, but a few years later the collection was dispersed and only two now remain in family ownership. Any water-colour by Birket Foster of

Venice that comes onto the market should be checked with the above titles for the possibility of its having originated with the Seely commission and therefore having a date of not before about 1870 and not later than early 1877. Numbers 68, 78, 91, 96, and 105 as listed in the Nottingham exhibition were illustrated in the Cundall biography, with the addition of a work entitled 'Palazzo Gussoni'.

APPENDIX 5

Birket Foster Centenary Special Loan Exhibition – Laing Art Gallery, Newcastle upon Tyne, 1925

The exhibition consisted of 167 items, but a full list of these is not shown as many of the exhibits are now in public collections and have already been listed, mentioned in the text, or included among the illustrations, e.g. 'Wandering Minstrels', etc. About 20 remain in family ownership, including views of Newcastle, Edinburgh and Rothesay Bay in possession of Spence family connections. A drawing of 'Low Lights, North Shields' dated 1844 relates to the Birket Foster letter on p. 19 and was loaned by Philip Spence. It is now owned by of his son Charles Spence. 'The Falls of Tummel' as loaned by Mrs E. Glasson is now in possession of her daughter, Miss Sarah G. A. Glasson. 'Monte Carlo' – a slightly unexpected subject for Birket Foster – was loaned by the widower of Birket Foster's elder daughter, who also lent 'Glencoe', as exhibited at the Brussels International Exhibition in 1897. Items 55-98 consisted of water-colours from the Seely Collection, listed in detail on p. 200. Exhibits 112-122 were catalogued as drawings and included 'The Omnibus' – the earliest known example from the hand of Birket Foster – and 'George Hudson's Train passing over Dean Street Arch', 1848 (both drawings loaned by descendants of Robert Spence). Exhibits 123-167 showed mostly etchings, engravings and various miscellaneous items such as a fan painted by Birket Foster for his second wife, the letter to Robert Foster as quoted on p. 171 and a painting of the kitchen at The Hill by A. W. Cooper.

The author is in possession of a catalogue of the above exhibition which was kindly presented by the Laing Art Gallery.

APPENDIX 6

Catalogue details of the sale of remaining works of Birket Foster, as held at Christie, Manson and Woods on 26-7 June 1899

First day's sale

Early Pencil Drawings:
1 Crag End; Rothbury; Beddington, etc. (13)
2 Rochester; Edinburgh; Windsor; Eton. etc. (9)
3 Melrose Abbey; Bywell; Croxteth Hall; Carisbrooke, etc. (6)
4 Tynemouth Priory; Bywell; Brinkburn Priory and Porch; St Margaret's Church, York (4)
5 Eastbourne; Folkestone; Bridlington Quay; Holy Island, etc. (5)
6 Ovingham Hall; Ordsall Hall, etc. (4)
7 Stirling Castle; Flodden Field; Ben Ledi; Doune Castle; etc. (9)

8 Views in the English Lake District (13)
9 Walton-on-Thames; Harbottle; Jarrow, etc. (4)
10 The Tower of London; The Pool of London; Hull; On the Thames (4)
11 New Brighton Fort; North Shields; Cullercoats (3)
12 North and South Shields; Tynemouth Priory; Lighthouse, Tynemouth. (3)
13 Views of the Rhine: done as illustrations for Longfellow's *Hyperion* – a set of 63

English Scenery
Sketch Books:
14 Four sketch books, containing pencil views of the Thames, Rye, Ludlow, Hereford, Worcester, Carmarthen and the Isle of Wight
15 Three sketch books, containing pencil views of Shrewsbury, Bridgnorth, Haddon, Maidenhead, Cookham, Peterborough, Newcastle, etc.
16 Three sketch books, with pencil views of Putney, Chelsea, Deal, Canterbury, Ramsgate, Naworth Castle, etc.
17 A sketch book, with Bolton Abbey, Rocks at Torquay, and two others, coloured; Berkeley Castle, Tewkesbury, Ashby-de-la-Zouche, Peak Castle, Chester, etc. – in pencil
18 A sketch book, containing views of Lyme Regis, Windsor High Street, and two others, coloured; pencil drawings of Eton College, etc.
19 A sketch book, containing views of Huntingdon and one other, coloured; pencil views of Maidenhead, Bray, Cookham, Offord, St Ives, etc.
20 A sketch book, illustrating the cathedrals of England, with pencil views of Oxford, Carlisle, Manchester, Truro, Chester, Liverpool, Bristol, St. Asaph, Bangor, Exeter, etc.
21 A sketch book, containing a coloured drawing of a castle on a lake; and pencil views of King's Lynn, Aldeburgh, Orford, etc.
22 A sketch book, with a coloured sketch of fishermen at Southwold; and pencil views of Carisbrooke, etc.
23 A sketch book, containing 'The Mumbles' – coloured; and pencil views of Manorbier Castle, Tenby, Pembroke, Oystermouth, etc.
24 A sketch book, containing five coloured drawings of Lancaster Sands, shipping, peacocks, etc.; and pencil studies of figures, etc.
25 A sketch book, containing coloured views of Eyemouth, Dunfermline, Newhaven; pencil sketches of Holyrood; and various pastoral subjects
Pencil Drawings: In folio
26 Windsor Castle; A Thames View; and a Bridge (3)
27 Rochester; Tilbury from Gravesend, etc. (4)
28 Haddon Hall; Tintern Abbey; Newark Abbey (3)
29 Robin Hood's Bay; Guildford; Gad's Hill Place, Okehampton; Bedford; etc. (6)
30 Views of Oxford (2)
Water-colour Drawings: in folio
31 Southwold; At Runswick (2)
32 Horning Ferry, Norfolk
33 Rocks, Ilfracombe; Hastings Beach; and the Thames from Charlton (3)
34 Southwold; and At Walberswick (2)
35 Stanwell; Dover; Longstone; and Farne Island (4)
36 Warkworth Hermitage; and Penshurst (2)
37 Warkworth Castle, 1846
38 Bamborough Castle

Water-colour Drawings: Framed

39 Cowper's Summer House at Olney ($6\frac{1}{2} \times 8''$)
40 At the Golden Grove, Chertsey ($5\frac{1}{2} \times 8\frac{1}{2}''$)
41 Eton College ($4 \times 5\frac{1}{2}''$)
42 At Paignton, Devon ($5\frac{1}{2} \times 8\frac{1}{2}''$)
43 At Kingskerswell, Devon ($5\frac{1}{2} \times 8\frac{1}{2}''$)
44 Cottage at Paignton, Devon ($5\frac{1}{2} \times 7\frac{1}{2}''$)
45 At Southwold ($7\frac{1}{2} \times 10\frac{1}{2}''$)
46 At Faningford, Isle of Wight ($7\frac{1}{4} \times 9\frac{3}{4}''$)
47 Robin Hood's Bay ($7 \times 10''$)
48 Caversham ($5 \times 10\frac{1}{2}''$)
49 At Freshwater, Isle of Wight ($8 \times 12\frac{1}{4}''$)
50 At Walberswick ($8 \times 10\frac{1}{2}''$)
51 Morecambe Bay ($6 \times 8\frac{1}{2}''$)
52 Sand Pits, Hambledon ($6\frac{1}{2} \times 9''$)
53 Rocks at Tynemouth, Northumberland ($9\frac{1}{4} \times 13\frac{1}{2}''$)
54 The Pond at The Hill, Witley ($14 \times 10''$)
55 Rokeby, Yorkshire ($12\frac{1}{2} \times 17\frac{1}{2}''$)
56 Elstead, Godalming ($11\frac{1}{2} \times 16''$)
57 Busse's Cottage, Hambledon ($7 \times 9\frac{1}{2}''$)
58 Cottage at Hambledon, Surrey ($8 \times 10\frac{1}{2}''$)
59 Alnwick Castle, 1846 ($10\frac{1}{2} \times 17\frac{1}{2}''$)
60 The Golden Grove, Chertsey ($13\frac{1}{2} \times 19''$)
61 Old Chain Pier, Brighton ($5\frac{1}{4} \times 6\frac{3}{4}''$)
62 Hambledon, Surrey ($9 \times 13\frac{3}{4}''$)
63 Newbiggin by the Sea, Northumberland ($7 \times 9\frac{3}{4}''$)
64 At Bonchurch, Isle of Wight ($10 \times 15\frac{1}{2}''$)
65 A Castle on the East Coast ($12 \times 17''$)
66 A Welsh Stream ($7 \times 9''$)
67 Walberswick, Suffolk ($7 \times 11''$)
68 On Hambledon Common ($7 \times 10''$)
   Exhibited at Brussels, 1897
69 The Weald of Surrey ($10 \times 14''$)
70 Southwold from the Black Ferry ($7\frac{1}{2} \times 12''$)
71 Rocks at Boscastle, Cornwall ($8 \times 14''$)

Scotch (*sic*) Scenery

Sketch Books:

72 Two sketch books containing coloured views of Mull from Oban, and Ben Nevis, and numerous pencil sketches
73 Four sketch books with pencil views of the Bass Rock, Melrose, Abbotsford, Edinburgh, Callander, etc.
74 A sketch book containing a coloured drawing of The Birthplace of George Stephenson, and pencil views of Iona, Connel Ferry, etc.
75 A sketch book with a coloured view of Edinburgh, and various pencil sketches for the Scotland series; also a few views in Italy
76 A sketch book containing two coloured views near Dalmally, and pencil sketches of Loch Leven, Annan, Corby Castle, Port Carlisle, etc.

Water-colour Drawings: In folio

77 Scotch Cottages and Boats; Highland Cottage (2)
78 Peat Bog, Banavie; and Ben Nevis from Banavie (2)
79 Flowerdale, Gairloch
80 Haroldswick, Shetland; and Lerwick, 1845 (2)
81 Scalloway; and A Castle (2)

Framed:

82 Inverlochy Castle - vignette ($4 \times 5''$)
83 Near Taynuilt ($4\frac{3}{4} \times 8\frac{1}{2}''$)
84 Ben Nevis ($5\frac{1}{2} \times 7\frac{1}{2}''$)
85 Getting Peats ($5\frac{1}{2} \times 9''$)
86 A Reel ($8 \times 11\frac{1}{2}''$)
87 Keppoch, Arisaig ($6\frac{1}{2} \times 10\frac{1}{2}''$)
88 Rocks, Dunbar ($4\frac{3}{4} \times 11\frac{1}{2}''$)

89 At Loch Awe ($8 \times 10\frac{1}{2}''$)
90 Keppoch Farm, Arisaig ($6 \times 10''$)
91 Cottages, Ichrachan, Taynuilt ($8 \times 11''$)
92 Loch Awe ($9 \times 13\frac{1}{4}''$)
93 Girl washing at a Brook near Loch Awe ($9\frac{1}{4} \times 7\frac{1}{2}''$)
94 Cottages at Balmacara ($7 \times 10\frac{1}{2}''$)
95 The Bass Rock ($4\frac{1}{2} \times 6''$)
96 On the East Coast of Scotland ($12 \times 18''$)
97 A Highland River ($10 \times 13''$)
98 Waterfall, Loch Achray ($12 \times 10''$)
99 At Loch Awe ($10\frac{1}{2} \times 15''$)
100 Ben Venue, Loch Achray ($10\frac{1}{2} \times 15''$)
101 Loch Maree, from the Polewe Road ($9\frac{1}{2} \times 15\frac{1}{2}''$)
Sketch for the large drawing painted for J.H. Foster, Esq.
102 Glencoe ($11 \times 16''$)
Sketch for a drawing in possession of Mrs Birket Foster
103 Old Mill, near Braemar ($11 \times 8\frac{3}{4}''$)
104 Ben Nevis ($7 \times 15\frac{1}{2}''$)
105 Mull, from Oban ($6\frac{1}{2} \times 13''$)
106 Old Mill, Braemar ($8\frac{1}{4} \times 11''$)
107 Edinburgh ($7 \times 4\frac{3}{4}''$)
108 The Abbey of Arbroath ($7\frac{1}{2} \times 10\frac{1}{2}''$)
109 St Andrews ($6 \times 10''$)
110 Hayfield, Taynuilt ($6\frac{3}{4} \times 10\frac{1}{2}''$)
111 Highland Cottages, Near Taynuilt ($8 \times 10\frac{1}{2}''$)
112 Ben Cruachan ($8 \times 10\frac{1}{2}''$)
113 A Ruined Chapel, Arisaig ($10\frac{1}{2} \times 15''$)
114 The Hermitage Bridge, near Dunkeld ($21\frac{1}{2} \times 17''$)
115 Loch Awe ($11 \times 17\frac{1}{2}''$)

Continental Scenery

Sketch Books:

116 A sketch book with a coloured view of Naes Romsdal Fiord; and pencil views of Christiansund, Trondhjem, Merok and Nykirke, etc.
117 A sketch book, containing six coloured views of Creels, Vesuvius, Castles and Cottages, and pencil sketches for Blowing Bubbles, The Organ Grinder, etc.

Pencil Drawings: In folio

118 A Swiss Lake; A Gorge; and A Street Scene (3)
119 Views in Lucerne (3)
120 A View on the Rhine

Water-colour drawings: In Folio

121 Windmill, Dort, Holland; Dutch Boats - on grey paper (3)

Framed:

122 A View in a Swiss Village - on grey paper ($9\frac{1}{2} \times 7''$)
123 Dort ($6 \times 9\frac{1}{2}''$)
124 Antwerp ($12 \times 8\frac{1}{2}''$)
125 Freiburg (sketch for the picture painted for M. Gambart)
126 Heidelberg ($8\frac{1}{2} \times 12''$)

Views at Tangiers:

127 Tangiers ($5\frac{1}{2} \times 11''$)
128 A Well, Tangiers ($6 \times 7''$)
129 The Gate of The Citadel, Tangiers ($8\frac{1}{2} \times 6''$)
130 Street in Tangiers ($11\frac{1}{2} \times 9''$)
131 A Market, Tangiers ($8 \times 11\frac{1}{2}''$)
132 A Well, Tangiers ($10 \times 9\frac{1}{2}''$)

Pictures

[Note: from this term the inference is that the works were in oils]

133 Dedham ($9\frac{3}{4} \times 13\frac{1}{2}''$)
134 The Loch ($9\frac{1}{2} \times 14''$)

135 A Meadow (13 × 18″)
136 A Cottage Door (8 × 6″)
137 The Timber-Waggon (9 × 12½″)
138 Hounds Breaking Cover (42 × 36″)

END OF FIRST DAY'S SALE

Second day's sale

Miscellaneous Subjects

Sketch Books:

139 Four sketch books containing pencil studies of land-scapes, cathedrals, figures, etc.
140 Four sketch books containing pencil studies of land-scapes, pastoral subjects, figures, etc.
141 A sketch book containing 'The Pedlar' and 'Sunset at Sea' – coloured; and pencil sketches of children, etc.
142 A sketch book containing Highland Drovers, Hop-Pickers, and two others – coloured; and numerous pencil drawings and designs
143 Two sketch books, containing five coloured sketches of flowers, etc. and numerous pencil sketches
144 Three sketch books containing four coloured sketches of flowers, milk-cans, etc. and pencil views of Clifton, Melrose, Cockington, etc.
145 A sketch book containing A Sweet-Shop Window – coloured; and pencil views of Lyme Regis, Lucerne, etc.

Pencil Drawings: In folio

146 Landscape and figure studies (8)
147 Cathedrals, churches, etc. (6)
148 Landscapes, cottages, windmills, etc. (9)
149 Views of towns, mansions, etc. (7)
150 River scenes, etc. (7)
151 River scenes, bridges, etc. (7)
152 Castles, ruined abbeys, etc. (7)
153 Harbour and river scenes, with shipping, etc. (5)
154 Woody landscapes and bird's-eye views, etc. (5)

Water-colour drawings: In Folio

155 Lily and Roses; and Basket of Roses
156 Garlands, First of May; and Bluebells
157 A Cavern by the Sea; Study of a Roof; and Study of Sky
158 A Harvest-Cart; and Sunset
159 A Cottage Porch; A Waterfall; and Study of Rock
160 A Ruined Castle; and A Landscape; Sunset
161 Studies of Trees, etc.
162 Moonlight; and Sea and Sand
163 Study of Rocks; and Tumbling Water
164 A Birch Stem; and A Sky Study
165 A Gap in the Hedge; and A Flock of Sheep
166 A River Scene; and A Woodland Stream
167 Windmills
168 A River Scene, with distant castle
168A Bamborough Castle

Framed:

169 Sunset at Sea (4 × 5½″)
170 A Windmill (11¼ × 6″)
171 Sunset (5¾ × 8″)
172 Fish (7½ × 10½″)
173 A Farmyard (5 × 7″)
174 Rocks (5 × 7½″)
175 A Boat (4½ × 7½″)
176 A Cottage Study (7½ × 10″)
177 A Ruined Abbey (7 × 10″)

178 A Hay-Cart (6 × 11″)
179 A Coast Scene (9½ × 13½″)
180 A Shady Lane (8½ × 11½″)
181 Roses, in a blue vase (8¾ × 6¾″)
182 Dog-Fish and Skate (7½ × 7″)
183 Melons – two in one frame (5 × 9″)

French Scenery (*sic*)

Sketch Books:

184 A sketch book, containing coloured views of Hyères, La Garde, Antibes, Fréjus, Roccabruna, Bordighera and Albenga, and other views in the Riviera in pencil
185 A sketch book, with coloured views of Hyères, La Ciotat, Alves, Hyères and Pisa, and pencil sketches on the Mediterranean coast
186 Two sketch books, containing views of cathedrals at Rouen, Caen, Honfleur, Lisieux, and views of Normandy and Brittany – pencil
187 Four sketch books, containing views of Chartres, Orleans, Paris, etc. and studies of figures and animals in Brittany

Drawings: In folio

188 Rouen; Notre Dame; and Dinan, etc. – pencil (6)
189 A Forge; Market Girl; Children at a Shrine, etc. – pencil (4)
190 A Market Scene; A Clothes Stall; Girl Knitting, etc. – pencil (3)
191 Paris – water-colour

Water-colour Drawings: Framed

192 Marseilles, from Estaque (4¾ × 7″)
193 Brittany Woman and Cow – vignette (4½ × 3½″)
194 French Fishwives: Calais (5 × 6″)
195 Mentone (9½ × 14″)
196 Pardon Day: Quimper (11 × 15″)
[Note: Sketch for the more finished work]
197 A Fountain: Toulon (7 × 9″)
198 Mont St. Michel (5 × 7″)
199 Procession of Pardon Day: Quimper, Brittany (16 × 21½″)

Italian Scenery

Sketch Books:

200 A sketch book, with ten coloured views of Tivoli, Nemi, Castel Gandolfo, Sorrento, Verona, etc.; and pencil views of Isola Bella, Isola Piscatore, Streza, and Sesto Calende, etc.
201 A sketch book containing views of Lake Como and Argegno (2) and pencil sketches of Verona, Florence, Venice, etc.

Pencil Drawings: In folio

202 Turin; At Naples; and A Colosseum (3)
203 Isola Piscatore, Lago Maggiore; and Views in the Italian Lakes (3)
204 Bellagio, Lake Como etc.
205 Canale, San Giuseppe, Venice, etc. (2)
206 The Lagoons; S. Giorgio Maggiore; and The Giudecca (3)
207 The Dogana; The Balcony of a Palace; and Figures at Wells (6)
208 Looking over the Rialto

Water-colour Drawings: in folio

209 Fishing Boats, Venice; and A Venetian Sail
210 Campo Santo, Pisa

Water-colour Drawings: Framed

211 Desenzano, Lago di Garda (5 × 7½″)
212 Citadella, Pisa (3½ × 5″)

213 Burano, Venice ($8 \times 7''$)
214 Verona ($6 \times 9''$)
215 A Flower Shop: Venice ($7 \times 9''$)
216 The Market Place, Verona ($9\frac{3}{4} \times 6''$)
217 An Italian Lake Scene ($17 \times 27\frac{1}{2}''$)

Spanish Scenery

Sketch Books:
218 A sketch book containing 'The Pilar del Toro Calle Elbira, Granada' and 'Francisca' – coloured; and pencil sketches of Toledo, Gibraltar, etc.
219 Two sketch books with three coloured views and pencil drawings of Seville, Cape St. Vincent, Gibraltar, etc.
220 Four sketch books containing pencil views in Seville, Tangiers, Burgos, Venice, etc.

Water-colour Drawings: In folio
221 The Alhambra, from Generaliffe; and Figure at the Little Mosque, Alhambra
222 A Window in the Little Mosque; and A Balcony, Alhambra
223 Granada from the Alhambra
224 Returning from Market; A Market Place; and Figures at a Fountain – pencil

Water-colour Drawings: Framed
225 A Market in Seville ($4 \times 5\frac{1}{2}''$)
226 The Alhambra, from the Top of the Generaliffe ($5\frac{1}{2} \times 8\frac{1}{2}''$)
227 Sorrento ($4\frac{3}{4} \times 7''$)
228 The Alhambra ($7 \times 10\frac{1}{2}''$)
229 A Patio, Seville ($10 \times 8''$)
230 The Little Mosque, Alhambra ($8\frac{1}{4} \times 10\frac{1}{2}''$)
231 The Sierra Nevada, from the Alhambra ($10 \times 15''$)
232 The Alhambra ($7\frac{1}{2} \times 10\frac{1}{2}''$)
233 Two Figures at the Little Mosque, Alhambra ($8 \times 7''$)
234 The Moors' Market ($8 \times 5''$)
235 Gipsies: Alhambra ($7 \times 4\frac{1}{2}''$)
236 The Rock of Gibraltar ($9 \times 13\frac{1}{2}''$)
237 Seville ($9 \times 11''$)
238 A Spaniard: Alhambra ($7\frac{1}{4} \times 4\frac{1}{2}''$)
239 In a Garden of the Alhambra ($8\frac{1}{2} \times 11''$)
240 A Market in Seville ($23 \times 33''$)

Pastoral and Figure Subjects

Sketch Books:
241 A sketch book, containing a coloured drawing 'Watering the Garden' and numerous pencil sketches
242 Two sketch books, containing two coloured pastoral sketches, various views on the Italian coast, and studies of figures in pencil
243 Two sketch books, with three coloured drawings, and numerous pencil studies and views at Wallingford, Stratford-on-Avon, Caversham, etc.
244 Three sketch books containing pencil studies of pastoral subjects and figures

Pencil Drawings: In folio
245 Cottages and Children; Sea Dabblers, etc. (8)
246 Going to School; Down the Hill; Gathering Wild Roses, etc. (10)
247 The Fiddler; Gathering Apples, etc. (3)
248 The Broom Seller; The Skipping Rope, etc. (4)
249 Crossing the Stream – a study on the reverse

Water-colour Drawings: In folio
250 In a Meadow; and Stepping Stones
251 Children and a Cottage; and A Village Inn
252 A Devonshire Lace-Maker; Gathering Blackberries, etc. (4)

253 A Cottage Girl; and A Sulky Child (2)
254 Barking Time
256 A Farmyard
256 A Fiddler
257 Illustration to Gray's Elegy; and A Landscape with children and sheep

Water-colour Drawings: Framed
258 The First of May is Garland Day ($4\frac{1}{2} \times 6''$)
259 Cottages, Children and Brook ($4\frac{1}{2} \times 6''$)
260 Watering flowers ($3\frac{1}{2} \times 5''$)
261 What's O'clock? ($5 \times 7''$)
262 Blowing Bubbles ($4\frac{1}{2} \times 6''$)
263 Cart and Flock of Sheep ($5\frac{1}{2} \times 8\frac{1}{2}''$)
264 The Ford ($9\frac{1}{2} \times 13''$)
265 Barking Time ($10 \times 14''$)
266 An Illustrated Paper ($6 \times 7\frac{1}{2}''$)
[The last drawing that the artist finished]
267 The Kitten ($8 \times 10''$)
[One of the drawings in hand at the artist's death]
268 Barking Time ($10 \times 14''$)
269 The Drinking Trough ($6 \times 8''$)
[One of the artist's last finished drawings]
270 Figures by a Stream ($10\frac{1}{2} \times 15''$)
271 Children at a Brook ($16\frac{1}{2} \times 13\frac{1}{2}''$)
[Study for a work painted for Edmund Evans]
272 The Last Load ($12 \times 19''$)

Note: Total sum obtained for the sale of these works:– £5,324/16/6d. Individual prices may be obtained on application to the author, but monetary values have so much changed as to render these without relevance to the present day.

APPENDIX 7

Catalogue of work by Birket Foster in public collections

Below are given provincial locations of examples of work, as listed in this section. Information in brackets indicates that a specific topographical subject is included in work by Birket Foster in that collection.

Aberdeen (Hambledon)
Aberystwyth
Accrington
Bath
Bedford (St Michael's Mount)
Belfast (Lyme Regis, Falls of Tummel)
Birkenhead
Birmingham (Worms Cathedral, Birmingham, Freiburg, Berne, Loch Awe)
Blackburn (Holywell, Florence, Littlehampton, Venice)
Blackpool (Mont St Michel)
Bolton (Woking, Surrey)
Bournemouth (Swiss Scene)
Bradford (Witley, Hastings)
Brighton (Tynemouth)
Bristol (Stoke Poges)
Burnley (Seville)
Bury (Rottingdean)
Cambridge (Venice, Granada)
Cardiff
Dudley
Edinburgh
Exeter (Cullercoats)
Glasgow

Halifax
Hartlepool
Hereford (Lake Como)
Hitchin (Hitchin Market Place)
Huddersfield
Ipswich (Ipswich)
Leeds (Cromer)
Liverpool (Stratford-on-Avon)
Manchester (Manchester, Hampstead, Balmacara, Dunkeld, Dolceaqua, Pisa)
Newcastle (Newcastle, Tynemouth, Gateshead, Cullercoats, Ben Nevis, Arundel, Venice, Quimper, Verona, Chalfont St. Giles, Elstow, Taymouth, Ilfracombe)
Newport (Ben Venue and Loch Katrine)
Norwich (Broxbournebury Park, Herts)
Oxford (on the Rhine)
Paisley
Port Sunlight (Hambledon)
Preston (Dunstanborough Castle, Bellaggio)
Rochdale (Guildford Common)
St Helens (Streatley-on-Thames)
Sheffield (Kimbolton, Mentone, Chartres, Stolzenfels, Ilfracombe, Rouen, Stoke Poges)
Southport
Sunderland (Venice)
Walsall
Warrington (Bonchurch, Isle of Wight)
Wigan
Windsor – Eton College (Hindhead, Venice)
Wolverhampton
Worthing
York (Bootham Bar, York)

Measurements should be taken as indicating height before width. Very slight variations in the equivalents between Imperial and Metric may occur as a result of individuals rounding these figures up or down. Information that a work is 'signed with monogram' indicates the letters 'B F' in the device as shown on most of the illustrated examples, e.g. Ill. 40. Monogram positions are not included, as this information can only be of use if a work is to hand. An analysis of monogrammed works shows that there is no predisposition to either left or right. The use of the term 'Studio stamp' is well explained in Christie's catalogue, 26 June 1899, thus: 'The remaining works of the late Birket Foster, R.W.S. have been stamped with the initials "B F" with the exception of the pencil drawings in the Sketch Books and 63 Views of the Rhine done for Longfellow's *Hyperion*'. This studio mark consists of B.F. in neat sepia capitals, which are placed within a slightly oval-shaped circle.

THE VICTORIA AND ALBERT MUSEUM, SOUTH KENSINGTON, LONDON SW7 2RL

529-1882 The Milkmaid ($11\frac{3}{4} \times 17\frac{1}{2}''$ – 29.8 × 44.5 cms) Ill. 40. Water-colour, signed 'B.F. 1860' The official postcard of this work has now been discontinued, but is reproduced in this form by the Medici Society. Also reproduced pl. 9 of the *Catalogue of the Jones Collection*, Part III, 1923.

523-1882 Santa Maria della Salute, Grand Canal, Venice ($7\frac{1}{4} \times 10\frac{3}{4}''$ – 18.4 × 26.0 cms) Water-colour, signed with monogram. Reproduced in the *Catalogue of the Jones Collection*, as above.

524-1882 San Giorgio Maggiore, Venice ($7\frac{1}{4} \times 10\frac{1}{4}''$ – 18.4 × 26.0 cms) Water-colour, signed with monogram.

Reproduced as above. Also in *Water-colour Painting in Britain* by Martin Hardie – B.T. Batsford.

1108-1886 Young Gleaners Resting ($11\frac{7}{8} \times 17\frac{5}{8}''$ – 30.2 × 44.8 cms) Ill. 41. Water-colour, signed with monogram. Dixon Bequest (Bethnal Green Museum). Reproduced in *The Magazine of Art* vol. XV, p. 244.

1119-1886 Coast Scene, sunset and windy sky ($4\frac{7}{8} \times 7''$ – 14.6 × 17.8 cms) Water-colour, signed. Dixon Bequest (Bethnal Green Museum).

1219-1886 Landscape with Water-sunset ($5\frac{3}{4} \times 8\frac{1}{2}''$ – 14.6 × 21.6 cms) Water-colour, signed. Dixon Bequest (Bethnal Green Museum).

1221-1886 Children Running down Hill ($13\frac{1}{4} \times 27\frac{5}{8}''$ – 33.6 × 70.2 cms) Water-colour, signed. Reproduced in *Water-colours in the Dixon Bequest*, 1923, pl. XX.

1224-1886 Landscape with Cattle ($7\frac{1}{4} \times 10\frac{5}{8}''$ – 18.4 × 27.0 cms) Water-colour, signed. Reproduced as above, pl. XXI.

1225-1886 Landscape with Cattle and Bridge ($8\frac{1}{4} \times 12\frac{1}{4}''$ – 21 × 31.2 cms) Water-colour, signed. Reproduced as above, pl. XXVI.

65-1895 A Dell in Devonshire ($9\frac{3}{4} \times 19\frac{1}{2}''$ – 24.8 × 49.5 cms) Water-colour. Reproduced in *The Art Journal*, 1908, p. 90.

E. 534-1929 Winter scene, with village church, sheltered by trees ($3 \times 2\frac{3}{4}''$ – 7.6 × 7 cms) Sepia, heightened with white, inscribed: 'Xmas with the Poets – 2nd. Ed.' This is a design for a headpiece in *Christmas with the Poets*, 1851, p. 194. Donated by Harold Hartley.

E. 549-1948 A traveller with staff in a mountain landscape ($5 \times 8\frac{1}{2}''$ – 12.7 × 21.6 cms) Signed in ink 'Birket Foster' and inscribed 'Vignette for the title page of Goldsmith's Traveller' – *not* used in the 1859 colour edition.

E. 550-1948 A preacher addressing a group of Scots in a mountainous landscape ($5\frac{3}{4} \times 4\frac{1}{8}''$ – 14.6 × 10.5 cms) Pencil, wash and Chinese White, signed 'Birket Foster' in ink. Inscribed: 'A design for Grahame's Sabbath' (see list of illustrated books).

P. 19-1943 The Chair Mender ($10\frac{1}{4} \times 7\frac{3}{4}''$ – 26 × 19.7 cms) Water-colour, signed, with monogram. Donated by The Viscountess Wakefield, in memory of her husband, The Viscount Wakefield of Hythe.

E. 515-1948 September: A Country Fair ($7\frac{1}{8} \times 6\frac{1}{8}''$ – 18 × 15.5 cms) Pencil and wash, signed B. Foster and inscribed 'Country Fair'. Preliminary drawing for the illustration on p. 38 of *The Illustrated London Almanack* 1849 (see Ill. 8 for finished engraving). Bequeathed by H.H. Harrod.

Also bequeathed by H.H. Harrod:– Various pencil sketches, with reference numbers, as follows:– E. 513-1948 to E. 563-1948.

E. 16-1911 A volume containing 20 sketches by Birket Foster for 'A Voyage Round the World' in *Poems of James Montgomery* (see list of illustrated books). The poem with the finished sketches is bound in the volume, which was from the collection of Edward Dalziel, whose book plate is inserted.

P. 5-1922. Sketch book with 30 leaves, containing numerous studies of figures, landscapes, etc. Several sketches are studies for the same theme, i.e. a group with a donkey crossing a stream. Inscribed on the inside of the front cover 'Birket Foster to Sharpley Bainbridge'. Pen and pencil.

E. 1975-1946. to E. 1977-1946 Three sketch books, including one which is almost certainly lot 20 in the 1899

artist's sale, i.e. sketches of cathedral towns. Donated by Miss Ida M. Gabriel.

E. 1379-1481-1954 Sketches (103) of landscapes, buildings, figures in regional costume, harbour scenes, boats and carts, made principally in north-western France, including views of Amboise, Nantes, Quimper, Saint-Malo, Angers, Dinan, Saumur, Morlaix, Mont Saint-Michel, Saint Servan, Pont l' Abbé, Blois, Falaise, and sketches of the west portal of Quimper Cathedral; views of Mentone, Toulon, Beauvais and sketches of the west portals of Rheims Cathedral; views of Antwerp, Cadiz, Naples, on the Rhine and in Switzerland, including a view of the Castle at Chillon, Lake Geneva. Some sheets with slight sketches on the back. Mounted in a volume containing 106 sheets of white wove paper, half bound in brown morocco, gold tooled, marble boards.

Pencil and wash (various sizes). Most inscribed with titles and some with colour notes. E. 1393, 1469, dated respectively 8 May 1875 and 19 May 1872. Inscribed in ink on label on the spine of the volume 'Birket Foster Sketches'.

THE TATE GALLERY, MILLBANK, LONDON SWIP 4RG

1977 Cottage at Hambledon ($16\frac{3}{4} \times 25''$ - 42.5×63.5 cms). Ill. 45. Water-colour, signed with monogram. Bequest of C. Fraser 1905.

4950 Eel Bucks ($4 \times 5\frac{1}{2}''$ - 10.2×14.0 cms) Water-colour, signed with monogram.

4950 Smithy ($4 \times 5\frac{1}{2}''$ - 10.2×14.0 cms) Water-colour, signed with monogram. This is a direct version of pl. no. 12 in *Pictures of English Landscape* but the composition has been extended to the right to include a figure in typical late style. Both works probably dated about 1890. Bequest of R.H. Williamson.

The Tate Gallery also holds 'The Country Inn' - an engraved print from the block for the illustration in *Pictures of English Landscape*, item from the provenance of George Dalziel (ref. 4016).

UNIVERSITY OF LONDON, COURTAULD INSTITUTE GALLERIES, WOBURN SQUARE, LONDON WC1H 0AA

Witt no. 3079 View of Jarrow ($10\frac{1}{4} \times 14''$ - 26×35.6 cms) Lead pencil, water-colour with body colour on buff paper. Inscribed: Jarrow/B F.

Witt no. 4039 A Peacock ($3\frac{1}{8} \times 3\frac{1}{4}''$ - 7.9×8.2 cms) Water-colour on light blue paper.

Witt no. 4478A Girl Feeding Chickens ($5\frac{1}{8} \times 4\frac{1}{8}''$ - 13×10.5 cms) Lead pencil signed with monogram.

Witt no. 4478B Girl and Goat ($5\frac{3}{4} \times 4\frac{1}{4}''$ - 14.6×10.8 cms) Lead pencil, signed with monogram.

Witt no. 4478C A Woman and Two Children at a Rabbit Hutch ($5\frac{1}{2} \times 4\frac{1}{4}''$ - 14×10.9 cms) Lead pencil, signed with monogram.

Witt no. 4478D A woman and two children in a field ($5\frac{3}{4} \times 4\frac{1}{4}''$ - 14.6×10.8 cms) Lead pencil signed with monogram.

CITY OF LONDON LIBRARIES, GUILDHALL ART GALLERY, LONDON EC2P 2EJ

No. 886 The Hillside ($12 \times 17''$ - 30.5×43.2 cms) Water-colour-bequeathed by J.T. Slater, 1909.

No. 887 The Hen Coop ($7 \times 10''$ - 17.8×25.4 cms) Water-colour - bequeathed by J.T. Slater.

No. 1043 Richmond Bridge ($4 \times 5''$ - 10.1×12.7 cms) Water-colour, signed with monogram. Donated by Sir William Lancaster, 1926.

No. 1347 Seascape ($6 \times 9''$ - 15.2×22.8 cms) Water-colour, signed with monogram. Donated by Miss T.A.C. Durning Lawrence, 1946.

No. 1497 A girl driving cattle across a stream ($5 \times 7''$ - 12.7×17.7 cms) Bequeathed by John E.S. Dallas, 1953.

NATIONAL MARITIME MUSEUM, ROMNEY ROAD, GREENWICH SE10 9NF

Illustrations to Southey's *Life of Nelson*, published by David Bogue, 1854. Pencil and wash. Set of four, as follows:
1 Nelson birdsnesting
2 Nelson put on board a prize
3 Departure from Portsmouth
4 Nelson wounded at the Nile

Set of seven, as above subject:
1 Burnham Church
2 Nelson and the bear
3 Nelson boarding the Lowestoft
4 Nelson playing with Mrs Nisbet's child
5 Nelson at Syracuse
6 Admiral Hotham's action
7 Nelson's arrival at Naples

CITY OF ABERDEEN, ART GALLERY AND MUSEUM, SCHOOLHILL, ABERDEEN AB9 1FQ

Ref. 21.9.33 The Way Down the Cliff ($11\frac{5}{8} \times 17\frac{3}{4}''$ - 29.5×45.1 cms) Water-colour, signed with monogram. Exhibited: Society of Painters in Water-colours, 1867. Reproduced, 'Masters in Colour', Medici Calendar, 1981.

21.9.34 At Hambledon ($3\frac{3}{8} \times 4\frac{3}{4}''$ - 8.6×12.1 cms) Pencil and water-colour, inscribed with monogram and 'Hambledon/Sketch for a picture'. Bequeathed by Alexander Webster, 1921.

01.1.45 Birket Foster - self portrait. Water-colour, inscribed with monogram. This is worked directly from a photograph taken by William Foster, as reproduced in the biography by H.M. Cundall (1906). In the McDonald Collection of Artists' Portraits.

THE NATIONAL LIBRARY OF WALES, ABERYSTWTH, DYFED SY23 3BU

PD 6739 River Scene with figure standing in a punt ($3\frac{3}{8} \times 4\frac{3}{4}''$ - 8.6×12 cms).

PD 6740 Country Lane with houses in the distance ($3\frac{3}{8} \times 4\frac{3}{4}''$ - 8.6×12 cms).
Both items are water-colour with body colour and both are signed with monogram.

BOROUGH OF HYNDBURN, HAWORTH ART GALLERY, HAWORTH PARK, MANCHESTER ROAD, ACCRINGTON, LANCASHIRE

The Old Chair Mender ($14 \times 21\frac{1}{2}''$ - 35.5×54.5 cms) see Colour Ill. E. Water-colour and body colour, signed with monogram. Donated to the gallery as part of the estate of Miss Haworth.

Woman washing clothes in a stream ($9\frac{1}{8} \times 8''$ - 23.2×20.3 cms) Water-colour and body colour, signed with monogram. Also thought to have been from the provenance of Miss Haworth (the benefactor who presented the gallery).

BATH CITY COUNCIL, VICTORIA ART GALLERY, BRIDGE STREET, BATH BA1 2EW

26:20 Landscape with Cows ($3 \times 3\frac{3}{4}''$ - 7.6×9.5 cms) Pencil drawing, signed 'B. Foster'. Alfred Jones Gift, 1926.

40:28 Landscape – a country road with a flock of sheep ($4\frac{1}{2} \times 6\frac{1}{2}''$ – 11.4 × 16.5) Water-colour, unsigned. Presented by Miss A. A. Weeks, 1940.

NORTH BEDFORDSHIRE BOROUGH COUNCIL, THE CECIL HIGGINS ART GALLERY, CASTLE CLOSE, BEDFORD MK 40 3NY

1 Return of the Lifeboat with St. Michael's Mount in the distance ($8 \times 11\frac{1}{2}''$ – 20.3 × 29.2 cms) Ill. 80. Water-colour and pencil, heightened with white.

2 Illustration for *The Traveller* by Oliver Goldsmith. Water-colour sketch showing preliminary reverse sketch.

ULSTER MUSEUM, BOTANIC GARDENS, BELFAST BT9 5AB

782 Bringing Daddy's Dinner ($7\frac{1}{8} \times 5\frac{1}{4}''$ – 18.1 × 13.3 cms) Water-colour, heightened with white and signed with monogram.

783 Lyme Regis ($7\frac{7}{8} \times 9\frac{1}{2}''$ – 20 × 24.1 cms) Pencil with water-colour and white on thin white card, with a vignetted composition. Signed with monogram.

784 Falls of the Tummel ($6\frac{1}{2} \times 7\frac{1}{2}''$ – 16.5 × 19.1 cms) Water-colour on thin white card. Vignetted composition, signed with monogram.

1191 A Pedlar ($17\frac{1}{2} \times 26\frac{3}{4}''$ – 44.4 × 67.9 cms). Ill. 92. Water-colour and gouache. Signed.

1560 The Haymakers ($20\frac{7}{8} \times 32\frac{1}{4}''$ – 53.1 × 81.9 cms) Water-colour with gouache. Signed with monogram. Exhibited: Laing Art Gallery, Newcastle upon Tyne, Birket Foster Special Centenary Loan Exhibition, 1925.

1639 Going to Market ($11\frac{5}{8} \times 29\frac{1}{8}''$ – 29.5 × 74 cms) Water-colour with gouache, signed with monogram.

All the above works were donated in 1936 by Lady Cleaver in memory of her husband, Sir James Frederick Cleaver.

METROPOLITAN BOROUGH OF WIRRAL, WILLIAMSON ART GALLERY AND MUSEUM, SLATEY ROAD, BIRKENHEAD, MERSEYSIDE

BIGM: 1729 The First Voyage ($7\frac{7}{8} \times 10''$ – 20 × 25.4 cms) Water-colour, signed with monogram. The work was purchased from Frost and Reed, Bristol, who had acquired the item from the Barnet Lewis sale. At this time the firm also had 'Crossing the Ford' and 'Crossing the Brook', as illustrated in the Cundall biography. 'The First Voyage' depicts three children on a breakwater, sailing a toy boat in a sea pool.

BIRMINGHAM MUSEUM AND ART GALLERY, BIRMINGHAM B3 3DH

550'04 Worms Cathedral ($8\frac{3}{4} \times 12\frac{3}{4}''$ – 22.3 × 32.4 cms) Water-colour and body colour.

116'31 By the River ($6\frac{1}{2} \times 6''$ – 16.5 × 15.2 cms) Water-colour and body colour.

747'37 Bringing Home the Cattle ($12\frac{3}{4} \times 17\frac{3}{4}''$ – 32.4 × 45.1 cms) Water-colour and body colour.

2'49 The Arrival of Queen Victoria at Birmingham Town Hall. Water-colour, dated 15 June 1858 (engraved in *The Illustrated London News*, 26 June 1858).

180'53 Study of a French serving maid, Hotel des Voyageurs – as inscribed on reverse. ($8\frac{1}{2} \times 4\frac{1}{8}''$ – 21.6 × 10.4 cms) See p. 145.

181'53 Children by a Pool ($6\frac{1}{4} \times 5\frac{3}{8}''$ – 15.9 × 13.6 cms) Water-colour.

182'53 Old Fountain, Freiburg ($6\frac{1}{2} \times 3\frac{13}{16}''$ – 16.5 × 9.7 cms) Pencil and water-colour.

Milk Carts, Berne ($3\frac{5}{16} \times 4\frac{10}{16}''$ – 8.4 × 11.7 cms) Water-colour.

Loch Awe: Sunset ($7\frac{1}{4} \times 10\frac{3}{4}''$ – 18.4 × 27.3 cms) Water-colour.

The City of Birmingham is also in possession of a photograph of Birket Foster in costume (P427'78) – in Part V of the set entitled 'The Studio': a collection of photographic portraits of living artists taken in the style of the Old Masters by an amateur (no date).

BOROUGH OF BLACKBURN, BLACKBURN MUSEUM AND ART GALLERY, LIBRARY STREET, BLACKBURN

Holywell, near Newcastle ($13\frac{3}{4} \times 9\frac{5}{8}''$ – 35 × 24.4 cms) Water-colour, signed with monogram. Bequeathed by R.E. Hart, 1946. Exhibited: Worthing Art Gallery and Museum, 1979.

Arran and Bute ($26\frac{1}{4} \times 11\frac{3}{4}''$ – 66.6 × 29.8 cms) Water-colour, signed with monogram, dated 1866. Bequeathed by E.L. Hartley, 1954.

Florence ($4\frac{1}{16} \times 5\frac{3}{4}''$ – 10.2 × 14.6 cms) Hartley Bequest, 1954. Exhibited: Worthing Art Gallery and Museum, 1979.

Near Littlehampton ($7\frac{1}{16} \times 2\frac{3}{4}''$ – 18 × 7 cms) Water-colour, signed with monogram and inscribed 'Near Littlehampton'. Hartley Bequest, 1954. Exhibited: Worthing Art Gallery and Museum, 1979.

The Rialto, Venice ($12 \times 8\frac{1}{4}''$ – 30.5 × 21 cms) Water-colour, signed with monogram. Hartley Bequest, 1954. Exhibited: Worthing Art Gallery and Museum, 1979.

Summertime ($12\frac{13}{16} \times 9''$ – 32.5 × 22.8 cms) Water-colour, signed with monogram. Exhibited: Worthing Art Gallery and Museum, 1979.

Landscape with Cottage ($10\frac{7}{16} \times 7\frac{11}{16}''$ – 26.5 × 19.5 cms) Purchased in June 1884 from W. Harrison of Salmesbury Old Hall, near Preston.

BLACKPOOL BOROUGH COUNCIL, GRUNDY ART GALLERY, QUEEN STREET, BLACKPOOL, FY1 1PX

75 Mont St Michel ($21 \times 18''$ – 55.2 × 43.7 cms) Water-colour, with vignetted composition.

BOLTON METROPOLITAN BOROUGH, MUSEUM AND ART GALLERY, CIVIC CENTRE, BOLTON BL 11 SA

A Farmstead ($7 \times 10''$ – 17.8 × 25.4 cms) Water-colour, signed with monogram.

Children Playing in a Meadow ($9 \times 13\frac{3}{4}''$ – 22.9 × 34.9 cms) Water-colour with touches of gouache, signed with monogram.

An Old Oak ($8\frac{1}{4} \times 6\frac{3}{4}''$ – 21 × 17.2 cms) Pencil and water-colour.

At Woking, Surrey ($5\frac{5}{8} \times 7\frac{3}{8}''$ – 14.3 × 18.8 cms) Water-colour with touches of gouache – inscribed in pencil on the mounting card: 'At Woking. Surrey/19 June 1884'.

RUSSELL – COTES ART GALLERY AND MUSEUM, EAST CLIFF, BOURNEMOUTH BH1 3AA

711 The Bird's Nest ($3\frac{3}{4} \times 5\frac{1}{2}''$ – 9.5 × 14 cms) Water-colour, signed with monogram. Bequeathed by Alfred Ives, 1936.

285 Swiss Scene ($6\frac{3}{4} \times 3\frac{1}{2}$ – 17.2 × 8.9 cms) Pencil and water-colour. Collection of Sir Merton Russell-Cotes.

CITY OF BRADFORD METROPOLITAN COUNCIL, CARTWRIGHT HALL, LISTER PARK, BRADFORD, WEST YORKSHIRE DB9 4NS

56/71.3 Crossing the Stream ($7 \times 10''$ – 17.8 × 25.4 cms) Water-colour, signed with monogram.

56/71 A Cottage near Witley, Surrey ($9\frac{3}{4} \times 13\frac{1}{2}''$ – 24.8 × 34.3 cms) Water-colour, signed with monogram.

56/71.2 Gathering Wild Roses ($10 \times 14''$ – 25.4 × 35.5 cms) Water-colour, signed with monogram. Exhibited: Manchester Jubilee Exhibition, 1887.

This water-colour appears to be the original on which the chromolithograph (Ill. 70) is based. The colouring and treatment is deliberately strong. Birket Foster would be aware of the needs of the colour printer, as this work was executed to the commission of the Art Union of London specially for reproduction as a chromolithograph (1864).
56/71.4 Near Hastings – Waiting for Daddy's Boat (8½ × 11″ – 21.6 × 27.9 cms) Water-colour, signed with monogram.

All the above works transferred from the Central Library, Bradford in 1971.

CITY OF BRISTOL MUSEUM AND ART GALLERY, QUEEN'S ROAD, BRISTOL BS8 1RL
The Girl with the Orange (38¾ × 59¼″ – 98.5 × 150.5 cms) Ill. 78. Oil on canvas, signed with monogram. Donated by Sir John Wills, July 1971. Exhibited: Bristol City Art Gallery – 'Harvest Time' August–Sept 1971; Bristol City Art Gallery and Glynn Vivian Art Gallery, Swansea, 1975 – 'Victorian and Edwardian Paintings'.
The Harrow (13¾ × 33¾″ – 35 × 85.8 cms) Ill. A – colour. Water-colour, and gouache, signed with monogram. Bequest of Jessie and Robert Bromhead, 1935.
A local Surrey paper (extract incomplete – probably about 1900) mentioned this work as being on loan to an unnamed exhibition in the area, as follows: 'Mr A. Bilbrough has contributed some very fine ones, amongst them 'The Harrow' by Birket Foster. It depicts a number of children with a pony by a pond, the colouring being very beautiful. It is interesting to note that the daughter of the accomplished artist now lives in Twickenham'. i.e. Ellen Glasson (née Foster). The child with a basket over her arm has very much the appearance of having been modelled by Ellen, who was frequently used as a figure in the water-colour drawings.
K1241 Going to Market (8½ × 14″ – 21.6 × 35.6 cms) Water-colour and gouache, signed with monogram in red. Bequest of Jessie and Robert Bromhead, 1935. Reproduced in colour as 'The Market Cart', Plate 13 *In Rustic England*, published by Hodder and Stoughton, 1906. (From the chromolithograph of this water-colour, published by George Rowney and Co.)
K1243 Summer Time (8 × 13⅜″ – 20.3 × 34 cms) Water-colour, signed with monogram in red. Bequest of Jessie and Robert Bromhead, 1935. Reproduced in colour, plate 8, *In Rustic England*, from the chromolithograph of this water-colour, published by George Rowney and Co.
K2812 A Woodland Stream (6⅛ × 4½″ – 15.5 × 11.5 cms) Water-colour, heightened with white, signed with monogram. Inscribed on back of mount: 'A Surrey Stream' (modern hand). Authenticated by the British Museum, 1939. Purchased 1961.
K2207 Study for **The Mother's Lament** and linked with illustrations for this song, as published in *The Illustrated London News* (Musical Supplement, 24 January 1852). (See p. 31). Ill. 15. This example is an uncut engraver's block, showing original drawing in pencil and Chinese White. Size of block 7 × 9½″ – 17.8 × 24.1 cms. Donated by Mrs Tetley 1942.
M63399 Stoke Poges Church (4 × 3⅝″ – 10.2 × 9.2 cms) Pencil and wash drawing, heightened with white on board. Vignette showing view between arching trees, over stile, through churchyard, church to left in distance. This sketch is the exact reverse of the illustration on p. 5 of 'Elegy written in a country churchyard' by Thomas Gray, edition

published for Joseph Cundall by Sampson Low, 1854. Donated by Miss Wayne (Mrs F. Kerr) 1938.

THE BOROUGH OF BRIGHTON, ART GALLERY AND MUSEUMS, BRIGHTON BN1 1UE
Billy Mill, Tynemouth (9¼ × 14¼″ – 23.5 × 36.2 cms) Water-colour, signed with monogram. Bequeathed by A.G.E. Godden, June 1933. Exhibited: Worthing Art Gallery and Museum, 1979.

BURNLEY BOROUGH COUNCIL, TOWNELEY HALL ART GALLERY AND MUSEUM, BURNLEY, BB11
WA/CO 94 Seville (30 × 26″ – 76.2 × 66 cms) Water-colour, signed with monogram. Purchased from R. Haworth, Blackburn, 1933. Label on reverse: 'No. 1 Seville, Birket Foster, The Hill, Witley, Surrey'.
WA/CO 100 Wandering Minstrels (25 × 20½″ – 63.5 × 52 cms). Ill. 104. Water-colour, signed with monogram. Purchased from R. Haworth, Blackburn, 1937. Exhibited: Laing Art Gallery and Museum, Newcastle upon Tyne, Birket Foster Special Centenary Loan Exhibition, 1925. Lent by 'A Wallasey Gentleman'.

METROPOLITAN BOROUGH OF BURY, ART GALLERY AND MUSEUM, MANCHESTER ROAD, BURY, LANCASHIRE, BL9 0DR
65 Rottingdean, near Brighton (13½ × 28¼″ – 34.3 × 71.7 cms). Colour Illustration B. Water-colour, signed with monogram and dated 1865.
66 A Surrey Lane (8 × 12″ – 20.2 × 30.5 cms) Water-colour, signed 'B. Foster' in the style that appears as the signature in engraved illustrations. This work is probably dated about 1858 or a little earlier. Both works from the Wrigley Collection, 1901.

THE FITZWILLIAM MUSEUM, CAMBRIDGE, CB2 1RB
1525 Venice (8⅞ × 5⁵⁄₁₆″ – 22.5 × 13.4 cms) Pencil and water-colour, signed twice in pencil with initials and also has studio stamp.
1526 The Alhambra (7⅞ × 10¾″ – 20 × 27.4 cms) Pencil and water-colour, with studio stamp. Both items donated by The Friends of the Fitzwilliam Museum, 1929.

NATIONAL MUSEUM OF WALES, CATHAYS PARK, CARDIFF, CF1 3NP
3109 The Distribution of Coals (6 × 9¾″ – 15.2 × 24.8 cms) Pen and ink, tinted with water-colour. Original drawing for the subject as used by *The Illustrated London News* 1850. Formerly in the J. Pyke Thompson collection of British water-colours which was donated to Cardiff in 1898 and acquired by the National Museum of Wales in 1912.

DUDLEY METROPOLITAN BOROUGH, 3 ST. JAMES'S ROAD, DUDLEY, WEST MIDLANDS DY1 1HU
90/1937 House by a Stream (3½ × 4½″ – 8.9 × 11.4 cms) Water-colour with studio stamp. Purchased 1904.

NATIONAL GALLERY OF SCOTLAND, THE MOUND, EDINBURGH, EH2 2EL
D4504 Children with a Donkey (9½ × 13⅞″ – 24.1 × 35.2 cms) Ill. 89. Water-colour, The pose of the boy on the donkey is directly modelled from a photograph of Birket Foster's youngest son, Harry.
D5023/2 Briar Roses (7 × 5½″ – 17.8 × 14 cms) This water-colour sketch has all the appearance of having been a study from the tangled bank of wild flowers which Birket Foster allowed to grow in the garden of The Hill.

ROYAL ALBERT MEMORIAL MUSEUM, QUEEN STREET, EXETER EX4 3RX

62/1924.98 Boat, Figures and Sea ($7\frac{5}{8} \times 10\frac{5}{8}''$ – 19.4 × × 27 cms) Water-colour, heightened with white, signed with monogram and on verso stencilled '375/n'. Bought from A. Tooth and Son by Sir Harry Veitch and bequeathed by him in 1924, with example below.

62/1924.96 At Cullercoats ($7\frac{9}{16} \times 10\frac{1}{8}''$ – 19.1 × 25.7 cms) Water-colour, heightened with white, signed with monogram and inscribed: 'B.F. Cullercoats'. Exhibited: Royal Albert Memorial Museum, 1969. Worthing Museum and Art Gallery, 1979. Reproduced: Catalogue of Pictures and Sculpture, Royal Albert Memorial Museum, 1926.

CITY OF GLASGOW DISTRICT COUNCIL, ART GALLERY AND MUSEUM, KELVINGROVE, GLASGOW G3 8AG

1216 A View on the Rhine – the Lorelei Rocks. Water-colour, signed with monogram. ($7 \times 11''$ – 17.7 × 28 cms.) Presented by the executors of Henry Calcott.

53-8c Hastings ($3\frac{7}{8} \times 5\frac{1}{2}''$ – 9.9 × 14 cms) Water-colour, signed with monogram. Presented by Mrs E. Maitland Ramsey, 1953; also two examples listed below.

53-8d On the Thames, sunset ($5 \times 7''$ – 12.7 × 17.8 cms) Water-colour, signed with monogram.

53-8e Rustic Anglers ($7 \times 10''$ – 17.8 × 25.4 cms) Water-colour, signed with monogram.

METROPOLITAN BOROUGH OF CALDERDALE, BANKFIELD MUSEUM, BOOTHTOWN ROAD, HALIFAX HX3 6HG

159 Haymaking ($7\frac{5}{8} \times 5\frac{13}{16}''$ – 19.3 × 14.8 cms) Water-colour, signed with monogram.

160 An Italian River ($5\frac{15}{16} \times 8\frac{13}{16}''$ – 15 × 22.4 cms) Water-colour, signed with monogram. The subject is Venetian – the Giudei Canal and St Maria in the background.

161 Landscape ($6\frac{5}{8} \times 5''$ – 16.8 × 12.7 cms) All 3 items presented by Alderman William Smith in 1907.

BOROUGH OF HARTLEPOOL, GRAY ART GALLERY AND MUSEUM, CLARENCE ROAD, HARTLEPOOL CLEVELAND TS24 8BT

In the woods ($7\frac{1}{2} \times 10''$ – 19 × 25.4 cms) Water-colour, signed with monogram. Shows silver birches with rabbits and a stream in the foreground. Donated by Major T.A. Jobson 1926.

METROPOLITAN BOROUGH OF ST. HELENS, CENTRAL LIBRARY, VICTORIA SQUARE, ST. HELENS WA10 1DY

Near Streatley on Thames ($10\frac{3}{16} \times 20\frac{1}{4}''$ – 25.8 × 51.4 cms) Water-colour, signed with monogram. Ill. 44.

A Surrey Cottage ($11\frac{3}{4} \times 18\frac{3}{8}''$ – 29.8 × 46.6 cms) Water-colour – illustrated in *Birket Foster* by H.M. Cundall, 1906. Guy and Margery Pilkington Collection.

HEREFORD CITY MUSEUMS, BROAD STREET, HEREFORD HR4 9AU

6863 Two sketch book leaves (each $3\frac{3}{8} \times 5\frac{1}{2}''$ – mounted together). Foy Church and Rectory, inscribed: Foy June 1870.

5276 Lake Como ($3\frac{3}{8} \times 5\frac{5}{8}''$ – 9.8 × 14.3 cms) Water-colour, not signed.

5277 Italian Scene ($4 \times 6''$ – 10.2 × 15.2 cms) Water-colour, not signed.

NORTH HERTFORDSHIRE DISTRICT COUNCIL, HITCHIN MUSEUM, PAYNES PARK, HITCHIN, HERTS SG5 1EQ

Hitchin Market Place ($8\frac{3}{4} \times 6\frac{1}{4}''$ – 22.2 × 15.9 cms) Pencil sketch approximately 50% covered with water-colour, inscribed and signed with monogram. Presented by the executors of Mrs W.P. Ransom in 1950. Exhibited: Worthing Museum and Art Gallery 1979.

Note: The Hitchin Museum also holds a photograph of Birket Foster in middle life showing him examining a drawing in his studio. Inscribed on reverse: Cundall, Downes and Co. 168, New Bond Street and 10 Bedford Place, Kensington. Probably the work of Joseph Cundall and contemporary with the first edition of *Summer Scenes* 1866 for which Cundall photographed the illustrations.

KIRKLEES METROPOLITAN COUNCIL, LIBRARIES AND MUSEUMS, PRINCESS ALEXANDRA WALK, HUDDERSFIELD HD1 2SU

Children in a field ($7\frac{1}{2} \times 10\frac{1}{2}''$ – 19 × 26.7 cms) Water-colour, signed with monogram.

BOROUGH OF IPSWICH, IPSWICH MUSEUM, SUFFOLK

Ipswich from Bishop's Hill ($8\frac{1}{4} \times 12\frac{3}{4}''$ – 21 × 32.3 cms). Pencil drawing with touches of sepia, wash and white. Signed 'B. Foster'. Purchased 1923.

CITY OF LEEDS, CITY ART GALLERY, LEEDS

No. 558/24. Rocks on the Greta ($15 \times 20\frac{1}{8}''$ – 38.1 × 51.1 cms) Water-colour and gouache. Signed with monogram. Bought 1924. Witt Library Neg. Number – 801/40(36).

No. 1.9./48. View of Cromer ($5\frac{5}{8} \times 3\frac{15}{16}''$ – 14.3 × 10 cms). Water-colour, signed with monogram. Illustrated in the *Catalogue of the Nettlefold Collection*, 1933, vol. II. p. 78. Witt Negative – 801/28 (35).

MERSEYSIDE COUNTY COUNCIL, WALKER ART GALLERY, WILLIAM BROWN STREET, LIVERPOOL L3 8EI

171 The Stile ($7\frac{3}{4} \times 7''$ – 19.7 × 17.8 cms) Water-colour, signed with monogram. Bequeathed by Mrs Margaret Harvey 1878. Exhibited: Worthing Art Gallery and Museum 1979.

169 A Lock near Stratford on Avon ($8\frac{7}{16} \times 11\frac{5}{8}''$ – 21.5 – 29.5 cms) Water-colour, signed with monogram and inscribed: 'Stratford on Avon' Bequeathed by Henry S. Young 1931. Exhibited: Probably as no. 384 'Lock, Stratford on Avon' – Society of Painters in Water-colours, Winter 1868.

1455 Blackberries ($7\frac{1}{8} \times 5\frac{1}{2}''$ – 18.1 × 14 cms). Ill. 83. Water-colour, signed with monogram. Bequeathed by Henry S. Young in 1931 (previously sold from the collection of Lt. Col. J. B. Gaskell – Christie's, 1926).

The Cottage Garden ($7\frac{7}{8} \times 10\frac{15}{16}''$ – 20 × 27.8 cms) Water-colour, signed with monogram. Bequeathed by George Audley 1932.

1051 Happy Days ($11 \times 8''$ – 28 × 20.3 cms) Water-colour, signed with monogram. Bequeathed by George Audley, 1932. Exhibited: Worthing Art Gallery and Museum 1979.

170 Landscape with Sheep ($11\frac{15}{16} \times 17\frac{7}{8}''$ – 30.3 × 45.4 cms) Water-colour signed with monogram. Bequeathed by Mrs Margaret Harvey, 1878.

786 The Fairy Tale ($7\frac{3}{16} \times 9\frac{7}{16}''$ – 18.4 × 24.1 cms) Water-colour, signed with monogram and inscribed: 'A Story Book'. Bequeathed by George Audley in 1932. Previously sold at Christie's, December 1910 as 'The Story Book'.

787 The Young Angler ($6\frac{1}{16} \times 8\frac{1}{16}''$ – 15.4 × 20.5 cms) Water-colour signed with monogram and inscribed 'An Angler'. Bequeathed by George Audley, 1932. Exhibited: Worthing Museum and Art Gallery 1979.

209

706 A Stranded Boat ($5\frac{1}{16}$ × $7\frac{5}{8}''$ – 12.9 × 19.4 cms) Water-colour signed with monogram, also studio stamp. Probably as lot no. 175 'A Boat' – see sale of remaining works, p. 203.

CITY OF MANCHESTER, CITY ART GALLERY, MOSLEY STREET, MANCHESTER M2 3JL

1934.400 A Brook ($30\frac{1}{2}$ × $24\frac{9}{16}''$ – 77.5 × 62.4 cms) Oil on canvas. John E. Yates Bequest 1934.

1917.27 A River Scene ($7\frac{3}{4}$ × $10\frac{13}{16}''$ – 19.7 × 27.5 cms) Water-colour. James Blair Bequest 1917.

1917.32 Haytime ($8\frac{7}{8}$ × $14''$ – 22.5 × 35.5 cms) Water-colour. James Blair Bequest 1917.

1917.37 Hampstead ($6\frac{1}{16}$ × $9''$ – 15.4 × 22.8 cms) Water-colour. James Blair Bequest 1917.

1917.265 Landscape with Sheep ($6\frac{1}{8}$ × $9\frac{3}{16}''$ – 15.5 × 23.4 cms) Water-colour. James Gresham Bequest 1917.

1934.402 Washing Day at Balmacara ($6\frac{13}{16}$ × $10\frac{5}{8}''$ – 17.3 × 27 cms) Water-colour. John E. Yates Bequest 1934.

1941.61 Manchester Cathedral ($4\frac{7}{8}$ × $5\frac{5}{8}$ – 12.3 × 14.3 cms) Water-colour. G. Beatson Blair Bequest 1941.

1947.124 The Hermitage Bridge, Dunkeld ($21\frac{7}{8}$ × $17\frac{1}{8}''$ – 55.5 × 43.5 cms) Water-colour. G. Beatson Blair Bequest 1934.

Note: The bequest of G. Beatson Blair also included a scrapbook of sketches, inscribed: 'To Mary Brown from her uncle Birket Foster – 1864'. This was the year of Birket Foster's second marriage and the marriage of Mary ('Polly') Brown to Edmund Evans. It seems possible that the book was a little souvenir for Polly of all the happy years that she had been a part of the Foster household. There are 55 pieces by Birket Foster in this album, which also includes work by J. D. Watson, Kate Greenaway, Walter Crane and Hablot K. Browne ('Phiz'). Examples by Birket Foster include designs for book covers, as already mentioned in the text and studies for *The Illustrated London News*; also some sketches in the Newcastle area, in Italy and a Swiss scene, as well as such subjects as Apples and Hazlenuts, Snowdrops and a Decorative Design with wild roses and a butterfly, which is the preliminary drawing for the frontispiece of *Common Wayside Flowers*. See also 'Greenwich Fair' – Ill. 16. Some of these sketches were reproduced in *Birket Foster* by H. M. Cundall, 1906.

WHITWORTH ART GALLERY, UNIVERSITY OF MANCHESTER, WHITWORTH PARK, MANCHESTER M15 6ER

D 12. 1937 The Sea Shore ($7\frac{7}{8}$ × $10\frac{5}{8}''$ – 20 × 27 cms) Water-colour and body colour, with surface scratching, signed with monogram. Exhibited: Manchester Royal Jubilee Exhibition, 1887. Bequeathed by Jesse Haworth, 1937. Reproduced as 'Children by the Sea' in *Birket Foster*, H. M. Cundall, 1906.

16. 1910 Dolce Aqua ($5\frac{1}{2}$ × $3\frac{7}{8}''$ – 14 × 9.9 cms) Water-colour, pencil and body colour, signed with monogram. Bequeathed by C. F. Cox 1910.

14. 1910 The Old Mill ($13\frac{3}{8}$ × $10\frac{7}{8}''$ – 34 × 27.7 cms) Water-colour and body colour, signed with monogram. Kay-Cox Bequest 1910. A drawing entitled 'An Old Water Mill' was shown with the Royal Society of Painters in Water-colours in 1881. The composition was etched by Birket Foster for reproduction in *The Art Journal* – opposite p. 32, 1881. This shows a very similar version to the Whitworth drawing.

D.17. 1910 The Citadella, Pisa ($5\frac{1}{2}$ × $3\frac{7}{8}''$ – 14 × 8.6

cms) Water-colour and body colour, signed with monogram. Kay-Cox Bequest 1910.

TYNE AND WEAR COUNTY COUNCIL, ART GALLERIES AND MUSEUMS, LAING ART GALLERY, HIGHAM PLACE, NEWCASTLE UPON TYNE NE1 8AG (including Shipley Art Gallery)

15-17 *Tynemouth ($5\frac{1}{2}$ × $12''$ – 14 × 40.5 cms) Ill. 39. Water-colour, signed and dated: B. Foster 1855. Given by Robert Spence, *son* of Robert Spence, whose correspondence with Birket Foster is published in this book. Donated 1915.

16-59 *Old Windmill on Windmill Hills, Gateshead ($5\frac{7}{8}$ × $8\frac{3}{4}''$ – 14.9 × 22.2 cms) Pencil and water-colour, signed, inscribed and dated: B F/unfinished/17 June 1870. Purchased 1916.

B.8001* A View in Surrey (9 × $14''$ – 22.8 × 35.5 cms) Water-colour, signed with monogram. Purchased 1917.

19-43 *Newcastle upon Tyne from Windmill Hills ($5\frac{3}{4}$ × $9''$ – 14.6 × 22.8 cms) Water-colour, dated about 1871-2. Purchased 1919.

30-241. Coquet Island ($5\frac{1}{4}$ × $8''$ – 13.4 × 20.3 cms) Water-colour, signed and inscribed: Coquet Island/B. Foster. Purchased 1930.

34-1 *Cullercoats (7 × $16\frac{1}{4}''$ – 17.7 × 41.2 cms) Water-colour, signed with monogram. Donated in 1934 by Miss M. E. Evans ('Lily'), daughter of Edmund Evans.

B 8002 *Venice ($5\frac{3}{4}$ × $3\frac{3}{4}''$ – 14.6 × 9.5 cms) Water-colour, signed with monogram. Exhibited: Leicester Art Gallery, 'The Victorian Vision of Italy', 1968. Donated by George E. Henderson in 1934.

36-3* Ben Nevis ($46\frac{1}{2}$ × $31''$ – 119 × 78.7 cms) Water-colour, signed with monogram. Exhibited: Royal Society of Painters in Water-colours, 1891. See p. 162. Bequeathed by Lord Kirkley, 1936.

36-37 Arundel Park (9 × $12''$ – 22.8 × 30.5 cms) Pencil and water-colour. Provenance: Mrs Edmund Evans (the former Polly Brown) in 1906 and donated by Dr H. A. Powell, through the National Art Collections Fund in 1936. Reproduced in *Birket Foster* by H. M. Cundall, p. 20.

D. 2687 Children playing on the shore: castle in the background ($5\frac{1}{2}$ × $3\frac{7}{8}''$ – 14 × 9.8 cms) Signed with monogram. Given by George Henderson 1934.

B 659 'Emma taking the billet from the hard hand of Madelaine' (3 × $2''$ – 7.6 × 5 cms) Pencil, wash and body colour, inscribed in pencil 'How will this do?' Subject as engraved by Henry Vizetelly in Longfellow's *Hyperion*, published by David Bogue, second edition, p. 88. Purchased 1976.

B658 'His jaded steed the armed knight/Reined up before the abbey gate' (4 × $2\frac{1}{2}''$ – 10.2 × 6.3 cms) Pencil, wash and body colour. Engraved by Henry Vizetelly in *Christmas with the Poets* – 'Christmas comes but once a year' (Thomas Miller, p. 165).

C 13234 A Highland Bothy ($10\frac{7}{8}$ × $15\frac{3}{8}''$ – 27.6 × 39.1 cms) Water-colour, signed with monogram. Bequeathed by George E. Henderson 1937.

D. 2684 Quimper, Brittany ($5\frac{1}{4}$ × $3\frac{1}{4}''$ – 13.3 × 8.2 cms) May have been exhibited as 'Washing Place, near Quimper, Brittany' with the Royal Society of Painters in Water-colours, 1889. Bequeathed by George E. Henderson 1937.

D 2685 Verona ($4\frac{1}{2}$ × $6\frac{1}{4}''$ – 11.4 × 15.8 cms) Water-colour, signed with monogram. Exhibited: Leicester Art Gallery, 'The Victorian Vision of Italy', 1968. Given by George E. Henderson 1934.

37-141* **Milton's Cottage at Chalfont St. Giles,
Buckinghamshire** ($5\frac{5}{8}$ × $8\frac{1}{4}''$ - 14.2 × 21 cms) Water-
colour, signed with monogram. Shows a distant view to
the cottage over fields, unlike a very close-up version, as
photographed by William Foster, about 1890. Exhibited:
Royal Society of Painters in Water-colours, 1893. Bequeathed by George E. Henderson 1937.
C1- 3170 **Elstow, Bedfordshire, birthplace of John
Bunyan** ($5\frac{7}{8}$ × $8''$ - 14.3 × 20.3 cms) Exhibited: Royal
Society of Painters in Water-colours, 1893. Bequeathed
by George E. Henderson. 1937.
714 **Near Taymouth** ($4\frac{5}{8}$ × $8\frac{1}{2}''$ - 11.7 × 21.6 cms)
Water-colour, with studio stamp. Given by H. C. Richard-
son 1947. Collection: Shipley Art Gallery.
767 **Early Drawing: A Well** ($7\frac{7}{8}$ × $12''$ - 20 × 30.5 cms)
Inscription on reverse: 'Early drawing by Birket Foster'.
Fairly convincing provenance. From the estate of the late
George Wilson. Collection: Shipley Art Gallery
591 **Near Ilfracombe, Devon** ($4\frac{7}{8}$ × $7\frac{1}{8}''$ - 12.4 × 18
cms) Water-colour. Given by H. C. Richardson, 1928.
Collection: Shipley Art Gallery
Note: *Items exhibited at the Special Loan Exhibition of
Works by Birket Foster, Laing Art Gallery, 1925.

BOROUGH OF NEWPORT, NEWPORT MUSEUM AND ART GAL-
LERY, JOHN FROST SQUARE, NEWPORT, GWENT NPT IPA
33-68 **Ben Venue and Ellen's Island, Loch Katrine**
(6 × $8''$ - 15.2 × 20.3 cms) Water-colour, signed with
monogram. As reproduced facing p. 110 in *Birket Foster*
by H. M. Cundall, 1906.

CASTLE MUSEUM, NORWICH, NR1 3JU
Broxbournebury Park, Herts ($6\frac{7}{8}$ × $6''$ - 17.4 × 15.2
cms) Pencil on page from a sketch book, joined across
middle. Signed with monogram and inscribed and dated:
Broxbournebury Park/Sept.r 1861. Ref. 26,928. Presented
by M. C. W. Duffett, 1928.

THE ASHMOLEAN MUSEUM, DEPARTMENT OF WESTERN ART,
OXFORD OX1 2PH
A Catch of Fish and Lobster Pots on a Seashore (7
× $10\frac{7}{8}''$ - 17.8 × 27.6 cms) Water-colour and body colour
over pencil, with studio stamp. Virtue-Tibbs Bequest Purchase, 1963. Exhibited: Ashmolean Museum, Exhibition
of English Drawings from the collection of the late Sir
Bruce Ingram, 1963.
Nocturnal View on the Rhine ($7\frac{1}{8}$ × $11''$ - 18.2 × 27.9
cms) Water-colour over pencil. Signed with monogram.
Purchased 1941.

RENFREW DISTRICT COUNCIL, MUSEUM AND ART GALLERY,
PAISLEY, PA1 2BA
D57 **Country Scene** (5 × $4''$ - 12.7 × 10.2 cms)
Water-colour sketch, not signed or dated, but obviously a
preliminary study for an illustration and authentic.
Presented by the McIntyre Family 1947.

THE LADY LEVER ART GALLERY, PORT SUNLIGHT, MERSEYSIDE
Seaweed Gatherers ($5\frac{15}{16}$ × $8\frac{13}{16}''$ - 15 × 22.4 cms)
Water-colour, signed with monogram. Exhibited: Empire
Loan Exhibiting Society, 1948.
A Riverside Church with figures and sheep - sunset.
Water-colour.
On the Common, Hambledon, Surrey (6 × $8''$ - 15.2
× 20.3 cms) Water-colour, signed with monogram.

BOROUGH OF PRESTON, HARRIS MUSEUM AND ART GALLERY,
MARKET SQUARE, PRESTON, PR1 2PP
Dunstanborough Castle (38 × $56''$ - 96.5 × 142.2 cms)
Presented by J. R. Smith, 1922.
Bellagio, Lake Como ($4\frac{5}{8}$ × $6''$ - 11.7 × 15.2 cms)
Haslam Bequest 1947.

METROPOLITAN BOROUGH OF ROCHDALE, ROCHDALE ART GAL-
LERY, ESPLANADE, ROCHDALE
442 **On Guildford Common** ($5\frac{7}{8}$ × $8\frac{3}{4}''$ - 15 × 22.3
cms). Ill. 107. Water-colour, signed with monogram. Don-
ated by J. S. Littlewood, 1919.
689 **Girl at Well** ($6\frac{1}{4}$ × $7\frac{1}{4}''$ - 15.8 × 18.5 cms) Water-
colour, signed with monogram in ink. Donated by Horace
G. Holden, 1947.
749 **Dead Fishes** ($4\frac{3}{4}$ × $6\frac{1}{2}''$ - 12 × 16.5 cms) Water-
colour, signed with monogram. Still Life, purchased with
the Bright Bequest, 1955.
See also:
585 **The Young Rower** (40 × $30''$ - 101.6 × 76.2 cms)
Oil on canvas, signed: L. Glasson, 1932. Exhibited: Royal
Academy, no. 669, 1932. Gift from A. W. Kay-Menzies,
1932. The above work by Lancelot Myles Glasson (1894-
1959) *grandson* of Birket Foster is discussed on pp. 187-8.

CITY OF SHEFFIELD, MUSEUMS AND ART GALLERIES, SURREY
STREET, SHEFFIELD
(Graves Art Gallery and Mappin Art Gallery)
410 **Wornditch, Kimbolton** ($7\frac{7}{8}$ × $10\frac{1}{2}''$ - 19.3 × 26.7
cms) Water-colour, signed with monogram. Labels on
verso show that the work was formerly in possession of
Henry Foster, from the collection of Frances Foster, who
labelled the item: The Stream/by Birket Foster/Frances
Foster. Exhibited: Birket Foster Centenary Loan Exhibition, Laing Art Gallery, 1925, as the property of Henry
Foster, 7 South Parade, Whitley Bay, Northumberland.
392 **Mentone** ($9\frac{3}{8}$ × $14\frac{1}{8}''$ - 23.8 × 35.8 cms) Water-
colour, with studio stamp. Provenance: bought by Alder-
man Graves, Christie's 9 July 1930. Graves Gift.
3173 **The Little Nurse** (5 × $4''$ - 12.7 × 10.2 cms)
Water-colour, signed with monogram. Bequest of Dr J.
Ward, 1941.
1954 **Chartres** ($3\frac{7}{8}$ × $5\frac{3}{4}''$ - 9.9 × 14.7 cms) Water-
colour signed with monogram. Bequest of Dr J. Ward,
1941.
482 **Children at Play** ($5\frac{1}{2}$ × $4\frac{1}{8}''$ - 14 × 10.4 cms)
Water-colour, signed with monogram. Graves Gift 1935.
506 **Evening** ($5\frac{1}{4}$ × $7\frac{7}{8}''$ - 13.3 × 19.3 cms) Water-
colour, signed with monogram. Provenance: Christie's 25
April 1930, as 'Sheep on the banks of the river'. Graves
Gift.
430 **Feeding the Pig** ($7\frac{3}{8}$ × $10\frac{3}{8}''$ - 18.7 × 26.3 cms)
Water-colour, signed with monogram. Christie's, 6 May,
1932. Graves Gift. Exhibited: Water-colours from the
Graves Art Gallery, 1948. Victorian Paintings, Tawney
House, Matlock, 1967. Nottingham University, Department of Fine Art, 1967.
437 **Stolzenfels on the Rhine** ($8\frac{1}{2}$ × $12''$ - 21.6 × 30.5
cms) Water-colour, signed with monogram. Graves Gift.
440 **Ilfracombe** ($6\frac{1}{4}$ × $10\frac{1}{4}''$ - 17.1 × 26 cms) Water-
colour, signed with monogram. Graves Gift, 1935.
475 **Rouen** ($4\frac{1}{2}$ × $6''$ - 11.4 × 15.2 cms) Water-colour,
signed in pencil with monogram and inscribed: 'Birket
Foster/View of Rouen.' (Vignetted composition) Provenance: Christie's 25 April, 1930. Graves Gift.
336 **The Ruined Mill** ($8\frac{3}{4}$ × $7\frac{1}{8}''$ - 22.2 × 18.1 cms) Oil

on millboard, signed with monogram. Labelled on reverse: 'Purchased by Mr Garland, B. Foster Sale of sketches'. Graves Gift, 1935.

1136 The Porch, Stoke Church and Monument to Gray, Stoke (both $3\frac{1}{2} \times 4\frac{1}{2}''$ - 8.9 × 11.4 cms) Pair of early water-colour drawings. No. 1 Signed B. Foster, dated 1845, and inscribed: 'The Porch, Stoke Church', No. 2. Signed and dated 1845 and inscribed 'Monument to Gray/ Stoke'. Graves Gift.

756 At the Church Door ($3\frac{3}{8} \times 3\frac{1}{4}''$ - 8.5 × 8.2 cms) Water-colour. Graves Gift.

TYNE AND WEAR COUNTY COUNCIL, SUNDERLAND MUSEUM, BOROUGH ROAD, SUNDERLAND

B 8826 Entrance to the Grand Canal Venice ($10\frac{1}{4} \times 15\frac{1}{4}''$ - 26.0 × 38.7 cms) Water-colour, signed with monogram in pen and ink. Dated about 1868. Purchased in 1976 with a grant from the Victoria and Albert Museum.
C6391 Landscape with Cottages ($7\frac{1}{8} \times 12\frac{1}{8}''$ - 18.1 × 30.8 cms) Water-colour, signed 'B. Foster' in paint. Purchased 1949.

METROPOLITAN BOROUGH OF SEFTON, THE ATKINSON ART GALLERY, LORD STREET, SOUTHPORT, MERSEYSIDE PR8 1DH

30 Old Abbey ($5\frac{1}{4} \times 6\frac{3}{4}''$ - 13.3 × 17.2 cms) Water-colour, signed with monogram. Bequeathed by Miss Ball, 1898.
473 Going to Market ($7\frac{3}{4} \times 5\frac{1}{4}''$ - 19.7 × 13.3 cms) Water-colour, signed with monogram. Bequeathed by J. H. Bell, 1929
456, 478. Two water-colours entitled *Country Scene*, signed with monogram and also bequeathed by J. H. Bell.

WALSALL METROPOLITAN BOROUGH, CENTRAL LIBRARY, LICHFIELD STREET, WALSALL, WS1 1TR

Children Playing in a Wood ($5\frac{3}{4} \times 9\frac{7}{8}''$ - 14.5 × 25.0 cms) Water-colour, heightened with body colour. Signed with monogram and dated '67. The picture is No. GR.94 in the Garman Ryan Catalogue, published in March 1976. Formerly in possession of Lady Epstein.

WARRINGTON BOROUGH COUNCIL, MUSEUM AND ART GALLERY, BOLD STREET, WARRINGTON, WA1 1JG

Ref. 48'967. At Bonchurch, Isle of Wight ($9\frac{1}{4} \times 14''$ - 23.5 × 35.5 cms) Ill. 46. Water-colour, signed with monogram. Purchased from J. H. Booth with aid of a grant from the Victoria and Albert Museum.

METROPOLITAN BOROUGH OF WIGAN, TURNPIKE GALLERY, LEIGH, GREATER MANCHESTER

The Shepherd Boy ($5\frac{1}{2} \times 4\frac{1}{2}''$ - 14 × 11.4 cms) Water-colour.

Gathering Apples ($7\frac{1}{2} \times 6\frac{1}{2}''$ - 19 × 6.5 cms) Both are bequest of Thomas Dootson, a noted benefactor of the former Borough of Leigh. Water-colour collection transferred to the Metropolitan Borough of Wigan in 1974.

ETON COLLEGE COLLECTION, ETON COLLEGE, WINDSOR, BERKSHIRE, SL4 6DB.

On the Grand Canal Venice ($6\frac{3}{8} \times 9\frac{1}{4}''$ - 16.2 × 23.4 cms) Water-colour, signed with monogram.
Witley Common, from Hindhead ($4\frac{7}{8} \times 7''$ - 12.4 × 17.8 cms) Water-colour with body colour.

METROPOLITAN BOROUGH OF WOLVERHAMPTON, ART GALLERY AND MUSEUM, LICHFIELD STREET, WOLVERHAMPTON WV1 1DU

W.108 Seapiece ($3\frac{3}{8} \times 5\frac{1}{2}''$ - 8.6 × 14 cms)
W.844 Coastal Scene ($3\frac{15}{16} \times 5\frac{1}{8}''$ - 10 × 13 cms)
W.845 Stormy Sea and Headland ($3\frac{15}{16} \times 5\frac{1}{8}''$ - 10 × 13 cms)
W.864 Lockgates and Church Spire ($3\frac{3}{4} \times 5\frac{1}{8}''$ - 9.5 × 13 cms)
W.847 Two Barges, evening ($3\frac{1}{2} \times 5\frac{1}{8}''$ - 9 × 13 cms)
The above water-colours are all signed with monogram. All are foxed, with the exception of item W. 108.

WORTHING BOROUGH COUNCIL, MUSEUM AND ART GALLERY, WORTHING, SUSSEX, BN11 1HQ.

The Hen Coop ($7\frac{7}{8} \times 11''$ - 20 × 27.9 cms) Water-colour, signed with monogram. Exhibited: 'Myles Birket Foster' - Worthing Museum and Art Gallery, 1979.

CITY OF YORK, ART GALLERY, EXHIBITION SQUARE, YORK, YO1 2EW

Bootham Bar, York ($3\frac{15}{16} \times 5\frac{1}{2}''$ - 10 × 14 cms) Water-colour and body colour, signed with monogram. Purchased in 1961 with the aid of the York Civic Trust.

IN THE COLLECTION OF HER MAJESTY THE QUEEN, ROYAL LIBRARY, WINDSOR CASTLE, BERKSHIRE (Ill. 105)

RL.14256 A Highland Burn ($8\frac{1}{4} \times 5\frac{1}{2}''$ - 21 × 14 cms) Water-colour, signed 'Birket Foster'. This work was photographed by William Foster and has 'Duchess of York' pencilled in the album as the subsequent owner. The future Queen Mary was Duchess of York from 1893 to 1901. It is believed that 'A Highland Burn' may have been presented as part of a gift from some institution on the occasion of the marriage of the Duke and Duchess of York (6 July 1893).

The following is intended only as a short selection from collections outside the United Kingdom
NATIONAL GALLERY OF IRELAND, MERRION SQUARE WEST, DUBLIN 2, EIRE

Mountain view with farmhouse ($7\frac{3}{8} \times 11\frac{1}{8}''$ - 18.8 × 28.1 cms). (Ill. 1). Water-colour, inscribed on reverse: 'Birket Foster/Drawn when he was *eleven* years old/Given me by D. Foster, Esq.,/W.S.' William Smith Bequest 1877.

ART GALLERY OF NEW SOUTH WALES, ART GALLERY ROAD, SYDNEY, NEW SOUTH WALES, AUSTRALIA 2000

Barking, Springtime ($29\frac{1}{8} \times 42\frac{1}{8}''$ - 74.0 × 107.0 cms) Water-colour, signed with monogram. Purchased 1887.
The Magpie ($7\frac{7}{8} \times 11''$ - 20.0 × 28.0 cms) Water-colour, with body colour, signed with monogram and inscribed in pencil: 'The Magpie'. On verso: landscape brush sketch. Albert and Katey Nathan Bequest 1941.
The Art Gallery of New South Wales is also in possession of 'The Fight: St. George Kills the Dragon' - panel no. 6 in the series commissioned from Burne-Jones by Birket Foster for the dining room at The Hill, Witley.

ART GALLERY OF SOUTH AUSTRALIA, NORTH TERRACE, ADELAIDE, SOUTH AUSTRALIA 5000.

O.492 Evening, Upper Thames
O.493 Sunny Hours
Two unsigned examples attributed to Birket Foster.

SOUTH AFRICAN NATIONAL GALLERY, PO. BOX 2420, CAPE TOWN 8000, SOUTH AFRICA

1519 Sunset (9 × 13″ - 22.8 × 33 cms)

1523 Tantallon Castle (5⅛ × 8⅛″ - 13 × 20.5 cms)

1524 Girl and a Pitcher (7 × 5″ - 17.7 × 12.7 cms)

1537 Children Playing outside a Cottage (7⅞ × 10¾″ - 20 × 27.3 cms)

Note the above works are in water-colour and body-colour and are part of the Sir Abe Bailey Bequest left to the gallery in 1942.

YALE CENTER FOR BRITISH ART, 1080 CHAPEL STREET, BOX 2110, YALE STATION, NEW HAVEN, CONNECTICUT 06520 USA

B1975.3.1137 Lago Maggiore, Italy (8⅛ × 12¼″ - 20.6 × 31.1 cms) Water-colour over pencil, signed with monogram. Purchased from John Baskett in 1970. Paul Mellon Collection.

B1975.4.1186-8 Three Studies on the Venetian Lagoon (mounted with Foster's 'Three Studies of Gondolas') All water-colour over pencil, not inscribed and of small size. Originally in collection of Martin Hardie, author of *Water-Colour Painting in Britain*, published by B. T. Batsford. Paul Mellon Collection.

B1975.4.1189-91 Three Studies of Gondolas All water-colour over pencil, not inscribed and of small size. Also from the collection of Martin Hardie. Paul Mellon Collection.

B1975.4.1192 The Water Cart (3¼ × 3⅝″ - 8.3 × 9.2 cms) Water-colour over pencil, not inscribed. Originally in the collection of Martin Hardie. Paul Mellon Collection.

The Hayrick (30½ × 26½″ - 77.5 × 67.3 cms) Water-colour with body colour and traces of pencil, signed with monogram. Exhibited: British Water-colour Drawings in the collection of Mr and Mrs Paul Mellon, The Art Gallery of Greater Victoria, Canada, 1971.

The Balloon (2¹³⁄₁₆ × 5⅞″ - 7.2 × 15 cms) Water-colour with body colour over pencil on beige paper.

The Yale Center for British Art also holds a boxed collection of four water-colour drawings and 39 hand-coloured engravings, e.g. illustrations to Goldsmith's Poems (chiefly 'The Deserted Village'). Identification numbers: Drawings: B1977.14.1914-17 Engravings: B1977.14.1918-1956. Paul Mellon Collection.

HENRY E. HUNTINGTON LIBRARY AND ART GALLERY, SAN MARINO, CALIFORNIA 91108 USA

1 Amble, Northumberland - beach scene (7 × 4″ - 17.8 × 10.2 cms) Water-colour.

2 Donkey and Cart (11¾ × 8½″ - 29.8 × 21.5 cms) Water-colour, unfinished with odd pencil sketches on same sheet.

3 Farm Yard Sketch (7 × 5″ - 17.8 × 12.7 cms) Water-colour.

4 View from Punch Bowl, Hindhead (6½ × 5″ - 16.5 × 12.7 cms) Water-colour.

5 Italian Street Scene (4½ × 3¾″ - 11.5 × 9.5 cms) Water-colour.

6 Gurnards - two fish only (7½ × 3¾″ - 19 × 9.5 cms) Water-colour, signed with monogram and inscribed 'Gurnard/Brighton 1874'. Exhibited: Birket Foster Loan Exhibition at L. and W. Vokins Gallery, 14-16, Great Portland Street, London.

7 St. Maurice (10 × 7″ - 25.4 × 17.7 cms) Pencil and water-colour.

8 Skating in Hyde Park (2½ × 5¼″ - 6.3 × 13.3 cms) Water-colour. Fine Art Society, 1947. Originally in the collection of Mrs William Foster.

9 Paddington Station (2¼ × 5¼″ - 5.7 × 13.3 cms) Water-colour, also from the above collection.

Note: Items 1-9 form part of the Gilbert Davis Collection which was acquired by the Henry E. Huntington Library and Art Gallery and also contains interesting examples by William Callow, R.W.S. (see book by Jan Reynolds, B. T. Batsford, 1980).

10 Autumn (3½ × 4⅜″ - 8.9 × 11.1 cms) Grey washes heightened with white. Purchased by the Trustees, 1969

11 Chillon (6¾ × 9¾″ - 17.2 × 24.8 cms) Pencil and water-colour, inscribed in pencil with title. Purchased 1946.

12 Design for 'Old Christmas' (7 × 4½″ - 17.7 × 11.4 cms) Grey washes, heightened with white - drawing for *Christmas with the Poets*. Purchased by the Trustees, 1969

13 Illustration for Longfellow's *Evangeline* (2¾ × 3⅞″ - 7 × 9.8 cms) Pencil and grey wash, heightened with white. Purchased 1971

*The Henry E. Huntington Library also holds three sketch books containing work by Birket Foster, as follows:

71.13A 17 Drawings of Italian Travels. Pencil (pages - 4½ × 7¼″ - 11.4 × 18.3 cms).

71.13B Drawings mainly of English landscape and genre (pages - 5⅜ × 7¼″ - 13.6 × 18.4 cms). Pencil.

71.13C 20 Drawings of British Coastal Scenes (pages - 5⅜ × 7¼″ - 13.6 × 18.4 cms). Pencil. Purchased 1971.

Note: Public collections frequently acquire works by donation and it is an undoubted fact that in this manner some spurious Birket Fosters have found a place in the catalogues of museums and art galleries. One such item is illustrated, as an example, but others have also been identified and deliberately left out of this section. However, it was not practicable for all collections to be personally inspected by the author and the basic details are as supplied in good faith by the museums and galleries listed, with some additional comments.

APPENDIX 8

Alphabetical list of work by other artists in possession of Birket Foster during the time that he lived at The Hill, Witley - 1863-93

Unless otherwise stated, all these pictures were subsequently sold by Birket Foster at Christie's on 28 April 1894. Items marked with * were later sold at Christie's on 2 December 1921. In the 1894 sale the highest price for an individual lot was obtained for 'Venice: under the Rialto' by James Holland - £330/15/0. Specimen prices only are included in the following list. Total sum obtained: £6,461/17/6 (after commission). Medium: water-colour, unless otherwise stated. Descendants of the family have photographs of many of these works. Collectors should apply to the author if more detailed descriptions or information should be required.

W. J. Blacklock. Cottage and Trees.

Sir Edward Burne-Jones, A.R.A. Seven oil panels - The Story of St. George and the Dragon:
1. A Petition to the King

2. The King's Daughter
3. Moritura
4. Going to Death
5. The Princess Tied to the Tree (Ill. 64)
6. St. George Kills the Dragon
7. The Return
See also pp. 97, 99 and 176.
History of Saint Frideswide – eight oil panels in the form of a screen. Bought from Birket Foster by G. W. Robertson. (See pp. 104–6).

John Burr, A.R.W.S.
A Sleeping Boy.

***William Callow, R.W.S.**
Caen (unframed) Lot 35–1921 (with 'Farmyard Studies', 'The Maypole', and 'The Popinjay' by R. Hill – four studies in one frame).

George Cattermole, R.W.S.
The Oratory at Naworth Castle.
Manfred (a man in armour).
In the armoury.
Venice (as glimpsed in Ill. 65).
Convent Hospitality.

George Dodgson, R.W.S.
Beech Trees (– sold as 'Knowle Park')

Edward Duncan, R.W.S.
The Inchcape Bell, 1859.
Sunset at Sea, After a Storm.

***Pierre Edouard Frère.**
Child by a stove – sold as 'Warming her Hands' – oil on panel.

Sir John Gilbert, R.A., P.R.W.S.
'I am slain by a fair cruel maid.' – study for an illustration.

William Hogarth.
Sketch of Miss Fenton as Polly Peacham.

James Holland, R.W.S.
Venice: Under the Rialto (£330/15/0 – 1894). See also p. 108.
Venice (as exhibited at Burlington House, 1891).
Roses and Larkspurs (flowers in a tumbler).
Azalea – sold as 'Flowers in a blue and white dish'.

William Henry Hunt, R.W.S.
Chaffinch's Nest and Wild Rose (£115/15/0 – 1894). Ill. 65.
Red Ware Jug and Eggs.
May Blossom and Eggs.
Primroses and Egg.
Wild Roses and Egg (£135/9/0).
Snowdrops (oval composition).
Greengages and Orleans Plums.
Black Grapes, Peaches and Strawberries.
*Hare and Partridge – sold as Lot 37 in 1921 for a mere £2/2/0.
*Hastings Castle.
See also p. 173.

E.K. Johnson, R.W.S.
The Anxious Mother (£94/10/0) See Ill. 58. (dated 1875).

W.L. Leitch, R.I.
Fir Trees – sold as 'A Classical Composition'.
Como – sold as 'An Italian Composition'.

Sir Edwin Landseer, R.A.
Water-colour sketch of a horse, cart and driver. Note: not included in either sale.

John F. Lewis, P.R.W.S., R.A.
The Hhareem. See Ill. 55 and p. 101. Dated 1850 – exhibited Burlington House, 1891. Lot 25 in 1894 sale, but bought in at £183/10/0. Sold in 1921 sale for £131/15/0. Collection: Victoria and Albert Museum.
The Mendicant: Interior of a Turkish house, with figures. Dated 1863 – also exhibited as above.
Figure (sketch) – sold as 'A Turkish Soldier', but a photograph of the original shows this to have been a water carrier.
Eastern Woman – sold as 'A Greek Girl'.

John Linnell, Sen.
A Pastoral Scene, with boys tending sheep. Dated 1853 (£152/5/0 – 1894 sale).
The Barley Harvest. Dated 1863 (£203/14/0).
Both the above specially commissioned by Birket Foster.
Fen Country. Lot 30 – bought in at £55/13/0 in 1894 sale, but sold in 1921 (lot 51) for only £23/2/0.

H.S. Marks, R.A.
Shakespeare's Seven Ages of Man – designed for the summer house which was situated as part of the terrace at The Hill, Witley. Set of 7 oil panels (£73/10/0 in 1894 sale).
Little Boy Blue – oil panel.
Nursery Rhymes – set of eight panels in oils. Queen of Hearts; Humpty Dumpy, Four and Twenty Tailors, etc. See position in Ill. 60.
Nursery Rhymes – set of three panels in oils. Baa! Baa! Black Sheep, Queen Amuse, There was a Little Man.

Sir John E. Millais, R.A.
Gareth and Lynette
The Seamstress
Old Letters
Mary, Queen of Scots
Moonlight

Sir William Quiller Orchardson, R.A.
Portrait of the second Mrs Birket Foster. (Ill. 72) Exhibited no. 223 at the Royal Academy in 1868. Now in possession of Mrs L.M. Glasson
*Mrs Birket Foster and Miss Ellen Foster (black and white)

Samuel Palmer, R.W.S.
The Morning of Life
Sunset

G.J. Pinwell, R.W.S.
The Princess and the Ploughman
Also, after Pinwell: The Elixir of Love.

F.W. Topham, R.W.S.
A Spanish Grape Seller (a girl)

J.M.W. Turner, R.A.
Sidon (5 × 8″). Sold in the 1894 sale for £273
Lake of Geneva – no measurements, not in any sale of Birket Foster's possessions
Loch Lomond (8½ × 10½″) £46/4/-.
Set of six water-colour drawings on blue-grey tinted paper, as follows:
In the Rhone Valley (5¼ × 7¼″) Lot 40 – £68/5/-
In the Rhone Valley (as above) Lot 41 – £94/10/-
On the Moselle (5¼ × 7¼″) – £42
Ehrenbreitstein (5¼ × 7¼″) – £75/12/-
Amalfi (5¼ × 7¼″) – £50/8/-
Luxembourg (5¼ × 7¼) – £84

Frederick Walker, A.R.A.
The Chaplain's Daughter (5½ × 8″) – £320/5/-. Ill. no. 75.
Exhibited at the Royal Jubilee Exhibition, Manchester, 1887. Burlington House, 1891
The Lido, Venice
Palace in Venice (Orchardson at the window). In possession of Mrs L.M. Glasson
*An Avenue, with seated girl.
*At the Hill, Witley
Ellen Foster (see Ill. 74). In possession of Mrs L.M. Glasson
Also: Original drawing for the poster for Wilkie Collins' *Woman in White*

Index

Numerals in italics indicate pages on which an illustration occurs.

The content of the Appendixes is not covered in this Index, so as to avoid lists of page references of unhelpful length; the Appendixes give information in a manner which should make for ease of consultation, details being presented in the manner in which they would be available if the reader has the original reference to hand.